Consumer Credit

The College of Law
of England and Wales

Other titles available from Law Society Publishing:

Bankruptcy (forthcoming, 2012)
Vernon Dennis

Commercial Law Handbook
Editor: David Berry

Company Law Handbook (2nd edn)
Stephen Griffin

Data Protection Handbook (2nd edn)
General Editor: Peter Carey

Drafting Commercial Agreements
Stuart Cakebread

Drafting Employment Contracts (2nd edn)
Gillian Howard

Employment Law Handbook (5th edn)
Henry Scrope, Daniel Barnett and Keira Gore

Freedom of Information Handbook (3rd edn)
General Editors: Peter Carey and Marcus Turle

Intellectual Property Law Handbook
Editor: Lorna Brazell

Titles from Law Society Publishing can be ordered from all good bookshops or direct (telephone 0870 850 1422, email **lawsociety@prolog.uk.com** or visit our online shop at **www.lawsociety.org.uk/bookshop**).

CONSUMER CREDIT

Law, Practice and Precedents

Russell J. Kelsall

The Law Society

© The Law Society 2012
Crown copyright material in Precedents 1 to 5 and 21 in the Appendix and on the accompanying disk is reproduced with the permission of the Controller of Her Majesty's Stationery Office

ISBN-13: 978-1-85328-874-6

Published in 2012 by the Law Society
113 Chancery Lane, London WC2A 1PL

Typeset by Columns Design XML Ltd, Reading
Printed by CPI Group (UK) Ltd., Croydon, CR0 4YY

The paper used for the text pages of this book is FSC® certified. FSC (the Forest Stewardship Council®) is an international network to promote responsible management of the world's forests.

Contents

ix

Preface

Consumer credit is an area which is not afraid of change. It has been subject to persistent change over the last 10 years or so. Significant changes to agreements arrived, quickly followed by the Consumer Credit Act 2006, which phased in changes over two years. Even then, lurking in the background, was the European Union's Consumer Credit Directive which, eventually, was fully implemented on 1 February 2011. It was therefore with some trepidation, mixed with the enthusiasm and (some may say) blind optimism only a consumer credit lawyer could have, that I accepted the challenge of writing this text. I did not expect it to be an easy process but I hope I have achieved my aim of providing an accessible and practical text on the law of consumer credit and consumer hire.

Looking forward, the pace of change shows no sign of letting up. There is, on the horizon, the transfer of the Office of Fair Trading's function to the Financial Conduct Authority and the Government's planned review of the regulatory architecture. If writing this text has taught me anything, it is that the consumer credit industry has spent a considerable amount of time trying to understand the vast regulatory regime and, on the whole (with multiple agreements and voluntary terminations being, perhaps, two main exceptions), it works pretty well. For my own part, I would not advocate a transfer to a Financial Services Authority-style rulebook which, as we know from the rules on payment protection insurance, appears to create uncertainty. In the meantime, the European Union proposes to release a new Consumer Credit Directive so, whatever the outcome of the Government's review, lenders will no doubt have to redesign their systems in the short-term.

It is impossible to thank everyone who has helped me in the production of this text. I must, however, make some special mentions. Thanks go to my endlessly patient colleagues at Squire Sanders; they have put up with my thoughts and comments on consumer credit without too many complaints! I must also thank Aamir Khan at Lloyds Banking Group for kindly agreeing to write Chapter 11. Many thanks must also go to David Bowden and Ian Harding at Lloyds Banking Group – Asset Finance for sending me copies of the various decisions involving Black Horse Ltd (and, of course, running those cases to trial and appellant courts – the text may have been somewhat shorter without them). Thanks also to Simon Blackett and his team at Law Society Publishing, who have gently reminded me when I have missed my deadlines. My explanation that a fast-moving area of law meant the text needed constant re-writes has no doubt worn somewhat thin! Without their prompting, this book may never have been finished. Last, but by no means least, I must thank my long-suffering wife, Nicola, and my son, Benjamin, who have tolerated my 'double life'. As a small token of my appreciation, it is to both of them that this book is dedicated.

I have tried to state the law as at 14 November 2011. If there are any errors or omissions, they are, of course, my own. If anyone has any comments, these would be welcomed.

Russell J. Kelsall
Leeds
December 2011

Table of cases

Table of statutes

Table of statutory instruments

Table of European legislation

Abbreviations

APR	annual percentage rate
ASA	Advertising Standards Authority
BIS	Department for Business Innovation & Skills
BPMMR 2008	Business Protection from Misleading Marketing Regulations 2008, SI 2008/1276
CAP	Committee of Advertising Practice
CAP Code	British Code of Advertising, Sales Promotion and Direct Marketing
CC(A)R 1983	Consumer Credit (Agreements) Regulations 1983, SI 1983/1553
CC(A)R 2010	Consumer Credit (Agreements) Regulations 2010, SI 2010/1014
CC(Ad)R 2004	Consumer Credit (Advertisements) Regulations 2004, SI 2004/1484
CC(Ad)R 2010	Consumer Credit (Advertisements) Regulations 2010, SI 2010/1970
CC(CNCD)R 1983	Consumer Credit (Cancellation Notices and Copies of Documents) Regulations 1983, SI 1983/1557
CC(DI)R 2004	Consumer Credit (Disclosure of Information) Regulations 2004, SI 2004/1481
CC(DI)R 2010	Consumer Credit (Disclosure of Information) Regulations 2010, SI 2010/1013
CC(EA)O 1989	Consumer Credit (Exempt Agreements) Order 1989, SI 1989/869
CC(EA)O 2007	Consumer Credit (Exempt Agreements) Order 2007, SI 2007/1168
CC(EDTN)R 1983	Consumer Credit (Enforcement, Default and Termination Notices) Regulations 1983, SI 1983/1561
CC(EUD)R 2010	Consumer Credit (EU Directive) Regulations 2010, SI 2010/1010
CC(IRDLC)R 2007	Consumer Credit (Information Requirements and Duration of Licences and Charges) Regulations 2007, SI 2007/1167
CC(NCR)(E)R 1983	Consumer Credit (Notice of Cancellation Rights) (Exemptions) Regulations 1983, SI 1983/1558

CC(NVA)R 1977	Consumer Credit (Notice of Variation of Agreements) Regulations 1977, SI 1977/328
CC(RACI)R 1983	Consumer Credit (Running-Account Credit Information) Regulations 1983, SI 1983/1570
CC(RP)R 1983	Consumer Credit (Realisation of Pawn) Regulations 1983, SI 1983/1568
CC(TCC)R 1980	Consumer Credit (Total Charge for Credit) Regulations 1980, SI 1980/51
CC(TCC)R 2010	Consumer Credit (Total Charge for Credit) Regulations 2010, SI 2010/1011
CCA 1974	Consumer Credit Act 1974
CCA 2006	Consumer Credit Act 2006
CCD	Consumer Credit Directive (87/102/EEC)
CMCs	claims management companies
CPR	Civil Procedure Rules 1998, SI 1998/3132
CPUTR 2008	Consumer Protection from Unfair Trading Regulations 2008, SI 2008/1277
CRAs	credit reference agencies
ECCI	European Consumer Credit Information
EEA	European Economic Area
FA 1976	Finance Act 1976
FCA	Financial Conduct Authority
FS(DM)R 2004	Financial Services (Distance Marketing) Regulations 2004, SI 2004/2095
FSA	Financial Services Authority
FSMA 2000	Financial Services and Markets Act 2000
GLO	Group Litigation Order
HAA 1985	Housing Associations Act 1985
ICOB	Insurance: Conduct of Business Rules
ICTA 1970	Income and Corporation Taxes Act 1970
OFT	Office of Fair Trading
PD	Practice Direction
PPI	payment protection insurance
RAO 2001	Financial Services and Markets Act 2000 (Regulated Activities) Order 2001, SI 2001/544
SECCI	Standard European Consumer Credit Information
SGA 1979	Sale of Goods Act 1979

CHAPTER 1

Introduction, definitions, and credit and hire agreements

1.1 INTRODUCTION

The Consumer Credit Act 1974 (CCA 1974) is one of the most fascinating but complex pieces of legislation. Lord Justice Clarke said in *McGinn* v. *Grangewood Securities Ltd* [2002] EWCA Civ 522 that:

> [s]implification of a part of the law which is intended to protect consumers is surely long overdue so as to make it comprehensible to layman and lawyer alike. At present it is certainly not comprehensible to the former and is scarcely comprehensible to the latter.

It is, therefore, perhaps unsurprising that so much litigation and argument has followed.

Unfortunately, since Lord Justice Clarke expressed his view on CCA 1974 it has been significantly amended at least three times: first, with the changes to the Consumer Credit (Agreements) Regulations 1983, SI 1983/1553 (which came into effect on 31 May 2005); secondly, with the changes that came into effect by the Consumer Credit Act 2006 (which amended CCA 1974); and, thirdly, the most recent changes as a result of the Consumer Credit Directive (87/102/EEC) (which came into effect on 1 February 2011). This chapter and, indeed, this text, aims to help practitioners tackle consumer credit so, whilst it may not be an easy topic to grapple with, it is certainly more comprehensible.

1.2 KEY DEFINITIONS

Section 189(1) of CCA 1974 introduces a number of key definitions which are applied throughout CCA 1974 and also appear in regulations made under CCA 1974. Section 189(1) also usefully refers the reader, where a definition is not in s.189(1), to where it appears in CCA 1974. In this chapter (which is intended to be an overview for the rest of this text), we look at some of those definitions. Any successful consumer credit lawyer will always keep these definitions in mind when tackling problems. The key definitions are as follows:

- 'appropriate method' means (a) post or (b) transmission in the form of an electronic communication in accordance with s.176A(1);
- 'associate' is construed in accordance with s.184. This, in turn, says:
  - for individuals, an associate is the individual's husband or wife or civil partner; a relative of the individual, the individual's husband or wife or civil partner; or the husband or wife or civil partner of a relative (which is also defined by s.184(5)) of the individual or the individual's husband or wife or civil partner;
  - for partnerships, an associate is any person with whom a person is in partnership, and the husband, wife or civil partner or a relative of any individual with whom he is in partnership;
  - for a body corporate, an associate is another body corporate if the same person is a controller of both, or a person is a controller of one and persons who are his associates, or he and persons who are his associates, are controllers of the other; or if a group of two or more persons is a controller of each company, and the groups either consist of the same persons or could be considered as consisting of the same persons by treating (in one or more cases) a member of either group as replaced by a person of whom he is an associate;
  - for a body corporate, it is an associate of another person if that person is a controller of it or if that person and persons who are his associates together are controllers of it;
- 'authorised business overdraft agreement' means a debtor-creditor agreement which provides authorisation in advance for the debtor to overdraw on a current account, where the agreement is entered into by the debtor wholly or predominantly for the purposes of the debtor's business. This definition is also supplemented by s.189(2A);
- 'authorised non-business overdraft agreement' means a debtor-creditor agreement which provides authorisation in advance for the debtor to overdraw on a current account where (a) the credit must be repaid on demand or within three months and (b) the agreement is not entered into by the debtor wholly or predominantly for the purposes of the debtor's business. This definition is also supplemented by s.189(2A);
- 'business' includes a profession or trade. This definition is also supplemented by s.189(2);
- 'cancellable agreement' means a regulated agreement which, by s.67, may be cancelled by the debtor or hirer. We discuss cancellable agreements in Chapter 4 at **4.12**;
- 'cash' includes money in any form;
- 'conditional sale agreement' means an agreement for the sale of goods or land under which the purchase price or part of it is payable by instalments, and the property in the goods or land is to remain in the seller (despite the fact that the

buyer is to be in possession of the goods or land) until such conditions as to the payment of instalments or otherwise as may be specified in the agreement are fulfilled;

- 'consumer credit agreement' has the meaning given by s.8, and includes a consumer credit agreement which is cancelled under s.69(1), or becomes subject to s.69(2), so far as the agreement remains in force. We discuss consumer credit agreements at **1.3.1** below;
- 'consumer credit business' means any business being carried on by a person so far as it comprises or relates to (a) the provision of credit by him or (b) otherwise his being a creditor, under regulated consumer credit agreements;
- 'consumer hire agreement' has the meaning given by s.15. We discuss consumer hire agreements at **1.3.2** below;
- 'consumer hire business' means any business being carried on by a person so far as it comprises or relates to (a) the bailment or (in Scotland) the hiring of goods by him or (b) otherwise his being an owner, under regulated consumer hire agreements;
- 'controller', in relation to a body corporate, means a person (a) in accordance with whose directions or instructions the directors of the body corporate or of another body corporate which is its controller (or any of them) are accustomed to act, or (b) who, either alone or with any associate or associates, is entitled to exercise, or control the exercise of, one-third or more of the voting power at any general meeting of the body corporate or of another body corporate which is its controller;
- 'copy' is construed in accordance with s.180;
- 'court' means (for England and Wales) the county court;
- 'credit' is construed in accordance with s.9. We discuss the problematic concept of credit at **5.6.3**;
- 'credit-broker' means a person carrying on a business of credit brokerage. We discuss credit-brokers at **2.3.4**;
- 'credit brokerage' has the meaning given by s.145(2). We discuss credit brokerage at **2.3.4**;
- 'credit information services' has the meaning given by s.145(7B). We discuss credit information services at **2.3.9**;
- 'credit intermediary' has the meaning given by s.160A. This is a person who in the course of a business:

  – carries out, for a consideration that is, or includes, a financial consideration, any of the following activities: (a) recommending or making available prospective regulated consumer credit agreements, other than agreements secured on land, to individuals; (b) helping individuals by undertaking other preparatory work for such agreements; or (c) entering into regulated consumer credit agreements, other than agreements secured on land, with individuals on behalf of creditors; and
  – does not do so as a creditor.

A credit intermediary must by s.160A(2) disclose in certain adverts (discussed at **3.7.12**) and in certain documentation whether he is acting independently and, in particular, whether he works exclusively with a creditor. If the credit intermediary carries on such an activity for a debtor, the intermediary must secure that any financial consideration payable to him by the debtor for the activity is disclosed to the debtor and then agreed in writing before the regulated consumer credit agreement is concluded (s.160A(4)). Credit intermediaries who fail to comply with the requirements of s.160A commit a criminal offence (s.160A(6));

- 'credit limit' has the meaning given by s.10(2). We discuss the concept of the credit limit at **5.6.3**;
- 'creditor' means the person providing credit under a consumer credit agreement or the person to whom his rights and duties under the agreement have passed by assignment or operation of law, and in relation to a prospective consumer credit agreement, includes the prospective creditor;
- 'credit reference agency' has the meaning given by s.145(8). We discuss credit reference agencies at **2.3.10**;
- 'credit-sale agreement' means an agreement for the sale of goods, under which the purchase price or part of it is payable by instalments, but which is not a conditional sale agreement;
- 'credit-token' has the meaning given by s.14(1). We discuss credit-tokens at **1.4.7** below;
- 'credit-token agreement' means a regulated agreement for the provision of credit with the use of a credit-token. We discuss credit-token agreements at **1.4.7** below;
- 'debt-adjusting' has the meaning given by s.145(5). We discuss debt-adjusting at **2.3.5**;
- 'debt administration' has the meaning given by s.145(7A). We discuss debt administration at **2.3.8**;
- 'debt-collecting' has the meaning given by s.145(7). We discuss debt-collecting at **2.3.7**;
- 'debt-counselling' has the meaning given by s.145(6). We discuss debt-counselling at **2.3.6**;
- 'debtor' means the individual receiving credit under a consumer credit agreement or the person to whom his rights and duties under the agreement have passed by assignment or operation of law, and in relation to a prospective consumer credit agreement includes the prospective debtor;
- 'debtor-creditor agreement' has the meaning given by s.13. We discuss debtor-creditor agreements at **1.4.6** below;
- 'debtor-creditor-supplier agreement' has the meaning given by s.12. We discuss debtor-creditor-supplier agreements at **1.4.5** below;
- 'default notice' has the meaning given by s.87(1). We discuss default notices at **7.3.1**;
- 'default sum' has the meaning given by s.187A;

- 'deposit' means (except in ss.16(10) and 25(1B)) any sum payable by a debtor or hirer by way of deposit or down-payment, or credited or to be credited to him on account of any deposit or down-payment, whether the sum is to be, or has been, paid to the creditor or owner or any other person, or is to be, or has been, discharged by a payment of money or a transfer or delivery of goods or by any other means;
- 'electronic communication' means an electronic communication within the meaning of the Electronic Communications Act 2000;
- 'embodies' and related words are construed in accordance with s.189(4). This states that a document embodies a provision if the provision is set out either in the document itself or in another document referred to in it;
- 'enforcement authority' has the meaning given by s.161(1);
- 'enforcement order' means an order under ss.65(1), 105(7)(a) or (b), 111(2) or 124(1) or 124(2). We discuss enforcement orders at **10.2** and **10.3**;
- 'executed agreement' means a document, signed by for the parties, embodying the terms of a regulated agreement, or such of them as have been reduced to writing;
- 'exempt agreement' means an agreement specified in or under ss.16, 16A, 16B or 16C. We discuss exempt agreements at **1.3.3** below;
- 'fixed-sum credit' has the meaning given by s.10(1)(b). We discuss fixed-sum credit at **1.4.2** below;
- 'future arrangements' are construed in accordance with s.187;
- 'give' means to deliver or send by an appropriate method. We discuss service at **7.4**;
- 'goods' has the meaning given by s.61(1) of the Sale of Goods Act 1979;
- 'hire-purchase agreement' means an agreement, other than a conditional sale agreement, under which (a) goods are bailed or (in Scotland) hired in return for periodical payments by the person to whom they are bailed or hired and (b) the property in the goods will pass to that person if the terms of the agreement are complied with and one or more of the following occurs: (i) the exercise of an option to purchase by that person, (ii) the doing of any other specified act by any party to the agreement, (iii) the happening of any other specified event;
- 'hirer' means the individual to whom goods are bailed or (in Scotland) hired under a consumer hire agreement, or the person to whom his rights and duties under the agreement have passed by assignment or operation of law, and in relation to a prospective consumer hire agreement includes the prospective hirer;
- 'individual' means a natural person but also includes (a) a partnership consisting of two or three persons not all of whom are bodies corporate; and (b) an unincorporated body of persons which does not consist entirely of bodies corporate and is not a partnership;
- 'land' includes an interest in land;
- 'land mortgage' includes any security charged on land;
- 'licence' means a licence under CCA 1974, Part III (see **Chapter 2**);

- 'licensed' in relation to any act, means authorised by a licence to do the act or cause or permit another person to do it;
- 'linked transaction' has the meaning given by s.19(1). We discuss linked agreements at **1.3.6** below;
- 'modifying agreement' has the meaning given by s.82(2). We discuss modifying agreements at **6.13**;
- 'multiple agreement' has the meaning given by s.18(1). We discuss multiple agreements at **1.3.5** below;
- 'negotiator' has the meaning given by s.56(1);
- 'non-commercial agreement' means a consumer credit agreement or a consumer hire agreement not made by the creditor or owner in the course of a business carried on by him;
- 'notice' means notice in writing;
- 'notice of cancellation' has the meaning given by s.69(1);
- 'open-end' in relation to a consumer credit agreement, means of no fixed duration;
- 'owner' means a person who bails or (in Scotland) hires out goods under a consumer hire agreement or the person to whom his rights and duties under the agreement have passed by assignment or operation of law, and in relation to a prospective consumer hire agreement, includes the prospective bailor or person from whom the goods are to be hired;
- 'pawn' means any article subject to a pledge. We discuss pawn agreements at **9.7**;
- 'pawn-receipt' has the meaning given by s.114;
- 'pawnee' and 'pawnor' include any person to whom the rights and duties of the original pawnee or the original pawnor, as the case may be, have passed by assignment or operation of law;
- 'pledge' means the pawnee's rights over an article taken in pawn;
- 'prescribed' means prescribed by regulations made by the Secretary of State;
- 'pre-existing arrangements' is construed in accordance with s.187;
- 'principal agreement' has the meaning given by s.19(1);
- 'protected goods' has the meaning given by s.90(7). We discuss protected goods at **7.3.5**;
- 'redemption period' has the meaning given by s.116(3). We discuss the redemption period at **9.7.3**;
- 'regulated agreement' means a consumer credit agreement, or consumer hire agreement, other than an exempt agreement, and 'regulated' and 'unregulated' are construed accordingly;
- 'regulations' means regulations made by the Secretary of State;
- 'relative' means, except in s.184, a person who is an associate by virtue of s.184(1);
- 'representation' includes any condition or warranty, and any other statement or undertaking, whether oral or in writing;

- 'restricted-use credit agreement' and 'restricted-use credit' have the meanings given by s.11(1). We discuss these concepts at **1.4.3** below;
- 'running-account credit' is construed in accordance with s.10. We discuss running-account credit at **1.4.1** below;
- 'security', in relation to an actual or prospective consumer credit agreement or consumer hire agreement, or any linked transaction, means a mortgage, charge, pledge, bond, debenture, indemnity, guarantee, bill, note or other right provided by the debtor or hirer, or at his request (express or implied), to secure the carrying out of the obligations of the debtor or hirer under the agreement (see **Chapter 9**);
- 'security instrument' has the meaning given by s.105(2);
- 'serve on' means deliver or send by an appropriate method to. We discuss service at **7.4**;
- 'signed' is construed in accordance with s.189(3). This states that any provision of CCA 1974 requiring a document to be signed is complied with by a body corporate if the document is sealed by that body;
- 'small agreement' has the meaning given by s.17(1), and 'small' in relation to an agreement within any category is construed accordingly. We discuss small agreements at **1.3.4** below;
- 'standard licence' has the meaning given by s.22(1)(a);
- 'supplier' has the meaning given by ss.11(1)(b) or 12(c) or 13(c) or, for an agreement falling within s.11(1)(a), means the creditor, and includes a person to whom the rights and duties of a supplier (as so defined) have passed by assignment or operation of law, or (in relation to a prospective agreement) the prospective supplier;
- 'surety' means the person by whom any security is provided, or the person to whom his rights and duties in relation to the security have passed by assignment or operation of law;
- 'technical grounds' is construed in accordance with s.189(5). This states that an application dismissed by the court or the Office of Fair Trading (OFT) will, if the court or the OFT (as the case may be) so certifies, be taken to be dismissed on technical grounds only;
- 'time order' has the meaning given by s.129(1). We discuss time orders at **10.4**;
- 'total charge for credit' means a sum calculated in accordance with regulations made under s.20(1). We discuss the total charge for credit at **5.6.4**;
- 'total price' means the total sum payable by the debtor under a hire-purchase agreement or a conditional sale agreement, including any sum payable on the exercise of an option to purchase, but excluding any sum payable as a penalty or as compensation or damages for a breach of the agreement;
- 'unexecuted agreement' means a document embodying the terms of a prospective regulated agreement, or such of them as it is intended to reduce to writing;
- 'unlicensed' means without a licence, but applies only in relation to acts for which a licence is required;

- 'unrestricted-use credit agreement' and 'unrestricted-use credit' have the meanings given by s.11(2). We discuss these concepts at **1.4.4** below;
- 'working day' means any day other than (a) Saturday or Sunday, (b) Christmas Day or Good Friday, (c) a bank holiday within the meaning given by the Banking and Financial Dealings Act 1971, s.1.

1.3 TYPES OF AGREEMENTS

1.3.1 Consumer credit agreements

The starting point for what is a consumer credit agreement is found in CCA 1974, s.8. This underwent significant change in April 2008 which, most importantly, removed the limit of £25,000 for all regulated consumer credit agreements. There is now no such limit. Section 8(1) defines a consumer credit agreement as an agreement between an 'individual' (as defined in s.189(1)) (called 'the debtor') and any other person (called 'the creditor') under which the creditor provides the debtor with credit of any amount. Section 8(3) states that a consumer credit agreement is a regulated agreement unless it is exempt by virtue of ss.16–16C (or regulations made under those sections). We discuss exempt agreements at **1.3.3** below.

The relatively broad wording of s.8(1) can cause significant practical difficulties. For example, it potentially covers any agreement between an individual and another person (who does not need to be a finance company) providing credit. We will look in detail of the meaning of the word 'credit' at **5.6.3**. There is some help in CCA 1974, s.189(2) which states that a person is not to be treated as carrying on a particular type of business merely because occasionally he enters into transactions belonging to a business of that type. It is submitted, therefore, that occasional loans made by employers to employees, or parents to children, are unlikely to be regulated by CCA 1974. To ensure that they are not, solicitors advising persons proposing to lend monies should ensure that, first, their client is aware of the risk (and the consequences of an agreement being declared a regulated agreement) and, second, that the risk can be avoided if the terms are negotiated so that it is an exempt agreement.

1.3.2 Consumer hire agreements

The starting point for a consumer hire agreement is found in CCA 1974, s.15. Like the definition of a consumer credit agreement, s.15 has similarly undergone significant change in April 2008 with, also importantly, the removal of the limit of £25,000 for all consumer hire agreements. Section 15(1) defines a consumer hire agreement as an agreement made by a person with an 'individual' (called the 'hirer') for the bailment or (in Scotland) the hiring of goods (because in Scotland an owner hires goods while in England and Wales an owner bails goods) to the hirer, being an agreement which:

- is not a hire-purchase agreement; and
- is capable of lasting for more than three months.

By s.15(2), a consumer hire agreement is a regulated agreement unless it is exempt by virtue of CCA 1974, ss.16–16C (or regulations made under those sections). We discuss exempt agreements at **1.3.3** below.

Section 15(1) therefore contains a clear distinction between hire-purchase agreements (which are consumer credit agreements) and consumer hire agreements. Hire-purchase agreements differ significantly from hire agreements: a hire-purchase agreement gives the debtor an option to buy the goods but a hire agreement does not give the hirer any such option (the goods will always be returned to the owner). The leading case on what is a hire-purchase agreement is the House of Lords' decision in *Helby* v. *Matthews* [1895] AC 471.

1.3.3 Exempt agreements

Introduction

Exempt agreements play a crucial role in CCA 1974. Without them, a number of agreements would be classed as regulated agreements meaning the creditor or owner would need to comply with the detailed requirements of CCA 1974. To overcome this issue, CCA 1974 introduces a concept of 'exempt agreements'. Such agreements are completely excluded from the requirements of CCA 1974 except for the unfair relationship provisions (which apply to credit agreements, not hire agreements – see **10.11**). More recently, there has been an increase in the number of exemptions under CCA 1974 following the introduction of ss.16A–16C. We now turn to look at those requirements.

General exemptions

Until 6 April 2008, s.16 of CCA 1974 and the Consumer Credit (Exempt Agreements) Order 1989, SI 1989/869 (CC(EA)O 1989) contained the only exemptions from CCA 1974. From 6 April 2008, we have further exemptions contained in ss.16A–16C of the amended CCA 1974 and the Consumer Credit (Exempt Agreements) Order 2007, SI 2007/1168 (CC(EA)O 2007).

Section 16 and CC(EA)O 1989

CCA 1974, s.16 is another example of complicated drafting. It requires the practitioner to consider both s.16 and CC(EA)O 1989 to work out what exemptions remain. The combined effect of those provisions is that the main classes of exemption are:

- mortgages with local authorities and other specified bodies;
- agreements with a limited number of payments;

- agreements with specific rates of interest;
- agreements with a connection outside the UK; and
- agreements for metering equipment for gas, water or electricity.

CERTAIN MORTGAGES

By art.2(1) of CC(EA)O 1989, CCA 1974 does not regulate consumer credit agreements which fall within s.16(2). This, in turn, is limited by CC(EA)O 1989, art.2(2) to agreements where:

- the creditor is: (i) a body specified in CC(EA)O 1989, Sched.1, Part I; or (ii) a deposit taker within the meaning of CCA 1974, s.16(10); and
- the agreement is:

  - a debtor-creditor-supplier agreement:

    - financing: (i) the purchase of land; or (ii) the provision of dwellings on any land, and secured by a land mortgage on that land (i.e. within CCA 1974, s.16(2)); or
    - financing a transaction which is a linked transaction for: (i) an agreement falling within s.16(2)(a); or (ii) a debtor-creditor agreement secured by any land mortgage financing the purchase of any land or the provision of dwellings on any land (i.e. within CCA 1974, s.16(2)(c)),

    and secured by a land mortgage on the land referred to in s.16(2)(a) or, as the case may be, the land purchased or acquired for the provision of dwellings within s.16(2)(c);
  - a debtor-creditor agreement secured by any land mortgage to finance:

    - the purchase of land; or
    - the provision of dwellings or business premises on any land; or
    - (subject to art.2(3)), the alteration, enlarging, repair or improvement of a dwelling or business premises on any land;

  - a debtor-creditor agreement secured by any land mortgage to refinance the debtor's existing indebtedness (whether to the creditor or another person) under any agreement by which the debtor was provided with credit for any of the purposes of:

    - the purchase of land;
    - the provision of dwellings or business premises on any land; or
    - (subject to art.2(3)), the alteration, enlarging, repair or improvement of a dwelling or business premises on any land.

The limitation imposed in CC(EA)O 1989, art.2(3) means that it only applies where:

- by art.2(3)(i), the creditor is the creditor under:

  - an agreement (whenever made) by which the debtor is provided with credit for the purchase of land or the provision of dwellings or business premises on any land; or
  - an agreement (whenever made) refinancing an agreement under which the debtor is provided with credit for any of those purposes,

  being, in either case, an agreement relating to the land upon which any dwelling or business premises are to be altered, enlarged, repaired or improved and secured by a land mortgage on that land; or

- by art.2(3)(ii), where a debtor-creditor agreement to finance the alteration, enlarging, repair or improvement of a dwelling, secured by a land mortgage on that dwelling, is made as a result of any such services as are described in s.4(3)(e) of the Housing Associations Act 1985 (HAA 1985) which are certified as having been provided by:

  - a local authority;
  - a housing association within the meaning of HAA 1985, s.1 or the Housing (Northern Ireland) Order 1981, SI 1981/156, art.114;
  - a body established by such a housing association for the purpose of providing such services as are described in HAA 1985, s.4(3)(e);
  - a charity;
  - the National Home Improvement Council;
  - the Northern Ireland Housing Executive;
  - a body, or a body of any description, that has been approved by the Secretary of State under the Local Government and Housing Act 1989, s.169(4)(c).

By art.2(4), if the creditor is a body specified in Part II of Sched.1 to CC(EA)O 1989, then art.2(1) applies only to an agreement specified in that Part in relation to that body and made under an enactment or for a purpose so specified.

By art.2(5), if the creditor is a body specified in Part III of Sched.1 to CC(EA)O 1989, then art.2(1) applies only to an agreement of a description falling within art.2(2)(a)–(c), being an agreement advancing money on the security of a dwelling-house.

NUMBER OF PAYMENTS

By art.3(1) of CC(EA)O 1989, CCA 1974 does not regulate any of the following consumer credit agreements:

- by art.3(1)(a), a debtor-creditor-supplier agreement for fixed-sum credit (unless it is, by art.3(2), an agreement to finance the purchase of land, an agreement for conditional sale or hire-purchase or an agreement secured by pledge (other than a pledge of documents of title or of bearer bonds)) under which:

- the total number of payments to be made by the debtor does not exceed four;
- those payments must be made within a period not exceeding 12 months beginning with the date of the agreement (the key phrase here is 'not exceeding': it is submitted that an agreement for 12 months from the date of the agreement falls within this exemption); and
- the credit is provided without interest and without any other charges (i.e. interest free credit);

• by art.3(1)(a), a debtor-creditor-supplier agreement for running-account credit (unless it is, by art.3(2), an agreement to finance the purchase of land, an agreement for conditional sale or hire-purchase or an agreement secured by pledge (other than a pledge of documents of title or of bearer bonds)):

- which requires payments to be made by the debtor for specific periods of no longer than three months;
- which requires one payment to be made by the debtor to repay the whole amount of the credit provided in each period; and
- where no or 'insignificant charges' are payable for the credit;

• by art.3(1)(b), a debtor-creditor-supplier agreement financing the purchase of land under which:

- the debtor does not need to make more than four payments; and
- the credit is provided without interest and without any other charges;

• by art.3(1)(c), a debtor-creditor-supplier agreement for fixed-sum credit to finance a premium under a contract of insurance for any land or to anything on that land where:

- the creditor is the creditor under an agreement secured by a land mortgage on that land which either is an exempt agreement by virtue of CCA 1974, s.16(1) or of CC(EA)O 1989, art.2, or is a personal credit agreement which would be an exempt agreement by virtue of either of those provisions if the credit provided were not to exceed £15,000;
- the amount of the credit is to be repaid within the period to which the premium relates, not being a period exceeding 12 months;
- the credit is provided without interest and without any other charges; and
- the number of payments to be made by the debtor does not exceed 12;

• by art.3(1)(d), a debtor-creditor-supplier agreement for fixed-sum credit where:

- the creditor is the creditor under an agreement secured by a land mortgage on that land which either is an exempt agreement by virtue of CCA 1974, s.16(1) or of CC(EA)O 1989, art.2, or is a personal credit agreement which would be an exempt agreement by virtue of either of those provisions if the credit provided were not to exceed £15,000;

– the agreement is to finance a premium under a contract of life insurance which provides, in the event of the death before the credit under the secured agreement has been repaid of the person on whose life the contract is effected, for payment of a sum not exceeding the amount sufficient to pay the sums which, immediately after that credit has been advanced, would be payable to the creditor in respect of that credit and of the total charge for that credit;

– the credit is provided without interest and without any other charges; and

– the number of payments to be made by the debtor does not exceed 12.

By virtue of art.3(1A) of CC(EA)O 1989 there are some tweaks to these exemptions for consumer credit agreements secured on land. These are where:

• the agreement is a debtor-creditor-supplier agreement for fixed-sum credit within art.3(1)(a), there is no requirement for the credit to be provided without interest and without any other charges (art.3(1A)(a));

• the agreement is a debtor-creditor-supplier agreement for running-account credit within art.3(1)(a), there is no requirement for the specific periods to be three months and the requirement for no or 'insignificant charges' are payable for the credit is deleted (art 3(1A)(b));

• the agreement is a debtor-creditor-supplier agreement financing the purchase of land within art.3(1)(b), there is no requirement for the credit to be provided without interest and without any other charges (art.3(1A)(c));

• the agreement is a debtor-creditor-supplier agreement for fixed-sum credit to finance a premium under a contract of insurance for any land or to anything on that land within art.3(1)(c), the third requirement for the credit to be provided without interest and charges is replaced by a requirement that there is no charge forming part of the total charge for credit under the agreement other than interest at a rate not exceeding the rate of interest from time to time payable under the land mortgage mentioned in the first condition (art.3(1A)(d)); and

• the agreement is a debtor-creditor-supplier agreement for fixed-sum credit within art.3(1)(d), the third requirement for the credit to be provided without interest and charges is replaced by a requirement that there is no charge forming part of the total charge for credit under the agreement other than interest at a rate not exceeding the rate of interest from time to time payable under the land mortgage mentioned in the first condition (art.3(1A)(e)).

RATE OF INTEREST

Under CC(EA)O 1989, art.4, CCA 1974 does not regulate the following:

- a debtor-creditor agreement where the creditor is a credit union (defined in art.4(4)) and the rate of the total charge for credit (calculated in accordance with the Consumer Credit (Total Charge for Credit) Regulations 2010, SI 2010/1011 (CC(TCC)R 2010) or, if appropriate, the Consumer Credit (Total Charge for Credit) Regulations 1980, SI 1980/51 (CC(TCC)R 1980)) does not exceed 26.9 per cent (art.4(1)(a));
- (subject to CC(EA)O 1989, art.4(2) and (2A)) a debtor-creditor agreement which is an agreement of a type offered to a particular class, or particular classes, of individuals and not offered to the public generally, and under the terms of which the only charge included in the total charge for credit is interest which cannot at any time exceed the sum of 1 per cent and the highest of the base rates published by the banks named in art.4(3), being the latest rates in operation on the date 28 days before any such time (art.4(1)(b)).
- (subject to CC(EA)O 1989, art.4(2) and (2A)) a debtor-creditor agreement (art.4(1)(c)), which is an agreement of a type offered to a particular class, or particular classes, of individuals and not offered to the public generally, under which there can be no increase after the relevant date in the rate or amount of any item which is included in the total charge for credit or which would be included but for CC(TCC)R 1980, reg.14, and where the rate of the total charge for credit does not exceed the sum of 1 per cent and the highest of the base rates published by the banks named in art.4(3), being the latest rates in operation on the date 28 days before the date on which the agreement is made.

By art.4(2), the exemptions in art.4(1)(b) and (c) do *not* apply to an agreement under which the total amount to be repaid by the debtor to discharge his indebtedness for the amount of credit provided may vary according to a formula which is specified in the agreement and which has effect by reference to movements in the level of any index or to any other factor.

By art.4(2A), where an agreement mentioned in art.4(1)(b) or (c) is not an agreement offered by a creditor who is an employer to a debtor as an incident of employment with the creditor, or is not an agreement secured on land, then those sub-paragraphs do *not* apply to the agreement unless the following conditions (contained in art.4(2B)) are satisfied:

- the agreement is offered under an enactment with a general interest purpose; *and*
- the rate of interest (if any) on the credit which may be provided under the agreement is either:
  - at a rate which is lower than that prevailing on the market, or
  - at a rate which is not higher than that prevailing on the market where the other terms on which credit may be provided are more favourable for the debtor than those prevailing on the market.

The provisions of CC(EA)O 1989, art.4(2A) came into force on 1 February 2011 as a result of the Consumer Credit Directive. The revisions (which are entirely new) have dramatically reduced the ability to offer exempt agreements at a low interest.

CONNECTION OUTSIDE THE UK

By virtue of CC(EA)O 1989, art.5, CCA 1974 does not regulate a consumer credit agreement made:

- for goods or services between the UK and a country outside the UK or within a country or between countries outside the UK, being an agreement under which credit is provided to the debtor in the course of a business carried on by him; or
- between a creditor (who must either be a Federal Credit Union (as defined in the Federal Credit Union Act of the United States of America of 26 June 1934), American Book Distributors Inc. or NationsBank of Texas, NA) and a debtor who is:

  - a member of any of the armed forces of the United States of America;
  - an employee not habitually resident in the UK of any of those forces; or
  - any such member's or employee's wife or husband or any other person (whether or not a child of his) whom he wholly or partly maintains and treats as a child of the family.

METERING EQUIPMENT FOR GAS, WATER OR ELECTRICITY

Under CC(EA)O 1989, art.6, CCA 1974 does not regulate consumer hire agreements (but does regulate consumer credit agreements) for the metering of gas, water or electricity where the owner is a body corporate authorised by or under any enactment to supply electricity, gas or water. It is, therefore, important for electricity, gas or water suppliers to provide equipment under a hire agreement and not a hire-purchase agreement.

High net worth debtors and hirers

Until 6 April 2008, CCA 1974 did not recognise the concept of high net worth debtors or hirers. Instead, provided that the agreement was a regulated agreement, the debtor's or hirer's financial position was largely irrelevant. From 6 April 2008, we now have such a two-tier system. By s.16A(1), the Secretary of State was given powers to order that CCA 1974 does not regulate a consumer credit agreement or a consumer hire agreement. The Secretary of State made such an order in CC(EA)O 2007.

The framework is set out in CCA 1974, s.16A(1). It applies where:

- the debtor or hirer is a 'natural person';

- the agreement includes a declaration made by him saying that he does not want the protection and remedies that would be available to him under CCA 1974 if the agreement were a regulated agreement;
- a statement of high net worth has been made in relation to him; and
- that statement is current in relation to the agreement and a copy of it was provided to the creditor or owner before the agreement was made.

Section 16A is supplemented by CC(EA)O 2007. By CC(EA)O 2007, art.2, CCA 1974 does not regulate a consumer credit agreement or consumer hire agreement where:

- the debtor or hirer is a natural person;
- from 1 February 2011 and for consumer credit agreements other than agreements secured on land, the agreement is for credit which exceeds £60,260;
- the agreement includes a declaration made by him complying with CC(EA)O 2007, art.3 and Sched.1;
- a statement of high net worth complying with CC(EA)O 2007, arts.4, 5 and Sched.2 has been made in relation to him;
- the statement was made during the period of one year ending with the day on which the agreement was made; and
- before the agreement was made a copy of that statement was provided to the debtor or hirer and, if the statement was not made by the creditor or owner, to the creditor or owner.

Under CC(EA)O 2007, art.3, the declaration must be:

- set out in the consumer credit agreement or consumer hire agreement no less prominently than other information in the agreement and be readily distinguishable from the background medium; and
- signed by the debtor or hirer, unless the agreement is so signed.

There is no explanation of what is meant by the phrase 'unless the agreement is so signed'. It is therefore advisable that even if the agreement is signed, the declaration is also separately signed.

By CC(EA)O 2007, art.4(1) (and subject to art.5), a statement of high net worth must be signed by any of the following:

- the creditor or owner; or
- an accountant who is a member of any of the following bodies:
    - the Institute of Chartered Accountants in England and Wales;
    - the Institute of Chartered Accountants of Scotland;
    - the Institute of Chartered Accounts in Ireland;
    - the Association of Chartered Certified Accountants;
    - the Chartered Institute of Management Accountants;
    - the Chartered Institute of Public Finance and Accountancy; or

- a professional body for accountants established in a jurisdiction outside the United Kingdom.

The limitation imposed by art.5 is that a person who is: (i) the creditor or owner; (ii) an employee or agent of the creditor or owner or a person who otherwise acts for the creditor or owner in relation to the consumer credit agreement or consumer hire agreement; or (iii) an associate of the creditor or owner, may only make a statement of high net worth if the creditor or owner is a person who has permission under Part IV of the Financial Services and Markets Act 2000 to accept deposits. This is, of course, usually limited to retail banking institutions. It is also unclear whether an accountancy firm may sign the declaration in its firm's name (rather than the name of the individual accountant). It is suggested that if a firm can be a member of any of those bodies, it probably can sign the declaration.

It is also important to remember that:

- a declaration of high net worth can only be made where the natural individual has received during the previous financial year net income totalling an amount of not less than £150,000 and/or had throughout that year net assets with a total value of not less than £500,000 (which, importantly, does not include the value of the debtor's or hirer's primary residence or any loan secured on the that residence) by virtue of CCA 1974, s.16A(2);
- a declaration of high net worth cannot be made by the debtor or hirer by virtue of CCA 1974, s.16A(3)(a);
- where an agreement has two or more debtors or hirers, a separate statement of high net worth must have been made for all of them by virtue of CCA 1974, s.16A(5);
- an exempt agreement can still be challenged by the unfair relationship provisions in CCA 1974, ss.140A–D (discussed at **10.11**) by virtue of CCA 1974, s.16A(8).

Precedents

For a precedent form of declaration of high net worth by the debtor or hirer, see **Precedent 1**.
For a precedent statement of high net worth, see **Precedent 2**.

Business exemption

Before the repeal of the £25,000 'limit' for consumer credit agreements and consumer hire agreements on 6 April 2008, many business loans to 'individuals' (as defined by s.189) were (by the size of the lending) outside the scope of CCA 1974. The abolition of the £25,000 limit therefore had the potential to turn a substantial number of business loans into regulated agreements. To counter this issue, a further exemption for businesses was introduced on 6 April 2008. It does not act retrospectively.

By s.16B(1), CCA 1974 does not regulate:

- a consumer credit agreement by which the creditor provides the debtor with credit exceeding £25,000; or
- a consumer hire agreement that requires the hirer to make payments exceeding £25,000,

if the agreement is entered into by the debtor or hirer wholly or predominantly for the purposes of a business carried on, or intended to be carried on, by him.

The key question, when deciding whether the exemption applies, is therefore whether the agreement is entered into by the debtor or hirer wholly or predominantly for the purposes of a business carried on, or intended to be carried on, by him. This is a question of fact and may, in some cases, cause creditors some difficulties. CCA 1974, s.16B(2) goes some way to helping solve that problem by stating that if an agreement includes a declaration made by the debtor or hirer recording that the agreement is entered into by him wholly or predominantly for the purposes of a business carried on, or intended to be carried on, by him, there is a presumption that it is entered into for business purposes and is therefore not regulated. Creditors or owners should therefore ensure that business loans, as a matter of course, include such a declaration. There is also a prescribed form of declaration, contained in CC(EA)O 2007, Sched.3. These regulations were made under CCA 1974, s.16B(4).

Under CC(EA)O 2007, art.6 the form of declaration must:

- comply with Sched.3;
- be set out in the consumer credit agreement or consumer hire agreement no less prominently than other information in the agreement and be readily distinguishable from the background medium; and
- be signed by the debtor or hirer or where the debtor or hirer is a partnership or unincorporated body of persons be signed by or for the debtor or hirer, unless the agreement is so signed.

Precedent

For a precedent form of declaration of business use, see **Precedent 3**.

The presumption of business use is, however, rebuttable. By virtue of CCA 1974, s.16B(3), it does not apply if (when the agreement is entered into) the creditor or owner, or any person who has acted for the creditor or owner in connection with the entering into of the agreement knows, or has reasonable cause to suspect, that the agreement is not entered into by the debtor or hirer wholly or predominantly for the purposes of a business carried on, or intended to be carried on, by him. It is therefore important for creditors or owners to ensure that anyone who could be seen to be acting for them has made enquiries to establish the purpose of the loan. This may be achieved by a standard form being completed by any third party confirming the enquiries made (and the debtor's or hirer's response to that enquiry). This could then be returned with the application for the loan.

Investment properties exemption

From 31 October 2008, and by s.16C(1) and (2), CCA 1974 does not regulate a consumer credit agreement if, at the time the agreement is entered into, any sums due under it are secured by a land mortgage on land where less than 40 per cent of the land is used, or is intended to be used, as, or in connection with, a dwelling:

- by the debtor or a person connected with the debtor; or
- in the case of credit provided to trustees, by an individual who is the beneficiary of the trust or a person connected with such an individual.

Section 16C(2) is supplemented:

- by s.16C(3), which states that the area of any land which comprises a building or other structure containing two or more storeys is to be taken to be the aggregate of the floor areas of each of those storeys; and
- by s.16C(4), which states that a person is 'connected with' the debtor or an individual who is the beneficiary of a trust if he is:

  - that person's spouse or civil partner;
  - a person (whether or not of the opposite sex) whose relationship with that person has the characteristics of the relationship between husband and wife; or
  - that person's parent, brother, sister, child, grandparent or grandchild.

It is important to remember, however, that CCA 1974, s.126, which prevents the enforcement of land mortgages without a court order, still applies to an agreement which would, but for s.16C, be a regulated agreement (s.16C(5)). Creditors or owners under such agreements must therefore obtain a court order before recovering possession of the land.

1.3.4 Small agreements

The curious provisions on small agreements are contained in CCA 1974, s.17. By s.17(1), a small agreement is:

- a regulated consumer credit agreement for credit not exceeding £50, other than a hire-purchase or conditional sale agreement; or
- a regulated consumer hire agreement which does not require the hirer to make payments exceeding £50,

being an agreement which is either unsecured or secured by a guarantee or indemnity only (whether or not the guarantee or indemnity is secured).

If the consumer credit agreement is for running-account credit then the test is whether the credit limit exceeds £50. If it does, it cannot be a small agreement (s.17(2)).

By s.17(3), where two or more small agreements are made at or about the same time between the same parties and it appears probable that they would instead have been made as a single agreement but for the desire to avoid the provisions of s.17, then CCA 1974 applies to the small agreements as if they were regulated agreements other than small agreements.

Section 17(4) contains a similar provision where a creditor or owner tries to split the agreements up between various entities (i.e. ABC Finance 1 Limited, ABC Finance 2 Limited, etc.) where those entities are group companies.

The effect of s.17(3) and (4) is therefore key: they prevent a creditor or owner from splitting a number of agreements into small agreements to avoid some of the protection of CCA 1974. Section 17 makes it clear that such an avoidance technique will not be allowed.

1.3.5 Multiple agreements

Perhaps one of the most complex provisions of CCA 1974 is s.18 which deals with multiple agreements. Its perceived purpose is, much like the effect of s.17(4) for small agreements, apparently simple: to stop creditors or owners combining a number of agreements together so that the amount of credit exceeds the former statutory caps for regulation of £15,000 and, more recently, £25,000. Since the repeal of the financial cap, there have been compelling calls for the repeal of s.18. Unfortunately, it remains on the statutory book.

By s.18(1), s.18 applies to an agreement (called a 'multiple agreement') if its terms are such as:

- to place a part of it within one 'category' of agreement mentioned in CCA 1974, and another part of it within a different 'category' of agreement, or within a 'category' of agreement not mentioned in CCA 1974 (s.18(1)(a)); or
- to place it, or a part of it, within two or more 'categories' of agreement mentioned in CCA 1974 (s.18(1)(b)).

The effect of part of an agreement falling within s.18(1) is that, by s.18(2), that part is treated for the purposes of CCA 1974 as a separate agreement. By s.18(3), if an agreement falls within s.18(1)(b), it is treated as an agreement in each of the categories and CCA 1974 accordingly applies to it. If part of an agreement is to be treated as a separate agreement by s.18(2) then, by s.18(4), the multiple agreement will (with any necessary modifications) be construed accordingly. For example, any sum payable under the multiple agreement, if not apportioned by the parties, will for the purposes of proceedings in any court relating to the multiple agreement be apportioned by the court as may be required.

Section 18(5) provides an important limitation to s.18 for creditors under running-account credit: it states that a term of the agreement allowing the credit limit to be exceeded temporarily is not to be treated as a separate agreement or as an agreement providing fixed-sum credit for the excess. There is a less important limitation contained in s.18(6): it states that CCA 1974 does not apply to a multiple agreement so far as the agreement relates to goods if under the agreement payments are made for the goods in the form of rent (other than a rentcharge) issuing out of land.

Despite CCA 1974, s.189(1) including a considerable number of definitions, it does not define the words 'category' or 'part'. This has caused a considerable amount of debate, and litigation, by debtors seeking to arguing that their agreement is a multiple agreement requiring two separately documented agreements and the creditor's or owner's failure to document in this way makes the agreement (if before 6 April 2007) irredeemably unenforceable.

Until recently, there have been a number of conflicting county court and High Court decisions. The Court of Appeal has, however, recently considered the issue of multiple agreements in *Southern Pacific Mortgage Ltd* v. *Jayne Elizabeth Heath* [2009] EWCA Civ 1135. Ms Heath owed a property in Worksop subject to a charge in favour of the Halifax. The balance outstanding was around £19,000. She applied for and obtained a loan from a creditor for around £28,000. It was a condition of the loan that Ms Heath's existing loan with the Halifax would be paid off on completion and the debt would be secured against her property as a second charge. Ms Heath accepted the terms and entered into an agreement with the new lender. Upon completion, her mortgage with the Halifax was redeemed and Ms Heath received the balance of around £9,000 to spend as she wished.

The lender later assigned its agreement with Ms Heath to Southern Pacific Mortgage Ltd. The total credit advanced exceeded £25,000 (the statutory limit at the time of the loan) meaning, on the face of it, the agreement was not regulated by CCA 1974 or subject to the Consumer Credit (Agreements) Regulations 1983, SI 1983/1553 (CC(A)R 1983). The Court of Appeal correctly stated that the issue for it to decide was whether the transaction (not the credit) fell under s.18, meaning it had to be split into parts and require separate documentation. The court noted that if Ms Heath's argument was correct (i.e. that the agreement was a multiple agreement because there were two loans: one for restricted-use credit to pay off the Halifax loan and another for unrestricted-use credit which Ms Heath was free to spend as she wished), it would pose substantial practical difficulties. For example, if part of the loan was to be used to pay off an existing debt then the amount may not be easy to work out: it would often alter on a daily basis. To state the precise figure on the agreement may therefore be difficult, meaning (if the agreement was regulated) it may be unenforceable. This, Lord Justice Lloyd said, must be a relevant consideration.

The Court of Appeal dismissed Ms Heath's appeal and said, in particular, that:

- the starting point is the terms of the loan. From this, one must work out whether the agreement is one advance, under which there are two or more parts in different categories, or whether it (or part of it) falls into two or more categories;
- it was wrong to start from the proposition that if there seemed to be more than one disparate category (i.e. restricted-use credit to pay off the Halifax advance and unrestricted-use credit for the balance) then the agreement must fall into two or more parts;
- instead, the question is whether the agreement falls into one or more categories, not the credit provided under it;
- the use of the word 'category' was the same in s.18(1)(a) and (b) and meant disparate categories (for example, restricted-use and unrestricted-use or running-account credit and fixed-sum credit): it did not mean compatible categories (like unrestricted-use, debtor-creditor and running-account credit);
- s.18(1)(b) recognised that the agreement as a whole could fall within more than one category without being an agreement in parts (which would require separate documentation).

Taking these considerations into account, Ms Heath's loan was not split between the amount to be paid towards the Halifax charge and the amount which Ms Heath was free to use. Instead, there was simply a term of the agreement requiring part of the loan to be used to pay off the outstanding mortgage. This was not a multiple agreement and it would be an artificial exercise for the court to notionally apportion the monies between the two categories. Given the decision in *Heath* and the removal of the £25,000 limit, the repeal of s.18 is long overdue.

1.3.6 Linked transactions

CCA 1974, s.19 tackles an important definition: linked transactions. This is referred to throughout CCA 1974 and is extremely important for cancellable agreements. By s.19(1) a transaction entered into by the debtor or hirer, or a relative of his, with any other person (the 'other party'), except one providing security, is a linked transaction for the actual or prospective regulated agreement (called the 'principal agreement') of which it does not form part if:

- the transaction is entered into in compliance with a term of the principal agreement; or
- the principal agreement is a debtor-creditor-supplier agreement and the transaction is financed, or to be financed, by the principal agreement; or
- the other party is:
  - the creditor or owner, or his associate;
  - a person who, in the negotiation of the transaction, is represented by a credit-broker who is also a negotiator in antecedent negotiations for the principal agreement;

– a person who, at the time the transaction is initiated, knows that the principal agreement has been made or contemplates that it might be made,

and that person initiated the transaction by suggesting it to the debtor or hirer, or his relative, who enters into it:

– to induce the creditor or owner to enter into the principal agreement; or
– for another purpose related to the principal agreement; or
– where the principal agreement is a restricted-use credit agreement, for a purpose related to a transaction financed, or to be financed, by the principal agreement.

The importance of linked transactions is set out in CCA 1974, s.19(3): this makes it clear that a linked transaction entered into before the making of the principal agreement has no effect unless and until that agreement is made. By s.19(4), regulations may exclude linked transactions from the effect of s.19(3).

Example

Miss Goodman wants to buy a new motor car but does not have the funds to buy it. She visits her local motor dealer who offers to sell a motor car she is interested in for £7,000 and apply for credit with a third party creditor. The motor dealer also offers to service the motor car for the next three years for £300 if she enters into the agreement today. The motor dealer is happy for the cost to also be financed by the creditor. After searching for an appropriate creditor, Miss Goodman is offered credit for £7,300 and enters into the agreement. Because the hire purchase is a debtor-creditor-supplier agreement and the maintenance contract is financed by that agreement, the maintenance agreement is a linked transaction.

1.4 TYPES OF CONSUMER CREDIT AGREEMENTS

1.4.1 Running-account credit

Under CCA 1974, s.10(1)(a), running-account credit is a facility under a consumer credit agreement where the debtor receives from time to time (whether in his own person, or by another person) from the creditor or a third party any of the following:

- cash;
- goods; or
- services,

to an amount or value such that, taking into account payments made by or to the credit of the debtor, the credit limit (if any) is not at any time exceeded.

Section 10 contains further provisions relevant to running-account credit. The credit limit is defined by s.10(2) as the maximum debit balance which is allowed to stand under the consumer credit agreement. Section 10(2) also disregards any term of the agreement allowing that maximum to be temporarily exceeded.

For any provision under CCA 1974 that specifies an amount of credit (excluding s.17(1)(a)), running-account credit is taken as not exceeding the amount specified in that provision (called the 'specified amount') if:

- the credit limit does not exceed the specified amount (s.10(3)(a)); or
- whether or not there is a credit limit, and if there is, regardless of the fact that it exceeds the specified amount (s.10(3)(b)):

    - the debtor is not enabled to draw at any one time an amount which, so far as it represents credit, exceeds the specified amount; or
    - the agreement provides that, if the debit balance rises above a given amount (not exceeding the specified amount), the rate of the total charge for credit increases or any other condition favouring the creditor or his associate comes into operation; or
    - at the time the agreement is made it is probable, having regard to the terms of the agreement and any other relevant considerations, that the debit balance will not at any time rise above the specified amount.

The most obvious example of a running-account regulated consumer credit agreement is a credit card. Under the terms of the agreement, the debtor is typically entitled to drawdown (from time to time) credit so long as the balance under the agreement does not exceed a pre-arranged (or pre-notified) credit limit. Another popular example is credit terms for suppliers of goods. In these types of cases, the supplier will allow a debtor to buy goods from time to time using a running-account regulated consumer credit agreement. The balance will vary from time to time (much like a credit card) and the debtor will repay the credit in instalments. Suppliers wanting to offer such a facility but wishing to avoid regulation need to ensure that any agreement falls within one of the exemptions. These are discussed at **1.3.3** above.

1.4.2   Fixed-sum credit

CCA 1974, s.10(1)(b) provides that fixed-sum credit is any facility (other than those caught by s.10(1)(a) – see **1.4.1**) under a consumer credit agreement where the debtor is entitled to receive credit (whether in one amount or by instalments). The most obvious examples of fixed-sum credit are loans. Under the terms of a typical agreement, the creditor will advance a sum of money to the debtor. The debtor will be required to repay that sum, together with interest and other charges, over a set period. There is often no opportunity for the debtor to re-drawdown credit when some has been repaid. At the end of the term, the balance is zero.

1.4.3   Restricted-use credit

A restricted-use credit agreement is a regulated consumer credit agreement (CCA 1974, s.11(1):

- to finance a transaction between the debtor and the creditor, whether forming part of that agreement or not (s.11(1)(a)); or
- to finance a transaction between the debtor and a person (known as the 'supplier') other than the creditor (s.11(1)(b)); or
- to refinance any existing indebtedness of the debtor's, whether to the creditor or another person (s.11(1)(c));

and 'restricted-use credit' is construed accordingly.

There are two important qualifications to s.11(1):

- First, by s.11(3), an agreement does not fall within s.11(1) if the credit is provided in such a way that it leaves the debtor free to use it as he chooses, even though certain uses would contravenc that or any other agreement.
- Second, by s.11(4), an agreement may fall within s.11(1)(b) even though the identity of the supplier is unknown at the time the agreement is made.

The most obvious example of an agreement falling under s.11(1)(a) is a hire-purchase agreement. Under the terms of the hire-purchase agreement, the creditor will allow the debtor to use the goods (in exchange for regular monthly payments) and give him an option to buy the goods at the end of the term. To allow the creditor to supply the goods to the debtor under the agreement, the creditor will have bought the goods from the supplier. It is important to remember, however, that a hire-purchase agreement finances a transaction between the creditor and the debtor: the supplier simply sells the goods to the creditor.

In a similar theme, a good example of an agreement caught by s.11(1)(b) is a loan provided by a creditor to a debtor to allow him to buy specific goods from a third party supplier. This often happens where a debtor visits a third party supplier, perhaps a motor vehicle supplier, and wants to acquire the goods using a loan (perhaps because the rate of interest is better). For the fixed-sum loan agreement to fall within s.11(1)(b), it must be agreed that the funds will finance the purchase of the motor vehicle (i.e. the agreement must specifically state that the monies must be used to buy the motor vehicle). If the loan is simply advanced following the debtor's expression that he intends to buy a motor vehicle, it is submitted that is not enough to fall within s.11(1)(b). Such an agreement will be unrestricted-use credit as the debtor could (because he is not compelled by the agreement) use the funds for other purposes.

Finally, only agreements which include a term requiring the repayment of existing debts will fall within s.11(1)(c). If there is simply an understanding that the credit will be used to repay existing debts, that is not enough: *National Westminster Bank plc* v. *Story and another* [1999] Lloyd's Rep Bank 261 (CA).

1.4.4 Unrestricted-use credit

By CCA 1974, s.11(2), an unrestricted-use credit agreement is a regulated consumer credit agreement which does not fall within s.11(1). The phrase 'unrestricted-use credit' is construed accordingly.

1.4.5 Debtor-creditor-supplier agreements

CCA 1974, s.12 provides that a debtor-creditor-supplier agreement is a regulated consumer credit agreement which is:

- a restricted-use credit agreement which falls within s.11(1)(a) (by s.12(a)); or
- a restricted-use credit agreement which falls within s.11(1)(b) and is made by the creditor under pre-existing arrangements, or in contemplation of future arrangements, between the creditor and the supplier (by s.12(b)); or
- an unrestricted-use credit agreement which is made by the creditor under pre-existing arrangements between the creditor and a person (the 'supplier') other than the debtor in the knowledge that the credit is to be used to finance a transaction between the debtor and the supplier (by s.12(c)).

There are, once again, typical agreements that fall into each subsection of s.12. These mirror the examples discussed at **1.4.3** (i.e. hire-purchase or conditional sale agreements for s.12(a) and restricted-use loans to buy specific goods for s.12(b)). There is, however, an important distinction between s.12(b) and s.11(1)(b) as the former requires the agreement to be made under pre-existing arrangements, or contemplated future arrangements, between the creditor and supplier. Evidence will therefore be needed to support any argument that an agreement falls within s.12(b), although this will usually be satisfied if a supplier has copies of blank loan agreements with a third party creditor at its premises. Section 12(c) appears to be a sweep up provision which is, in practice, normally avoided by creditors as the debtor is free to spend such credit as he wishes.

1.4.6 Debtor-creditor agreements

Under CCA 1974, s.13, a debtor-creditor agreement is a regulated consumer credit agreement which is:

- a restricted-use credit agreement which falls within s.11(1)(b) but is not made by the creditor under pre-existing arrangements, or in contemplation of future arrangements, between himself and the supplier (by s.13(a)); or
- a restricted-use credit agreement which falls within s.11(1)(c) (by s.13(b)); or
- an unrestricted-use credit agreement which is not made by the creditor under pre-existing arrangements between himself and a person (the 'supplier') other than the debtor in the knowledge that the credit is to be used to finance a transaction between the debtor and the supplier (by s.13(c)).

Section 13 is largely the opposite of s.12: if an agreement does not fall within s.12 it will probably fall within s.13.

1.4.7 Credit-token agreements

A credit-token is a card, check, voucher, coupon, stamp, form, booklet or other document or thing given to an individual by a person carrying on a consumer credit business (CCA 1974, s.14), who undertakes that:

- on the production of it (whether or not some other action is also required) he will supply cash, goods and services (or any of them) on credit (s.14(1)(a)); or
- where, on the production of it to a third party (whether or not any other action is also required), the third party supplies cash, goods and services (or any of them), he will pay the third party for them (whether or not deducting any discount or commission), in return for payment to him by the individual (s.14(1)(b)).

Section 14(2) makes it clear that a credit-token agreement is a regulated agreement for the provision of credit for use with the credit-token. By s.14(4), the use of an object to operate a machine provided by the person giving the object or a third party will be treated as the production of the object to the creditor.

The obvious examples of credit-token agreements are credit cards. these can be used to pay for goods or services or, in many cases, to obtain cash from a cash machine (which brings s.14(4) into play).

CHAPTER 2

Licensing

2.1 INTRODUCTION

For businesses involved in all types of credit business, the Consumer Credit Act 1974 (CCA 1974) provides a detailed regulatory framework to determine whether a consumer credit licence is needed. If a business is carrying on regulated business requiring a licence, and it has failed to obtain such a licence, it commits a criminal offence. The problem is further complicated where it provides credit or a creditor provides credit following an introduction by an unlicensed credit-broker: in such a case, the debt is unenforceable. We now turn to look at those requirements.

2.2 WHO NEEDS A LICENCE?

The key question is whether a business needs a consumer credit licence. Under CCA 1974, s.21(1) a licence is required to carry on:

- a 'consumer credit business';
- a 'consumer hire business'; or
- an 'ancillary credit business'.

There is an exception, in s.21(2), which states that a local authority does not need a licence to carry on a business. There is also a further exception contained in s.21(3) which states that a body corporate does not need a licence to carry on business where it has been named by a public general Act to do so.

2.3 DEFINITIONS

2.3.1 Overview

CCA 1974, s.189(1) provides:

- a 'consumer credit business' is defined as any business being carried on by a person so far as it comprises or relates to:
    - the provision of credit by him; or

- – otherwise his being a creditor under regulated consumer credit agreements (as defined in s.8);
- a 'consumer hire business' is defined as any business being carried on by a person so far as it relates to or comprises:
  - – the bailment of any goods by him; or
  - – otherwise his being an owner under regulated consumer hire agreements (as defined in s.15);
- an 'ancillary credit business' is defined as having the meaning given to it by s.145(1). This, in turn, defines it as any business so far as it comprises or relates to:
  - – credit brokerage;
  - – debt-adjusting;
  - – debt-counselling;
  - – debt-collecting;
  - – debt administration;
  - – the provision of credit information services; or
  - – the operation of a credit reference agency.

These definitions are extremely important as any creditor applying for a consumer credit licence will need to tell the Office of Fair Trading (OFT) what type of activity it undertakes. We therefore look at some practical examples of each activity.

2.3.2 Consumer credit business

Given its definition, anyone providing credit under a regulated consumer credit agreement will need a licence to undertake consumer credit business. Typical examples include fixed-sum loan agreements, hire-purchase agreements and running-account agreements.

2.3.3 Consumer hire business

Given its definition, owners providing leasing facilities (with no provision for the hirer to exercise a right or option to purchase the goods) will fall into this category provided that they are bailing goods under a regulated consumer hire agreement. Typical examples include contract hire agreements.

2.3.4 Credit brokerage

By CCA 1974, s.145(2), credit brokerage is effecting the introductions of individuals (as defined in CCA 1974) wishing to:

- obtain credit from lenders carrying on:

- business as a consumer credit business;
- a business which comprises or relates to consumer credit agreements being (otherwise than by virtue of CCA 1974, s.16(5)(a)) exempt agreements; or
- a business which comprises or relates to unregulated agreements where the applicable law is outside the UK and if the applicable law were the law of the UK then it would be a regulated consumer credit agreement,

or in the case of a debtor wishing to obtain credit for the purchase of residential property, in which the debtor or his relative is, or will be, living, to any person carrying on business in the provision of such credit to be secured on the property; or

- obtain goods on hire to persons carrying on:

  - a business as a consumer hire business;
  - a business which comprises or relates to consumer hire agreements being (otherwise than by virtue of CCA 1974, s.16(6)), exempt agreements; or
  - a business which comprises or relates to unregulated agreements where the applicable law is outside the UK and if the applicable law were the law of the UK then it would be a regulated consumer hire agreement; or

- obtain credit or goods on hire to other credit-brokers.

At the time of writing, the OFT are consulting on detailed guidance for brokers and intermediaries.

2.3.5 Debt-adjusting

Under CCA 1974, s.145(5), debt-adjusting is (in relation to debts due under consumer credit agreements or consumer hire agreements):

- negotiating with the creditor or owner, on the debtor's or hirer's behalf, terms for the discharge of a debt; or
- taking over, in return for payments from the debtor or hirer, his obligations to discharge a debt; or
- any similar activity concerned with the liquidation of a debt.

By s.146(5B) and (6), it is not within the definition of debt-adjusting if the introduction is made to:

- an authorised person, within the meaning of the Financial Services and Markets Act 2000 (FSMA 2000), who has permission under FSMA 2000 to enter into a relevant agreement as lender or home purchase provider (as the case may be); or
- a qualifying broker,

with a view to that individual obtaining credit under an agreement which is secured by a land mortgage or is, or forms part of, a regulated home purchase plan but only if entering into the agreement as lender or home purchase provider (as the case may be) is a regulated activity for the purposes of FSMA 2000 (a 'relevant agreement').

It should be remembered that debt-adjusting applies to consumer credit or hire agreements (whether regulated or exempt). If a business is debt-adjusting exempt agreements, it will still need a licence.

Examples of debt-adjusters include any third party that attempts to resolve a debtor's liability under a consumer credit or hire agreement. There are many such organisations out there and debtors must ensure that anyone offering such a service has a consumer credit licence. It also arguably includes a family member who contacts the creditor to try and negotiate terms (not necessarily binding terms) of repayment.

2.3.6 Debt-counselling

By s.145(6) of CCA 1974, debt-counselling is the giving of advice to debtors or hirers about the liquidation of debts due under consumer credit agreements or consumer hire agreements. It does not apply, by s.146(5C) and (6), where a person gives advice to debtors about the liquidation of debts if:

- the debt in question is due under a relevant agreement (as discussed at **2.3.5** above); and
- giving that advice is a regulated activity for the purposes of FSMA 2000.

There is a further exclusion in s.146(6) which excludes anything done by a person in relation to a debt arising under an agreement if any of the following conditions are satisfied:

(aa)   that he is the creditor or owner under the agreement, or
(c)   that he is the supplier in relation to the agreement, or
(d)   that he is a credit-broker who has acquired the business of the person who was the supplier in relation to the agreement, or
(e)   that he is a person prevented by subsection (5) from being treated as a credit-broker, and the agreement was made in consequence of an introduction (whether made by him or another person) which, under subsection (5), is to be disregarded.

Section 146(5) of CCA 1974 provides a disregard for introductions effected by an individual by canvassing off trade premises if it results in either a debtor-creditor-supplier agreement falling within CCA 1974, s.12(a) or is a regulated consumer hire agreement and:

(a)   the introductions are not effected by him in the capacity of an employee, and
(b)   he does not by any other method effect introductions falling within section 145(2).

Like debt-adjusting, it should be remembered that debt-counselling applies to consumer credit or hire agreements (whether regulated or exempt). If a business is debt-counselling exempt agreements, it will still need a licence.

Examples of a debt-counsellor will be similar to those provided at **2.3.5** above dealing with debt adjustors. The OFT has published guidance to debt-adjusters and counsellors in its 'Debt Management Guidance' (OFT 366). The latest copy of this report is dated September 2008 and available from the OFT website (**www.oft.gov.uk/shared_oft/business_leaflets/credit_licences/oft366.pdf**). At the time of writing, the OFT is currently consulting on substantially revised guidance.

2.3.7 Debt-collecting

By CCA 1974, s.145(7), debt-collecting is the taking of steps to secure payment of debts due under consumer credit agreements or consumer hire agreements. CCA 1974, s.146(6) provides an exemption to this definition. We discussed s.146(6) at **2.3.6** above. It should (once again) be remembered that debt-collecting is not limited to a regulated agreement and equally applies to exempt consumer credit and hire agreements. The OFT has published advice to debt collectors entitled 'Debt Collection Guidance' (OFT 664Rev). The latest copy of this report is dated July 2003 but it was revised in October 2011. It is available from **www.oft.gov.uk/ shared_oft/consumer_leaflets/credit/OFT664Rev.pdf**.

Examples of debt collectors would include solicitors (although solicitors with a current practising certificate are (thankfully in the writer's view!) covered by the Law Society's Group Licence) and debt collection agencies.

2.3.8 Debt administration

Debt administration is the taking of steps to:

- perform duties under a consumer credit agreement or consumer hire agreement for a creditor or owner; or
- exercise or to enforce rights under such agreements for the creditor or owner,

so far as such steps are not debt-collecting (CCA 1974, s.145(7A)).

By s.146(7), it is not debt administration where a person takes steps to perform duties, or to exercise or enforce rights, under an agreement on the creditor's or owner's behalf if any of the conditions mentioned in s.146(6) are satisfied for that person. These exclusions are discussed at **2.3.6** above.

Examples of debt administrators include third party processing companies that, for example, issue statutory notices to debtors for creditors or manage the payments made by the debtors as they 'perform duties': businesses that simply process post are unlikely to fall within this definition.

More tricky situations arise under the second limb. For example, many creditors letting goods under a hire-purchase or conditional sale agreement will often instruct a third party to repossess those goods. In such a case, is the third party exercising or enforcing rights under such an agreement (which would require a licence) or is it simply exercising an owner's legal right to repossess goods after a bailment ends (which does not require a licence)? It is submitted that businesses in such a case should (given the criminal sanctions) apply for a consumer credit licence to avoid issues being raised by debtors.

2.3.9 Provision of credit information services

Under CCA 1974, s.145(7B), a person provides credit information services if:

- he takes any of the following steps for an individual:

    - finding out if a credit information agency (other than that person if he is one) holds information relevant to the individual's financial standing;
    - finding out the contents of such information held by such an agency;
    - securing the correction of, the omission of anything from, or the making of any other kind of modification of such held information;
    - securing that an agency which holds such information (a) stops holding it or (b) does not provide it to another person; or

- he gives advice to an individual in relation to the taking of any such steps.

By s.145(7D), a 'credit information agency' means (for the purposes of s.145(7C)) a person carrying on:

- a consumer credit business or a consumer hire business;
- so far as it comprises or relates to credit brokerage, debt-adjusting, debt-counselling, debt-collecting, debt administration or the operation of a credit reference agency;
- a business which would be a consumer credit business except that it comprises or relates to consumer credit agreements being, otherwise than by virtue of CCA 1974, s.16(5)(a), exempt agreements; or
- a business which would be a consumer hire business except that it comprises or relates to consumer hire agreements being, otherwise than by virtue of s.16(6), exempt agreements.

An example of a business carrying on this type of activity is one that offers to review and update a debtor's credit file. This is, from a debtor's point of view, a very useful activity as it is likely to improve his credit rating. Debtors thinking of asking a business to carry out such an activity should ensure it has an appropriate consumer credit licence.

2.3.10 Operation of a credit reference agency

By s.145(8), a credit reference agency is a person carrying on a business providing information relevant to the financial standing of individuals, being information collected by the agency for that purpose.

From this definition, it seems that at least two types of activities are excluded:

- first, if a business collects information about limited companies then it is excluded (as this definition only relates to individuals); and
- second, if a business provides information which has not been collected for the purpose of providing information about an individual's financial standing then it is excluded. For example, an employer providing information about an employee's bank accounts or salary would not need a licence as that information was collected to allow it to pay the employee. Similarly, a bank providing information about its customer's conduct of its account would not need a licence as that information was collected to allow the bank to provide retail banking services.

Examples of credit reference agencies will therefore be few and far between. The definition will, of course, include the three main credit reference agencies in the UK: Experian Limited, Equifax Limited and Callcredit Limited.

2.4 EUROPEAN PASSPORTS

Given the UK's membership of the European Economic Area (EEA), a business from outside the UK but inside the EEA may apply for a 'European Passport'. If it does so, it can provide credit in the UK without the need for a consumer credit licence. To obtain a 'European Passport', a business must satisfy three conditions by virtue of FSMA 2000, Sched.3, para.13:

- First, the UK's Financial Services Authority (FSA) must have received a notice from the business's home regulator consenting to it opening a branch in the UK (the 'consent notice').
- Second, the consent notice must be given in accordance with the relevant single market directive, identify the activities to which the consent relates and include such other information as may be prescribed.
- Third, the FSA must have either:
  - given the business (as long as it is an investment firm as defined in art.4.1.1 of the Markets in Financial Instruments Directive (2004/39/EC)) notice or two months have passed since the date beginning when the consent notice was given; or
  - told the business (unless it is an investment firm) of the applicable provisions and two months have passed beginning with the date when the FSA received the consent notice.

While a business with a European Passport does not need a licence, it must otherwise comply with CCA 1974 and its regulations. It is likely that when the FSA's powers transfer to the provisionally named Financial Conduct Authority (FCA), the legislation will remain the same except for the insertion of 'FCA' in place of 'FSA'.

2.5 TYPES OF LICENCES

There are two types of licences issued by the OFT:

- a 'standard licence' (which is issued more regularly); and
- a 'group licence'.

The main difference between the two is that a standard licence is issued to a particular person, business or company (i.e. the licence holder) and entitles that person or entity to carry on the activities stated in the licence. A group licence, on the other hand, covers such persons and activities described in the licence. The OFT will rarely grant a group licence and it is not appropriate for a business, wishing to set up a number of group companies to carry on licensable business, to apply for a group licence. Such a company must apply for a standard licence for each individual company. For the purposes of this chapter, we concentrate on standard licences rather than group licences.

Example

ABC Finance Ltd wishes to set up in business lending monies to individuals which will be secured against their properties as second charges. For other reasons, it wishes to use ABC Finance Ltd as a holding company and lend up to £1 million from a subsidiary company, ABC Finance (No.1) Ltd, lend up to £3 million from another subsidiary company, ABC Finance (No.2) Ltd, and lend up to £5 million from another subsidiary company, ABC Finance (No.3) Ltd.

In this case, it is very unlikely that ABC Finance Ltd will be granted a group licence. It therefore follows that it must obtain a standard licence for each subsidiary company, namely ABC Finance (No.1) Ltd, ABC Finance (No.2) Ltd and ABC Finance (No.3) Ltd. If the holding company, ABC Finance Ltd, carries on any licensable business, it should also obtain a separate standard licence. It is submitted that it would be sensible to do so in any event given the consequences of carrying on licensable activities without a licence in place.

Under CCA 1974, s.37(1), a licence is not assignable or transmissible on the licence holder's death, bankruptcy or incapacity (under the Mental Capacity Act 2005): it is personal to the licence holder. This does not, however, prevent a company holding a licence and the shares being sold to a third party. In such a case, the buyer must remember that notifications need to be given to the OFT within the prescribed period. We will discuss this in more detail at **2.12.1**. The terms of the licence will also say whether it has effect indefinitely or for a limited period of time. If it is limited, the licence will state that period. If it is indefinite, the OFT will often review it.

2.6 STANDARD LICENCES: DURATION

Under CCA 1974, s.22(1C), there is a presumption that a standard licence will last indefinitely unless the applicant asks for a limited period, or the OFT considers there is a good reason why it should be limited for a specific period.

Even if a person is covered by a group licence, they may still obtain a standard licence (s.22(7)).

The application for a standard licence must (by s.24A), for each type of business, state whether the applicant is applying for the licence to cover the carrying on of that type of business:

- with no limitation; or
- only so far as it falls it within one or more descriptions of business.

The concept of indefinite licences was introduced on 6 April 2008. Until then, standard licences were issued for five years. Licence holders who need to renew their licences will now be granted indefinite licences.

2.7 GROUP LICENCES: DURATION

There is a presumption that a group licence will last for a specific period unless the OFT considers there is good reason why it should last for an indefinite period (CCA 1974, s.22(1D)). The OFT may only issue a group licence by s.22(5) if it appears to it that the public interest is better served by doing so rather than requiring individuals of the group to apply separately for standard licences. The most obvious example is the group licence issued to The Law Society. If one had not been issued, any firm of solicitors carrying out debt-collection activities would have needed to apply for an individual standard licence. For many firms, this would have increased their own running costs and some solicitors may have been ignorant of the need to apply for a licence. A group licence has also been issued to the National Association of Citizens' Advice Bureaux: many of their activities are, of course, licensable ones.

2.8 BUSINESS NAMES

Under CCA 1974, s.24, a business can only carry on licensable activities using the names on its licence. Licence holders must ensure that all business names are included on the licence.

Example

ABC Finance Ltd wishes to set up in business lending monies to individuals which will be secured against their properties as second charges. For other reasons, it wishes to use ABC Finance Ltd as a holding company and lend up to £1 million from a subsidiary company, ABC

Finance (No.1) Ltd, lend up to £3 million from another subsidiary company, ABC Finance (No.2) Ltd, and lend up to £5 million from another subsidiary company, ABC Finance (No.3) Ltd.

In this case, each company, namely ABC Finance (No.1) Ltd, ABC Finance (No.2) Ltd and ABC Finance (No.3) Ltd, will need a consumer credit licence. If the holding company, ABC Finance Ltd, carries on any licensable business, it should also obtain a separate standard licence. Each company will also need to ensure that any trading names, like 'ABC' or 'ABC Finance' or any other name, are added to the licence.

By CCA 1974, s.25(1AD), an applicant will not be issued with a licence unless he satisfies the OFT that the name or names under which he would be licensed is, or are, not misleading or otherwise undesirable. Applicants are well advised to search the register before applying to see if there is any potential for confusion. To reduce the risk of an issue being raised, the OFT will often give an initial view on a prospective name. Such a view is not, however, conclusive and the OFT retains the right to refuse to grant a licence in any business name.

2.9 CATEGORIES OF LICENSABLE ACTIVITIES

Before applying for a licence, a business needs to work out which of the categories of licensable activities it needs a licence for. The types of business are listed in CCA 1974, s.24A(4) and the OFT breaks these down into the following categories:

Category A: consumer credit business
Category B: consumer hire business
Category C: credit brokerage
Category D: debt-adjusting
Category E: debt-counselling
Category F: debt-collecting
Category G: debt administration
Category H: credit information services (excluding credit repair)
Category H1: credit information services (including credit repair)
Category I: credit reference agency
Category Z: canvassing of debtor-creditor-supplier agreements or regulated consumer hire agreements off trade premises.

It is generally advisable, for any business applying for a consumer credit licence, to seek a licence in all categories that it intends, or possibly intends, to do business in except Category I (i.e. credit reference agency unless, of course, the business *is* a credit reference agency). By doing so, the business will reduce its risk of regulatory steps being taken for unlicensed activities.

2.10 APPLICATION FOR A CONSUMER CREDIT LICENCE: STANDARD LICENCES

2.10.1 Making the application

Applicants for a standard licence can either apply online or by post using the standard forms produced by the OFT. Those wishing to apply online need to visit the OFT's website (currently **https://www2.crw.gov.uk/LIVE/CCL/OnlineForm .aspx**) and be able to pay the fee by debit or credit card. Those wishing to apply using a paper application will need to ask the OFT to send a copy by email. Applicants (or their lawyers) should ensure the right form is completed as there are two standard forms: one for sole traders and another for companies, partnerships and other organisations (excluding a sole trader).

2.10.2 Time period for determination of application

The OFT's website 'recommends all applicants apply online' and its target on low-risk cases is to process 90 per cent of them within 25 working days. If the application is high risk, the OFT's target is to process 75 per cent of them within 35 working days. Applicants for a licence must therefore leave sufficient time before starting business to apply for a licence. It is submitted that a sensible time frame for most applications is at least two to three months.

2.10.3 The application

Under CCA 1974, s.24A(1), an application for a standard licence must state whether the applicant is applying for a licence to cover the carrying on of that category of business with no limitation or only so far as it falls within one or more descriptions of business. If the application falls into this latter category, the applicant must set out a description or descriptions of the business in question. The categories are those set out at **2.9** above.

2.10.4 Grant of a licence

If an application is made and the OFT is satisfied that the applicant is a 'fit person' to carry on the category of business applied for with no limitation, and the name or names on the proposed licence are not misleading or otherwise undesirable, then he is entitled to be issued with a standard licence for that category and without limitation (CCA 1974, s.25(1), (1AD)). If an applicant applies for a licence to cover only a type of business limited to a certain description and the OFT is satisfied that the applicant is a 'fit person' to carry on that type of business (as limited in the application) then he is also entitled to a licence (s.25(1AA)).

The issue becomes more problematic when the OFT decides that the applicant is a fit person but not to the extent sought in the application. The OFT's decision is then subject to s.25(1AB). This states that the applicant is entitled to be issued with a licence if:

- the OFT is satisfied that the applicant is a fit person to carry on that category of business so far as it falls within the description or descriptions in question;
- the applicant could have applied for the licence to be limited in that way; and
- the licence would not cover any activity which was not covered by his application.

This creates a 'half-way house' for applicants. Before the revisions to CCA 1974, if an applicant was not fit then he would not get a licence. If the applicant is fit for something then he must now get a licence for that activity. By CCA 1974, s.27(1), if the OFT decides to grant the licence in part then it will, before determining the application, tell the applicant and give its reasons. It will also invite the applicant to make representations to the OFT under s.34. If the OFT grants the application in terms different from those applied for then, whether or not the applicant appeals, the OFT will issue the licence in its approved terms unless the applicant gives notice telling the OFT that it does not want a licence in those terms (s.27(2)).

2.10.5   Fitness test

The fitness test is one of the cornerstones of licensing. It appears in CCA 1974, s.25(2), (2A) and (2B). When considering an application, the OFT must consider any matters appearing to be relevant including:

- the applicant's skills, knowledge and experience in consumer credit, consumer hire or ancillary credit businesses (s.25(2)(a));
- such skills, knowledge and expertise of other persons the applicant will work with in any business that would be carried on by him under the licence (s.25(2)(b));
- practices and procedures the applicant intends to implement (s.25(2)(c));
- evidence that tends to show that the applicant, or any of its employees, agents or associates (whether past or present) or, where the applicant is a body corporate, any persons appearing to the OFT to be a controller of the body corporate or any associate, has:

  - committed any offence involving fraud, dishonesty or violence;
  - contravened any provision of CCA 1974, FSMA 2000, Sched.1A, para.13, or Part XVI of FSMA 2000 to the extent that it relates to the consumer credit jurisdiction or any other enactment regulating the provision of credit to individuals or other transactions with individuals;
  - contravened similar provisions in any other EEA state;

- practised discrimination on grounds of sex, colour, race or ethnic or national origins in, or connection with, the carrying on of any business; or
- engaged in business practices appearing to the OFT to be deceitful, oppressive or otherwise unfair or improper (whether lawful or not) and including practices in the carrying on of a consumer credit business which involve 'irresponsible lending'.

The OFT can therefore potentially consider a considerable part of an applicant's business. Historically, the OFT has rarely delved too deep into an application unless it has concerns. The extension of the fitness test may lead to more investigations but, in a system which is already under a lot of pressure, it is submitted that such a proactive approach by the OFT may be asking too much. This should not, of course, encourage applicants to leave out relevant parts which may be unhelpful. Such conduct is almost certainly a criminal offence and is likely to lead to the OFT revoking the licence.

So far, the OFT has issued guidance entitled 'Consumer Credit Licensing: General Guidance for Licensees and Applicants on Fitness and Requirements' (OFT 969) dated January 2008 (available at **www.oft.gov.uk/shared_oft/ business_leaflets/credit_licences/oft969.pdf**). Given the importance of the fitness test, we now turn to look at some of the issues that the OFT will consider under CCA 1974, s.25(2) and (2A).

Applicant's skills, knowledge and experience

It often helps an applicant if he has skills, knowledge and experience in relation to consumer credit, consumer hire or ancillary credit businesses. It should not, however, be assumed that those without any previous knowledge will be unable to obtain a licence: but they will need to demonstrate an understanding of the obligations under CCA 1974.

Participator's skills, knowledge and experience

If an applicant has other people involved in the business with knowledge of consumer credit, consumer hire or ancillary credit businesses, he is able to rely upon it. For example, if an applicant employs staff or consultants who have knowledge, skills and experience from other business, this can be taken into account. Retaining external consultants, perhaps an experienced consumer credit solicitor, barrister or compliance officer, is also likely to support an application.

Practices and procedures

It will be extremely helpful, and in most cases vital, to have written evidence of practices and procedures. This is not just limited to the consumer credit legislation but is likely to extend to all consumer protection legislation and codes of conduct. It is notable that s.25(2)(c) is drafted in such a way that it looks at the practices and procedures that the applicant 'proposes' to implement: it is therefore forward looking. Given the OFT's broad remit, however, an applicant would be ill advised to simply suggest that if a licence is obtained certain practices and procedures will be implemented.

Evidence of commission of any offence involving fraud or other dishonesty or violence

This provision attempts to stamp out the old moneylenders and loan sharks who would use (and, in some cases, continue to use) rather unscrupulous techniques to secure repayment. It should be noted that it simply requires the OFT to consider evidence of the commission of an offence. While it does not state whether evidence of a conviction is necessary, para.2.5 of the OFT's guidance on 'Consumer Credit Licensing' states that it will consider:

> ... criminal offences committed by you or your associates, particularly involving violence, fraud or dishonesty, whether or not they lead to prosecution or a conviction

Applicants who do have previous convictions may be able to take advantage of the Rehabilitation of Offenders Act 1974 which deals with 'spent' convictions. While it is arguable that spent convictions should not be relevant, the OFT's guidance suggests that they will be relevant.

Contravened provisions

The OFT will look at whether an applicant has breached any provisions. Paragraph 2.5 of the OFT's guidance on 'Consumer Credit Licensing' states that the OFT will consider any breach of CCA 1974 and any other consumer protection law, which would include the Consumer Protection from Unfair Trading Regulations 2008, SI 2008/1277, the Unfair Terms in Consumer Contracts Regulations 1999, SI 1999/2083, and the Consumer Protection (Distance Selling) Regulations 2000, SI 2000/2334.

Practised discrimination on grounds of sex, colour, race or ethnic origins in connection with the carrying on of any business

A more general point is that the OFT will look at whether an applicant has practised discrimination. Paragraph 2.5 of the OFT's guidance on 'Consumer Credit Licensing' states that it does not matter whether that practice (if it exists) involved licensable activities or not. It therefore follows that the OFT will consider the business as a whole, not just the part of the business which applies for the licence.

Engaged in business practices appearing to OFT as deceitful or oppressive or otherwise unfair or improper (whether lawful or not)

This is perhaps one of the broader aspects of fitness because it allows the OFT to consider deceitful, oppressive, unfair or improper business practices whether lawful or not. Even if, therefore, an applicant has engaged in conduct which did not breach any law but the OFT took a dislike to it, the OFT could take the view that this meant the applicant was not fit to hold a licence.

Irresponsible lending

Following the amendments made to CCA 1974 by the Consumer Credit Act 2006 (CCA 2006), CCA 1974, s.25(2B) now allows the OFT to consider whether a consumer credit business has been carried on involving 'irresponsible lending'. The OFT has issued guidance entitled 'Irresponsible Lending – OFT Guidance for Creditors' (OFT 1107) dated March 2010 (revised in February 2011). This is currently available on its website (**www.oft.gov.uk/shared_oft/consultations/oft1107con.pdf**). The Irresponsible Lending guidance is detailed so all creditors must ensure that they consider, and implement, the guidance.

Second charge lending

While it is not a specific principle of fitness, creditors providing credit to debtors under regulated consumer credit agreements secured on residential property will need to be aware of the OFT's guidance entitled 'Second Charge Lending – OFT Guidance for Lenders and Brokers' (OFT 1105) dated July 2009 (available at **www.oft.gov.uk/shared_oft/business_leaflets/general/oft1105.pdf**). For secured lending, this guidance supersedes the OFT's 'Non-Status Lending Guidance' (OFT 192v2).

2.10.6 Duration of a licence and renewal charges

If a standard licence is granted, it is for an indefinite period unless the applicant asks for the licence to be limited to a specific period or the OFT thinks there are good reasons to limit the duration of the licence (CCA 1974, s.22(1C)). Until 6 April 2008, licences were issued for a fixed term of five years and, if the licence holder wanted to continue undertaking the licensable activity, had to be renewed. From 6 April 2008, a licence holder does not need to renew its licence but is now under an obligation, by s.28A(1), to pay before the end of the payment period (currently every five years) a renewal fee to the OFT. The amount of the fee is determined by the OFT and approved by the Secretary of State and the Treasury. Information on the OFT's latest charges is available at **www.oft.gov.uk/OFTwork/credit-licensing/fees-refunds-payments**.

By virtue of CCA 1974, s.28B(1), a licence holder can apply only once to the OFT for an extension in time to pay the renewal fee. The OFT must be satisfied that there is a good reason for granting the extension and, if it is, it will grant an extension. It is submitted that an extension will only be granted in exceptional circumstances: licence holders should therefore ensure fees are paid on time. If fees are not paid on time, the licence holder's licence will (by s.28C(3)) terminate unless the licence holder has applied for an extension under s.28 and that application has yet to be determined. In those cases, the licence only terminates if the OFT refuses the extension and has told the licence holder of its decision.

2.10.7 Refusal of an application

By s.27(1), if the OFT is minded to refuse all of the application (we have already discussed partial refusal at **2.10.4** above), it will, before determining the application, tell the applicant and give its reasons. It will also invite the applicant to make representations to the OFT under CCA 1974, s.34.

If a consumer credit EEA firm (see **2.4** above) applies for a standard licence and the activities covered by the application are all 'permitted activities', then the OFT must refuse to issue the licence (CCA 1974, s.27A(1)). By s.27A(5), a 'permitted activity' means an activity for which the firm has, or could obtain, permission under FSMA 2000, Sched.3, para.15. If, however, a consumer credit EEA firm applies for a standard licence and only some of the activities are 'permitted activities' (and not all) then the applicant does not need to satisfy the OFT that it is a fit person to carry on that type of business so far as it would involve any of the 'permitted activities' (CCA 1974, s.27A(3)). This is a good example of the OFT avoiding treading on the FSA's toes. This issue may, of course, disappear if the OFT and the FSA merge into the FCA.

2.10.8 OFT's power to impose requirements on individual licensees

If a person applies for a standard licence and, while considering the application the OFT takes the view that if the licence sought was issued, it may wish to impose requirements under CCA 1974, s.33A because it is dissatisfied with the applicant, then the OFT may, before issuing the licence, follow the steps set out in CCA 1974, s.33D or s.34(1) or (2). The OFT's powers are discussed at **2.12.5** below.

2.11 THE CONSUMER CREDIT REGISTER

The OFT is required by CCA 1974, s.35(1) to establish and maintain a register containing particulars of:

- applications not yet determined for issue, variation or renewal of licences, or for ending the suspension of a licence;

- licences that are in effect, or have at any time been suspended or revoked or terminated by s.28C, with details of any variation of the terms of a licence;
- requirements imposed under ss.33A and 33B which are in effect or which have been in effect, with details of any variations of those requirements;
- decisions given by it under CCA 1974 and any appeal from those decisions; and
- such other matters (if any) as it thinks fit.

The OFT's consumer credit register is available at **www2.crw.gov.uk/pr/Default.aspx**.

2.12 AFTER OBTAINING A LICENCE

2.12.1 Duty to notify of changes

It is important to remember that once a business has a licence, it must ensure that the OFT remains up to date. CCA 1974, s.36 imposes an obligation on licence holders to:

- give notice to the OFT, within 21 working days after a change takes place in any of the particulars entered in the register (not resulting from action taken by the OFT), of the change (s.36(1));
- give notice to the OFT, within 21 working days after:
  - any change in the officers of a body corporate, or an unincorporated body of persons, which is the licensee under a standard licence (s.36(2)(a)(i));
  - any change in the officers of a body corporate which is a controller of a body corporate which is a licensee under a standard licence (s.36(2)(a)(ii));
  - a body corporate which is a licensee under a standard licence becomes aware that a person has become or ceased to be a controller of the body corporate (s.36(2)(b)); or
  - any change takes place in the members of a partnership which is a licensee under a standard licence (including a change on the amalgamation of the partnership with another firm, or a change meaning the number of partners is reduced to one) (s.36(2)(c)).

Because a licence holder may not be aware of changes in its controller, s.36(3) requires (within 14 working days after any change takes place in the officers of a body corporate which is a controller of another body corporate which is a licensee under a standard licence) the controller to give the licensee notice of the change. Within 14 working days of a person becoming or ceasing to be a controller of a body corporate which is a licensee under a standard licence, that person must give notice to the OFT (s.36(4)). If notice is not given in time, that person commits a criminal offence (s.39(3)). The concept of a controller is notoriously one of the more difficult aspects of CCA 1974. The definition under CCA 1974 is given at **1.2**. If an applicant or licence holder is in any doubt, it should err on the side of caution and adopt a wide definition of 'controller'.

From 6 April 2008, three further provisions were imposed:

- If the OFT issues a general notice requiring information or documents (either before or after the issue of a standard or group licence), the licensee must provide that further information or documents within the period specified by the notice (CCA 1974, s.36A).
- The OFT may impose a requirement on a licensee under a standard licence or the original applicant for a group licence (but only if the request is reasonably required for the OFT's functions under CCA 1974 and relates to a relevant act or omission as set out in s.36B(6)) to provide information or documents within a reasonable period specified in the notice (CCA 1974, s.36B).
- The OFT may by notice to a licensee under a standard licence or the original applicant for a group licence (but only if the request is reasonably required for the OFT's functions under CCA 1974 and relates to a relevant act or omission as set out in s.36B(6)) require him to allow the OFT access to premises specified in the notice for the purpose of observing the carrying on of a business by the licensee or to inspect the licensee's documents relating to that business (which was specified or described in the notice and situated on the premises). The OFT must explain why access is needed (CCA 1974, s.36C).

The OFT issued a general notice (GN75) on 27 March 2008 that requires licence holders who apply for, renew or vary their licence after 6 April 2008 to update the OFT, within 28 days, of any changes to the information provided in response to specified questions in that application. This notice is available at **www.oft.gov.uk/ shared_oft/business_leaflets/consumer_credit/General_Notice_No_75.pdf**. GN75, importantly, includes an obligation to notify the OFT of any finding by a court of an unfair relationship. Failing to provide notification of changes to information provided in the application may result in a fine of up to £50,000.

If the licence holder has failed to do something he was required to do under s.36B or s.36C then, following an application by the OFT, the county court may (by s.36E) require the defaulting party:

- to do the thing that it appears he failed to do within such time specified in the order;
- otherwise to take such steps to remedy the consequences of the failure as may be specified.

If the defaulter is a body corporate, a partnership or an unincorporated body of persons which is not a partnership then the order may require any officer who is (wholly or partly) responsible for the failure to meet the costs of the application (s.36E(3)).

2.12.2   Renewal

By virtue of CCA 1974, s.29(1), if the licensee under a standard licence of limited duration, or the original applicant for, or any licensee under, a group licence of limited duration, wants the OFT to renew the licence, whether on the same terms (except as to expiry) or on varied terms, he must, before the date specified in the licence, make an application to the OFT for its renewal. This application can be done online by visiting **https://www2.crw.gov.uk/LIVE/CCL/OnlineForm. aspx**. By s.29(2), the OFT may (of its own motion) renew any group licence.

CCA 1974, s.29(3) makes the general point that ss.21–28C apply to the renewal of a licence as they apply to the issue of a licence with the exception that s.28 does not apply to a person who was already excluded in the licence up for renewal. By s.29(4), a licence continues (despite the fact it would, but for the application under s.29(1), have expired) until the application is determined and, where an appeal lies from the determination, until the end of the appeal period.

2.12.3   Variation

Variation by request

Under CCA 1974, s.30(1), the OFT may (if it thinks fit and following an application by the licensee) by notice to a licensee under a standard licence:

- if the licence covers the carrying on of a type of business only so far as it falls within one or more descriptions of business, vary the licence by:

  - removing that limitation;
  - adding a description of business to that limitation; or
  - removing a description of business from that limitation;

- if the licence covers the carrying on of a type of business with no limitation, vary the licence so that it covers the carrying on of that type of business only so far as it falls within one or more descriptions of business;
- vary the licence so that it no longer covers the carrying on of a type of business at all;
- vary the licence so that a type of business the carrying on of which is not covered at all by the licence is covered either with no limitation or only so far as it falls within one or more descriptions of business; or
- vary the licence in any other way except for the purpose of varying the descriptions of activities covered by the licence.

By s.30(2), the OFT may (if it thinks fit and following an application by the party who obtained the licence) by notice to the holder of the group licence, vary the terms in accordance with the application. The OFT may not, however, exclude a particular person from the group licence unless that person consents in writing. If a person is excluded (by name or description) from a group licence then the OFT may (by s.30(3) and following an application by that party), if it thinks fit, vary the terms of the licence so that it removes that exclusion. If it does so, it must give notice to that person. If a group licence is varied, general notice is given (s.30(5)).

If the OFT decides to refuse an application it must, before making a determination, give notice:

- telling the applicant that it is minded to refuse the application and give its reasons (s.30(4)(a)); and
- inviting the application to submit representations to the OFT to support its application in accordance with CCA 1974, s.34 (s.30(4)(b)).

Compulsory variation

CCA 1974, s.31 deals with the compulsory variation of licences. By s.31(1) if, at a time during the currency of a licence, the OFT forms the opinion that had the licence expired at that time (assuming, for indefinite licences, that it were a licence of limited duration) it would, on an application for its renewal or further renewal on the same terms, have been minded to grant the application but on different terms (meaning it should, for a standard licence, take the steps under s.30(1)(a)(ii) or (iii), (b), (c) and (e) or, for a group licence, vary the terms of the licence) then it is required to proceed as follows:

- For standard licences, the OFT must by notice:

    - tell the licensee of the variations the OFT is minded to make and give its reasons (s.31(2)(a)); and
    - invite the licensee to make representations (in accordance with s.34) responding to the proposed variations and the provision (if any) that should be included under s.34A if the OFT determines to vary the licence (s.31(2)(b)).

- For a group licence, the OFT must:

    - give general notice of the variations the OFT is minded to make and give its reasons (s.31(3)(a)); and
    - invite (in the notice) any licensee to make representations (in accordance with s.34) responding to the proposed variations (s.31(3)(b)).

- For a group licence issued on application, the OFT must also:

    - tell the original applicant of the variations the OFT is minded to make and give its reasons (s.31(4)(a)); and
    - invite the original applicant to make representations (in accordance with s.34) responding to the proposed variations (s.31(4)(b)).

- For group licences where the OFT is minded to vary the licence to exclude any person by name (other than the original applicant), it must also (in addition) take the appropriate steps under CCA 1974, s.28 (s.31(5)).

By s.31(1B), the OFT must also proceed in this way if it believes (having regard to CCA 1974, s.22(1B)–(1E)) that an indefinite licence should have a limited duration or a limited duration licence should have that duration shortened. If the licence is varied under s.31, it does not take effect before the end of the appeal period (s.31(7)).

2.12.4 Suspension and revocation

Principles

If at a time during the currency of a licence the OFT forms the opinion that if the licence had expired at that time (assuming for indefinite licences, that it were a licence of limited duration) it would have been minded not to renew it, it must proceed in accordance with CCA 1974, s.32(1).

For standard licences, the OFT must (by s.32(2)) give notice:

- telling the licensee that it is minded to revoke or suspend the licence (either until a specified date or indefinitely) and give reasons; and
- inviting the license holder to submit representations under s.34 dealing with (a) the proposed revocation or suspension and (b) the provision (if any) that should be included under s.34A if the OFT's determination is to revoke or suspend the licence.

For group licences, the OFT must (by s.32(3)):

- give general notice that is minded to revoke or suspend the licence (either until a specified date or indefinitely) and give reasons; and
- in the notice invite any licensee to submit to the OFT representations dealing with the proposed revocation in accordance with s.34.

For group licences issued on application, the OFT must also (by s.31(4)):

- tell the original applicant that it is minded to revoke or suspend the licence (either until a specified date or indefinitely) and give reasons; and
- invite the original applicant to submit to the OFT representations dealing with the proposed revocation in accordance with s.34.

The OFT must give notice of the revocation or suspension of a group licence by general notice (s.32(6)). The revocation or suspension does not take effect before the end of the appeal period (s.32(7)). It therefore follows that licensed activities may be carried out by a licence holder up to (and including) the last day for appealing.

Application to end suspension

If a licence is suspended rather than revoked, a licence holder may make an application to the OFT for the suspension to end. By CCA 1974, s.33(1), the OFT may (if it thinks fit) give notice to the licensee and end the suspension. It does not matter whether the suspension was for a fixed or indefinite period.

If, after receiving an application to end the suspension, the OFT's view is to refuse the application it will, before making its determination and by s.33(2), give notice:

- telling the applicant that it is minded to refuse the application and give its reasons; and
- inviting the applicant to submit representations to the OFT in accordance with CCA 1974, s.34.

If the suspension of a group licence is ended, the OFT must give general notice (s.33(3)). For group licences issued on application, the original applicant is given standing to make an application under s.33(4) and the OFT must tell the original applicant if a suspension of a group licence has ended (s.33(4)).

2.12.5   OFT's power to impose requirements

Individual licensees

By CCA 1974, s.33A, if the OFT is dissatisfied with any of the following matters:

(a)   a business being carried on, or which has been carried on, by a licensee or by an associate or a former associate of a licensee (s.33A(1)(a));

(b)   a proposal to carry on a business which has been made by a licensee or by an associate or a former associate of a licensee (s.33A(1)(b)); or

(c)   any conduct not covered by (a) or (b) of a licensee or of an associate or a former associate of a licensee (s.33A(1)(c)),

then it may, by s.33A(2), give notice to the licensee requiring it to do, not to do or to stop doing anything stated in the notice so that the OFT is no longer dissatisfied, or matters of the same or a similar kind do not arise.

The OFT may only give notice under s.33A(2) where the activity relates to a business which the licensee is carrying on, or proposing to carry on, under a licence of which he is a licensee. It cannot relate to any other activities because these are outside the OFT's regulatory jurisdiction. The OFT may, however, impose a requirement on a particular person rather than the licensee. If, for example, a particular employee or director is doing things, or not doing things, which make the OFT dissatisfied then it can specify that person in the notice. It does not matter if the OFT's dissatisfaction arose before or after the licensee became a licensee (s.33A(5)). Licence holders must therefore ensure that the OFT does not become dissatisfied with their approach in any way. By s.33A(7), the phrase 'associate' in s.33A also includes a business associate.

Supervisors of group licences

Under CCA 1974, s.33B(1), if the OFT is dissatisfied with the way in which a responsible person for a group licence is regulating or otherwise supervising, or has regulated or otherwise supervised, persons who are licensees under that licence or is proposing to regulate or otherwise to supervise such persons, then the OFT may (by virtue of s.33B(2)) give notice to the responsible person requiring him to do, not to do or to stop doing anything stated in the notice so that the OFT is no longer dissatisfied or matters of the same or a similar kind do not arise.

The OFT's powers under s.33B only apply to a responsible person's practices and procedures for regulating or otherwise supervising licensees under the licence for their carrying on of businesses under the licence (s.33B(3)). It does not matter if the OFT's dissatisfaction arose before or after the group licence was issued (s.33B(4)).

By s.33B(5), if a person applies for a group licence and, while dealing with the application, the OFT forms the opinion that if a group licence were to be issued, it would be minded to impose a requirement under s.33B, then the OFT must (before issuing the licence) do (in whole or part) anything that it must do under s.33D or s.34(1) or (2) for the imposing of the requirement.

Section 33B(6) defines that a person is a 'responsible person' for the group licence if he is the original applicant for it and he has a responsibility (whether by virtue of an enactment, an agreement or otherwise) for regulating or otherwise supervising persons who are licensees under the licence.

Supplementary provisions

CCA 1974, s.33C sets out supplemental provisions for requirements imposed by the OFT:

- a notice imposing a requirement under s.33A or s.33B may include provision about the time at, or by which, or the period during which, the requirement is to be complied with (s.33C(1)):
- a requirement imposed under s.33A or s.33B does not have effect after the licence it is imposed upon no longer has effect (s.33C(2));
- a person will not be required under s.33A or s.33B to compensate, or otherwise to make amends to, another person (s.33C(3));
- the OFT may by notice to the person on whom a requirement has been imposed under s.33A or s.33B vary or revoke the requirement (including any provision made under s.33C(1) relating to it) with effect from such date as may be specified in the notice (s.33C(4));
- the OFT may exercise its power under s.33C(4) for a requirement either on its own motion or on the application of a person falling within s.33C(6) or (7) (s.33C(5)).

A person falls within s.33C(6) in relation to a requirement if he is the person on whom the requirement is imposed. A person falls within s.33C(7) in relation to a requirement if:

(a)   the requirement is imposed under section 33A;

(b)   he is not the person on whom the requirement is imposed;

(c)   the requirement is framed by reference to him by name; and

(d)   the effect of the requirement is –

    (i)   to prevent him being an employee of the person on whom the requirement is imposed;

    (ii)   to restrict the activities that he may engage in as an employee of that person; or

    (iii)   otherwise to prevent him from doing something, or to restrict his doing something, in connection with a business being carried on by that person.

Procedure for requirements

CCA 1974, s.33D deals with the procedural aspects of requirements under ss.33A–33C. By s.33D(1), the OFT is required to follow certain procedures before making a determination to:

- impose a requirement on a person under s.33A or s.33B; or
- refuse an application under s.33C(5) for a requirement imposed under either of those sections; or
- vary or revoke a requirement so imposed.

The OFT must give notice to the person on whom the requirement is imposed or who is referred to in the notice by telling him, with reasons, that it is minded to make the determination and inviting him to submit to it representations to under CCA 1974, s.34.

    The OFT does not, however, need to give notice where the proposed determination is in the same terms as a proposal made by that person to the OFT (whether as a part of an application or otherwise) (s.33D(4)).

Guidance on imposing requirements

By s.33E(1), the OFT must prepare and publish guidance on how it exercises, or proposes to exercise, its powers under ss.33A–33C. So far, the OFT has not published separate guidance but paragraphs 4.5–4.13 of the 'Consumer Credit Licensing: General Guidance for Licensees and Applicants on Fitness and Requirements' (OFT 969), dated January 2008, provides some limited guidance (available at **www.oft.gov.uk/shared_oft/business_leaflets/credit_licences/oft969.pdf**).

2.13 REPRESENTATIONS TO THE OFT

Applicants invited to submit representations to the OFT under s.34 must make them within 21 days after the notice containing the invitation is given or is published (or such longer period as the OFT allows). The representations can be made in writing but the applicant can state that it wishes to make oral representations. If it does, the OFT must fix a hearing (s.34(1)). By s.34(2), the OFT is bound to consider any representations it receives when reaching its determination. Once it has made its determination, the OFT will give notice to the applicant or, if the invitation was given by general notice, will give notice of its determination by general notice.

2.14 WINDING UP OF A STANDARD LICENSEE'S BUSINESS

From 6 April 2008, CCA 1974, s.34A addresses an important issue where the OFT makes one of the following determinations:

- to refuse to renew a standard licence in accordance with the terms of the application for its renewal;
- to vary such a licence under CCA 1974, s.31; or
- to suspend or revoke such a licence.

To allow the licensee to transfer or wind up its business subject to such a determination, the OFT now has the power by s.34A (if it thinks fit) to include as part of that determination a provision authorising the licensee to carry on for a specified period:

- specified activities; or
- activities of specified descriptions,

which, because of that determination, the licensee is no longer able to carry on. This overcomes the problem of licensees being subject to a determination and then having to act quickly to either transfer or wind up their existing books of business. This is a particular issue for credit or hire providers who may need to transfer their books to another creditor owner. The OFT has a wide discretion under s.34A(3) and (4) and largely exercises that discretion as it thinks fit. For example, it may require other persons to run the business for a specified period or require the licensee to give the OFT access to premises at particular points in time.

2.15 SURRENDER OF A LICENCE

By CCA 1974, s.37(1A), a licence terminates if the licensee gives the OFT notice under s.37(1B). This procedure is straightforward and can be quickly completed using the OFT's website (at **https://www2.crw.gov.uk/LIVE/CCL/Online Form.aspx**). By s.37(4), group licences may not be surrendered under s.37.

2.16 CRIMINAL OFFENCES

It is important to remember that if a business does not have a proper licence in place, it may commit a criminal offence. Under CCA 1974, s.39, a person commits an offence if:

- he engages in any activities requiring a licence when he does not have a licence which covers those activities (s.39(1));
- he carries on business under a name which is not specified in the licence (s.39(2)); and
- he fails to give to the OFT or a licensee notice under s.36 within the required period (s.39(3)).

2.17 POWER TO IMPOSE CIVIL PENALTIES

2.17.1 Minded to impose a penalty

Before imposing a penalty on a person under CCA 1974, s.39A, the OFT must give (by s.39B(1)) a notice to that person:

- telling him that it is minded to impose a penalty;
- stating the proposed amount;
- stating its reasons for being so minded and the reasons for the amount;
- stating the proposed period for payment; and
- inviting him to make submissions under s.34.

2.17.2 Imposing a penalty

By s.39A(1), the OFT, where it is satisfied that a person (called the 'defaulter') has failed or is failing to comply with a requirement imposed on him under ss.33A, 33B or 36A, may by notice to him (called a 'penalty notice') impose a penalty of an amount it thinks fit. This should not exceed £50,000 (s.39A(3)). By s.39A(2), the penalty notice must:

- state the amount of the penalty;
- explain why the penalty is being imposed and the reasons for the amount of it;
- state how the payment of the penalty may be made to the OFT; and
- state when the payment must be made (which cannot be earlier than the end of the period during which an appeal may be brought under s.41).

If the penalty is not paid, it carries interest (currently at 8 per cent a year) and is recoverable by the OFT (s.39A(5)). The OFT (when deciding whether to impose a penalty) must have regard to:

- any penalty or fine that has been imposed on that person by another body for the conduct giving rise to the person's failure (s.39B(2)(a)); and

- other steps that the OFT has taken (or might take) under Part III of CCA 1974 for that conduct (s.39B(2)(b)).

2.18 APPEALS

2.18.1 Standing to appeal

If the OFT makes a determination then, in certain circumstances, the aggrieved person may be able to appeal the decision to the First-tier Tribunal (Consumer Credit) (which replaced the short-lived Consumer Credit Appeals Tribunal). Under CCA 1974, s.41, the following persons are entitled to appeal:

- the applicant where his application to issue, renew or vary a licence in accordance with the terms of the application has been refused;
- the person excluded from a group licence;
- the licensee where there has been a compulsory variation, suspension or revocation of a standard licence;
- the original applicant or any licensee where there has been a compulsory variation, suspension or revocation of a group licence;
- the applicant where there has been a refusal to end the suspension of a licence in accordance with the terms of the application;
- where there has been a determination to: (a) impose a requirement under s.33A or s.33B; (b) refuse an application under s.33C(5) in relation to a requirement imposed under either of those sections; or (c) vary or revoke a requirement so imposed, a person who falls within CCA 1974, s.33C(6) or (7) in relation to the requirement unless the OFT was not required to give notice to him for the determination under s.33D(4);
- the applicant where there is a refusal to make an order under CCA 1974, ss.40(2), 148(2) or 149(2) in accordance with the terms of the application;
- the person on whom the penalty is imposed where a penalty is imposed under s.39;
- the consumer credit EEA firm concerned where there is an imposition of, or refusal to withdraw, consumer credit prohibition under FSMA 2000, s.203; and
- the consumer credit EEA firm concerned where there is an imposition of, or refusal to withdraw, a restriction under FSMA 2000, s.204.

2.18.2 Procedure rules

The Tribunal Procedure (First-tier Tribunal) (General Regulatory Chamber) Rules 2009, SI 2009/1976 apply to the proceedings in the Tribunal. These are currently available at **www.justice.gov.uk/downloads/guidance/courts-and-tribunals/tribunals/tribunals-rules-2009-at010411.pdf**.

2.18.3 Tribunal's powers

The Tribunal must determine the appeal under CCA 1974, s.41 by way of a rehearing of the determination appealed against: (s.41ZB(1)). In essence, this means that the aggrieved party gets a second bite of the cherry. By s.41ZB(2), the Tribunal may do one or more of the following:

(a) confirm the determination appealed against;
(b) quash that determination;
(c) vary that determination;
(d) remit the matter to the OFT for reconsideration and determination in accordance with the directions (if any) given to it by the tribunal;
(e) give the OFT directions for the purpose of giving effect to its decision.

For appeals against the imposition of a penalty, the Tribunal has (by s.41ZB(3)) no power to increase the penalty but may extend the period within which the penalty must be paid (including cases where the time for paying has already passed).

CHAPTER 3

Seeking business

3.1 INTRODUCTION

There is considerable conflict between the role of advertising, which is often to encourage a person to buy goods or services, and the role of legislation relating to advertising, which tries to ensure that a consumer or buyer is not misled. In this chapter, we look at the important topic of seeking business and, in particular, consumer credit advertising. Whilst we will briefly consider other provisions that apply to all kinds of advertising, the main thrust of this chapter is to consider the provisions set out in the Consumer Credit (Advertisements) Regulations 2004, SI 2004/1484 (CC(Ad)R 2004) and the Consumer Credit (Advertisements) Regulations 2010, SI 2010/1970 (CC(Ad)R 2010). CC(Ad)R 2010 largely replaced CC(Ad)R 2004 on 1 February 2011 (except for advertising for credit secured on land and subject to transitional orders). For practitioners not familiar with the genesis of CC(Ad)R 2010, these revoked and replaced an earlier set of regulations (bearing the same name). For the purpose of this chapter, CC(Ad)R 2010 are those regulations that are numbered SI 2010/1970.

3.2 KEY DEFINITIONS

For the purposes of this chapter, the following definitions are crucial:

- *Advertisement*: by CCA 1974, s.189(1), this includes every form of advertising, whether in a publication, by television or radio, by display of notices, signs, labels, showcards or goods, by distribution of samples, circulars, catalogues, price lists or other material, by exhibition of pictures, models or firms, or in any other way.
- *Advertiser*: by CCA 1974, s.189(1), this is any person indicated by the advertisement as willing to enter into transactions to which the advertisement relates.
- *Dealer*: by CC(Ad)R 2004, reg.1(2) and CC(Ad)R 2010, reg.1(3), this is, for hire-purchase, credit sale or conditional sale agreements under which he is not the creditor, a person who sells or proposes to sell goods, land or other things to the creditor before they form the subject matter of such an agreement and, for any other agreement, means a supplier of such goods or his agent.

- *Representative APR*: by CC(Ad)R 2010, reg.1(3), this is the APR at or below which the advertiser reasonably expects, at the date on which the credit advertisement is published, that credit would be provided on at least 51 per cent of the consumer credit agreements which will be entered into as a result of the advertisement. For these purposes, in the case of a credit advertisement which falls within CCA 1974, s.151(1), 'advertiser' means the person carrying on the business of credit brokerage.
- *Typical APR*: by CC(Ad)R 2004, reg.1(2), this is the APR at or below which the advertiser reasonably expects, at the date on which the advertisement is published, credit would be provided on at least 66 per cent of the agreements entered into as a result of the advertisement. If the advertisement is by a credit-broker, the 'advertiser' means the person carrying on the business of credit-brokerage.

3.3 APPLICATION

Under CCA 1974, s.43(1), any advertisement which is published for the purposes of a business carried on by an advertiser which indicates that it is willing either to provide credit or to enter into an agreement for the bailment or hiring of goods is subject to Part IV of CCA 1974. CC(Ad)R 2004 and CC(Ad)R 2010 do *not* apply to consumer hire agreements.

3.4 EXEMPT ADVERTISEMENTS

CCA 1974, s.43(2)–(5) provide exemptions to the general principle set out in s.43(1) as follows:

- where the advertiser does not carry on any of the following (s.43(2)):

    - a consumer credit or consumer hire business; or
    - a business in the course of which it provides credit to individuals secured on land; or
    - a business which compromises or relates to unregulated agreements where:

        - the applicable law to the agreement is the law of a country outside of the UK; and
        - if the law applicable to the agreement were the law of part of the UK, it would be a regulated agreement;
- where the credit is only available to a body corporate (s.43(3)(b));
- if it is a communication of an invitation or inducement to engage in investment activity within the meaning of the Financial Services and Markets Act 2000 (FSMA 2000), s.21 (other than an exempt generic communication which is

defined by s.43(3B) as a communication of an invitation or inducement to engage in investment activity to which the FSMA 2000, s.21(1) does not apply) (s.43(3A));

- where the advertisement indicates that the advertiser is not willing to enter into any consumer hire agreements then s.43(1)(b) is not engaged (s.43(4));
- where an order is made by the Secretary of State (s.43(5)).

The Consumer Credit (Exempt Advertisements) Order 1985, SI 1985/621, is such an order made under CCA 1974, s.43(5). The exemptions contained in art.2 of the Order are as follows:

(a) advertisements for certain debtor-creditor-supplier consumer credit agreements under which the number of payments to be made by the debtor do not exceed a certain number (i.e. those agreements falling within art.3(1)(a), (c) and (d) of the Consumer Credit (Exempt Agreements) Order 1985 (CC(EA)O 1985));

(b) advertisements for a debtor-creditor consumer credit agreement offered to a particular class or classes of people and where the only charge for credit is interest which cannot at any time exceed the sum of 1 per cent above the highest base rate of the banks listed in CC(EA)O 1985, art.4(3) (i.e. an agreement falling within CC(EA)O 1985, art.4(1)(b));

(c) advertisements for consumer credit agreements which are exempt because of their connection with a country outside the UK (i.e. an agreement falling within CC(EA)O 1985, art.5);

(d) advertisements for consumer hire agreements made by certain public bodies (i.e. an agreement falling within CC(EA)O 1985, art.6);

(e) advertisements for agreements which would be consumer credit agreements if the credit provided under it did not exceed £15,000 (bizarrely, this amount was not changed when the limit in CCA 1974, s.8 was increased and, more recently, abolished) and is an advert that would otherwise fall within any of (a) to (c) set out above;

(f) advertisements for agreements which would be consumer hire agreements if the credit provided under it did not exceed £15,000 and is an advertisement that would otherwise fall within (d) set out above.

3.5 FORM AND CONTENT OF ADVERTISEMENTS

By virtue of CCA 1974, s.44, the Secretary of State was given the power to make regulations dealing with the form and content of advertisements subject to Part IV. The Secretary of State initially made the Consumer Credit (Advertisement) Regulations 1989 but these were repealed and replaced on 31 October 2004 by CC(Ad)R 2004 (see **3.1** above). These, in turn, were partially repealed and replaced by CC(Ad)R 2010. We now turn to look at those provisions.

3.6 CC(AD)R 2004

3.6.1 Introduction

Following the introduction of CC(Ad)R 2010, which came fully into force on 1 February 2011, the impact of CC(Ad)R 2004 has somewhat lessened. By reg.1A of CC(Ad)R 2004, these regulations still play an important role in regulating advertisements for consumer credit agreements secured on land from 1 February 2011. Otherwise, CC(Ad)R 2010 generally applies. It is also important to remember that, until 28 May 2008, consumer hire advertisements were also subject to CC(Ad)R 2004 but, following the introduction of the Consumer Protection from Unfair Trading Regulations 2008, SI 2008/1277 (CPUTR 2008), are no longer subject to CC(Ad)R 2004 or, indeed, CC(Ad)R 2010. They are, of course, and similar to consumer credit advertising, subject to other advertising controls including CPUTR 2008.

3.6.2 Exemptions

Under CC(Ad)R 2004, reg.10, CC(Ad)R 2004 does not apply to advertisements:

- which make it clear, either expressly or implicitly, that a person is only willing to provide credit or enter into an agreement for the bailment of goods for the purposes of another person's business;
- if it is a communication of an invitation or inducement to engage in investment activity (other than an exempt generic communication which is defined by reg.10(4)) within the meaning of FSMA 2000, s.21;
- if it is a communication of an invitation or inducement to enter into a regulated mortgage contract within art.61 of the Financial Services and Markets Act 2000 (Regulated Activities) Order 2001, SI 2001/544 (RAO 2001) or a regulated home purchase plan within the meaning of RAO 2001, art.63F.

This last exemption is really designed to ensure that the division between regulation by the FSA and CCA 1974 is maintained. This will no doubt change in the future with the proposals to combine the OFT, which supervises CCA 1974, with the FSA. In the meantime, and in short, first charge mortgages are generally not subject to CCA 1974 or CC(Ad)R 2004 but, instead, subject to regulation by FSMA 2000 and regulations made under it.

3.6.3 Basic duty

Under CC(Ad)R 2004, reg.2, a person who causes a credit advertisement to be published must ensure that the advertisement complies with all applicable requirements of CC(Ad)R 2004. The advertisement must, by reg.3, also:

- be in plain and intelligible language;

- be easily legible or, if given orally, clearly audible; and
- state the advertiser's name.

It is likely that the requirement for an advert to be in plain and intelligible language will be satisfied if 'plain English' is used. Lawyers are often notorious for using unnecessarily complex words, phrases or grammar. Using the Plain English Campaign's 'The A–Z of Alternative Words' (available at **www.plainenglish.co.uk/ free-guides.html**) will certainly help overcome some of these issues.

3.6.4 Content of a consumer credit advert

If a consumer credit advert contains any of the following information (in broad terms):

- the frequency, number and amounts of repayments or, if the credit is running-account credit, the frequency of repayments and the amount either as a fixed amount or a statement explaining how that amount will be calculated (CC(Ad)R 2004, Sched.2, para.5); or
- a statement indicating the description and amount of any other charges (excluding default charges) or how such charges are calculated (CC(Ad)R 2004, Sched.2, para.6); or
- the total amount payable by the debtor, for fixed-sum credit repayable at specific intervals or in specific amounts other than situations where the total of the advance payments, the amount of credit repayable and the total charge for credit is not more than the cash price (CC(Ad)R 2004, Sched.2, para.7),

then the advert must also (by reg.4(1)):

- include all of the other items of information (except where the information is inapplicable) listed in CC(Ad)R 2004, Sched.2; and
- specify the advertiser's postal address at which it may be contacted unless the advert:

  - is published on the television or by radio broadcast;
  - is at the dealer's or creditor's premises and cannot be taken away;
  - includes the dealer's name and address; and
  - includes the credit-broker's name and address.

3.6.5 Prominence of Schedule 2 information

If the requirement to show the information under CC(Ad)R 2004, Sched.2 is engaged then the items of information must be given equal prominence and shown together as a whole (reg.4(2)). There are a number of ways of achieving this: the most obvious is by either printing the text of the information required by the Schedule in bold or making the font a different size. The OFT has published guidance in the form of 'frequently asked questions' (OFT 746: available at

www.oft.gov.uk/shared_oft/business_leaflets/consumer_credit/oft746.pdf),
which provides some useful help. It is, however, submitted that the OFT's guidance
goes some way beyond the requirements of CC(Ad)R 2004.

3.6.6   Variations to information

If any of the information is contained in a book, catalogue, leaflet or any other
document, and is likely to vary over time, then the requirement under CC(Ad)R
2004, reg.4(2) for the information to be 'shown together as a whole' is satisfied if:

- it is set out together as a whole in a separate document issued with the book,
  catalogue, leaflet or other document (i.e. is an insert into that document)
  (reg.4(3)(a));
- the other information in the credit advertisement is shown together as a whole
  in the book, catalogue, leaflet or other document (reg.4(3)(b)); and
- the book, catalogue, leaflet or other document identifies the separate document
  in which the information that is likely to vary is set out (reg.4(3)(c)).

These provisions are often used where a creditor changes its rates on a month-by-
month basis to ensure its profit margins are maximised.

3.6.7   Dealer's seasonal or calendar publications

Given the reduction in CC(Ad)R 2004's remit from 1 February 2011, it is unlikely
that reg.5 will provide much benefit to creditors. Regulation 5 does, however,
provide an exception to the requirements under reg.4. This only applies, however,
where:

- a credit advertisement is contained in, or in a separate document issued with, a
  publication published by or for a dealer for goods or services which may be sold
  or supplied by that dealer in a seasonal or calendar period stated in the
  document (i.e. Christmas booklets);
- the credit advertisement contains the information specified in reg.5(2); and
- no other indication is given that another person was willing to provide credit.

The information specified in reg.5(2) is:

- the name and postal address of the creditor, credit-broker or dealer with or
  without a statement of his occupation or the general nature of his occupation;
  and
- an indication that individuals may obtain on request details of the terms that the
  proposed advertiser is prepared to do business on.

It therefore follows that reg.5 is a very limited exception to the requirement to
comply with reg.4. Indeed, the advert may simply contain words along the following lines:

Credit provided by SSH Finance plc of 2 Park Lane, Leeds, LS3 1ES; terms available upon request.

3.6.8 Dealer's publications relating to credit under a debtor-creditor-supplier agreement

Under CC(Ad)R 2004, reg.6, if an advert deals with credit proposed to be advanced under a debtor-creditor-supplier agreement, and the advert is published by, or for, a dealer for goods or services which may be sold or supplied by him, the information will be taken for the purpose of reg.4(2) to be shown as a whole if:

- the advertisement clearly indicates (by reg.6(a)):
  - the cash price alone; or
  - the cash price, any advance payment and the information specified in paras.5–7 of Sched.2 and (except for the agreements where the total amount payable by the debtor is not greater than the cash price for the goods of services acquired using the credit under the agreement) the annual percentage rate (APR),

  in close proximity to every description of, or reference to, goods or services to which the information in the publication relates; and
- the remaining information in the advertisement is presented so it is readily comprehensible as a whole by a prospective debtor and an indication is given in close proximity to any of that information that it relates to all or specified descriptions of goods and services (by reg.6(b)); and
- except as mentioned by reg.6(a), no information relating to the providing of credit is shown together with the cash price.

3.6.9 Security

Given the ambit of CC(Ad)R 2004 from 1 February 2011, reg.7 perhaps contains some of the most important provisions. In short, it states that if security is, or may be, required as a condition of advancing credit then the advertisement must also state that security is or may be required and specify the nature of that security.

This is typically achieved by creditors stating that all loans must be secured on, for example, a debtor's home. Other examples include 'log book loan' lenders (but those are now, of course, subject to CC(Ad)R 2010) which take security for the loan by the use of a bill of sale: such creditors must make it clear that the customer's vehicle is needed as security for the loan.

If the security comprises or may comprise a mortgage or charge on the debtor's home then the advertisement must by reg.7(2)(a) contain (unless reg.7(2)(c) applies) the following warning:

YOUR HOME MAY BE REPOSSESSED IF YOU DO NOT KEEP UP REPAYMENTS ON A MORTGAGE OR ANY OTHER DEBT SECURED ON IT.

If the advertisement suggests that credit is available to pay off debts due to other creditors, the warning in reg.7(2)(a) must be preceded by the following warning:

THINK CAREFULLY BEFORE SECURING OTHER DEBTS AGAINST YOUR HOME.

If, however, the credit agreement is or would be an agreement of the kind described in reg.7(3) then the advert must contain the following warning:

CHECK THAT THIS MORTGAGE WILL MEET YOUR NEEDS IF YOU WANT TO MOVE OR SELL YOUR HOME OR YOU WANT YOUR FAMILY TO INHERIT IT. IF YOU ARE IN ANY DOUBT, SEEK INDEPENDENT ADVICE.

The agreements caught by reg.7(3) are:

(a)   any credit agreement under which no instalment repayments secured by the mortgage on the debtor's home, and no payment of interest on the credit (other than interest charged when all or part of the credit is repaid voluntarily by the debtor), are due or capable of becoming due while the debtor continues to occupy the mortgaged land as his main residence; and

(b)   any credit agreement –

(i)   which is secured by a mortgage which the creditor cannot enforce by taking possession of or selling (or concurring with any other person in selling) the mortgaged land or any part of it while the debtor continues to occupy it as his main residence, and

(ii)   under which, although interest payments may become due, no full or partial repayment of the credit secured by the mortgage is due or capable of becoming due while the debtor continues to occupy the mortgaged land as his main residence.

If the credit advertisement is for a mortgage or other loan secured on a property and repayments are made in currency other than sterling, then the advert must contain, by reg.7(4), the following warning message:

CHANGES IN THE EXCHANGE RATE MAY INCREASE THE STERLING EQUIVALENT OF YOUR DEBT.

The warnings required by reg.7(2) and (4) must (by reg.7(6)) be given greater prominence in the advertisement than is given to any rate of charge other than the typical APR, or any indication or incentive of a kind referred to in reg.8(1)(c) (e.g. an indication that credit is available to those who may be restricted on the credit they can obtain) or reg.8(1)(d) (i.e. where an incentive is provided), and be given no less prominence in the advertisement than is given to any of the information required to be listed under CC(Ad)R 2004, Sched.2.

By reg.7(8), none of these requirements, except for the information that must be included under reg.7(1) (i.e. a statement that security may be needed or a statement explaining the nature of the security), need be included in an advertisement which:

- is published by a television or radio broadcast in the course of programming the primary purpose of which is not advertising;
- is published by exhibition of a film (other than exhibition by television broadcast); or
- contains only the name of the advertiser.

3.6.10 APR

Perhaps the most significant requirement under CC(Ad)R 2004, given its aim to allow consumers to compare products, is the requirement to state the typical APR by virtue of CC(Ad)R 2004, reg.8. By reg.8(1), a credit advertisement must state the typical APR if it:

- states any other rate of charge;
- includes any of the information listed in CC(Ad)R 2004, Sched.2, paras.5–7;
- indicates in any way, including by means of a name or an address used by the business for electronic communication, that:
  - credit is available to persons who might otherwise have had restricted access to credit (for example, by using a trade name or a domain name like www.unrestrictedcredit.co.uk); or
  - any of the terms on which the credit is available is more favourable than terms applied in any other case or by any other creditor (for example, by claiming that the credit offered is the cheapest in the market); or
- includes any incentive to apply for credit or to enter into an agreement under which credit is provided (the OFT's 'frequently asked questions' (OFT 746) gives some examples on this).

Creditors are only allowed to give a range of APRs in limited circumstances. Regulation 8(2) allows a creditor to do so where it states, with equal prominence, both:

- the APR that the advertiser reasonable expects, at the date that the advertisement is published, would be the lowest APR at which credit would be provided to not less than 10 per cent of the agreements entered into as a result of that advertisement; and
- the APR which the advertiser reasonably expects, at the same date, would be the highest APR at which credit would be provided under any of the agreements entered into as a result of that advertisement.

Creditors must, of course, have enough evidence to back up their claims if they are later challenged by the OFT or Trading Standards.

Regulation 8(3)–(5) sets out the rules for displaying the APR. In short, they are as follows:

- the APR should be displayed on the advert as '% APR' (reg.8(3));

- if the APR is subject to change, it should be accompanied (either before or following the APR) by the word 'variable' (reg.8(4));
- the typical APR must:
  - be accompanied by the word 'typical' (reg.8(5)(a));
  - be presented together with any of the information required by Sched.2 (reg.8(5)(b));
  - be given greater prominence in the advertisement than (i) any other rate of charge, (ii) any of the information required by Sched.2 and (iii) any indication or incentive of the kind referred to in reg.8(1)(c) or (d) (reg.8(5)(c));
    if the advert is printed or in electronic form which includes any of the information required by Sched.2, be shown in characters at least one and a half times greater in size than other characters.

Regulation 8(6) contains an exemption which states that if the agreement is a debtor-creditor agreement allowing the debtor to overdraw on a current account under which the creditor is the Bank of England or an authorised deposit taker then, instead of showing the typical APR, the creditor may include a statement of:

- a rate, expressed to be a rate of interest, being a rate determined as the rate of the total charge for credit calculated on the assumption that only interest is included in the total charge for credit; and
- the nature and amount of any other charge included in the total charge for credit.

Schedule 1 to CC(Ad)R 2004 also sets out:

- assumptions for calculating the total charge for credit and the APR for running-account credit (Sched.1, para.1); and
- tolerances for the disclosure of the APR (Sched.1, paras.2–4).

Given the similarities of the provisions on tolerances between CC(Ad)R 2004 and the Consumer Credit (Agreements) Regulations 1983, SI 1983/1553, readers are referred to **5.9.2** for a more detailed look at these rules.

3.6.11 Restrictions on phrases and words

CC(Ad)R 2004, reg.9 imposes restrictions on the phrases and words that may be used in credit advertisements. There is a complete ban on using:

- the word 'overdraft' or any similar expression which describes any agreement for running-account credit unless the agreement allows the debtor to overdraw on a current account (reg.9(1)(a));
- the phrase 'interest free' or any similar expression suggesting that a customer is liable to pay no more than he would have to pay if he was a cash buyer unless the total amount payable by the debtor does not exceed the cash price (reg.9(1)(b));

- the phrase 'no deposit' or any similar expression unless no advance payment is actually required (reg.9(1)(c));
- the phrases 'loan guaranteed' or 'pre-approved' or any similar expression unless the agreement is free from any conditions over the debtor's credit status (reg.9(1)(d));
- the words 'gift', 'present' or any similar expression unless there are no conditions which require the debtor to return the credit or items that are the subject of the claim (reg.9(1)(e)); and
- for any repayments, the expression 'weekly equivalent' or any similar expression or any expression of any other periodical equivalent unless weekly payments or other periodical payments are provided under the agreement (reg.9(2)).

3.6.12 Schedule 2 information

Schedule 2 to CC(Ad)R 2004 sets out the information to be included (where relevant) in a credit advertisement, as follows:

- Amount of credit: the credit advertisement must state the amount of credit which may be provided under a consumer credit agreement or an indication of one or both of the maximum and minimum amount of credit that may be provided (Sched.2, para.1).
- Deposit of money in an account: the credit advertisement must state any requirement to place on deposit any sum of money in any account with any person (Sched.2, para.2).
- Cash price: if the credit is provided under a debtor-creditor-supplier agreement for goods, services, land or other things having a particular cash price, the acquisition of which is to be financed by credit, the credit advertisement must state the cash price of such goods, services, land and other things (Sched.2, para.3).
- Advance payment: the credit advertisement must state whether an advance payment is required and, if so, the amount or minimum amount of that payment expressed as a sum of money or a percentage (Sched.2, para.4).
- Frequency, number and amount of repayments of credit: running-account credit: the credit advertisement must state the frequency of the repayments under the advertised transaction and the amount of each repayment stating whether it is a fixed or minimum amount, or a statement indicating the manner in which that amount will be determined. The amount of any repayment may be expressed as a sum of money or as a specified proportion of a specified amount (including the amount outstanding from time to time) (Sched.2, para.5(1)).
- Frequency, number and amount of repayments of credit: non-running-account credit: the credit advertisement must state the frequency, number and amounts of repayments of credit. The amount of any repayment may be expressed as a

sum of money or as a specified proportion of a specified amount (including the amount outstanding from time to time) (Sched.2, para.5(2)).

- Other payments and charges: the credit advertisement must state the description and amount of any other payments and charges which may be payable under the advertised transaction (Sched.2, para.6(1)). This is subject to two points:

    1. if the debtor's liability cannot be established at the date of the advertisement's publication, there must be a statement indicating the description of the payment and the circumstances in which the liability to make it will arise (Sched.2, para.6(2));
    2. the requirements of Sched.2, para.6(1) or (2) do not apply to any charge payable to the creditor or any other person under the transaction upon the debtor's failure (or his relative's failure) to do, or not do, anything which he is required to do or not do (Sched.2, para.6(3)).

- Total amount payable by the debtor: if the credit advertisement is for fixed-sum credit provided under a consumer credit agreement which is repayable at specified intervals or in specified amounts, and the total of the following three items: (i) advance payments; (ii) the amount of credit repayable by the debtor; and (iii) the amount of the total charge for credit, is not more than the cash price, then there must be a statement of the total amount payable (Sched.2, para.7).

3.7 CC(AD)R 2010

3.7.1 Introduction

CC(Ad)R 2010 came into force on 1 February 2011, subject to a grace period for existing adverts under reg.12, and (like CC(Ad)R 2004) apply to 'credit advertisements'. This definition is unchanged and, therefore, if an advertisement was regulated by CC(Ad)R 2004, it will now generally be regulated by CC(Ad)R 2010 (subject to some exceptions the main being consumer credit agreements secured on land). It is also important to remember that (like the position under CC(Ad)R 2004) hire agreements are not subject to CC(Ad)R 2010 but are subject to CPUTR 2008. All advertisements are subject to general advertising regulations.

3.7.2 Exemptions

By virtue of reg.11, CC(Ad)R 2010 does not apply to a credit advertisement which expressly or by implication indicates clearly that a person is willing to provide credit for the purposes of another person's business, and does not indicate (whether expressly or by implication) that a person is willing to provide credit otherwise than for the purposes of such a business.

The regulations do not apply if the advert is a communication of an invitation or inducement (reg.11(3)):

- to engage in investment activity within the meaning of FSMA 2000, s.21 other than an exempt generic communication (which is a communication to which s.21(1) of FSMA 2000 does not apply, as a result of an order being made under s.21(5), because it does not identify a person as providing an investment or carrying on an activity to which the communication relates);
- to enter into a regulated home purchase plan within the meaning of RAO 2001, art.63F.

Nor do the regulations apply to an advert for a consumer credit agreement secured on land (reg.11(5)).

3.7.3   Basic duty

Under reg.2, a person who causes a credit advertisement to be published (other than an exempt advert) must ensure that the advertisement complies with all applicable requirements of CC(Ad)R 2010. The advertisement must, by reg.3, also:

- use plain and intelligible language;
- be easily legible or, if given orally, clearly audible; and
- state the advertiser's name.

It is likely that the requirement for an advert to be in plain and intelligible language will be satisfied if 'plain English' is used (see **3.6.3** above). In short, using the Plain English Campaign's 'The A–Z of Alternative Words' (available at **www.plain english.co.uk/free-guides.html**) will certainly help overcome some of these issues.

3.7.4   Content of a consumer credit advert

If a credit advertisement includes a rate of interest or an amount relating to the cost of the credit (whether expressed as a sum of money or a proportion of a specified amount), the advertisement must by CC(Ad)R 2010, reg.4(1) also contain:

- (subject to reg.4(2)) standard information by means of a 'representative example' in accordance with reg.5;
- the advertiser's postal address unless it is a credit advertisement:
    - published by television or radio broadcast;
    - in any form on the premises of a dealer or creditor (not being advertisements in writing which customers are intended to take away);
    - which includes the name and address of a dealer; or
    - which includes the name and a postal address of a credit-broker.

A representative example is not required under reg.4(1)(a) where reg.6(1) applies and the credit advertisement does not indicate a rate of interest or other amount relating to the cost of the credit other than the representative APR (reg.4(2)).

3.7.5 Representative example

If a representative example is required by CC(Ad)R 2010, reg.4(1)(a) then it must, by reg.5(1) and subject to reg.5(5), include the following information:

- the rate of interest, whether fixed, variable or both (reg.5(1)(a));
- the nature and amount of any other charge included in the total charge for credit (reg.5(1)(b));
- the total amount of credit (reg.5(1)(c));
- the representative APR (see the definition at **3.2** above) (reg.5(1)(d));
- in the case of credit in the form of a deferred payment for specific goods, services, land or other things, the cash price and the amount of any advance payment (reg.5(1)(e)); and
- except where the consumer credit agreement is an open-end agreement:

    - the duration of the agreement (reg.5(1)(f)(i)); and
    - the total amount payable by the debtor and the amount of each repayment of credit (reg.5(1)(f)(ii)).

The information required by reg.5(1)(a)–(c), (e) and (f) must be that which the advertiser reasonably expects (at the date on which the credit advertisement is published) to be representative of consumer credit agreements to which the representative APR applies and which are expected to be entered into as a result of the advertisement (reg.5(2)). For credit advertisements falling within CCA 1974, s.151(1), 'advertiser' means (for this purpose) the person carrying on the business of credit brokerage.

Regulation 5(2) is supplemented by reg.5(3) which makes it clear that the phrase 'agreements to which the representative APR applies' in the case of reg.5(1)(e) means agreements providing credit for the purchase of specific goods, services, land or other things to which the representative APR applies.

If the consumer credit agreement allows for different ways of drawing down credit at different rates then, for the purposes of reg.5(1)(a), the rate of interest is assumed to be the highest rate applied to the most common drawdown mechanism for the product to which the agreement relates (reg.5(4)).

By reg.5(7), the rate of interest is an annual rate of interest.

By reg.5(5), the information required by reg.5(1)(d) and (2) does not apply to an authorised non-business overdraft agreement.

3.7.6 Presentation and prominence of representative example

Under CC(Ad)R 2010, reg.5(6), the standard information contained in the representative example must be:

- specified in a clear and concise way;
- accompanied by the words 'representative example';
- presented together with each item of information being given equal prominence; and
- given greater prominence than any other information relating to the cost of the credit in the credit advertisement except for any statement relating to an obligation to enter into a contract for an ancillary service referred to in reg.8(1), and any indication or incentive of a kind referred to in reg.6(1).

3.7.7 Other advertisements requiring representative APR

By CC(Ad)R 2010, reg.6(1), a credit advertisement must state the representative APR if the advertisement:

- indicates in any way, including by the name given to the business or by the address used by the business for the purpose of electronic communication, that:

  - credit is available to persons who might otherwise have had restricted access to credit (for example, by using a trade name or a domain name like www.unrestrictedcredit.co.uk); or
  - any of the terms on which the credit is available is more favourable (either for a limited period or generally) than terms applied in any other case or by any other creditor (for example, by claiming that the credit offered is the cheapest in the market); or

- includes any incentive to apply for credit or to enter into an agreement under which credit is provided.

If there is a need to show the representative APR then it must be given greater prominence than any of the incentives or indications mentioned in reg.6(1) (reg.6(2)). The real thrust of reg.6 is therefore to ensure that the representative APR stands out more than the incentive or indication.

Regulation 6(1) does not, however, apply to credit advertisements for an authorised non-business overdraft agreement (reg.6(3)).

3.7.8 APR

Under CC(Ad)R 2010, reg.7 the APR must be recorded in the advertisement as '% APR' (reg.7(1)).

If the APR is subject to change, it must be accompanied by the word 'variable' (reg.7(2)) and the representative APR must be accompanied by the word 'representative' (reg.7(3)).

The Schedule to CC(Ad)R 2010 also sets out:

- assumptions for calculating the total charge for credit and the APR for running account credit (para.1); and
- tolerances for the disclosure of the APR (paras.2–4).

Given the similarities of the provisions on tolerances between CC(Ad)R 2010 and the Consumer Credit (Agreements) Regulations 2010, SI 2010/1014, see **5.15** for a more detailed look at these rules.

3.7.9 Ancillary services

There may be occasions when the credit is provided on the condition that the debtor takes certain additional services. For example, a hire-purchase agreement for a television may require, as a condition of advancing the credit, that the debtor takes out a maintenance agreement. CC(Ad)R 2010, reg.8(1) therefore makes it clear that such a credit advertisement must include a clear and concise statement about the ancillary service where:

- entry into that service contract is compulsory and a condition of obtaining the credit or of obtaining the credit on the advertised terms and conditions; and
- the cost of that ancillary service cannot be worked out in advance.

If reg.8(1) is engaged then the statement must (by reg.8(2)):

- be no less prominent than any standard information that must be included in the credit advertisement; and
- be presented together with any representative APR included in the credit advertisement.

Regulation 8(1) does not, however, apply to credit advertisements for an authorised non-business overdraft agreement (reg.8(3)).

It is therefore clear, once again, that CC(Ad)R 2010 requires complete clarity about the nature and terms of the credit being offered. If a creditor or advertiser is in any doubt, it is likely to be safer to err on the side of caution.

3.7.10 Security

Regulation 9 of CC(Ad)R 2010 is a much watered down version of the requirements under CC(Ad)R 2004. This is, perhaps, not surprising given that much of the security requirements under CC(Ad)R 2004 were for loans secured on land (which, of course, remain subject to CC(Ad)R 2004). Regulation 9 simply states that if a credit advertisement is for a facility for which security is or may be required then the advertisement must:

- state that security is or may be required; and
- specify the nature of the security.

Regulation 9 will therefore come into play for a fixed-sum loan agreement secured by a bill of sale over the debtor's motor vehicle (commonly known as log book loans). Creditors providing credit in such a way will (like the position under CC(Ad)R 2004) be required to state that the debtor's motor vehicle will be security for the loan.

3.7.11 Restrictions on phrases and words

Regulation 10 imposes restrictions on the phrases and words that may be used in credit advertisements. There is a complete ban on using:

- the word 'overdraft' or any similar expression which describes any agreement for running-account credit unless the agreement allows the debtor to overdraw on a current account (reg.10(1)(a));
- the phrase 'interest free' or any similar expression suggesting that a customer is liable to pay no more than he would have to pay if he was a cash buyer unless the total amount payable by the debtor does not exceed the cash price (reg.10(1)(b));
- the phrase 'no deposit' or any similar expression unless no advance payment is actually required (reg.10(1)(c));
- the phrases 'loan guaranteed' or 'pre-approved' or any similar expression unless the agreement is free from any conditions over the debtor's credit status (reg.10(1)(d));
- the words 'gift', 'present' or any similar expression unless there are no conditions which require the debtor to return the credit or items that are the subject of the claim (reg.10(1)(e)); and
- for any repayments, the expression 'weekly equivalent' or any similar expression or any expression of any other periodical equivalent unless weekly payments or other periodical payments are provided under the agreement (reg.10(2)).

3.7.12 Credit intermediaries

If a credit intermediary (which is defined by CCA 1974, s.160A(1) and discussed at **1.2**) publishes any advert intended for individuals not acting in the course of a business in any of the following activities (s.160A(2)):

(a) recommending or making available prospective regulated consumer credit agreements, other than agreements secured on land, to individuals,

(b) assisting individuals by undertaking other preparatory work in relation to such agreements, or

(c) entering into regulated consumer credit agreements, other than agreements secured on land, with individuals on behalf of creditors.

then he must by CCA 1974, s.160A(3) indicate the extent to which the intermediary is acting independently and, in particular, whether he works exclusively with a creditor.

3.8 ADVERTISING INFRINGEMENTS: RESPONSIBILITY FOR OTHER PARTIES

By s.47(1) of CCA 1974, if an advertiser commits an offence under s.44 or s.45, or would have been taken to commit an offence but has a defence under s.168, then a like offence is committed by:

- the publisher of the advertisement (s.47(1)(a)); and
- any person who, in the course of a business carried on by him, devised the advertisement, or a part of it relevant to the initial offence (s.47(1)(b)); and
- where the advertiser did not procure the publication of the advertisement, the person who did procure it (s.47(1)(c)).

Such a person is entitled to rely upon the defences contained in CCA 1974, s.168 (which are discussed at **3.13** above). If that person is also the publisher, he may have a supplemental defence, contained in s.47(2), where he can prove that:

- the advertisement was published in the course of a business carried on by him; and
- he received the advertisement in the course of that business and did not know, and had no reason to suspect, that its publication would be an offence.

Despite the substantial number of definitions in CCA 1974, s.189(1), there is no definition of the term 'publisher': it is therefore open to argument whether this should be restricted to one person or everyone involved in the publication process (including, for example, the creditor, the credit-broker (if any), the printer and the distributor). It should be remembered, by virtue of CCA 1974, s.171(3), the defendant must only prove his defence on the balance of probabilities.

3.9 ADVERTISEMENT OF GOODS THAT ARE NOT SOLD FOR CASH

Under CCA 1974, s.45, if an advertisement says that an advertiser will provide credit under a restricted-use credit agreement for goods or services to be supplied by any person, and at the same time as the advertisement is published, that person is not also willing to sell the goods or provide the services for cash, then the advertiser commits an offence. This is a fairly self-explanatory provision and covers situations where it is proposed that goods or services are *only* provided on credit: s.45 simply stops such a situation.

3.10 CANVASSING DEBTOR-CREDITOR AGREEMENTS OFF BUSINESS PREMISES

The combined effect of CCA 1974, ss.48 and 49 is to ban the canvassing of debtor-creditor agreements off trade premises. To fall within these sections, the following conditions must be satisfied:

- the canvasser is an individual (s.48(1));
- the canvasser must solicit the entry of another individual (called the 'consumer') as the debtor under a consumer credit agreement or the hirer under a consumer hire agreement;
- the canvasser must make oral representations to the consumer or another individual;
- those representations must be made during the canvasser's visit to any place except a place where a business is temporarily or permanently carried on by:
  - the creditor or owner;
  - a supplier;
  - the canvasser (including the canvasser's agent or employee); or
  - the consumer;
- the canvasser's visit must be for the purpose of making such oral representations to individuals who are at that place but not carried out in response to a request made on a previous occasion;
- the proposed agreement must be a debtor-creditor agreement.

If these conditions are satisfied then CCA 1974, s.49(1) makes it clear that it is an offence to canvass debtor-creditor agreements off trade premises. It is also an offence, by s.49(2), to solicit (rather than to canvass) the entry of an individual (as a debtor) into a debtor-creditor agreement during a visit carried out following a previous request where:

- the request was not made in writing and signed by or for the person making the request; and
- if no request for the visit had been made, the soliciting would have constituted the canvassing of a debtor-creditor agreement off trade premises.

Section 49(3) does, however, contain an important provision that s.49(1) and (2) do not apply to any soliciting for an agreement enabling the debtor to overdraw on a current account of any description kept with the creditor where:

- the OFT has determined that current accounts of that description kept with the creditor are excluded from s.49(1) and (2); and
- the debtor already has an account with the creditor (whether a current account or not).

During the recent (and substantial) increase in enforceability claims, there were a number of claims alleging that non-compliance with s.49(1) and/or (2) meant that the agreement was unenforceable. Such claims were always misconceived: it is worth remembering that CCA 1974, s.170(1) makes it clear that any breach of CCA 1974 incurs no criminal or civil sanction except to the extent (if any) expressly provided by or under CCA 1974. Section 49 simply creates a criminal offence.

3.11 CIRCULARS TO MINORS

The law has always sought to protect minors and CCA 1974 is no exception. Section 50(1) makes it an offence for a person who, with a view to financial gain, sends to a minor any document inviting him to:

- borrow money; or
- obtain goods on credit or hire; or
- obtain services on credit; or
- apply for information or advice on borrowing money or otherwise obtaining credit, or hiring goods.

It is important to note that the wording of s.50(1) makes it an offence to send 'any document': it is not limited to regulated agreements. It must therefore follow that the offence in s.50(1) applies to regulated and unregulated agreements. The wording 'with a view to financial gain' was also considered by the Divisional Court in *Alliance and Leicester Building Society* v. *Bubbs* (1993) 157 JP 706 where the creditor had sent a brochure advertising loans and included an application form. The small print included the words 'Loans are not available to applicants under 18 years of age' and the creditor's software stopped loans being approved to applicants under 18 years of age. The Divisional Court took the view that it was not the creditor's intention to obtain a financial gain from any person who at the time of receipt of the brochure was a minor. No offence therefore took place.

In addition to the general defences under CCA 1974, s.168 (see further **3.13** below), s.50(2) provides an additional defence for a person charged under s.50(1) where it can prove that he did not know, and had no reasonable cause to suspect, that the recipient of the circular was a minor. This is, however, subject to s.50(3) where there is a presumption of knowledge, for the defendant to disprove, where the circular is sent to a school or educational institution for minors. It should be noted that the phrase 'a person' suggest that anyone who falls within s.50(1) could be prosecuted.

3.12 BAN ON UNSOLICITED CREDIT-TOKENS

Credit-tokens, commonly in the form of credit cards, are a popular way of providing credit. CCA 1974, s.51(1) makes it an offence to send someone a credit-token if he has not asked for it. It is only possible to send a credit-token, unless the credit-token agreement is a small debtor-creditor-supplier agreement, following a request contained in a document signed by the party wanting the credit-token (s.51(2)). This is often achieved by the regulated agreement including wording confirming that the debtor wants to be issued with a credit-token. Section 51(1) does not, however, apply where the credit-token is supplied under an agreement already made or in renewal or replacement of a credit-token previously accepted (s.51(3)).

3.13 DEFENCES

3.13.1 The offence

Following the repeal of CCA 1974, s.46 on 28 May 2008 (pursuant to CPUTR 2008), the consequence of failing to comply with CC(Ad)R 2004 or, now, CC(Ad)R 2010, is that an offence is committed under CCA 1974, s.167(2). By Sched.1 to CCA 1974, the punishment is a sentence of two years or a fine of £400 or both.

3.13.2 The defence

The defence available to a party subject to a criminal prosecution under CCA 1974 is set out in s.168(1). It states that it is a defence for a person charged with any offence under CCA 1974 to prove that:

- his act or omission was due to a mistake, or to reliance on information supplied to him, or to an act or omission by another person, or to an accident or some other cause beyond his control; and
- he took all reasonable precautions and exercised all due diligence to avoid such an act or omission by him or any other person under his control.

To rely on such a defence, the person charged with the offence must (unless he obtains the court's permission) serve on the prosecutor, not less than seven clear days before the hearing, a notice giving such information identifying or helping in the identification of that other person as is in his possession (s.168(2)).

3.13.3 Liability of officers of a body corporate

If a body corporate commits an offence under CCA 1974 with the consent or connivance of, or because of neglect by, any individual, under s.69 the individual commits the like offence if at that time:

- he is a director, manager, secretary or similar officer of the body corporate; or
- he is purporting to act as such an officer; or
- the body corporate is managed by its members, of whom he is one.

3.13.4 Standard of proof

The standard or proof is generally the normal criminal standard (i.e. beyond reasonable doubt).

3.14 OTHER ADVERTISING CONTROLS

3.14.1 Introduction

For all consumer credit advertisements, or even for credit or hire not covered by the existing legislation (most notably consumer hire advertisements), there are other legislative controls which apply. The most obvious ones are the Consumer Protection from Unfair Trading Regulations 2008, SI 2008/1277 (CPUTR 2008) and the Business Protection from Misleading Marketing Regulations 2008, SI 2008/1276. There is also a system of voluntary regulation by the Advertising Standards Authority.

3.14.2 CPUTR 2008

Introduction

Until recently, there were various pieces of legislation covering complaints concerning trade descriptions, misleading pricing and misleading advertising. Since 26 May 2008, parts of the Trade Descriptions Act 1968, the Fair Trading Act 1973 and the Consumer Protection Act 1987 (which all impacted upon advertising) have been repealed and replaced by CPUTR 2008. CPUTR 2008 aim to tackle unfair trading practices. Broadly speaking, their effect is to allow consumers to make free and informed purchasing decisions and to stop aggressive selling techniques and practices like supplying misleading information before the consumer makes a purchasing decision.

What do CPUTR 2008 cover?

The regulations make criminal (and ban) 31 specific practices (which are always considered unfair). They also create three further criminal offences:

- misleading actions;
- misleading omissions; and
- aggressive sales techniques like those using coercion, harassment or 'undue influence' (i.e. pressure selling techniques).

General prohibition

Under CPUTR 2008, reg.3(1), unfair commercial practices are banned. Regulation 3(3) states that a commercial practice is unfair if:

- it contravenes the requirements of professional diligence; and
- it materially distorts or is likely to materially distort the economic behaviour of the average consumer towards the product.

This introduces an objective test (and a new concept) of the 'average consumer'. This is explained by CPUTR 2008, reg.2(2)–(6). The essence of those regulations is that if a commercial practice reaches, or is addressed to, a consumer or consumers then account must be taken of the relevant characteristics of such an average consumer including an assumption that he is reasonably well informed, reasonably observant and circumspect (reg.2(2)).

If a commercial practice is addressed to a particular group of consumers then the average consumer must be referenced to being a member of that group (reg.2(4)).

If a commercial practice reaches or is addressed to consumers of a group then if that group is particularly vulnerable to the practice or the underlying product because of their mental or physical infirmity, age or credulity in a way which the trader could reasonably be expected to foresee, and if the practice is likely to materially distort the economic behaviour only of that group, then reference to the average consumer must be read as referring to the average member of that group (reg.2(5)).

Regulation 2(6) does, however, make it clear that reg.2(5) is without prejudice to the 'common and legitimate advertising practice of making exaggerated statements which are not meant to be taken literally'.

Regulation 3(4) supplements reg.2(4) by also making a commercial practice unfair if it is:

- a misleading action under the provisions of reg.5;
- a misleading omission under the provisions of reg.6;
- aggressive under the provisions of reg.7; or
- listed in Sched.1.

Finally, CPUTR 2008, reg.4 creates a criminal offence where the owner of a code of conduct promotes any unfair commercial practice in its code of conduct.

Specific prohibition: banned practices

By a combination of reg.3(4)(d) and Sched.1 to CPUTR 2008, the following 31 practices are always considered unfair commercial practices:

- claiming to be signatory to a code of conduct when a trader is not;
- displaying a trust mark, quality mark or similar without obtaining authorisation from the issuing body of the mark;
- claiming a code of conduct has an endorsement from a public or other body when it does not;
- claiming that a trader or a product has been approved, endorsed or authorised by a public or private body when it has not, or making a claim without complying with any terms for that approval, endorsement or authorisation;
- inviting offers to buy products at a special price without saying whether any reasonable grounds exist for the trader believing that he will not be able to

supply the product or equivalent products at that price for a reasonable period (i.e. bait advertising);

- falsely stating that a product will only be available for a very limited time or that the terms of an offer will only be available for a very limited time to obtain an immediate decision from the consumer, or prevent them from having sufficient time or opportunity to make an informed choice;
- stating or creating the impression that a product can legally be sold when it cannot;
- stating that the consumer's legal rights are a distinct feature of the trader's offer;
- falsely claiming that a product is able to cure illnesses, dysfunction or malformations;
- making an invitation for consumers to buy goods at a specific price and then: (i) refusing to show those goods to the consumer; or (ii) refusing to take orders for it or deliver it within a reasonable time; or (iii) demonstrating a defective sample of the product with the intention of promoting a different product;
- making an inaccurate claim about the nature and extent of the risk to the personal security of the consumer and the consumer's family if the consumer does not buy the goods;
- requiring a consumer, who wishes to claim on an insurance policy, to produce documents which are not relevant to consider whether a claim is valid or not, or failing to respond to important correspondence with the aim of persuading the consumer not to exercise his legal rights;
- using editorial content in the material to promote a product where the trader has paid for the advert, without making it clear that the trader has paid for it;
- promoting a product similar to a product made by a competitor in such a way as to deliberately mislead the consumer into believing the product is made by a competitor when it is not;
- claiming that the trader is closing down or about to move premises when it is not;
- passing on inaccurate information on market conditions or the possibility of finding the product with the intention to cause the consumer to buy the goods at less favourable than normal market conditions;
- giving the impression, in marketing materials, that the consumer has already ordered goods when he or she has not;
- falsely claiming that he is not acting for the purposes of his trade or profession or falsely stating he is a consumer;
- including in an advert a 'buzz word' or catch phrase aimed at children to encourage them to buy the goods or persuade an adult to buy them;
- establishing a pyramid scheme;
- claiming a product will facilitate a consumer's winning of a game of chance;
- claiming to award a prize without it ever actually being awarded (or a reasonable equivalent);

- describing a product as 'free', 'gratis' or 'without charge' if a consumer has to pay anything other than the unavoidable cost of responding to the commercial practice and collecting or paying for delivery;
- creating a false impression that a consumer has won, or will win, when there is no prize or a consumer is required to incur a cost before collecting the prize;
- creating the impression that a consumer cannot leave the premises until a contract is formed;
- conducting personal visits to a consumer's home and ignoring the consumer's request to leave or not to return unless the trader is required to do so to enforce a contractual obligation;
- making persistent and unwanted solicitations to consumers by telephone, fax, email or other remote media except where it is necessary to enforce a contractual obligation;
- telling a consumer that if he or she does not buy the goods or services, the trader's job or livelihood will be in jeopardy;
- demanding immediate or deferred payment for goods when the consumer did not order the goods, unless they are supplied under the Consumer Protection (Distance Selling) Regulations 2000, SI 2000/2334, reg.19(7) (substitute goods);
- during pre-contract negotiations, offering to provide after-sales service to consumers in a language which is not actually provided;
- creating the false impression that after-sales service for a product is available in other EU states than the one in which the product is sold when it is not.

Specific prohibition: misleading actions

By virtue of reg.5(1) of CPUTR 2008, a commercial practice is a misleading action if it satisfies reg.5(2) or (3).

Regulation 5(2) makes a commercial practice misleading if:

- it provides false information in relation to the matters listed in reg.5(4), or if the overall impression in any way deceives, or is likely to deceive, the average consumer, even if that information is factually correct; and
- it causes, or is likely to cause, the average consumer to take a transactional decision he would not otherwise have taken.

Regulation 5(3) makes a commercial practice misleading if:

- any marketing of products (including comparative advertising) creates confusion with any other products, trademarks, trade names or other distinguishing features of a competitor; or
- it concerns the failure by a trader to comply with a code of conduct if the trader indicates in the commercial practice that he is bound by that code, the commitment is firm and capable of being verified, and it causes the average consumer to take a transactional decision he would not otherwise have taken.

The matters listed in CPUTR 2008, reg.5(4) (which are referred to in reg.5(2)) are:

(a)   the existence or nature of the product;
(b)   the main characteristics of the product (as defined in paragraph 5);
(c)   the extent of the trader's commitments;
(d)   the motives for the commercial practice;
(e)   the nature of the sales process;
(f)   any statement or symbol relating to direct or indirect sponsorship or approval of the trader or the product;
(g)   the price or the manner in which the price is calculated;
(h)   the existence of a specific price advantage;
(i)   the need for a service, part, replacement or repair;
(j)   the nature, attributes and rights of the trader (as defined in paragraph 6);
(k)   the consumer's rights or the risks he may face.

By reg.5(5), the main characteristics of the product for the purposes of reg.5(4)(b) include (but are not limited to):

(a)   availability of the product;
(b)   benefits of the product;
(c)   risks of the product;
(d)   execution of the product;
(e)   composition of the product;
(f)   accessories of the product;
(g)   after sale customer assistance concerning the product;
(h)   the handling of complaints about the product;
(i)   the method and date of manufacture of the product;
(j)   the method and date of provision of the product;
(k)   delivery of the product;
(l)   fitness for purpose of the product;
(m)   usage of the product;
(n)   quantity of the product;
(o)   specification of the product;
(p)   geographical or commercial origin of the product;
(q)   results to be expected from use of the product; and
(r)   results and material features of tests or checks carried out on the product.

By reg.5(6), the 'nature, attributes and rights' (mentioned in reg.5(4)(j)), as far as concern the trader, include the trader's:

(a)   identity;
(b)   assets;
(c)   qualifications;
(d)   status;
(e)   approval;
(f)   affiliations or connections;
(g)   ownership of industrial, commercial or intellectual property rights; and
(h)   awards and distinctions.

By reg.5(7), reference to the 'consumer's rights' in reg.5(4)(k) include rights the consumer may have under Part VA of the Sale of Goods Act 1979 or Part IB of the Supply of Goods and Services Act 1982.

Specific prohibition: misleading omissions

By CPUTR 2008, reg.6(1), a commercial practice is a misleading omission if, in its factual context and taking into account the following matters (listed in reg.6(2)):

- all the features and circumstances of the commercial practice;
- the limitations of the medium used to communicate the commercial practice (including limitations of space or time); and
- where the medium used to communicate the commercial practice imposes limitations of space or time, any measures taken by the trader to make the information available to consumers by other means,

the commercial practice omits information, hides information, provides 'material information' in a way which is unclear, unintelligible, ambiguous or untimely, or fails to identify its commercial intent, unless this is already apparent from the context and, as a result, causes, or is likely to cause, the average consumer to take a transactional decision he would not otherwise have taken.

'Material information' is defined (reg.6(3)) as the information which the average consumer needs, according to the context, to take an informed transactional decision and any information requirement which applies in relation to a commercial communication as a result of a Community obligation.

By reg.6(4), if a commercial practice is an invitation to buy, the following information will be material if not already apparent from the context in addition to any other information which is material information under reg.6(3):

(a) the main characteristics of the product, to the extent appropriate to the medium by which the invitation to purchase is communicated and the product;

(b) the identity of the trader, such as his trading name, and the identity of any other trader on whose behalf the trader is acting;

(c) the geographical address of the trader and the geographical address of any other trader on whose behalf the trader is acting;

(d) either –

   (i) the price, including any taxes; or
   (ii) where the nature of the product is such that the price cannot reasonably be calculated in advance, the manner in which the price is calculated;

(e) where appropriate, either –

   (i) all additional freight, delivery or postal charges; or
   (ii) where such charges cannot reasonably be calculated in advance, the fact that such charges may be payable;

(f) the following matters where they depart from the requirements of professional diligence –

   (i) arrangements for payment,
   (ii) arrangements for delivery,
   (iii) arrangements for performance,
   (iv) complaint handling policy;

(g) for products and transactions involving a right of withdrawal or cancellation, the existence of such a right.

Specific prohibition: aggressive commercial practices

A commercial practice is aggressive if (taking into account its factual context and all of its features and circumstances) it significantly impairs or is likely to significantly impair the average consumer's freedom of choice or conduct in relation to a product through the use of harassment, coercion or undue influence; and those actions cause, or are likely to cause, the average consumer to take a transactional decision he would not otherwise have taken (CPUTR 2008, reg.7(1)).

When deciding whether a commercial practice uses harassment, coercion or undue influence, under reg.7(2), the following will be considered:

(a) its timing, location, nature or persistence;
(b) the use of threatening or abusive language or behaviour;
(c) the exploitation by the trader of any specific misfortune or circumstance of such gravity as to impair the consumer's judgement, of which the trader is aware, to influence the consumer's decision with regard to the product;
(d) any onerous or disproportionate non-contractual barrier imposed by the trader where a consumer wishes to exercise rights under the contract, including rights to terminate a contract or to switch to another product or another trader; and
(e) any threat to take any action which cannot legally be taken.

Offences

Under CPUTR 2008, reg.8(1), a trader is guilty of an offence if:

(a) he knowingly or recklessly engages in a commercial practice which contravenes the requirements of professional diligence under regulation 3(3)(a); and
(b) the practice materially distorts or is likely to materially distort the economic behaviour of the average consumer with regard to the product under regulation 3(3)(b).

A trader is guilty of an offence if he engages in a commercial practice which is:

- a misleading action under reg.5 (CPUTR 2008, reg.9);
- a misleading omission under reg.6 (CPUTR 2008, reg.10);
- aggressive under reg.7 (CPUTR 2008, reg.11);
- set out in any of paras.1–10, 12–27 and 29–31 of Sched.1 (CPUTR 2008, reg.12).

Penalties

A person guilty of an offence under CPUTR 2008, regs.8, 9, 10, 11 or 12 will be liable, on summary conviction, to a fine not exceeding the statutory maximum (currently £5,000) or on conviction on indictment, to a fine or imprisonment for a term not exceeding two years or both (CPUTR 2008, reg.13).

Corporate defendants

If a person being prosecuted under CPUTR 2008 is a corporate body (i.e. a limited company) and the offence is proved to have been committed with the consent or connivance of an officer of the body, or to be attributable to any neglect on his part, then by CPUTR 2008, reg.15(1) the officer as well as the body corporate is guilty of the offence and liable to prosecuted in the same way.

Defences

As for many consumer criminal offences, the following defences are available:

- offence committed due to fault of another person (CPUTR 2008, reg.16);
- due diligence (i.e. the offence was caused by a mistake or reliance on information supplied by a third party) and the trader took all reasonable precautions to avoid the commission of the offence (CPUTR 2008, reg.17);
- innocent publication (i.e. if a person simply prints the advert) (CPUTR 2008, reg.18).

Enforcement

Like many other criminal laws which affect consumers, CPUTR 2008 are generally enforced by the Office of Fair Trading (OFT), usually through local Trading Standards Offices. Prosecutions must be brought within the earlier of three years from the date of the offence or one year from the date of discovery of the offence by a prosecutor. It is usual for the OFT to enforce its powers under CPUTR 2008 by combining them with its powers under Part 8 of the Enterprise Act 2002.

3.14.3 Business Protection from Misleading Marketing Regulations 2008

The Business Protection from Misleading Marketing Regulations 2008, SI 2008/1276 (BPMMR 2008), like CPUTR 2008, came into force on 26 May 2008. They primarily deal with business to business advertising and are largely beyond the scope of this text. They are, however, important for creditors wanting to compare their products against others. BPMMR 2008 define comparative advertising as 'advertising which in any way, either explicitly or by implication, identifies a competitor or a product offered by a competitor'. BPMMR 2008, reg.4 allows comparative advertising as long as all of the following conditions are met:

(a)   it is not misleading under regulation 3;
(b)   it is not a misleading action under regulation 5 of the Consumer Protection from Unfair Trading Regulations 2008 or a misleading omission under regulation 6 of those Regulations;
(c)   it compares products meeting the same needs or intended for the same purpose;
(d)   it objectively compares one or more material, relevant, verifiable and representative features of those products, which may include price;
(e)   it does not create confusion among traders –

(i)   between the advertiser and a competitor, or

(ii)   between the trade marks, trade names, other distinguishing marks or products of the advertiser and those of a competitor;

(f)   it does not discredit or denigrate the trade marks, trade names, other distinguishing marks, products, activities, or circumstances of a competitor;

(g)   for products with designation of origin, it relates in each case to products with the same designation;

(h)   it does not take unfair advantage of the reputation of a trade mark, trade name or other distinguishing marks of a competitor or of the designation of origin of competing products;

(i)   it does not present products as imitations or replicas of products bearing a protected trade mark or trade name.

It is an offence to engage in advertising that is misleading (which includes misleading comparative advertising) (BPMMR 2008, reg.6). The consequences of committing an offence, defences and penalties are largely the same under BPMMR 2008 as under CPUTR 2008.

3.14.4 Codes of Conduct

Not being content with legal regulation, the advertising industry has also developed a parallel system of self-regulation which is largely overseen by the Advertising Standards Authority (ASA) (either directly, in the case of non-broadcast media, or indirectly, being outsourced from Ofcom, for broadcast media). Whilst a detailed consideration of these self-regulatory controls is outside the scope of this text, we briefly consider those rules.

Broadcast media

The relevant codes for broadcast media are the TV Advertising Standards Code and the Radio Advertising Standards Code. It is important to remember that advertisers can, before publishing an advert, seek an initial view on its compliance from, in the case of TV advertising, Clearcast and, in the case of radio advertising, the Radio Advertising Clearance Centre. The ASA, given its authority to regulate broadcast media by Ofcom, tends to regulate broadcast media by investigating complaints, often made by the general public but (perhaps unsurprisingly) also made by competitors. It also undertakes a proactive role by undertaking a survey of advertisements on broadcast media. If the ASA determines that there is a breach of the TV Advertising Standards Code or the Radio Advertising Standards Code then it can:

- issue a notice on the ASA's website (at **www.asa.org.uk**);
- ask the advertiser to withdraw or amend the advertisement;
- ask the broadcaster to withdraw the advert;
- require the advertiser to have future adverts pre-approved;
- refer persistent breaches to the OFT (which can, in turn, take enforcement action or obtain an injunction under the Enterprise Act 2002) or Ofcom.

Non-broadcast media

The relevant code for non-broadcast media is the British Code of Advertising, Sales Promotion and Direct Marketing (CAP Code). Unlike broadcast media, it has two regulators: the ASA, which is, once again, given its authority by Ofcom, and the Committee of Advertising Practice (CAP), which has delegated authority from the ASA. Advertisers may seek an initial view on an advert's compliance. The ASA regulates and enforces non-broadcast media in the same way as it does for broadcast media except that it cannot refer persistent breaches to Ofcom. CAP, on the other hand, is responsible for reviewing, amending and enforcing the CAP Code. CAP's website (**www.cap.org.uk**) usefully includes an electronic version of the CAP Code together with guidance.

Challenging the ASA's decisions

If an advertiser wishes to challenge the ASA's decision, it must make an application for judicial review: *R* v. *Advertising Standards Agency, ex p DSG Retail Ltd t/a Dixons* [1997] COD 232. It is important to remember that the court's role is simply supervisory and it will only intervene when the ASA has acted illegally, irrationally or not followed a correct procedure.

CHAPTER 4

Before entering into a regulated agreement

4.1 INTRODUCTION

It will come as no surprise that there are numerous steps, obligations and duties that creditors and owners need to comply with, or be aware of, before entering into a regulated agreement. These include established principles of withdrawal and cancellation, liability for antecedent negotiations and additional steps for land mortgages. More recent additions to the consumer credit regime include the provision of pre-contract information, assessments of creditworthiness and providing adequate explanations. In this chapter, we will look at those provisions leaving issues concerning the form and content of the agreement, provision of copy documentation and improperly executed agreements to the next chapter.

4.2 PRE-CONTRACT INFORMATION

For over 30 years, the power contained in the Consumer Credit Act 1974 (CCA 1974), s.55(1) to make regulations setting out information to be disclosed to debtors or hirers before entering into a regulated agreement, lay dormant. In the last seven years, however, two sets of regulations have been made: the Consumer Credit (Disclosure of Information) Regulations 2004, SI 2004/1481 (CC(DI)R 2004) and the Consumer Credit (Disclosure of Information) Regulations 2010, SI 2010/1013 (CC(DI)R 2010). This has marked a significant move to increasing the amount of information provided to debtors or hirers before they enter into a regulated agreement.

4.3 CC(DI)R 2004

4.3.1 Introduction

After the Consumer Credit Directive (87/102/EEC) (CCD) came fully into force on 1 February 2011, the role of CC(DI)R 2004 has dramatically reduced. The 2004 Regulations came into force on 31 May 2005. If CC(DI)R 2004 applies, it sets out basic information that should be provided by the creditor or owner before entering into a regulated agreement.

4.3.2 Scope

By virtue of reg.2, CC(DI)R 2004 now applies to the following regulated agreements (unless such an agreement is a distance contract or the creditor or owner has opted to enter into the CCD and comply with CC(DI)R 2010):

- consumer credit agreements secured on land unless the agreement is subject to CCA 1974, s.58 (agreements subject to s.58 have their own disclosure requirements – see **4.10** below) (reg.2(1)(a));
- consumer hire agreements (reg.2(1)(b));
- consumer credit agreements under which the creditor provides the debtor with credit which exceeds £60,260 (reg.2(1)(c));
- consumer credit agreements entered into by the debtor wholly or predominantly for the purposes of a business carried on, or intended to be carried on, by him (reg.2(1)(d)); and
- small debtor-creditor-supplier agreements for restricted-use credit (reg.2(1)(e)).

For the purposes of an agreement falling within CC(DI)R 2004, reg.2(1)(d), CCA 1974, s.16B(2)–(5) applies.

4.3.3 Information

For the purposes of CC(DI)R 2004, reg.3(1), if the regulated agreement falls within reg.2(1) then the creditor or owner must disclose the information and statements of protection and remedies that are required to be given in the case of:

- a regulated consumer credit agreement, under reg.2 of the Consumer Credit (Agreements) Regulations 1983, SI 1983/1553 (CC(A)R 1983);
- a regulated consumer hire agreement, under CC(A)R 1983, reg.3;
- a modifying agreement which is, or is treated as, a regulated consumer credit agreement, under CC(A)R 1983, regs.2(3) and 7(2);
- a modifying agreement which is, or is treated as, a regulated consumer hire agreement, under CC(A)R 1983, regs.3(3) and 7(9).

If the agreement falls within CC(DI)R 2004, reg.2(1)(c), (d) or (e) the creditor must also provide a statement in accordance with CCA 1974, s.157(A1) saying that if it decides not to proceed with a prospective regulated consumer credit agreement then it must, when telling the debtor of this decision, tell the debtor that this decision has been reached on the basis of information from a credit reference agency and inform the debtor of the particulars of that agency (CC(DI)R 2004, reg.3(1A)).

The information and statements of protection required to be disclosed under reg.3(1) are the information and statements that will be included in the proposed regulated agreement except that, where any of the information is not known at the time of disclosure, the creditor or owner must disclose estimated information based on such assumptions as it may reasonably make (CC(DI)R 2004, reg.3(2)).

4.3.4 Method of disclosure

Given the requirement under reg.3 to provide disclosure, CC(DI)R 2004, reg.4 states that the information and statements must be:

(a) easily legible and, where applicable, of a colour which is readily distinguishable from the background medium upon which they are displayed;

(b) not interspersed with any other information or wording apart from subtotals of total amounts and cross references to the terms of the agreement;

(c) of equal prominence except that headings may be afforded more prominence whether by capital letters, underlining, larger or bold print or otherwise; and

(d) contained in a document which:

(i) is separate from the document embodying the relevant agreement (within the meaning of regulation 3) and any other document referred to in the document embodying that agreement;

(ii) is headed with the words 'Pre-contract Information';

(iii) does not contain any other information or wording apart from the heading referred to in sub-paragraph (ii);

(iv) is on paper or on another durable medium which is available and accessible to the debtor or hirer; and

(v) is of a nature that enables the debtor or hirer to remove it from the place where it is disclosed to him.

In practice, this essentially means that an almost identical copy of the proposed regulated agreement is provided to the debtor or hirer before or at the same time as presentation of the regulated agreement. It must, however, be a separate document (either on paper or in another durable medium which does allow it to be provided on a disc or as an electronic file). It is respectfully submitted that the pre-contract information provides little, if any, assistance to the prospective debtor or hirer: he or she simply receives essentially the same document twice. The failure to ensure that there was a prescribed time frame between giving the pre-contract information and the regulated agreement (as there is for secured loans under CCA 1974, s.58) means that the pre-contract information is often given to the debtor at the same time as the agreement.

4.3.5 Consequences of non-compliance with CC(DI)R 2004

The consequence of not complying, or not fully complying, with CC(DI)R 2004 is the same as applies to CC(DI)R 2010. Section 55(2) of CCA 1974 makes it clear that the agreement is enforceable against the hirer or debtor only with the court's permission under CCA 1974, s.127(1). There is, however, a further limitation contained in CCA 1974, s.55(2) which makes it clear that 'enforcement' for the purposes of CCA 1974, s.55 includes retaking of goods or land subject to the agreement. It therefore seems to follow that if CC(DI)R 2004 has not been complied with, the creditor should obtain an enforcement order before retaking possession of any goods or land (even if the goods are not protected by CCA 1974, s.90).

4.4 PRE-CONTRACT INFORMATION: CC(DI)R 2010

4.4.1 Introduction

Another consequence of the CCD was the introduction of CC(DI)R 2010. This sets out very detailed requirements on the pre-contract information to be provided to debtors under certain consumer credit agreements (and not hire agreements). It also introduces two new concepts: Standard European Consumer Credit Information (otherwise known as 'SECCI') and European Consumer Credit Information (ECCI).

4.4.2 Scope

By virtue of reg.2, CC(DI)R 2010 applies to all regulated consumer credit agreements except for:

- agreements subject to CCA 1974, s.58 (reg.2(2));
- an authorised non-business overdraft agreement which is for credit which exceeds £60,260 or secured on land (reg.2(3));
- by reg.2(4), an agreement (unless it falls within reg.2(5)):

    - under which the creditor provides the debtor with credit exceeding £60,260;
    - secured on land;
    - entered into by the debtor wholly or predominantly for the purposes of a business also carried on, or intended to be carried on, by him; or
    - made before 1 February 2011.

There are, of course, other exemptions from CC(DI)R 2010, which apply by virtue of CCA 1974. These are:

- exempt agreements within CCA 1974, ss.16–16C;
- non-commercial agreements by virtue of CCA 1974, s.74(1)(a); and
- authorised business overdraft agreements by virtue of CCA 1974, s.74(1)(b) and (1B).

CC(DI)R 2010 does, however, apply to agreements falling within reg.2(4) (which is not also an agreement mentioned in reg.2(2) or (3)) where a creditor or (where applicable) a credit intermediary discloses, or purports to disclose, the pre-contract credit information in accordance with CC(DI)R 2010 rather than in accordance with CC(DI)R 2004 or the Financial Services (Distance Marketing) Regulations 2004, SI 2004/2095.

If the agreement falls within CC(DI)R 2010, reg.2(4)(c) then CCA 1974, s.16B(2)–(5) applies.

4.4.3 Information: agreements other than telephone contracts, non-telephone contracts, excluded pawn agreements and overdraft agreements

Regulation 3 of CC(DI)R 2010 applies to an agreement other than:

- an agreement made by voice telephone communication where it is a distance contract and the debtor consents to the disclosure of the information referred to in reg.4(2) (reg.3(1)(a));
- an agreement made by voice telephone communication where it is not a distance contract and the creditor discloses the information referred to in reg.4(3) (reg.3(1)(aa));
- an agreement made using a means of distance communication other than a voice telephone communication, which does not enable the provision of the pre-contract credit information before the agreement is made and information is required by reg.5 (reg.3(1)(b));
- an excluded pawn agreement (which is defined in reg.1(2) as an agreement: (a) where the debtor is not a 'new customer' (see **4.4.9** below); and (b) where, before the agreement is made, the creditor has not received a request from the debtor for the pre-contract credit information under reg.9) (reg.3(1)(c)); and
- an authorised non-business overdraft agreement (reg.3(1)(d)).

For agreements other than those excluded by reg.3(1), the creditor must, in good time before the agreement is made, disclose to the debtor the pre-contract credit information (reg.3(2)). The creditor is not required to provide it where a credit intermediary has already provided it in compliance with reg.3(2) (reg.3(3)).

The pre-contract credit information comprises (CC(DI)R 2010, reg.3(4)):

(a) the type of credit,

(b) the identity and geographical address of the creditor and, where applicable, of the credit intermediary,

(c) the total amount of credit to be provided under the agreement and the conditions governing the draw down of credit. In the case of an agreement for running-account credit, the total amount of credit may be expressed as a statement indicating the manner in which the credit limit will be determined where it is not practicable to express the limit as a sum of money,

(d) the duration or minimum duration of the agreement or a statement that the agreement has no fixed or minimum duration,

(e) in the case of –

(i) credit in the form of deferred payment for specific goods, services or land, or

(ii) a linked credit agreement,

a description of the goods, services or land and the cash price of each and the total cash price,

(f)   the rate of interest charged, any conditions applicable to that rate, where available, any reference rate on which that rate is based and any information on any changes to the rate of interest (including the periods that the rate applies, and any conditions or procedure applicable to changing the rate),

(g)   where different rates of interest are charged in different circumstances the creditor must provide the information in paragraph (f) in respect of each rate,

(h)   the APR and the total amount payable under the agreement illustrated (if not known) by way of a representative example mentioning all the assumptions used in order to calculate that rate and amount,

(i)   the amount (expressed as a sum of money), number (if applicable) and frequency of repayments to be made by the debtor and, where appropriate, the order in which repayments will be allocated to different outstanding balances charged at different rates of interest,

(j)   in the case of an agreement for running-account credit, the amount of each repayment is to be expressed as (a) a sum of money; (b) a specified proportion of a specified amount; (c) a combination of (a) or (b); or (d) in a case where the amount of any repayment cannot be expressed in accordance with (a), (b) or (c), a statement indicating the manner in which the amount will be determined,

(k)   if applicable, any charges for maintaining an account recording both payment transactions and draw downs, unless the opening of an account is optional, and any charge payable for using a method of payment in respect of payment transactions or draw downs,

(l)   any other charges payable deriving from the credit agreement and the conditions under which those charges may be changed,

(m)   if applicable, a statement that fees will be payable by the debtor to a notary on conclusion of the credit agreement,

(n)   the obligation, if any, to enter into a contract for ancillary services relating to the consumer credit agreement, in particular insurance services, where the conclusion of such a contract is compulsory in order to obtain the credit or to obtain it on the terms and conditions marketed,

(o)   the rate of interest applicable in the case of late payments and the arrangements for its adjustment, and, where applicable, any charges payable for default,

(p)   a warning regarding the consequences of missing payments (for example, the possibility of legal proceedings and the possibility that the debtor's home may be repossessed),

(q)   where applicable, any security to be provided by the debtor or on behalf of the debtor,

(r)   the existence or absence of a right of withdrawal,

(s)   the debtor's right of early repayment under section 94 of the Act, and where applicable, information concerning the creditor's right to compensation and the way in which that compensation will be determined,

(t)   the requirement for a creditor to inform a debtor in accordance with section 157(A1) of the Act that a decision not to proceed with a prospective regulated consumer credit agreement has been reached on the basis of information from a credit reference agency and of the particulars of that agency,

(u)   the debtor's right to be supplied under section 55C of the Act on request and free of charge, with a copy of the draft agreement except where –

        (i)   the creditor is at the time of the request unwilling to proceed to the making of the agreement, or

        (ii)   the agreement is an agreement referred to in regulation 2(4)(a) to (c) or a pawn agreement, and

(v)   if applicable, the period of time during which the creditor is bound by the pre-contract credit information.

The requirement to provide a representative example of the APR by CC(DI)R 2010, reg.3(4)(h) is supplemented by reg.3(5). This sets out what must be considered and, importantly, where an agreement is for running-account credit with an unknown credit limit at the time of the disclosure, there is an assumption that the amount of credit is £1,200.

If repayments under a regulated consumer credit agreement do not give rise to an immediate reduction in the total amount of credit but are used to constitute capital, then the creditor or credit intermediary must provide, by CC(DI)R 2010, reg.3(6) and in a separate document to the pre-contract information, a clear and concise statement that such agreements do not provide for a guarantee of repayment of the total amount of credit drawn down under the credit agreement unless such a guarantee is given.

4.4.4   Information: telephone contracts

If an agreement is made by way of a voice telephone communication (regardless of whether it is a distance contract) and it is not an authorised non-business overdraft agreement, then CC(DI)R 2010, reg.4 applies (reg.4(1)).

If there is such an agreement, which is also a distance contract, then so long as the debtor explicitly consents, the creditor must disclose the following information before the agreement is made:

- the identity of the person in contact with the debtor and that person's link with the creditor (reg.4(2)(a));
- a description of the main characteristics of the credit agreement which includes the information set out in reg.3(4)(c), (d), (e), (f), (g), (h), (i) and (j) (see **4.4.3** above) (reg.4(2)(b));
- the total price to be paid by the debtor to the creditor for the credit including all taxes paid through the creditor or, if an exact price cannot be indicated, the basis for the calculation of the price allowing the debtor to check it (reg.4(2)(c));
- notice of the possibility that other taxes or costs may exist that are not paid through the creditor or imposed by the creditor (reg.4(2)(d));
- whether or not (by reg.4(2)(e)) there is:

  - a right to withdraw under CCA 1974, s.66A; or
  - a right to cancel under reg.9 of the Financial Services (Distance Marketing) Regulations 2004, SI 2004/2095 (FS(DM)R 2004) and, where there is such a right, its duration and the conditions for exercising it, including information on the amount which the consumer may be required to pay in accordance with FS(DM)R 2004, reg.13 as well as the consequences of not exercising that right;

- that other information is available on request and the nature of that information (reg.4(2)(f)).

If the agreement is not a distance contract then the creditor must, by CC(DI)R 2010, reg.4(3), disclose a description of the main characteristics of the credit agreement which includes the information set out in reg.3(4)(c), (d), (e), (f), (g), (h), (i) and (j) (see **4.4.3** above) by reg.4(3).

Under CC(DI)R 2010, reg.4(4), the creditor must disclose the pre-contract information in the way set out in reg.8 (see **4.4.8** below) immediately after the agreement is made.

4.4.5 Information: non-telephone distance contracts

Regulation 5 of CC(DI)R 2010 applies to an agreement, other than an authorised non-business overdraft agreement, made at the debtor's request and using a means of distance communication other than a voice telephone communication which does not allow the provision before the agreement is made of the pre-contract credit information.

The phrase 'at the debtor's request' is not defined by CC(DI)R 2010. It is, however, submitted that it should cover situations where the debtor makes the initial contact with the creditor. It is unlikely, however, to cover situations where the debtor responds to marketing material.

By reg.5(2), the creditor must disclose the pre-contract information in the way set out in reg.8 (see **4.4.8** below) immediately after the agreement is made.

4.4.6 Information: distance contracts for business purposes

Regulation 6 of CC(DI)R 2010 applies to an agreement which is a distance contract entered into by a debtor wholly or predominantly for the purpose of a business carried on, or intended to be carried on, by him (reg.6(1)). If, however, the agreement is an agreement to which regs.3, 4 or 5 apply, then the creditor may comply with those regulations by disclosing the pre-contract credit information immediately after the agreement is entered into by virtue of reg.6(2). For the purposes of reg.6(1), CCA 1974, s.16B(2)–(5) applies.

4.4.7 Information: distance contracts within regs.3, 4 and 5

Regulation 7 of CC(DI)R 2010 applies to an agreement which is:

- a distance contract to which regs.3, 4 or 5 apply; and
- which is not entered into by the debtor wholly or predominantly for the purposes of a business carried on, or intended to be carried on, by him.

Under reg.7(2), the creditor must ensure that:

- the information provided to the debtor under regs.3, 4 or 5 includes the contractual terms and conditions; and
- the information provided to the debtor on the contractual obligations which would arise if the distance contract were made accurately reflects the contractual obligations which would arise under the law presumed to be applicable to that contract.

If the agreement falls within reg.7(3) then CCA 1974, s.16B(2)–(5) applies for the purposes of reg.7(1).

4.4.8 Method of disclosure

By virtue of CC(DI)R 2010, reg.8(1), the pre-contract information must be disclosed using the SECCI contained in CC(DI)R 2010, Sched.1. Regulation 8(2) makes it clear that the SECCI must be in writing and of a nature which allows the debtor to remove it from the place where it is disclosed to him (for example, being printed on paper so it can be taken away).

The SECCI must be completed, by reg.8(3), in the following way:

- the relevant pre-contract credit information must be provided in the appropriate row;
- the form must be completed in accordance with any notes;
- the asterisks and notes may be deleted;
- gridlines and boxes may be deleted; and
- any information contained in the form must be clear and easily legible.

If the creditor provides in writing any additional information relating to the credit then it must be in a document which is separate from the SECCI (reg.8(4)).

For the difficult question of multiple agreements, reg.8(5) states that if a consumer credit agreement is a multiple agreement and contains more than one 'part' for the purposes of CCA 1974, s.18, the pre-contract credit information for each part may be provided in the same form so long as:

- information that is not common to each part of the agreement is disclosed separately within the relevant section of the form; and
- it is clear which information relates to which part.

4.4.9 Information: pawn agreements

Instead of requiring a creditor to provide a SECCI for pawn agreements, CC(DI)R 2010, reg.9(2) simply says that in good time before the pawn agreement is made (unless the debtor is a 'new customer'), the creditor must tell the debtor of his right to receive, free of charge and on request, the pre-contract information in the form of the SECCI.

Regulation 1 of CC(DI)R 2010 includes two important definitions:

- 'excluded pawn agreement' means an agreement (a) where the debtor is not a 'new customer' and (b) where, before the agreement is made, the creditor has not received a request from the debtor for the pre-contract credit information under CC(DI)R 2010, reg.9 (reg.1(2));
- 'new customer' means where the debtor has not entered into a pawn agreement with the creditor in the three years before the start of antecedent negotiations for the pawn agreement (reg.1(6)); and
- 'pawn agreement' means a consumer credit agreement under which the creditor takes an article in pawn (reg.1(2)).

It therefore follows that if a debtor is a 'new customer' then he must be given the information under CC(DI)R 2010, reg.3. If, however, the debtor is not a 'new customer' the creditor must only tell him, in good time before entering into the agreement, that he has the right to receive the SECCI. If he does so, but the debtor does not ask for it, there is no pre-contract information.

4.4.10 SECCI

Schedule 1 to CC(DI)R 2010 sets out the form of the SECCI. This is provided at **Precedent 4**. It must be completed in accordance with CC(DI)R 2010, reg.8(3), which is discussed at **4.4.8** above.

4.4.11 Information: authorised non-business overdrafts

Regulation 10 of CC(DI)R 2010 applies to authorised non-business overdraft agreements by virtue of reg.10(1). Regulation 10(2) requires the creditor to, in good time before an authorised non-business overdraft is made, disclose to the debtor the information required by reg.10(3) in the way set out in reg.11.

The information required by reg.10(3) (otherwise known as European Consumer Credit Information or ECCI) is as follows:

(a)   the type of credit,
(b)   the identity and geographical address of the creditor and, where applicable, of the credit intermediary,
(c)   the total amount of credit,
(d)   the duration of the agreement,
(e)   the rate of interest charged, any conditions applicable to that rate, any reference rate on which that rate is based and any information on any changes to the rate of interest (including the periods that the rate applies, and any conditions or procedure applicable to changing the rate),
(f)   where different rates of interest are charged in different circumstances the creditor must provide the information in paragraph (e) in respect of each rate,
(g)   the conditions and procedure for terminating the agreement,
(h)   where applicable, an indication that the debtor may be requested to repay the amount of credit in full on demand at any time,
(i)   the rate of interest applicable in the case of late payments and the arrangements for its adjustment, and, where applicable, any charges payable for default,
(j)   the requirement for a creditor to inform a debtor in accordance with section

157(A1) of the Act that a decision not to proceed with a prospective regulated consumer credit agreement has been reached on the basis of information from a credit reference agency and of the particulars of that agency,

(k)   the charges, other than the rates of interest, payable by the debtor under the agreement (and the conditions under which those charges may be varied),

(l)   if applicable, the period of time during which the creditor is bound by the information set out in this paragraph.

Regulation 10(4) makes it clear that there is no obligation to provide an ECCI where there is:

(a)   an agreement made by a voice telephone communication (whether or not it is a distance contract),

(b)   an agreement made at the debtor's request using a means of distance communication, other than a voice telephone communication, which does not enable the provision of the information required by paragraph (2) [i.e. the ECCI] before the agreement is made, or

(c)   an agreement that does not come within sub-paragraph (a) or (b) but where the debtor requests the overdraft be made available with immediate effect.

If an agreement is made by a voice telephone communication and is a distance contract then, if the debtor explicitly consents, the creditor must disclose by reg.10(5) the following information before the agreement is made:

(a)   the identity of the person in contact with the debtor and that person's link with the creditor,

(b)   a description of the main characteristics of the financial service including at least the information in paragraph (3)(c), (e), (f), (h) and (k),

(c)   the total price to be paid by the debtor to the creditor for the credit including all taxes paid via the creditor or, if an exact price cannot be indicated, the basis for the calculation of the price enabling the debtor to verify it,

(d)   notice of the possibility that other taxes or costs may exist that are not paid via the creditor or imposed by the creditor,

(e)   whether or not there is a right to cancel under regulation 9 of the Financial Services (Distance Marketing) Regulations 2004 and where there is such a right, its duration and the conditions for exercising it including information on the amount which the consumer may be required to pay in accordance with regulation 13 of those regulations, as well as the consequences of not exercising that right, and

(f)   that other information is available on request and the nature of that information.

If, however, the agreement is made by a voice telephone communication and is a distance contract but the debtor does not explicitly consent to disclosure of the information under reg.10(5) then the creditor must give the ECCI to the debtor before the agreement is made (reg.10(5A)).

If the agreement is made by a voice telephone communication but is not a distance contract then the creditor must disclose a description of the main characteristics of the financial service including at least the information in reg.10(3)(c), (e), (f), (h) and (k) before the agreement is made (reg.10(6)).

If the agreement is subject to reg.10 and is also a distance contract, then the creditor must ensure that the information provided to the debtor dealing with the contractual obligations under the agreement accurately reflects the contractual obligations which would arise under the law presumed to be applicable to that contract (reg.10(7)).

For agreements that do not come within CC(DI)R 2010, reg.10(4)(a) or (b) but under which the debtor asks the overdraft to be made immediately available, reg.10(8) imposes an obligation on the creditor to disclose the information in reg.10(3)(c), (e), (f), (h) and (k) before the agreement is made in the way set out in CC(DI)R 2010, reg.11. By reg.11(3), this information may be provided orally.

If there are two or more debtors then the creditor may comply with reg.10(5), (5A), (6) or (8) by disclosing the information to one debtor but only where all debtors have each given their consent to the creditor to do so.

4.4.12 Method of disclosure: authorised non-business overdrafts

Under CC(DI)R 2010, reg.11(1)(a), pre-contract information for authorised non-business overdrafts may be disclosed either using the ECCI contained in CC(DI)R 2010, Sched.3 or by giving it in writing as long as all the information is equally prominent.

The ECCI must be completed, by reg.11(2), in the following way:

- the relevant pre-contract credit information must be provided in the appropriate row;
- the form must be completed in accordance with any notes;
- the asterisks and notes may be deleted;
- gridlines and boxes may be deleted; and
- any information contained in the form must be clear and easily legible.

4.4.13 ECCI

Schedule 3 to CC(DI)R 2010 sets out the form of the ECCI. This is provided at **Precedent 5**. It must be completed in accordance with CC(DI)R 2010, reg.11(2), which is discussed at **4.4.12** above.

4.4.14 Modifying agreements

Subject to CC(DI)R 2010, reg.12(2)–(4), reg.12 applies to a modifying agreement that varies or supplements an earlier agreement and which is, or is treated under CCA 1974, s.82(3) as a regulated agreement (reg.12(1)).

Regulation 12(2)–(4) modifies the obligation under reg.12(1) as follows:

- by reg.12(2), if the modifying agreement modifies an earlier consumer credit agreement, the requirements of regs.3, 4 and 10 will be deemed to be satisfied if in good time before the modifying agreement is made the information specified in reg.3(4) (see **4.4.3**) or reg.10(3) (see **4.4.11**) is disclosed to the debtor for the earlier agreement which is varied or supplemented, and the creditor tells the debtor in writing that the other information in the earlier agreement remains unchanged;

- where FS(DM)R 2004 applies, the creditor complies with regs.7 and 8 of FS(DM)R 2004;
- by reg.12(3), if the modifying agreement is made in a way that does not allow the creditor to tell the debtor in writing that the other information in the earlier agreement remains unchanged, the creditor is deemed to have complied with that requirement if before the agreement is made, the creditor tells the debtor orally that the other information in the earlier agreement remains unchanged and this is confirmed to the debtor in writing immediately after the agreement is made;
- by virtue of reg.12(4), reg.12 does not apply to an excluded pawn agreement (discussed at **4.4.9** above).

4.4.15 Annual percentage rate (APR)

It is unsurprising that rules concerning the display of the APR on the pre-contract information (which appear in CC(DI)R 2010, Sched.2) are similar to the rules for its display on agreements and advertising. The rules are fairly straightforward:

- for running-account credit where the credit limit is not known at the time that the pre-contract information is disclosed but it is known that it will be subject to a maximum limit of less than £1,200, the credit limit will be assumed to be that maximum and not £1,200 (Sched.2, para.1);
- the APR stated on the agreement may exceed the actual APR by no more than 1 per cent or fall below the actual APR by no more than 0.1 per cent (Sched.2, para.2);
- there are other more detailed provisions dealing with tolerances in paras.3 and 4 of Sched.2. These cover tolerances where repayments are nearly equal and where the interval between the relevant date and the first repayment is greater than the interval between repayments.

4.4.16 Consequences of non-compliance with CC(DI)R 2010

The consequence of not complying, or not fully complying, with CC(DI)R 2010 is the same as the consequence of non-compliance with CC(DI)R 2004. Section 55(2) of CCA 1974 makes it clear that the agreement is enforceable against the hirer or debtor only with the court's permission under CCA 1974, s.127(1). There is, however, a further issue contained in s.55(2) which is that 'enforcement' for the purposes of s.55 includes retaking of goods or land subject to the agreement. It therefore seems to follow that if CC(DI)R 2010 has not been complied with, the creditor should obtain an enforcement order before retaking possession of any goods or land.

4.5 PRE-CONTRACTUAL EXPLANATIONS

4.5.1 Duty

The CCD introduced, from 1 February 2011, a concept of 'adequate explanations'. Section 55A(1) of CCA 1974 states that, before a regulated consumer credit agreement is made (other than an 'excluded agreement') the creditor must:

- provide the debtor with an 'adequate explanation' of the matters referred to in CCA 1974, s.55A(2) to place him in a position allowing him to assess whether the agreement is adapted to his needs and his financial situation (s.55A(1)(a)); and
- tell the debtor:

  - to consider the information disclosed under CC(DI)R 2004 or CC(DI)R 2010; and
  - where this information is disclosed in person to the debtor, that the debtor is able to take it away (s.55A(1)(b));

- give the debtor an opportunity to ask questions about the agreement (s.55A(1)(c)); and
- tell the debtor how to ask the creditor for further information and explanation (s.55A(1)(d)).

4.5.2 Exclusions

Under CCA 1974, s.55A(6), and for the purposes of s.55A, an agreement is an 'excluded agreement' if it is an agreement under which the creditor provides the debtor with credit which exceeds £60,260 or it is an agreement secured on land.

By s.55A(7), if a regulated consumer credit agreement is an agreement under which a person takes an article in pawn then:

- the obligation in s.55A(1)(a) only relates to the matters listed in s.55A(2)(d) and (e); and
- the obligations in s.55A(1)(b) and (d) do not apply.

In addition, the following credit agreements are excluded from CCA 1974, s.55A:

- agreements exempt under CCA 1974, ss.16–16C;
- non-commercial agreements (by virtue of CCA 1974, s.74(1));
- authorised business overdraft agreements (by virtue of its exclusion from CCA 1974, s.74(1B));
- authorised non-business overdraft agreements (as long as the credit is not repayable on demand or within three months) (by virtue of its exclusion from CCA 1974, s.74(1C)); and
- small debtor-creditor-supplier agreements for restricted-use credit (by virtue of CCA 1974, s.74(2)).

4.5.3 'Adequate explanation'

In accordance with CCA 1974, s.55A(2), the 'adequate explanation' needs to deal with the following:

(a)   the features of the agreement which may make the credit to be provided under the agreement unsuitable for particular types of use,

(b)   how much the debtor will have to pay periodically and, where the amount can be determined, in total under the agreement,

(c)   the features of the agreement which may operate in a manner which would have a significant adverse effect on the debtor in a way which the debtor is unlikely to foresee,

(d)   the principal consequences for the debtor arising from a failure to make payments under the agreement at the times required by the agreement including legal proceedings and, where this is a possibility, repossession of the debtor's home, and

(e)   the effect of the exercise of any right to withdraw from the agreement and how and when this right may be exercised.

These are rather high level concepts and there is little guidance explaining what the OFT expects a creditor (or a credit intermediary) to provide. It will therefore be interesting to see what guidance the OFT issues in due course. In the meantime, creditors are likely to be expected to exercise common sense and, if in any doubt, should err on the side of caution.

The advice and explanation may be given orally or in writing (s.55A(3)). If the explanation of the matters specified in s.55A(2)(a), (b) or (e) is given orally or in person to a debtor, then the explanation of the other matters, and the advice required to be given by s.55A(1)(b), must be given orally to him. It is assumed that this requirement is to ensure that creditors give a balanced view.

4.5.4   Credit intermediaries

The CCD also introduced the concept of a 'credit intermediary', which is found in CCA 1974, s.160A. In short, this is a person that carries on, in the course of business, any of the following (and not as a creditor):

•   recommending or making available prospective regulated consumer credit agreements, other than agreements secured on land, to individuals;

•   helping individuals by undertaking other preparatory work in relation to such agreements; or

•   entering into regulated consumer credit agreements, other than agreements secured on land, with individuals on behalf of creditors.

This plainly includes brokers and, most likely, motor traders looking to sell goods to customers using finance.

By CCA 1974, s.55A(5), if a credit intermediary has already complied with s.55A(1)–(4) then there is no need for the creditor to also comply with those requirements.

4.5.5 Consequences of non-compliance

There are no provisions in CCA 1974 which state that a failure to comply with CCA 1974, s.55A means the agreement is unenforceable or, indeed, that there is any other sanction. Given the clear wording of CCA 1974, s.170(1), it is submitted that there is no specific consequence for non-compliance. Creditors must, however, bear in mind that non-compliance is something the OFT could consider upon renewal of a consumer credit licence. It may also be something which a court may consider when deciding whether a relationship is fair or unfair.

4.6 ASSESSMENT OF CREDITWORTHINESS

4.6.1 Duty

The CCD also introduced, from 1 February 2011, a concept of 'creditworthiness'. Section 55B(1) of CCA 1974 imposes an obligation on a creditor before making a regulated consumer credit agreement other than an 'excluded agreement' to undertake an assessment of the debtor's creditworthiness.

Section 55B(2) also imposes an obligation on a creditor, before significantly increasing:

- the amount of credit to be provided under a regulated consumer credit agreement, other than an 'excluded agreement'; or
- a credit limit for running-account credit under a regulated consumer credit agreement, other than an 'excluded agreement',

to undertake an assessment of the debtor's creditworthiness. This will obviously come into play where credit card providers increase the debtor's credit limit.

4.6.2 Exclusions

For the purposes of CCA 1974, s.55B, an agreement is an excluded agreement if it is:

- an agreement secured on land (s.55B(4)(a)); or
- an agreement under which a person takes an article in pawn (s.55B(4)(b)).

It also does not apply to:

- agreements exempt under CCA 1974, ss.16–16C;
- non-commercial agreements (by virtue of CCA 1974, s.74(1));
- small debtor-creditor-supplier agreements for restricted-use credit (by virtue of CCA 1974, s.74(2)).

It is important to note that the requirement to assess creditworthiness therefore applies to consumer credit agreements for credit exceeding £60,260.

4.6.3 Creditworthiness assessment

The creditworthiness assessment must, by CCA 1974, s.55B(3), be based on sufficient information obtained from:

- the debtor (where appropriate); and
- a credit reference agency (where necessary).

This new provision in CCA 1974, s.55B raises interesting (and difficult) questions for creditors. Whilst the duty is limited to consumer credit agreements (other than excluded agreements) and does not apply to consumer hire agreements, it will be interesting to see the OFT's view on what documents are necessary to satisfy s.55B, particularly where the credit is a modest amount. In the case of pay day loan lenders, it is often rare for a credit reference agency to be consulted. It must, however, be the case that the greater the amount of credit that is applied for, the more likely it is that a creditor will need a more detailed assessment of the debtor's creditworthiness.

4.6.4 Consequences of non-compliance

There are no provisions in CCA 1974 which state that a failure to comply with s.55B means the agreement is unenforceable or, indeed, that there is any other sanction. Given the clear wording of CCA 1974, s.170(1), it is submitted that there is no consequence for non-compliance. Creditors must, however, bear in mind that non-compliance is something the OFT could consider upon renewal of a consumer credit licence. It may also be something which a court may consider when deciding whether a relationship is fair or unfair.

4.7 DRAFT CONSUMER CREDIT AGREEMENT

4.7.1 Duty

The CCD also introduced, from 1 February 2011, a right for the debtor to ask for a draft of the consumer credit agreement. Section 55C(1) of CCA 1974 imposes a duty on a creditor (if asked), before a regulated consumer credit agreement other than an 'excluded agreement' is made, give to the debtor without delay a copy of the prospective agreement (or such of its terms that have at that time been reduced to writing). Section 55C(2) goes on to say that there is no duty under s.55C(1) if, at the time the request is made, the creditor is unwilling to go ahead with the agreement.

There is no specific obligation in s.55C for the creditor to tell the debtor about his right to ask for a draft copy. It is submitted, however, that given the wide-ranging requirement for advice and explanations contained in s.55A, the creditor should tell the debtor of his right at that stage.

4.7.2   Exclusions

An agreement is an excluded agreement if it is an agreement:

- secured on land (CCA 1974, s.55C(4)(a));
- under which a person takes an article in pawn (s.55C(4)(b));
- under which the creditor provides the debtor with credit which exceeds £60,260 (s.55C(4)(c)); or
- entered into by the debtor wholly or predominantly for the purposes of a business carried on, or intended to be carried on, by him (s.55C(4)(d)).

If the agreement falls within s.55C(4)(d) then the provisions contained in CCA 1974, s.16B(2)–(5) apply.

4.7.3   Consequences of non-compliance

If a creditor fails to comply with CCA 1974, s.55C(1), the debtor is entitled to make a claim for breach of statutory duty under s.55C(3). It is difficult to see, however, what loss a debtor would suffer as a result of non-compliance with s.55C(1). The debtor could argue that he or she is entitled to an order requiring the creditor to provide the draft consumer credit agreement (but it is more than arguable that the creditor can rely on CCA 1974, s.170(1) to defeat such a claim) although the usefulness of such an order is, it is submitted, negligible.

4.8   ANTECEDENT NEGOTIATIONS

4.8.1   Introduction

For regulated agreements (but only in a limited circumstance for consumer hire agreements), CCA 1974, s.56 reverses the common law rules on agency in certain situations so that the negotiator is the creditor's deemed agent. This is a powerful tool for debtors or hirers and an important point to remember for creditors or owners.

4.8.2   When it applies

Under CCA 1974, s.56(1) 'antecedent negotiations' are any negotiations with the debtor or hirer:

- conducted by the creditor or owner in relation to the making of any regulated agreement (s.56(1)(a)); or
- conducted by a credit-broker in relation to goods sold or proposed to be sold by the credit-broker to the creditor before forming the subject matter of a debtor-creditor-supplier agreement within CCA 1974, s.12(a) (i.e. the dealer in a hire-purchase, conditional sale or credit sale agreement) (s.56(1)(b)); or

- conducted by the supplier in relation to a transaction financed or proposed to be financed by a debtor-creditor-supplier agreement within CCA 1974, s.12(b) or (c) (i.e. a dealer in any other situation under a debtor-creditor-supplier agreement including goods supplied under a credit card agreement) (s.56(1)(c)),

and 'negotiator' means the person by whom negotiations are so conducted with the debtor or hirer.

4.8.3 Effect

If negotiations are conducted with the debtor (and not a hirer under a regulated hire agreement) in a case falling within CCA 1974, s.56(1)(b) or (c) then, by s.56(2), they are deemed to be conducted by the negotiator as the creditor's agent as well as in his own capacity. This is vitally important for debtors as it reverses the common law rule for non-regulated agreements, set out by the House of Lords in *Branwhite* v. *Worcester Works Finance Ltd* [1969] 1 AC 552, that a dealer does not act as the finance company's agent. The same conclusion was reached for hire agreements by the Court of Appeal in *Woodchester Equipment (Leasing) Ltd* v. *British Association of Canned Preserved Food Importers and Distributors Ltd* [1995] CCLR 51 (CA).

4.8.4 When do antecedent negotiations begin?

By CCA 1974, s.56(4), antecedent negotiations begin when the negotiator and the debtor or hirer first enter into communication (including communication by advertisement). It also includes any representations made by the negotiator to the debtor or hirer and any other dealings between them.

4.8.5 Scope of deemed agency

The deemed agency's scope is rather wide. In *Forthright Finance Ltd* v. *Ingate (Carlyle Finance Ltd, third party)* [1997] 4 All ER 99, the Court of Appeal considered that the phrase 'in relation to' (mentioned in CCA 1974, s.56(1)(a)–(c)) meant there was a factual test of whether the negotiations were 'all part of one transaction'. If they were, they fell within s.56(1): it did not matter how the negotiations had been arranged. Instead, it was a decision of substance rather than form. It is unlikely, however, that the scope of deemed agency will extend to being held liable for any alleged breaches of a fiduciary relationship between the negotiator and the debtor.

The use of brokers, particularly in the asset finance market, has led to some interesting arguments over whether s.56(1) is engaged. Situations similar to the one in *Forthright Finance Ltd* v. *Ingate* (above) were historically straightforward and very common. For example, a customer has a car with outstanding finance of £5,000. She visits a motor trader and wants to part-exchange her car for a new model costing £10,000. Her existing vehicle is worth £6,000 so the dealer agrees to use the equity as a deposit for the new vehicle and pay off the existing finance. Further finance is agreed for the new car and the customer enters into a hire-purchase agreement. Instead of paying off the old finance, the dealer sells the old vehicle, pockets the sale proceeds and goes out of business. The old finance company then chases the customer for the outstanding balance. This is clearly where s.56(1)(b) and (2) come into play to protect the debtor and give her a claim against the new creditor.

The move to using brokers (either by consumers or dealers) has raised questions of whether CCA 1974, s.56(1) is still engaged in apparently 'traditional situations'. This issue came before the High Court in *Black Horse Ltd* v. *Langford* [2007] EWHC 907 (QB). Mr Langford wanted to part-exchange his existing motor car, a BMW Z3, which was acquired under a hire-purchase agreement with Black Horse Ltd (BH) for a new motor vehicle, a Lotus. A part-exchange price was agreed and the dealer agreed to pay off the existing finance to BH. Instead of approaching a finance company to finance the Lotus, it approached a broker. The broker (who Mr Langford did not know about) approached a finance company (which was, by coincidence, BH). BH agreed to provide credit to finance the acquisition of the Lotus under a hire-purchase agreement. The transaction completed (with the dealer selling the Lotus to the broker who, in turn, sold it to BH) but the dealer failed to pay the finance off on the BMW. BH issued proceedings against Mr Langford for the balance under the first hire-purchase agreement.

The High Court (on appeal from Huddersfield County Court) had to decide whether CCA 1974, s.56(1)(b) was engaged. Mr Justice Gray decided that s.56(1)(b) was not engaged: s.56(1)(b) applies 'only to the credit-broker who actually sells or proposes to sell the goods to the finance company'. Because the Lotus was sold by the dealer to the broker and then to BH, the goods were sold or proposed to be sold by the broker. Because the broker made no misrepresentations, the deemed agency provisions did not help Mr Langford.

4.8.6 Void agreements

By CCA 1974, s.56(3), an agreement is void if, and to the extent that, it purports in relation to an actual or prospective regulated agreement:

- to provide that a person acting as, or for, a negotiator is to be treated as the agent of the debtor or hirer; or
- to relieve a person from liability for acts or omissions of any person acting as, or for, a negotiator.

4.8.7 Creditor's claim

It is notable that a creditor faced with a claim by a debtor alleging, for example, a misrepresentation by the creditor's deemed agent under CCA 1974, s.56 has no statutory right to an indemnity (unlike the position under CCA 1974, s.75). There may be a recourse agreement between those parties but, if not, creditors may seek an indemnity or contribution from the deemed agent under the Civil Liability (Contribution) Act 1978.

4.9   WITHDRAWAL FROM A PROSPECTIVE REGULATED AGREEMENT

Section 57 of CCA 1974 makes it clear that a party may withdraw from a prospective regulated agreement at any point before it is completed. There are more detailed provisions for prospective land mortgages and these are discussed at **4.10** below. There is nothing revolutionary in this: it simply re-states the common law position that an offer can be withdrawn until it is accepted. There are, however, three important points:

- notice of withdrawal can be given either orally or in writing (s.57(2));
- the following are deemed agents of the creditor or owner for receiving any notice of withdrawal: a credit-broker or supplier who is the negotiator in antecedent negotiations and any person who, in the course of a business carried on by him, acts for the debtor or hirer in any negotiations for the agreement (s.57(3)); and
- the effect of withdrawal is the same as cancellation (s.57(4)).

The effect of withdrawal from a prospective regulated agreement is discussed at **4.12.5** below.

4.10   WITHDRAWAL FROM A PROSPECTIVE LAND MORTGAGE

4.10.1   Duty

Section 58 of CCA 1974 applies to prospective land mortgages (i.e. regulated agreements secured on land). Section 58(1) imposes an obligation on the creditor or owner, before sending an unexecuted agreement which is to be secured on land, to give an advance copy of the unexecuted agreement in the prescribed form. This must tell the debtor or hirer of his right to withdraw from the prospective agreement and how and when this right is exercisable. The creditor or owner must also, at the same time, send the debtor or hirer a copy of any other document referred to in the unexecuted agreement. This will include a copy of the mortgage deed.

4.10.2   Prescribed form

The advance copy will be an exact copy of the proposed regulated agreement except that:

- in place of the statutory heading required by the Consumer Credit (Agreements) Regulations 1983, SI 1983/1553 (CC(A)R 1983), the following words

107

should be included (the creditor or owner should, of course, pick the relevant word in the square brackets) by reg.4(1) of the Consumer Credit (Cancellation Notices and Copies of Documents) Regulations 1983, SI 1983/1557 (CC(CNCD)R 1983):

> Copy of proposed [credit][hire] agreement containing notice of your right to withdraw. Do NOT sign or return this copy.

- instead of any statement of rights of the debtor or hirer referred to in CC(A)R 1983, regs.2(3) and 3(3), Sched.2, Form 1 and Sched.4, the advance copy must include, by CC(CNCD)R 1983, reg.4(2), the following box:

YOUR RIGHT TO WITHDRAW

This is a copy of your proposed [credit][hire]* agreement which is to be secured on land. It has been given to you now so that you may have at least a week to consider its terms before the actual agreement is sent to you for signature. You should read it carefully. If you do not understand it, you may need to seek professional advice. If you do not wish to go ahead with it, you need not do so.

If you decide NOT to go ahead with the agreement you should inform [   ]** or, if you prefer, any supplier or broker involved in the negotiations. You can do this in writing or orally for example by telephone. If the agreement arrives for signature and you have decided NOT to go ahead. DO NOT SIGN IT. Then you will not be legally bound by the agreement.

[Note: Your notice of withdrawal will not affect [your contract for life assurance][your contract for insurance][your contract of guarantee][your contract to open a current account][your contract to open a deposit account].]* [The place where your financial obligations consequent upon withdrawal from this agreement are shown is [   ]***.]****]*

To complete this form, the creditor or owner must:

(a) delete the words in square brackets immediately before '*' where there are not applicable and the square brackets around the word which is relevant.

(b) insert in place of [   ]** the words 'the creditor' (for consumer credit agreements) or 'the owner' (for consumer hire agreements) or the expression by which the creditor or owner is referred to in the copy of the unexecuted agreement or an appropriate pronoun.

(c) insert in place of [   ]*** a clear reference to the place where these obligations appear.

(d) include the words in square brackets immediately before '****' where they are applicable.

4.10.3 Exceptions

By virtue of s. 58(2) of CCA 1974, s.58(1) does not apply to a restricted-use credit agreement to finance the purchase of the mortgaged land, or an agreement for a bridging loan in connection with the purchase of the mortgaged land or other land.

4.10.4 Procedure

Section 58 of CCA 1974 is supplemented by CCA 1974, s.61. This makes it clear that:

- if a creditor or owner does not comply with ss.58(1) and 61(2), the agreement is not properly executed (s.61(2)(a));
- the unexecuted copy of the agreement must be sent to the debtor or hirer by an appropriate method not less than seven days after the advance copy was given to him under s.58(1) (s.61(2)(b));
- from the date that the advance copy under s.58(1) is given to the debtor or hirer until the earlier of seven days after the day on which the unexecuted agreement was sent to the debtor under s.61(2)(b), or its return by the debtor or hirer after signature by him (known as the 'consideration period'), the creditor or owner must not approach the debtor or hirer (whether in person, by phone or letter or in any other way) except in response to a specific request by the debtor or hirer made after the beginning of the consideration period (s.61(2)(c));
- it is not properly executed unless no notice of withdrawal by the debtor or hirer was received by the creditor or owner before the sending of the unexecuted agreement (s.61(2)(d)).

The 'consideration period' is one of the key provisions of CCA 1974. It essentially gives the debtor 16 days (i.e. the two seven-day periods plus each day of service) to consider the documents without being contacted by the creditor or owner (or any broker). The documentation cannot change during the consideration period: if some of the terms are changed then the whole process must be re-started. Section 61(2)(c) is also likely to stop valuers contacting the debtor or hirer to arrange an inspection of the property. To overcome these problems, it is often the case that a summary sheet will be included with the advance copy under s.58(1). This will usually explain the procedure, tell the debtor or hirer that he cannot be contacted but he can contact the creditor or owner and ask the debtor or hirer to sign a form agreeing for a valuer to call.

4.10.5 Effect

Section 58 of CCA 1974 is vitally important for mortgage lending (often known as 'second charge lending'). The main reason why the debtor or hirer is given an 'advance copy' of the proposed agreement is to give him time to reflect before entering into the agreement. If the debtor or hirer was, instead, given a right to withdraw, it would cause significant practical difficulties because the creditor or owner would have to withdraw any application to register its charge. If the charge had already been registered, it would need to apply to the Land Registry for its removal.

4.11   AGREEMENT TO ENTER FUTURE AGREEMENT

Section 59(1) of CCA 1974 makes it clear that an agreement is void if it purports to bind a person to enter (either as a debtor or hirer) into a prospective regulated agreement. Section 59(2) does, however, allow the Secretary of State to make regulations excluding certain agreements. So far, there is only the Consumer Credit (Agreements to enter Prospective Agreements) (Exemptions) Regulations 1983, SI 1983/1552. By reg.2(2), the following agreements are excluded from CCA 1974, s.59(1):

- prospective consumer hire agreements for the bailment or (in Scotland) the hiring of goods where the goods are needed for the hirer's business or the hirer holds himself out as needing them for his business (reg.2(2)(a));
- prospective restricted-use credit agreements for fixed-sum credit to buy goods where the goods are needed by the debtor for the debtor's business or the debtor holds himself out as needing them for his business (reg.2(2)(b)).

In either case, there must be no face-to-face dealings with a negotiator or the agreement must be signed at one of the business premises of the creditor or owner, any party linked to the transaction or the negotiator in any antecedent negotiations.

The Court of Appeal recently considered CCA 1974, s.59(1) in *HSBC Bank plc* v. *Patrick Brophy* [2011] EWCA Civ 67. Mr Brophy received a pack of documents from HFC Bank Ltd (HFC), a member of the HSBC Group. This pack included a document headed 'Priority Application Form' which asked him to provide personal information if he wanted to apply for a credit card with HFC. Mr Brophy wished to do so. He therefore completed the application form. This form included a statutory heading saying that it was a 'Credit Agreement regulated by the Consumer Credit Act 1974' and included the statutory signature box. Clause 3 of the terms also said that the 'credit limit will be determined by us from time to time and notified to you'. Mr Brophy argued that the application form was no more than an invitation to treat or, alternatively, an agreement to enter into a prospective regulated agreement which was void by CCA 1974, s.59(1). The Court of Appeal disagreed: the application form was not an agreement of any kind unless and until it was signed by HFC, meaning that s.59 was not engaged.

4.12 CANCELLATION

4.12.1 When does it apply?

Section 67(1) of CCA 1974 is potentially wide-reaching. It allows a debtor or hirer to cancel a regulated agreement in accordance with CCA 1974 if antecedent negotiations included oral representations by, or by someone acting for, the negotiator in the presence of the debtor or hirer unless:

- the agreement is secured on land, or is a restricted-use credit agreement to finance the purchase of land or is an agreement for a bridging loan in connection with the purchase of land; or
- the unexecuted agreement is signed by the debtor or hirer at premises at which any of the following are carrying on any business (whether on a permanent or temporary basis):
  - the creditor or owner;
  - any party to a linked transactions (other than the debtor or hirer or a relative of his); or
  - the negotiator in any antecedent negotiations.

Key points to remember are:

- the oral representations must be made with the debtor or hirer in front of the negotiator and before the agreement is signed;
- the creditor or owner or dealer may be the negotiator in antecedent negotiations;
- a dealer will not be the negotiator in antecedent negotiations for a consumer hire agreement: *Lloyds Bowmaker Leasing Ltd* v. *MacDonald* [1993] CCLR 65;
- it is not enough for the representations to be made over the telephone: the use of the phrase 'in the presence of' is telling;
- the statement must be one of fact, or opinion or what will happen in the future which induces the debtor or hirer to enter into the regulated agreement: *Moorgate Services Ltd* v. *Kabir* [1995] CCLR 74;
- loans secured on land or for purposes of buying land are outside CCA 1974, s.67;
- the unexecuted agreement must be signed away from business premises.

4.12.2 When does it not apply?

The right to cancel under CCA 1974, s.67(1) does not apply, by virtue of s.67(2), if the debtor under a regulated consumer credit agreement has a right to withdraw under CCA 1974, s.66A. We discuss this right at **4.13** below.

There are also the following additional exclusions:

- exempt agreements (by virtue of CCA 1974, ss.16–16C);

- non-commercial agreements (by CCA 1974, s.74(1)(a));
- debtor-creditor agreements allowing the debtor to overdraw on a current account (by virtue of s.74(1)(b));
- debtor-creditor agreements to finance the making of such payments arising on, or connected with, the death of a person as may be prescribed (by s.74(1)(c)); and
- a small debtor-creditor-supplier agreement for restricted-use credit (by s.74(1)(d)),

4.12.3   Cooling-off period

Perhaps one of the most bizarre features of cancellation is the complicated rules on the duration of the cooling-off period. Section 68 of CCA 1974 says that the debtor or hirer may serve notice of cancellation between his signing of the unexecuted agreement and:

- the end of the fifth day after the day on which he received a copy of the executed agreement under CCA 1974, s.63(2) or a notice under CCA 1974, s.64(1)(b) that the agreement has completed; or
- if (by virtue of regulations made under s.64(4)) s.64(1)(b) does not apply, the end of the 14th day after the date on which he signed the unexecuted agreement.

The requirements to serve copies of the executed agreement are discussed at **5.17**.

4.12.4   Notice of cancellation

The general rule is contained in CCA 1974, s.69(1). It states that if the debtor or hirer under a cancellable agreement serves written notice within the cooling-off period, discussed at **4.12.3** above, on:

- the creditor or owner; or
- a person specified in the notice under CCA 1974, s.64(1); or
- a person who (whether by virtue of s.69(6) or otherwise) is the creditor's or owner's agent,

saying he wishes to withdraw from the agreement then that notice will cancel the agreement and any linked transaction and withdraw any offer by the debtor or hirer, or his relative, to enter into a linked transaction.

The wording of s.69(1) is clear: the debtor or hirer does not need to use a particular form. All he has to say is that he wants to 'cancel' his contract or otherwise pull out of the transaction.

4.12.5 Effect of withdrawal or cancellation

If a debtor or hirer cancels a cancellable regulated agreement, the consequences which follow are set out in CCA 1974, ss.70–73. By virtue of CCA 1974, s.57(4), the consequences are the same if the debtor or hirer withdraws from a prospective agreement.

Repayment of sums paid

Under CCA 1974, s.70(1) the cancellation of, or withdrawal from, a regulated and any linked transaction leads to the following consequences:

- any sum paid by the debtor or hirer (or any relative) under or in contemplation of the agreement or transaction becomes repayable to the debtor or hirer (or any relative);
- any sum, which but for the cancellation is, or would or might become, payable by the debtor or the hirer under the agreement or transaction, no longer is, and does not become, payable; and
- for debtor-creditor-supplier agreements falling within CCA 1974, s.12(b) (including fixed-sum restricted credit agreements for the purchase of goods), any sum paid to the supplier for the debtor by the creditor becomes repayable by the supplier to the creditor.

If the debtor or hirer has paid to a credit-broker a fee or commission then the amount repayable of that fee under s.70(1), if that fee exceeds £5, is the difference between the fee and £5 (s.70(6)). For example, if the broker's fee is £500 then the amount repayable is £495.

Section 70(1) does not, however, apply to any sum that would be payable by a debtor under an agreement for unrestricted credit. By s.70(5), the debtor remains liable to repay the credit and interest.

If the debtor or hirer (or his relative) is in possession of goods under a cancelled agreement then, by s.70(2), he has a lien over those goods until the sums paid under s.70(1) have been paid. This puts a debtor or hirer in a strong position to ensure the prompt repayment of monies.

The debtor or hirer is entitled, by s.70(3), to have the money repaid by the person to whom it was originally paid. This will normally be the creditor or owner so poses little difficulty. If, however, the agreement is a debtor-creditor-supplier agreement falling within CCA 1974, s.12(b) then the supplier is under a joint and several liability to repay the sums paid. If, therefore, the debtor brings proceedings against the creditor for repayment of monies, following cancellation or withdrawal, under a debtor-creditor-supplier agreement falling within CCA 1974, s.12(b), the creditor is statutorily entitled:

- by s.70(3) to make an additional claim (formerly called a Part 20 Claim) under the Civil Procedure Rules 1998, SI 1998/3132 (CPR); and

- by s.70(4) (and subject to any agreement between the supplier and the creditor) to be indemnified for loss suffered by the creditor in satisfying his liability under s.70(3) including costs reasonably incurred by the creditor in defending the debtor's proceedings.

Because the wording of s.70(4) mirrors the wording of CCA 1974, s.75(2), see **6.2.6** for consideration of how the indemnity works. In particular, note the consequences set out by Deputy District Judge Austin in *Kim Patricia Parker* v. *Black Horse Ltd & Browne & Sons (Loddon) Ltd t/a ESS Scooters* (unreported, Dartford County Court, 17 December 2010).

Repayment of credit

Following the cancellation of, or withdrawal from, a regulated agreement (unless it is a debtor-creditor-supplier agreement for restricted-use credit), the agreement remains in force to the extent that it relates to the repayment of credit and payment of interest (CCA 1974, s.71(1)). By virtue of CCA 1974, s.71(2), if, after the cancellation of a regulated consumer credit agreement, the debtor repays the whole or a portion of the credit before the expiry of one month after service of the notice of cancellation; or for credit repayable by instalments, before the date on which the first instalment is due, then no interest is payable on the amount repaid.

If the whole of the credit repayable by instalments is not paid on or before the date on which the first instalment is due, the debtor is not (by CCA 1974, s.70(3)) liable to repay any of the creditors until he receives a written request (in the prescribed form), signed by, or for, the creditor, stating the amounts of the remaining instalments.

By CCA 1974, s.71(4), a debtor or hirer may repay the credit (and any interest) to any person who could receive notice of cancellation under CCA 1974, s.69 except for any person who, in the course of a business carried on by him, acts for the debtor or hirer in any negotiations for the agreement.

Return of goods

Section 72 of CCA 1974 applies (by s.72(1)) to any agreement or transaction relating to goods which is:

- a restricted-use debtor-creditor-supplier agreement;
- a consumer hire agreement;
- a linked transaction to which the debtor or hirer under any regulated agreement is a party; or
- a linked transaction to which a relative of the debtor or hirer under any regulated agreement is a party,

and is cancelled after the debtor or (in the case of a consumer hire agreement) a hirer or a relative (in the case of a linked transaction to which the relative is a party) has acquired possession of the goods under the agreement or transaction.

Section 72(2) contains three definitions:

- the 'possessor' which is the person who has acquired possession of the goods as set out in s.72(1);
- the 'other party' which is the person from whom the possessor acquired possession; and
- the 'pre-cancellation period' which the period beginning when the possessor acquired possession and ending with the cancellation.

Section 72(3) imposes a duty on the possessor, throughout the pre-cancellation period, to retain possession of the goods and to take reasonable care of them. On cancellation, the possessor's duty changes, by virtue of s.72(4), to a duty (subject to any lien under s.70(2)) to restore the goods to the other party and, until he does, take reasonable care of the goods. Restoration is not, however, a requirement to return the goods to the other party: the possessor only needs to make them available at his own premises (i.e. the address stated on the agreement: s.72(10)) following a written request signed by or for the other party which is served on the possessor either before or at the time when the goods are collected from those premises (CCA 1974, s.70(5)).

The possessor may become discharged from his duty to retain the goods or deliver them to any person or take reasonable care of them If he delivers the goods to any person who could have been served with a notice of cancellation (other than any person who, in the course of a business carried on by him, acts for the debtor or hirer in any negotiations for the agreement), or sends the goods (at his own expense) to such a person, by the combined effect of CCA 1974, s.72(6) and (7). If the possessor decides to send the goods, he is under a duty to ensure that they arrive safely and are not damaged in transit.

There are, however, some time limits imposed by CCA 1974, s.72(8). In short:

- if the possessor receives a request under s.72(5) within 21 days of cancellation but unreasonable refuses or unreasonably fails to comply with the request, the duty to take reasonable care continues until the goods are returned;
- if the possessor does not receive a request under s.72(5) within 21 days of cancellation, his duty to take reasonable care ends after 21 days. After this period, the goods remain at the other party's risk.

If there is a breach of CCA 1974, s.72 then a claim may be brought for breach of statutory duty (s.72(11)).

By s.72(9), excluded from s.72 are the following:

- perishable goods;
- goods which by their nature are consumed by use and which, before the cancellation, were consumed;

- goods supplied to meet an emergency; or
- goods which, before the cancellation, had become incorporated in any land or thing not compromised in the cancelled agreement or a linked transaction.

Goods given in part exchange

Section 73 of CCA 1974 applies following the cancellation of a regulated agreement where, in antecedent negotiations, the negotiator agreed to take goods in part-exchange and those goods have been delivered to him (s.73(1)). The most obvious example is a motor car which is part-exchanged with a dealer. This motor car is not sold to the creditor: it is bought by the dealer who then applies the part-exchange amount against the cash price of the new vehicle.

Section 73(2) sets out the basic position: unless the part-exchanged goods are returned within 10 days beginning with the date of cancellation in substantially as good condition as they were in when delivered to the negotiator, the debtor or hirer is entitled to recover from the negotiator a cash payment of the part-exchange allowance. Two important points flow from s.73(2):

- it is submitted that the phrase 'substantially as good' means that only fair wear and tear is allowed: anything more means the goods are not 'substantially as good'; and
- the debtor or hirer is not given a choice if the part-exchanged goods are returned within 10 days: he must accept them back and cannot insist on cash being paid.

By s.73(5), the debtor or hirer also has a lien over the goods supplied under the regulated agreement for a period of 10 days beginning on the date of cancellation for:

- delivery of the part-exchanged goods in a condition substantially as good as when they were delivered to the negotiator; and
- a sum equal to the part-exchange allowance,

but the lien continues after this 10-day period for a sum equal to the part-exchange allowance only if it remains unpaid.

There is a statutory passing of title (if it has not already passed) to the part-exchanged goods upon receipt by the debtor or owner from the creditor or negotiator (or both of them jointly) of the part-exchange allowance (s.73(6)). This raises an interesting question of whether there are any implied terms for the passage of title. This has yet to be tested by the courts and, it is submitted, that there are no implied terms as the statutory transfer does not fall within the definition of a contract of sale under the Sale of Goods Act 1979.

Under s.73(3), if the agreement is a debtor-creditor-supplier agreement falling within CCA 1974, s.12(b) then the negotiator and the creditor are under a joint and several liability to pay the sum under s.73(2). If the debtor brings proceedings against the creditor, the creditor is statutorily entitled:

- by s.73(8) to make an additional claim (formerly called a Part 20 Claim) under the CPR; and
- by s.73(4) (and subject to any agreement between the negotiator and the creditor) to be indemnified for loss suffered by the creditor in satisfying its liability under s.72(3) including costs reasonably incurred by the creditor in defending the debtor's proceedings.

Because the wording of CCA 1974, s.73(4) mirrors the wording of s.75(2) (and, indeed, s.70(4)), see further **6.2.6** for consideration of how the indemnity works. In particular, readers will note the consequences set out by Deputy District Judge Austin in *Kim Patricia Parker* v. *Black Horse Ltd & Browne & Sons (Loddon) Ltd t/a ESS Scooters* (unreported, Dartford County Court, 17 December 2010).

4.13 WITHDRAWAL FROM A CONSUMER CREDIT AGREEMENT

4.13.1 Debtor's right

From 1 February 2011, CCA 1974, s.66A appeared on the statute book. Section 66A(1) provides a debtor under a regulated consumer credit agreement, other than an excluded agreement, with a right to withdraw from the agreement, without giving any reason, in accordance with the provisions of s.66A. This is an important right for debtors: they do not need to give any reason.

4.13.2 Exclusions

By CCA 1974, s.66A(14), the following consumer credit agreements are excluded from s.66A:

- an agreement for credit exceeding £60,260;
- an agreement secured on land;
- a restricted-use credit agreement to finance the purchase of land; or
- an agreement for a bridging loan in connection with the purchase of land.

4.13.3 Time period

The debtor has a period of 14 days to withdraw beginning on the 'relevant day' (CCA 1974, s.66A(2)). Section 66A(3) goes on to say that the 'relevant day' is the latest of the following:

- the day on which the agreement is made;
- where the creditor is required to tell the debtor of the credit limit under the agreement, the day on which the creditor first does so;
- where there is an obligation to supply a copy of the executed agreement under s.61A, the day on which the debtor receives a copy of the executed agreement

or on which the debtor is told that the agreement has been executed in accordance with s.61A(3);

- where there is an obligation to supply a copy of the executed agreement for an excluded agreement under s.63, the date on which the debtor receives a copy of the agreement under that section.

4.13.4 Method of withdrawal

Notice of the debtor's withdrawal can be given either orally or in writing (CCA 1974, s.66A(2)). It is therefore important for creditors to ensure that their agreements include a bespoke contact number or email address so that creditors can actively manage any withdrawals. Indeed, s.66A(4) makes it clear that oral notice must be given in the way set out in the agreement.

If notice of withdrawal is given electronically (perhaps by email or text) or by fax, then by CCA 1974, s.66A(5):

- it must be sent to the number or electronic address stated on the agreement; and
- it is deemed to have been received at the time it was sent (meaning CCA 1974, s.176A does not apply).

If the notice of withdrawal is given in writing and in any other form, then by s.66A(6):

- it must be sent by post to, or left at, the address stated on the agreement; and
- it is deemed to have been received at the time of posting or leaving (meaning CCA 1974, s.176A does not apply).

4.13.5 Consequences of withdrawal

If the debtor withdraws in time then by CCA 1974, s.66A(7):

- the agreement is treated as never having been entered into; and
- if an ancillary service is being provided by the creditor or by a third party on the basis of an agreement between a third party or a creditor (including, for example, installation services) then the ancillary service contract is treated as if it had never been entered into.

Because the agreement has not been entered into, by CCA 1974, s.66A(9) the debtor:

- must repay to the creditor any credit provided under the agreement and interest accrued on it at the rate provided under the agreement; and
- is not liable to repay to the creditor any compensation, fees or charges except any non-returnable charges paid by the creditor to a public administrative body.

The amount payable by the debtor under s.66A(9) must, by s.66A(10), be paid without delay and within 30 days beginning with the day after the debtor gave the creditor notice of withdrawal.

The creditor is under an obligation under s.66A(8) to tell any third party providing ancillary services that the debtor has withdrawn 'without delay'.

4.13.6 Creditor's rights following debtor's withdrawal

The more difficult issue for creditors arises when the debtor, who has acquired goods under a consumer credit agreement, has withdrawn and then fails to pay the purchase price. The question in this situation is whether the creditor has any rights against the goods. By virtue of CCA 1974, s.66A(7), the consumer credit agreement is treated as if it had not been entered into (meaning there is no need to serve a default notice or take steps to terminate the agreement), so it is submitted that the creditor remains the owner of the goods. This view is supported by CCA 1974, s.66A(11) which states (and is more fully explained at **4.13.7** below) that if the debtor withdraws from a conditional sale, hire-purchase or credit sale agreement but pays the sum payable under CCA 1974, s.66A(9)(a), then 'title to the goods purchased or supplied under the agreement is to pass to the debtor'. If the debtor was always the owner, there would be no need for this provision.

If this is the case, it follows that the creditor can take steps to recover possession of the goods and re-sell them either by self-help methods of recovery or, if the debtor refuses to return the goods, an application to the court for delivery-up of the goods following a written demand. If the net sale proceeds do not exceed the debtor's liability under CCA 1974, s.66A(9)(a) then, so long as the creditor takes reasonable steps to mitigate his loss, the creditor may also pursue a claim against the debtor for the difference.

4.13.7 Hire purchase, conditional sale and credit sale

If the agreement is for hire purchase, conditional sale or credit sale and:

- the debtor withdraws from the agreement under CCA 1974, s.66A after credit has been provided; and
- the sum payable under s.66A(9)(a) is paid in full by the debtor,

then title to the goods bought or supplied under the agreement passes to the debtor on the same terms that would have applied had the debtor not withdrawn from the agreement (CCA 1974, s.66A(11)).

It is submitted that the wording of CCA 1974, s.66A(11) is likely to cause some problems for both creditors and debtors. For example, if goods are acquired under a hire-purchase agreement then there are terms implied into the agreement under the Supply of Goods (Implied Terms) Act 1973. If, however, goods are supplied under a contract of sale then there are implied terms under the Sale of Goods Act 1979. This includes additional rights for consumers, contained in Part 5A of the Sale of Goods

Act 1979, including a legal right to repair or replacement and a reversed burden of proof for faults which arise during the first six months. Given the implications of CCA 1974, s.66A(7), it is unclear which legislation Parliament intended the supply to be subject to. No doubt this will be an issue for the courts to tackle in due course.

CHAPTER 5

Requirements of a regulated agreement

5.1 INTRODUCTION

For any practitioners familiar with the Consumer Credit Act 1974 (CCA 1974), the formalities for entering into a regulated agreement, including its form and content, are crucial to its enforceability. This concern has been lessened somewhat for agreements dated on or after 6 April 2007 following the repeal of CCA 1974, s.127(3) and (4). There are, however, a considerable number of traps for the unwary. Indeed, many of the recent consumer credit cases before the courts have alleged that the regulated credit or hire agreement is irredeemably unenforceable, because it fails to comply with the terms prescribed by Sched.6 to the Consumer Credit (Agreements) Regulations 1983, SI 1983/1553 (CC(A)R 1983) or it fails to include cancellation notices, or it is unenforceable without the court's permission under CCA 1974, s.127(1). Whilst these challenges have been largely unsuccessful, it is important to look at not only what must be in a regulated agreement, but the steps that a creditor or owner needs to take before entering into the agreement. We now turn to look at these in some detail.

It is important at this stage to say that the Consumer Credit Directive (87/102/EEC) (CCD), which has now been implemented by virtue of various statutory instruments, has had a significant impact upon consumer credit legislation. There is now an unfortunate two-tier system of regulation where certain agreements will be subject to CC(A)R 1983 and others will be subject to the Consumer Credit (Agreements) Regulations 2010, SI 2010/1014 (CC(A)R 2010). We will therefore discuss what sorts of agreements are still subject to CC(A)R 1983 and those that are subject to CC(A)R 2010. We then look at each set of regulations in some detail.

5.2 FORM AND CONTENT OF AGREEMENTS

Section 60(1) and (2) of CCA 1974 gives the Secretary of State power to make regulations prescribing the form and content of documents embodying regulated agreements. This is one of the most crucial provisions of CCA 1974 and has led to CC(A)R 1983 (as amended) and CC(A)R 2010.

If a person carrying on a consumer credit business or consumer hire business takes the view that it is impracticable for it comply with the requirements of

CC(A)R 1983 (as amended) and/or CC(A)R 2010 then it may, by CCA 1974, s.60(3), make an application to the Office of Fair Trading (OFT) for those requirements to be waived or varied. If the application is successful, the OFT will issue a notice. The OFT may, however, only issue a notice if it is satisfied that it would not prejudice the interest of debtors or hirers (CCA 1974, s.60(4)). It is notable that the OFT does not need to take into account the interest of other creditors or owners: it is entirely possible that the giving of such a notice will give the recipient a commercial advantage over its competitors.

An application under CCA 1974, s.60(3) can, however, only be made for the requirements to be waived or varied for the following agreements:

- consumer credit agreements secured on land;
- pawn agreements;
- consumer credit agreements for credit of more than £60,260;
- consumer credit agreements entered into by a debtor wholly or predominantly for the purposes of a business carried on, or intended to be carried on, by him; or
- consumer hire agreements.

5.3   PROPERLY EXECUTED AGREEMENTS

Section 61 of CCA 1974 requires an agreement to be properly executed. Under CCA 1974, s.65(1) an improperly executed agreement is only enforceable against the hirer or debtor with the court's permission. The circumstances in which the court can give permission are set out in CCA 1974, s.127 (discussed at **10.2**). Section 65(2) supplements s.65(1) by making it clear that a retaking of goods or land subject to a regulated agreement is an enforcement of the agreement.

Turning back to CCA 1974, s.61(1), an agreement is not properly executed unless:

- a document:
    - is in the prescribed form;
    - contains all of the prescribed terms;
    - conforms with the regulations made under s.60(1); and
    - is signed in the prescribed way by (or, in the case of a partnership or unincorporated body of persons, for) the debtor or hirer and by, or for, the creditor or owner;
- that document embodies all of the terms of the agreement other than implied terms; and
- the document is, when presented or sent to the debtor or hirer for signature, in such a state that all of its terms are readily legible.

If the agreement is also subject to CCA 1974, s.58(1) (discussed at **4.10** above) then there are additional requirements contained in CCA 1974, s.61(2). These are that:

- the requirements of CCA 1974, s.58(1) were complied with (see **4.10** above);
- the unexecuted agreement was sent, for signature, to the debtor or hirer by an 'appropriate method' not less than seven days after an advance copy of it was given to him under CCA 1974, s.58(1);
- during the 'consideration period', the creditor or owner did not approach the debtor or hirer (whether in person, by phone or letter or in any other way) except following a specific request made by the debtor or hirer after the beginning of the consideration period; and
- no notice of withdrawal by the debtor or hirer was received by the creditor or owner before the sending of the unexecuted agreement.

The 'consideration period' is defined by CCA 1974, s.61(3) as beginning with the giving of a copy under CCA 1974, s.58(1) and ending at the expiry of seven days after the date on which the unexecuted agreement (sent under CCA 1974, s.61(2)(b)) was sent for signature to the debtor or hirer, or on the return of the agreement signed by the debtor or hirer, whichever happens first.

5.4   WHEN DOES CC(A)R 2010 APPLY?

CC(A)R 2010 applies to certain agreements from 1 February 2011. It was possible for creditors to opt into CC(A)R 2010 before 1 February 2011 but few seem to have taken this opportunity. Regulation 2(1) of CC(A)R 2010 states that those regulations apply to all consumer credit agreements except for those listed in CC(A)R 2010, reg. 2(1A)–(5). The excluded credit agreements are therefore those:

- secured on land (other than an agreement subject to CCA 1974, s.58);
- under which the creditor provides to the debtor credit which exceeds £60,260; or
- entered into by the debtor wholly or predominantly for the purposes of a business carried on, or intended to be carried on, by him,

unless pre-contract information has been disclosed in compliance (or purported compliance) with the Consumer Credit (Disclosure of Information) Regulations 2010, SI 2010/1013.

   If the agreement is subject to CCA 1974, s.58 and:

- before the creditor gives the debtor the unexecuted agreement for signature the creditor gives the debtor a copy of the unexecuted agreement in compliance or purported compliance with CC(A)R 2010, regs.3, 7 and Scheds.1 and 2; and
- the copy of the unexecuted agreement includes a heading and notice as set out in reg.4(a)(ii) and (b)(ii) of the Consumer Credit (Cancellation Notices and Copies of Documents) Regulations 1983, SI 1983/1557,

then it will be subject to CC(A)R 2010. Otherwise, it will be subject to CC(A)R 1983.

5.5 WHEN DOES CC(A)R 2010 NOT APPLY?

In very broad terms, CC(A)R 2010 does not apply to any of the following agreements:

- agreements secured on land (unless the creditor opts into CC(A)R 2010);
- consumer hire agreements;
- agreements for credit exceeding £60,260; and
- business agreements.

5.6 FORM AND CONTENT OF CONSUMER CREDIT AGREEMENTS SUBJECT TO CC(A)R 1983

5.6.1 Introduction

Agreements that do not fall within the CCD must (by and large) comply with CC(A)R 1983. It is important to remember that the agreement must comply with the version of CC(A)R 1983 in force at the date of the agreement. CC(A)R 1983 has been subject to a few minor changes but there was a significant change as a result of the Consumer Credit (Agreements) (Amendment) Regulations 2004, SI 2004/1482, which came into force on 31 May 2005. Creditors or owners facing an enforceability challenge should therefore have, at the very least, a copy of CC(A)R 1983 both before and after these changes came into effect. For the purposes of this text, we consider CC(A)R 1983 as it stood after 1 February 2011 (given the tweaks made to CC(A) R 1983 following the introduction of CC(A)R 2010 as a result of the CCD) but make reference, where appropriate, to some of the provisions as they stood before they were amended (either on 31 May 2005 or 1 February 2011).

5.6.2 Layout of agreement

Perhaps one of the most important provisions of CC(A)R 1983 is contained in reg.2(4). This prescribes the layout of a regulated credit agreement and was introduced by the changes on 31 May 2005. It prescribes the document embodying a regulated consumer credit agreement must be set out in the following order:

(1) the nature of the agreement as set out in Sched.1, para.1;
(2) the parties to the agreement as set out in Sched.1, para.2;
(3) under the heading 'Key Financial Information', the financial and related particulars set out in Sched.1, paras.6–8B, 11–14 and 15–17;
(4) under the heading 'Other Financial Information', the financial and related particulars set out in Sched.1, paras.3–5, 9, 10, 14A and 18–19A;
(5) under the heading 'Key Information':

- the information set out in Sched.1, paras.20–24; and
- the statements of protection and remedies set out in Sched.2; and

(6)   the signature box and, where applicable, the separate box required by reg.2(7)(b),

and such information, statements of protection and remedies, signature and separate boxes must be shown together as a whole and must not be preceded by any information apart from trade names, logos or the reference number of the agreement or interspersed with any other information or wording apart from subtotals of total amounts and cross-references to the terms of the agreement. This is the so-called 'holy grail' rule.

5.6.3   Prescribed terms

Regulation 6(1) of CC(A)R 1983 provides that a regulated consumer credit agreement must contain the terms prescribed in CC(A)R 1983, Sched.6. This requirement does not mean that all of the terms in Sched.6 must be set out: it is only the terms that are relevant to the agreement in question. For example, if the agreement is an unrestricted-use fixed-sum debtor-creditor agreement then it need not include the term required by Sched.6, para.3 (i.e. the credit limit) as this is only necessary where the agreement is for running-account credit.

The terms prescribed by CC(A)R 1983, Sched.6 are summarised below.

Amount of credit (Sched.6, para.1 or para.2)

Under CC(A)R 1983, Sched.6, para.1, if an agreement is a restricted-use debtor-creditor-supplier agreement for fixed-sum credit:

- to finance a transaction comprising the acquisition of goods, services or land or other things specified in the agreement or identified and agreed on at the time at which the agreement is made;
- under which the total amount payable by the debtor is not greater than the total cash price; and
- under which there is no advance payment,

then the creditor must include a term stating the amount of credit, which may be expressed as the total cash price of the goods, services, land or other things, the acquisition of which is to be financed by credit under the agreement.

Under Sched.6, para.2, if the agreement is for fixed-sum credit but does not fall within para.1 (these provisions are mutually exclusive: if an agreement falls within para.1 it will not fall within para.2 and vice versa), then the agreement must state the amount of credit.

The term 'credit' is one which has caused a significant amount of litigation over the years. The reasons for such litigation are obvious: if the debtor can show that the agreement is for fixed-sum credit and the amount of credit is wrongly stated then, assuming the agreement pre-dates the repeal of CCA 1974, s.127(3) on 6 April 2007, it will be irredeemably unenforceable.

Despite the obvious importance of the term 'credit', it is (somewhat unfortunately) not clearly defined in CCA 1974. Section 189(1) of the Act simply says that it is 'construed in accordance with section 9' of CCA 1974. Section 9(1), in turn, says that credit 'includes a cash loan, and any other form of financial accommodation'. For hire-purchase agreements, s.9(3) gives an example. It says that the credit in such a case is the total amount for the goods minus the total of the deposit and the total charge for credit.

Example

Mr Jones obtains a motor car on hire purchase. The total amount payable under the agreement is £30,000. The deposit is £6,000 and the total charge for credit is £4,000. The amount of credit advanced to Mr Jones is therefore £20,000 (i.e. the total amount of £30,000 minus the deposit of £6,000 and the total charge for credit of £4,000).

There is a qualification to the definition in CCA 1974, s.9(4) which states that, for the purposes of CCA 1974, if an item enters into the 'total charge for credit' then it is not credit even if time is allowed for its payment. To find out whether an item forms part of the 'total charge for credit', practitioners will need to consult the rather cumbersome Consumer Credit (Total Charge for Credit) Regulations 1980, SI 1980/51 (CC(TCC)R 1980). The distinction between what is credit and what is part of the total charge for credit is of crucial importance: if the amount of credit is wrong then the agreement is unenforceable, either irredeemably if it is dated before 6 April 2007 or without a court order from 6 April 2007. Whether or not it is enforceable only with the court's permission will depend on the date of the agreement.

In *Wilson* v. *First County Trust Ltd (No.2)* [2001] EWCA Civ 633 the claimant, Mrs Wilson, pledged her motor vehicle to a pawn-broker. The agreement included a document fee of £250. Because time was given for its repayment, the creditor recorded the document fee as part of the 'credit' rather than the 'charge for credit'. After hearing submissions, the Court of Appeal decided the document fee formed part of the 'charge for credit'. The agreement therefore wrongly stated the amount of credit and was therefore unenforceable. The Court of Appeal said, however, that the provisions of CCA 1974, s.127(3) (which meant the agreement was irredeemably unenforceable) were contrary to the creditor's human rights. It therefore declared CCA 1974, s.127(3) as incompatible with the Human Rights Act 1998. This latter part of the Court of Appeal's judgment was successfully appealed to the House of Lords. It therefore follows that a document fee will be part of the 'charge for credit' even if time is allowed for its repayment.

There are two conflicting decisions of the Court of Appeal dealing with the payment of arrears under an earlier mortgage: *Watchtower Investments Ltd* v. *Payne and another* [2001] EWCA Civ 1159 and *McGinn* v. *Grangewood Securities Ltd* [2002] EWCA Civ 522. In *Watchtower*, the Court of Appeal decided that one of the objects of the credit was to pay off the arrears so this sum had correctly been included in the amount of credit. By contrast, in *McGinn*, the Court of Appeal decided that paying off the earlier arrears was not one of the objects of applying for the loan. The Court of Appeal therefore distinguished *McGinn* on this basis and decided that it had incorrectly included the amount to pay the arrears as the credit. The agreement was therefore unenforceable.

More recently, the Supreme Court (formerly the House of Lords) needed to consider whether a broker's fee, on which time was given for repayment and interest charged on it, was correctly recorded as part of the charge for credit and not credit in *Southern Pacific Securities 05-2 plc (formerly Southern Pacific Personal Loans Ltd)* v. *Walker and another* [2010] UKSC 32. The debtors argued that the provisions of CCA 1974, s.9(4) did not stop interest being charged on any 'charge for credit'. The Supreme Court dismissed the argument and expressed the view that any argument that:

- the amount of credit is £1,000 where a loan of £1,000 is repayable with interest and a broker fee of £50 is repayable without interest; and
- the amount of credit is £1,050 where a loan of £1,000 is repayable with interest and a broker fee of £50 is repayable with interest,

was nonsensical because it would involve the court adding the following wording to CCA 1974, s.9(4): 'unless interest is charged in which case it shall be treated as credit'. The agreement therefore correctly included the broker fee of £875 in the charge for credit rather than the amount of credit.

Credit limit (Sched.6, para.3)

Under CC(A)R 1983, Sched.6, para.3, if an agreement is for running-account credit (like a credit card) then there must be a term stating:

- the credit limit; or
- the manner in which it will be determined; or
- that there is no credit limit.

Plainly, there can hardly be a challenge where the agreement states 'the credit limit is £5,000' or 'there is no credit limit'. There have, however, been challenges by debtors on the requirement to state the manner in which the credit limit will be determined. The line of attack taken by debtors has often been that the exact method of determining the credit limit must be stated, even if this means going further than the requirements under CC(A)R 1983, Sched.1 (particularly para.8).

Until recently, there was no clear authority on Sched.6, para.4 or Sched.1, para.8. The closest that the courts had come was the Court of Appeal's decision in *Lombard Tricity Finance Ltd* v. *Paton* [1989] 1 All ER 918. However, such a challenge recently came before Mr Justice Flaux (on appeal), sitting as a judge of the High Court, in *Brophy* v. *HFC Bank Ltd* [2010] EWHC 819 (QB). In this decision, Mr Brophy had a regulated unrestricted running-account credit agreement with HFC

Bank Ltd. Its agreement stated, at clause 3, that the credit limit 'will be determined by us from time to time and notified to you'. Mr Brophy argued that whilst this complied with CC(A)R 1983, Sched.1, para.8(b), it did not comply with Sched.6. The court decided that this argument was illogical: in particular:

- it was not the purpose of Sched.6 to primarily inform the debtor: this was Sched.1's task;
- the purpose of Sched.6 (as the Court of Appeal stated in *Hurstanger Ltd* v. *Wilson* [2007] 1 WLR 2351) is to set out the bare minimum terms which must be included as an inflexible condition to enforceability;
- it would be very odd if Sched.6 required more information to be given than that required by Sched.1: this would be (to use the judge's words) to lead 'in effect to the tail of Schedule 6 wagging the much larger dog of Schedule 1'.

Mr Brophy appealed this decision to the Court of Appeal and judgment was handed down in *HSBC Bank plc* v. *Brophy* [2011] EWCA Civ 67. Lord Justice Moore-Bick, delivering the leading judgment, dismissed the appeal (essentially for the reasons given in the High Court) and added:

- there was 'no reason in principle why the same clause should not satisfy both requirements' of Scheds.1 and 6;
- paragraph 3 of Sched.6 was 'deliberately worded in broad terms in order to encompass the whole range of terms that might be employed to fix the credit limit';
- there was nothing in the wording of para.3 of Sched.6 to support the conclusion that it should require the creditor to spell out the factors it would take into account or the manner in which they would be evaluated;
- the expression 'the manner in which it will be determined' was deliberately broad and could cover situations where the parties may agree the credit limit where there is neither a fixed credit limit nor the absence of any credit limit;
- the wording of clause 3 was 'clear' and 'provides for [HFC Bank] to determine the credit limit from time to time at its discretion by notifying the debtor of its amount';
- how HFC decided the credit limit was 'entirely a matter for itself'; and
- there was no requirement on HFC to explain, at the time the debtor signs the agreement, the amount of credit or the formula that will be used to determine it.

A similar issue came before the Sheriff Court in Scotland in *Napier* v. *HFC Bank Ltd t/a The GM Card* (2010) SLT (Sh Ct) 174 where the debtor (again, under a regulated running-account credit agreement with HFC Bank Ltd) argued essentially the same point as Mr Brophy (i.e. that the exact method of determining the credit limit must be stated, even if this means going further that the requirements under CC(A)R 1983, Sched.1). The court, after considering the evidence, dismissed the claim and decided that the statement that the credit limit would be determined and notified from time to time complied with CC(A)R 1983, Sched.1, para.8 and Sched.6, para.3.

Rate of interest (Sched.6, para.4)

Under CC(A)R 1983, Sched.6, para.4 if an agreement is for running-account credit or fixed-sum credit falling within the exceptions in CC(A)R 1983, Sched.1, para.9(a)–(c), then the agreement must include a term stating the rate of any interest on the credit to be provided under the agreement.

It is important to remember that the requirement to state the rate of interest under CC(A)R 1983, Sched.6, para.4 applies only where the agreement is for running-account credit or fixed-sum credit falling within CC(A)R 1983, Sched.1, para.9(a)–(c). It does not apply where the rate of interest on a fixed-sum loan agreement is fixed (as this type of agreement does not fall within the exceptions in Sched.1, para.9(a)–(c)). Creditors providing fixed-sum loan agreements with a non-variable rate of interest do not, therefore, need to include a term stating the rate of interest under Sched.6, para.4. There is, however, a similar requirement to do so under Sched.1, para.9.

Paragraph 4 of Sched.6 has generated a significant amount of litigation in recent times. Much like Sched.6, para.3, there was no authority dealing with how the rate of interest must be documented. This ambiguity led to a number of challenges arguing that the creditor or owner had recorded the wrong rate of interest which meant a breach of the prescribed terms.

Such a challenge came before His Honour Judge Tetlow (sitting as a Circuit Judge in the county court) in *Brooks* v. *Northern Rock (Asset Management) plc (formerly Northern Rock plc)* [2009] GCCR 9901. Mrs Brooks argued (relying upon a computer program provided by a claims management company called the 'Checker Report') that her fixed-sum loan agreement (with a fixed rate of interest) was irredeemably unenforceable. The Checker Report worked by assuming the rate of interest recorded on the agreement is the 'nominal' rate (which is the rate of interest (a month in this case) multiplied by the number of instalments in a year (12 in this case)). Assuming a nominal rate of interest as 5.8 per cent, the Checker Report said that all of the other (agreed) figures on the agreement were wrong making the agreement irredeemably unenforceable. After considering submissions from the parties, HHJ Tetlow was unable to agree with Mrs Brooks and decided that:

- the Checker Report's method was (to use the judge's words) 'looking through the wrong end of the telescope'. The parties had agreed the monthly repayment and, from this, the APR had been calculated;
- Parliament had not provided any guidance on what the phrase 'interest' (used in CC(A)R 1983, Sched.1, para.9(2) and Sched.6, para.4) meant and it was not the court's function to try and fill the gap and make unenforceable an agreement which would otherwise be enforceable;
- the sole dissenting voice on what the phrase 'rate of interest' meant came from the new editors of *Goode: Consumer Credit Law and Practice*, LexisNexis Butterworths (then appearing at para 30.185 before its substantial revision). Such a view was wrong. Lenders can use either the 'nominal' or 'effective' rate of interest without the agreement becoming non-compliant;

- there is no logical reason why rounding of the 'rate of interest' (as opposed to the APR) should be prevented. In fact, a lender may round the 'rate of interest' or go to any number of decimal places without making the agreement non-compliant.

It therefore follows that the rate of interest may be recorded as either the 'nominal' or 'effective' rate of interest for the purposes of CC(A)R 1983, Sched.1, para.9 and Sched.6, para.4.

The decision in *Brooks* was quickly followed by the High Court's decision in *Joseph Sternlight* v. *Barclays Bank plc and others* [2010] EWHC 1865 (QB). Much like *Brooks*, the debtors under regulated running-account credit agreements argued that (after using a computer program which used the APR as the 'driver' for the other figures) each agreement had wrongly stated the 'rate of interest' as required by Sched.6, para.4. His Honour Judge Waksman QC rejected the suggestion that the APR was the 'driver' for the rate of interest. His reasons were:

- the borrowers' proposition had a 'surreal quality to it' as it led to the position that the borrower had agreed the expert's re-calculated rate and not the contractually agreed rate of interest;
- there was a very clear difference between the nature and function of the APR and the rate of interest: indeed, CC(A)R 1983 treats them as separate things. The borrowers' argument meant that a prescribed term would be 'driven' by prescribed information which was plainly contrary to the importance pre-scribed terms had been given in CC(A)R 1983 and CCA 1974, s.127;
- the APR need only be stated at the start of the agreement when it is produced and signed: it is therefore a guide for borrowers at that date. Lenders are, however, allowed to change the rate of interest. In such a case, the APR cannot act as the driver any more when the rate is varied;
- the view expressed by HHJ Tetlow in *Brooks* that the borrower's argument was 'looking through the wrong end of the telescope' was approved and applied by analogy to these cases: the rate of interest had been contractually agreed and there was no reason to say it should be any other figure.

Repayments (Sched.6, para.5 or para.6)

Under CC(A)R 1983, Sched.6, para.5, a consumer credit agreement must include a term stating how the debtor is to discharge his obligations under the agreement to make the repayments, which may be expressed by reference to a combination of any of the following:

- number of repayments;
- amount of repayments;
- frequency and timing of repayments;
- dates of repayments;

- the manner in which any of the above may be determined; or
- in any other way, and any power of the creditor to vary what is payable.

Under CC(A)R 1983, Sched.6, para.6, a consumer hire agreement must include a term stating how the hirer is to discharge his obligations under the agreement to pay the hire payments, which may be expressed by reference to a combination of any of the following:

- number of payments;
- amount of payments;
- frequency and timing of payments;
- dates of payments;
- the manner in which any of the above may be determined; or
- in any other way, and any power of the owner to vary what is payable.

Because these provisions are essentially same, with the only real difference being whether the agreement is a consumer credit or consumer hire agreement, we propose to deal with these requirements together. These provisions are deliberately broad and allow the creditor or owner a significant amount of latitude. They only require the creditor to explain repayments by reference to a 'combination' of these factors. The point made by Recorder Douglas QC (which was approved by the Court of Appeal in *Wilson* v. *Hurstanger Ltd* [2007] CCLR 2) that Sched.6 sets out 'certain basic minimum terms ... which the parties (with the benefit of legal advice if necessary) and/or the court can identify within the four corners of the agreement' is therefore an important one to be made.

5.6.4 Prescribed information

Under CC(A)R 1983, reg.2(1), a regulated consumer credit agreement must contain the information set out in column 2 of CC(A)R 1983, Sched.1. This requirement does not mean that all of the information in column 2 should be set out: it is only the information that is relevant to the agreement in question. For example, if the agreement is an unrestricted-use fixed-sum debtor-creditor agreement then it need not include the information required by CC(A)R 1983, Sched.1, para.3 as this is only necessary where the agreement is a restricted-use debtor-creditor-supplier agreement.

The information required by Sched.1 is summarised below.

Nature of the agreement (Sched.1, para.1)

Each agreement must include, in the top left corner, a description of the type of agreement that it is. The phrases are stated in CC(A)R 1983, Sched.1, para.1 and are (depending on the exact nature of the agreement):

Hire-Purchase Agreement regulated by the Consumer Credit Act 1974

Conditional Sale Agreement regulated by the Consumer Credit Act 1974

Fixed-Sum Loan Agreement regulated by the Consumer Credit Act 1974

Credit Card Agreement regulated by the Consumer Credit Act 1974

If none of these is relevant or appropriate then the following heading must be used:

Credit Agreement regulated by the Consumer Credit Act 1974

If the agreement also includes a pawn-receipt then the words ', and Pawn Receipt,' must immediately following the word 'Agreement'. For example, a fixed-sum loan agreement including a pawn-receipt would state:

Fixed-Sum Loan Agreement, and Pawn Receipt, regulated by the Consumer Credit Act 1974

If the agreement is a multiple agreement (within the meaning of CCA 1974, s.18) where at least part of it is not regulated by CCA 1974, then the word 'partly' must be added before 'regulated' unless the regulated and unregulated parts of the agreements are clearly separate. For example, a hire-purchase agreement partly regulated by CCA 1974 would state:

Hire-Purchase Agreement partly regulated by the Consumer Credit Act 1974

Finally, if the agreement is being secured on land then the words 'secured on' followed by the property's address must be added to the end of the heading. For example:

Fixed-Sum Loan Agreement regulated by the Consumer Credit Act 1974 secured on 2 Park Lane, Leeds, LS3 1ES

Parties to the agreement (Sched.1, para.2)

This provision is straightforward and requires every agreement to state:

- the name, postal address and, where appropriate, any other address of the creditor (CC(A)R 1983, Sched.1, para.2(1)); and
- the name, postal address and, where appropriate, any other address of the debtor (CC(A)R 1983, Sched.1, para.2(2)).

Description of goods, services, land, etc. (Sched.1, para.3)

For restricted-use debtor-creditor-supplier agreements for fixed-sum credit to finance a transaction which includes the debtor obtaining goods, services, land or other things stated in the agreement and agreed at the time the agreement is made, there must be a list or other description of those goods, services, land, etc.

The most obvious example falling within Sched.1, para.3 is a hire-purchase agreement under which the debtor acquires goods like a motor car. In such a case, to comply with para.3 the creditor should describe the goods or motor vehicle. An example may be: 'a BMW X3 motor car with registration No. A1 BCD and VIN/Chassis No. ABC123DEF456'.

Cash price (Sched.1, para.4)

If an agreement falls within CC(A)R 1983, Sched.1, para.3 the agreement must also state the cash price of the goods, services, land or other thing and the total cash price. Using the example of a motor vehicle under a regulated hire-purchase agreement, the cash price would be the vehicle's sale price. Any deposit must be disregarded and the cash price must include any VAT payable: *Rank Xerox* v. *Hepple* [1994] CCLR 1.

Advance payments (Sched.1, para.5)

If an advance payment is being made by a debtor (either to the creditor or to a third party) under any type of agreement before he is provided with the credit or before he enters into the agreement, the agreement must state the amount of the advance payment and, if the agreement is cancellable, the nature of the payment. Using the motor vehicle example, the advance payment would be the debtor's deposit (if any) or part-exchange allowance. It does not include, however, any deposit payable for the purchase of a land by the seller. In such a case, the advance payment is not required by the creditor or under the agreement: it is required by the seller.

Amount of credit (Sched.1, para.6 or para.7)

If the agreement falls within CC(A)R 1983, Sched.1, para.3 (i.e. restricted-use debtor-creditor-supplier agreements for fixed-sum credit to finance a transaction which includes the debtor obtaining goods, services, land or other things) but is not an agreement where:

- the total amount payable by the debtor is not greater than the total cash price required to be stated by Sched.1, para.4; and
- there is no advance payment falling within Sched.1, para.5,

then it must (by Sched.1, para.6) state the amount of credit to be provided under the agreement which is the difference between the cash price under para.4 and the advance payment under para.5 of Sched.1. This is not required, however, if the total amount payable is the same as the cash price. Agreements for fixed-sum credit that do not fall within Sched.1, para.3 must state the amount of credit to be provided under the agreement.

The issue of what is 'credit' has already been discussed at **5.6.3** above ('Amount of credit'). There is no difference in how 'credit' is treated under Sched.6 compared with Sched.1. Readers are therefore referred to **5.6.3** for a full consideration of what is 'credit' for the purposes of CCA 1974 and CC(A)R 1983.

Credit limit (Sched.1, para.8)

If an agreement is for running-account credit then under CC(A)R 1983 it must state the credit limit expressed as:

- a sum of money (Sched.1, para.8(a)); or
- a statement that the credit limit will be determined by the creditor from time to time under the agreement and that notice of it will be given by it to the debtor (Sched.1, para.8(b));
- a sum of money together with a statement that the creditor may vary the credit limit to such sum as he may from time to time determine under the agreement and that notice of it will be given by it to the debtor (Sched.1, para.8(c)); or
- in a case not falling within para.8(a)–(c), either a statement indicating the manner in which the credit limit will be determined and that notice of it will be given by the creditor to the debtor or a statement indicating that there is no credit limit.

The issue of the credit limit has already been discussed in **5.6.3** above. There are, however, more detailed requirements in how the credit limit must be stated under Sched.1, para.8 compared to Sched.6, para.3. For the reasons set out in the judgments discussed at **5.6.3** above (see 'Credit limit'), it is submitted that wording similar to that included in those agreements should satisfy Sched.1, para.8.

Term of the agreement (Sched.1, paras.8A and 8B)

If the agreement is for running-account credit of a fixed duration, it must state the duration of the agreement (CC(A)R 1983, Sched.1, para.8A). If the agreement is for fixed-sum credit, it must state the duration or minimum term of the agreement (para.8B).

Total charge for credit (Sched.1, paras.9 and 10)

For fixed-sum credit except agreements:

- which do not specify either the intervals between repayments or the amounts of repayments or both the intervals and the amounts;
- under which the total amount payable by the debtor to discharge his indebtedness for the amount of credit provided may vary according to any formula specified in the agreement having effect by reference to movements in the level of any index or to any other factor;

- which provide for a variation of, or allow the creditor to vary, (whether or not by reference to any index) the amount or rate of any item included in the total charge for credit after the relevant date; or
- under which the total amount payable by the debtor is not greater than the total cash price referred to in Sched.1, para.4,

the agreement must state:

- the total charge for credit, with a list of its constituent parts (Sched.1, para.9(1));
- the rate of interest on the credit to be provided under the agreement or, where more than one such rate applies, all the rates in all cases quoted on an annual basis with details of when each rate applies (Sched.1, para.9(2)); and
- a statement explaining how and when interest charges are calculated and applied under the agreement (Sched.1, para.9(3)).

Paragraph 9 of Sched.1 was substantially extended by the Consumer Credit (Agreements) (Amendment) Regulations 2004, SI 2004/1482, which came into force on 31 May 2005. Until then, the obligation under para.9 was simply to state the total charge for credit, with or without a list of its constituent parts.

We have already discussed that an item forming part of the total charge for credit cannot, by virtue of CCA 1974, s.9(4), also form part of the credit. For agreements subject to CC(A)R 1983, CC(TCC)R 1980 sets out a list, in reg.4, of items included in the charge for credit and a list, in reg.5, of items excluded from the charge for credit. For example, items included in the total charge for credit include interest, survey costs, legal fees, stamp duty and the premium payable for compulsory insurance whose sole purpose is to pay the credit in the event of death, illness, invalidity or unemployment. Items excluded are sums payable on default, sums payable in any event even if it was a cash transaction (most obviously installation or delivery charges) and all other premiums for insurance.

We have already discussed the issue on 'rate of interest' at **5.6.3** above.

Finally, HHJ Tetlow decided in *Brooks* v. *Northern Rock (Asset Management) plc (formerly Northern Rock plc)* [2009] GCCR 9901 that a statement saying the 'interest payable under this agreement will be debited to the account at the commencement of this agreement' satisfied Sched.1, para.9(3).

If the agreement is for running-account credit or fixed-sum credit falling within para.9(a)–(c), then by para.10 of Sched.1 the agreement must state:

- the total charge for credit with a list of its constituent parts and, in the case of running-account credit, the total charge for credit must be calculated on the same assumptions as are set out in Sched.7, para.1 for the purpose of calculating the APR in place of the assumptions contained in Part IV of CC(TCC)R 1980 that might otherwise apply (CC(A)R 1983, Sched.1, para.10(1));
- the total amount of other charges included in the total charge for credit for the credit to be provided under the agreement except that, where any such charge cannot be stated as an amount, the rate of the charge or the formula in

135

accordance with which it may be calculated and the total amount of the other such charges must be shown separately (Sched.1, para.10(2));

- a statement whether any interest rate to be shown under para.10(2) is fixed or variable (Sched.1, para.10(3)); and
- a statement explaining how and when interest charges are calculated and applied under the agreement (Sched.1, para.10(4)).

If a creditor is unable to exactly state the information required (where relevant) by CC(A)R 1983, Sched.1, paras.9–11 then it may give estimated information based upon the assumptions set out in para.10 (if applicable) or otherwise such assumptions as the creditor can reasonably make in all the circumstances and a statement of those assumptions must be set out in the agreement. Estimated information is often used in running-account debtor-creditor-supplier agreements (typically credit cards) where the charges vary depending on how the credit is used and how much of it is used.

Total amount payable (Sched.1, para.11)

For all agreements falling within CC(A)R 1983, Sched.1, para.9 there must be a statement of the total amount payable, being the total of any amounts to be shown under paras.5, 6 or 7, and 9 of Sched.1. If the information can only be estimated, the creditor is allowed to provide such information subject to the limitations set out under 'Total charge for credit' above.

Timing of repayments (Sched.1, para.12)

All agreements subject to CC(A)R 1983 must state the timing of repayments to be made under the agreement expressed by reference to one or more of the following:

- the dates on which each repayment is to be made (Sched.1, para.12(a));
- the frequency and number of the repayments and the date of the first repayment or a statement indicating the manner in which that date will be determined (Sched.1, para.12(b));
- a statement indicating the manner in which the dates of the repayments will be determined (Sched.1, para.12(c)).

The term 'repayments' is defined by CC(A)R 1983, reg.1(3) as the whole or any part of the credit, payment of the whole or any part of the total charge for credit or a combination of the two. These provisions seem to increase in flexibility as one works through them. Paragraph 12(a) is plainly satisfied by stating the date and can be combined with para.12(b) to give the following wording:

Repayments

You are required to repay the total amount payable by sixty monthly instalments of £350.00, each of which must be paid on or before the first day of each month. The first payment must be made on the date of this agreement.

Amount of repayments (Sched.1, paras.13, 14 and 14A)

All agreements except those falling within CC(A)R 1983, Sched.1, para.14 (which covers mortgage interest relief at source) must state the amount of each repayment under the agreement as (Sched.1, para.13(a)–(d)):

(a)   a sum of money;
(b)   a specified proportion of a specified amount (including the amount outstanding from time to time);
(c)   a combination of (a) and (b); or
(d)   in a case where the amount of any repayment cannot be expressed in accordance with (a), (b) or (c), a statement indicating the manner in which the amount will be determined.

If the agreement provides credit to be repayable by two or more instalments and the interest is of a type to which the Finance Act 1982, s.26 and Sched 7 applies (commonly known as MIRAS), then by CC(A)R 1983, Sched.1, para.14(a)–(d) the agreement must state the amount of each repayment to be made under the agreement (with or without the equivalent repayment after deduction of tax in accordance with MIRAS) expressed as:

(a)   a sum of money;
(b)   a specified proportion of a specified amount (including the amount outstanding from time to time);
(c)   a combination of para.14(a) and (b); or
(d)   in a case where the amount of any repayment cannot be expressed in accordance with para.14(a), (b) or (c), a statement indicating the manner in which the amount will be determined,

provided that, where the amounts to be paid by the debtor after deduction of MIRAS are the same, the requirements of Sched.1, para.14 may be satisfied by a statement indicating the lowest and highest amounts of the repayments to be made under the agreement before deduction of tax.

For all types where different interest rates or different charges or both are, or will be, at any time during the term of the agreement payable for:

• credit provided under the agreement for different purposes; or
• under each of the different parts of the agreement,

whether or not the agreement is a multiple agreement, Sched.1, para.14A states that there must be a statement of the order or proportions in which any amount paid by the debtor which is not sufficient to discharge the total debt then due under the agreement will be applied or appropriated by the creditor towards the discharge of the sums due: (i) for the amounts of credit provided for different purposes; or (ii) different parts of the agreement, as the case may be.

APR (Sched.1, paras.15–17)

Paragraph 15 of CC(A)R 1983, Sched.1 requires, for all agreements except those falling within para.16, information on the agreement's APR or a statement indicating that the total amount payable under the agreement is not greater than the total cash price of the goods, services, land or other things, the acquisition of which is to be financed by credit under the agreement (i.e. that there is no charge for credit at all).

By Sched.1, para.16, debtor-creditor-supplier agreements for running-account credit under which the debtor agrees to pay the creditor an amount specified in the agreement on specified occasions, there is a credit limit and charges for credit are either a fixed amount in respect of each transaction or calculated as a proportion of the price payable under a transaction financed by the credit, must state the APR for the agreement calculated on the following assumptions:

- the first assumption is that:

  - the debtor is provided with an amount of credit at the date of the making of the agreement which, taken with the amount of the charge for that credit ascertained at that date, is equal to the credit limit (para.16(2)(a)); and
  - the debtor repays the sum of the amounts referred to in para.16(2)(a) by payments of the amounts specified in the agreement on the occasions specified in the agreement and makes no other payment and obtains no further credit in relation to the account (para.16(2)(b)); and

- second, the same assumption set out in para.16(2) except that the sum of the amounts referred to in para.16(2)(a) must be taken to be one-third of the credit limit.

By Sched.1, para.17, agreements where the APR is based on a total charge for credit which is calculated to take account of relief available under the Income and Corporation Taxes Act 1970 (ICTA 1970), s.19 and the Finance Act 1976 (FA 1976), Sched.4 must include a statement indicating that it has been assumed when calculating the agreement's APR that relief may be available under ICTA 1970, s.19 and FA 1976, Sched.4 for premiums under certain policies of insurance without any deduction under ICTA 1970, s.21.

The APR must be stated to one decimal place and there are tolerances set out in CC(A)R 1983, Sched.7. These are discussed at **5.9.2** below.

It is important to remember that the APR is generated from the figures: not the other way around. Recently, the High Court considered another consumer credit challenge based on the wrong APR in *Joseph Sternlight* v. *Barclays Bank plc and others* [2010] EWHC 1865 (QB). In short, the borrowers re-calculated the figures based upon the APR (which was rounded to one decimal place) and argued that the agreement was irredeemably unenforceable. HHJ Waksman QC correctly noted that the APR is the result of calculations: it is not the driver for the figures.

Variable rates or items (Sched.1, paras.18–19A)

For agreements under which the rate or amount of any item included in the charge for credit will, or may, be varied (other than a variation as a result of an event which is certain to take place), then by CC(A)R 1983, Sched.1, para.18 there must be a statement indicating that in calculating the APR no account has been taken of any variation which may occur under the agreement of the rate or amount of any item entering into that calculation. The most obvious example is a variable rate of interest on the credit. The Court of Appeal's decision in *Lombard Tricity Finance Ltd* v. *Paton* [1989] 1 All ER 918 makes it clear that where the agreement allowed the creditor to vary on notice at its discretion, a statement saying it will do so is enough.

For agreements falling within Sched.1, para.18, there must also be (by Sched.1, para.19) a statement indicating the circumstances in which any variation may take place and, where that information can be found out at the time at which the document referred to in CCA 1974, s.61(1) is presented or sent to the debtor for signature, the time at which any such variation may occur.

If the agreement is land related and CC(TCC)R 1980, reg.15A applies then, by virtue of Sched.1, para.19A, it must.

- state the initial standard variable rate within the meaning of CC(TCC)R 1980, reg.15A(2); and
- explain what the rate is and that it has been taken into account when calculating the APR.

Security (Sched.1, paras.20 and 21)

If a debtor has given an item in pawn within the meaning of CCA 1974, s.114 (which is discussed at **9.7**), and no separate pawn-receipt is given then, by CC(A)R 1983, Sched.1, para.20, the agreement must indicate that an article has been taken in pawn and describe that item to allow it to be identified.

For all other agreements where security is provided by the debtor to secure the carrying out of obligations under the agreement, there must be, by Sched.1, para.21, a description of the security sufficient to indentify it and:

- a general description of any stocks and shares (including any right to become a stockholder or shareholder) to which it relates; and
- in any other case, a description of the subject matter to which it relates.

It is important to remember that Sched.1, para.22 only applies where security is given by the debtor: it does not, therefore, apply to security given by anyone else.

Charges (Sched.1, para.22)

For all agreements, CC(A)R 1983, Sched.1, para.22 requires:

- a list of any charges payable under the agreement to the creditor upon (as the case may be) failure by the debtor or a relative of his to do, or not do, something which he is required to do or not do (Sched.1, para.22(1));
- a statement indicating any item of the agreement which provides for charges not required to be shown under para.22(1) or not included in the total charge for credit (Sched.1, para.22(2)).

The information required by Sched.1, para.22 therefore includes charges for missed direct debit payments, service of notices, recovering possession of goods or land or payments made for the debtor (including insurance premiums, parking fines or repair costs).

Cancellation rights (Sched.1, para.23)

For all agreements that cannot be cancelled by the debtor under CCA 1974 or the Financial Services (Distance Marketing) Regulations 2004, SI 2004/2095, there must be a statement that the debtor has no right to cancel under CCA 1974 or the Financial Services (Distance Marketing) Regulations 2004.

Right of withdrawal (Sched.1, para.23A)

For agreements (unless CC(A)R 2010 applies) under which the creditor provides the debtor with credit exceeding £62,260 or entered into by the debtor wholly or predominantly for the purposes of a business carried on, or intended to be carried on, by him, there must be a statement of the debtor's right under CCA 1974, s.66A to withdraw from the consumer credit agreement including:

- the right to withdraw within 14 days without the debtor having to give any reason (CC(A)R 1983, Sched.1, para.23A(1));
- when the period of withdrawal begins and ends (Sched.1, para.23A(2));
- the requirement on the debtor to give the creditor notice, either orally or written, of his intention to withdraw (Sched.1, para.23A(3));
- contact details explaining how the debtor can give this notification (Sched.1, para.23A(4));
- the requirement for the debtor to repay the credit without delay and no later than 30 calendar days after giving notice of withdrawal (Sched.1, para.3A(5));
- the requirement to pay, without delay and no later than 30 calendar days after giving notice of withdrawal, the interest accrued from the date the credit was provided to the date of repaying it (Sched.1, para.23A(6));
- the amount of interest payable each day expressed as a sum of money (Sched.1, para.23A(7)).

The creditor does not need to give the information required by para.23A(7) where the agreement is for running-account credit and it is not practicable for the creditor to state the amount of interest payable each day. Instead, the agreement must state that if credit is drawn down during the withdrawal period, the creditor must inform the debtor, on request and without delay, of the amount of interest payable each day.

Amount payable on early settlement (Sched.1, para.24)

Under CC(A)R 1983, Sched.1, para.24, agreements for fixed-sum credit secured on land for a term of more than one month must:

- state examples based on the amount of credit provided under the agreement or the nominal amount of either £1,000 or £100, showing the amount that would be payable if the debtor exercises his right under CCA 1974, s.94 to discharge his indebtedness when:

  (a) a quarter of the agreement had passed;
  (b) half of the agreement had passed; and
  (c) three-quarters of the agreement had passed,

  or on the first repayment date after each of those dates;
- include a statement explaining that, in calculating the amounts shown, no account has been taken of any variation which might occur under the agreement and that the amounts are therefore only illustrative.

Statement of debtor's right of early repayment (Sched.1, para.24A)

For agreements (unless CC(A)R 2010 applies) under which the creditor provides the debtor with credit exceeding £62,260 or entered into by the debtor wholly or predominantly for the purposes of a business carried on, or intended to be carried on, by him, there must be a statement providing details of the debtor's right of early repayment under CCA 1974, s.94 including:

- the fact that the debtor has the right to repay early in full or part;
- the procedure for early repayment; and
- where applicable, details of the creditor's right to compensation under CCA 1974, s.95A and the manner in which it will be determined.

5.6.5 Statements of protection and remedies

Under CC(A)R 1983, reg.2(3) a regulated consumer credit agreement (other than 'exempted agreements') must contain statements of protection and remedies available to debtors under CCA 1974 set out in Sched.2. Like prescribed terms and information, the forms of statement that need to be included on the agreement are only those that are relevant to the agreement in question. For example, a fixed-sum loan agreement does not need to include Form 7 because this is only relevant to a hire-purchase or conditional sale agreement.

The forms of statement are as summarised below.

Form 1: Statement of your rights

If the agreement is subject to CCA 1974, s.58(1) then it must include a statement in the following form:

YOUR RIGHTS

Under the Consumer Credit Act 1974, you should have been given a copy of this agreement at least seven days ago so you could consider whether you wanted to go ahead. If the creditor did not give you a copy of this agreement he can only enforce it with a court order.

Form 2: Missing payments

All agreements must include a statement in the following form:

MISSING PAYMENTS

Missing payments could have severe consequences and make obtaining credit more difficult.

Form 3: Agreements secured on land

If the agreement is secured on land then it must include a statement in the following form:

YOUR HOME MAY BE REPOSSESSED

Your home may be repossessed if you do not keep up repayments on a mortgage or other debt secured on it.

Form 4: Cancellable agreement subject to CCA 1974, s.68(b)

If the agreement is a cancellable agreement subject to CCA 1974, s.68(b) then it must include a statement in the following form:

YOUR RIGHT TO CANCEL

You can cancel this agreement within FOURTEEN days (starting the day after you signed it) by giving WRITTEN notice to *.

If you intend to cancel, you should not use any goods you have under the agreement and you should keep them safe. You can wait for them to be collected and you do not need to hand them over until you receive a written request for them.

The creditor must, in place of the *, insert:

- the name and address of the person to whom the notice may be given; or
- an indication of the person to whom a notice may be given with clear reference to the place in the agreement where his name and address appears.

Form 5: Cancellable agreement not subject to Form 4 or Form 6

If the agreement is cancellable but is not caught by Form 4 or Form 6 then it must include a statement in the following form:

YOUR RIGHT TO CANCEL

Once you have signed this agreement you will have a short time in which you can cancel [it][that part of this agreement which is regulated by the Consumer Credit Act 1974]*. The creditor will send you exact details of how and when you can do this.

The creditor must delete the passage in square brackets which does not apply to the agreement. For example, if the agreement is partly regulated, the word '[it]' and the other square brackets must be deleted so it reads:

Once you have signed this agreement you will have a short time in which you can cancel that part of this agreement which is regulated by the Consumer Credit Act 1974. The creditor will send you exact details of how and when you can do this.

Alternatively, if the agreement is fully regulated by CCA 1974 then the creditor must delete the words '[that part of this agreement which is regulated by the Consumer Credit Act 1974]' and also remove the remaining square brackets so it reads:

Once you have signed this agreement you will have a short time in which you can cancel it. The creditor will send you exact details of how and when you can do this.

Form 6: Cancellable modifying agreement under CCA 1974, s.82(5)

If the agreement is a modifying agreement and is treated as being cancellable by virtue of CCA 1974, s.82(5) then it must include a statement in the following form:

YOUR RIGHT TO CANCEL

This agreement modifies an earlier agreement. Once you have signed this agreement your right to cancel [that part of]* the earlier agreement [which was regulated by the Consumer Credit Act 1974]* will be widened to cover the [regulated]* agreement as modified. The cancellation period itself will be unchanged. Details of how to cancel are given in your copy of this agreement.

The creditor must delete the passages in square brackets unless the modifying agreement is partly unregulated by CCA 1974. If the modifying agreement is wholly regulated by CCA 1974, it will therefore read:

This agreement modifies an earlier agreement. Once you have signed this agreement your right to cancel the earlier agreement will be widened to cover the agreement as modified. The cancellation period itself will be unchanged. Details of how to cancel are given in your copy of this agreement.

Form 7: Agreements for hire purchase or conditional sale of goods

For hire purchase or conditional sale agreements relating to goods (and not land) that do not fall within Form 8, there must be a statement in the following form:

TERMINATION: YOUR RIGHTS

You have a right to end this agreement. To do so, you should write to the person you make your payments to. They will then be entitled to the return of the goods and to [the cost of installing the goods plus half the rest of the total amount payable under this agreement, that is][half the total amount payable under this agreement, that is]* £x**. If you have already paid at least this amount plus any overdue instalments and have taken reasonable care of the goods, you will not have to pay any more.

If the amount is calculated in accordance with CCA 1974, s.100 then the creditor must select the appropriate wording in the square brackets (but delete the square brackets only) followed by * (i.e. 'the cost of installing the goods plus half the rest of the total amount payable under this agreement, that is' if there is an installation charge under the agreement or 'half the total amount payable under this agreement, that is' if there is not). If the agreement provides for an amount below the minimum prescribed by CCA 1974, s.100 then both the passages in the square brackets followed by * must be deleted.

The creditor must insert, in place of 'x**' the amount calculated in accordance with the provisions of CCA 1974, s.100 or such lower sum as the agreement may provide.

Form 8: Agreements modifying an agreement for hire purchase or conditional sale of goods

If the agreement modifies a hire-purchase or conditional sale agreement relating to goods (and not land) then it must include a statement in the following form:

TERMINATION: YOUR RIGHTS

You have the right to end this agreement. To do so, write to the person you make your payments to. They will then be entitled to the return of the goods and to [the cost of installing the goods plus half the total amount yet to be paid under the earlier agreement as modified by this agreement, that is][half the total amount payable under the earlier agreement as modified by this agreement, that is]* £x**. If you have already paid at least this amount, plus any overdue instalments and have taken reasonable care of the goods, you will not have to pay any more.

If the amount is calculated in accordance with CCA 1974, s.100, then the creditor must select the appropriate wording in the square brackets (but delete the square brackets only) followed by * (i.e. 'the cost of installing the goods plus half the total amount yet to be paid under the earlier agreement as modified by this agreement, that is' if there is an installation charge under the agreement or 'half the total amount payable under the earlier agreement as modified by this agreement, that is' if there is not). If the modified agreement provides for an amount below the minimum prescribed by CCA 1974, s.100 then both the passages in the square brackets followed by * must be deleted.

The creditor must insert, in place of 'x**' the amount calculated in accordance with the provisions of CCA 1974, s.100 or such lower sum as the modified agreement may provide.

Form 9: Conditional sale agreement secured on land

If the agreement is a conditional sale agreement secured on land (and not caught by Form 10) then it must include a statement in the following form:

TERMINATION: YOUR RIGHTS

Until the title to the land has passed to you, you have a right to end this agreement. To do so write to the person you make your payments to. They will then be entitled to the return of the land and to [half the total amount payable under this agreement, that is]* £x**. If, at the time you end this agreement, you have already paid at least this amount plus any overdue instalments and you have taken reasonable care of the land, you will not have to pay any more.

If the amount is calculated in accordance with CCA 1974, s.100, then the creditor must keep the wording in the square brackets (but delete the square brackets only) followed by * (i.e. 'half the total amount payable under this agreement, that is'). If the agreement provides for an amount below the minimum prescribed by CCA 1974, s.100 then the passage in the square brackets followed by * is to be deleted.

The creditor must insert, in place of 'x**' the amount calculated in accordance with the provisions of CCA 1974, s.100 or such lower sum as the agreement may provide.

Form 10: Agreements modifying conditional sale agreements relating to land

If the agreement modifies a conditional sale agreement relating to land then it must include a statement in the following form:

TERMINATION: YOUR RIGHTS

Until the title to the land has passed to you, you have a right to end this agreement. To do so write to the person you make your payments to. They will then be entitled to the return of the land and to [half the total amount payable under your earlier agreement as modified by this agreement, that is]* £x**. If you have already paid at least this amount plus any overdue instalments and taken reasonable care of the land, you will not have to pay any more.

If the amount is calculated in accordance with CCA 1974, s.100 then the creditor must keep the wording in the square brackets (but delete the square brackets only) followed by * (i.e. 'half the total amount payable under your earlier agreement as modified by this agreement, that is'). If the agreement provides for an amount below the minimum prescribed by CCA 1974, s.100 then the passage in the square brackets followed by * is to be deleted.

The creditor must insert, in place of 'x**' the amount calculated in accordance with the provisions of CCA 1974, s.100 or such lower sum as the agreement may provide.

Form 11: Agreements for hire purchase or conditional sale of goods

For hire-purchase or conditional sale agreements relating to goods (and not land) that do not fall within Form 12, there must be a statement in the following form:

REPOSSESSION: YOUR RIGHTS

If you do not keep your side of this agreement but you have paid at least [the cost of installing the goods plus one third of the rest of the total amount payable under this agreement, that is][one third of the total amount payable under this agreement, that is]* £x** the creditor may not take back the goods against your wishes unless he gets a court order. (In Scotland he may need to get a court order at any time.) If he does take the goods without your consent or a court order, you have the right to get back any money that you have paid under this agreement.

The creditor must select the appropriate wording in the square brackets (but delete the square brackets only) followed by * (i.e. either 'the cost of installing the goods plus one third of the rest of the total amount payable under this agreement, that is' or 'one third of the total amount payable under this agreement, that is').

The creditor must insert, in place of 'x**' the amount calculated in accordance with the provisions of CCA 1974, s.90.

Form 12: Agreements modifying an agreement for hire purchase or conditional sale of goods

If the agreement modifies a hire-purchase or conditional sale agreement relating to goods (and not land) then it must include a statement in the following form:

REPOSSESSION: YOUR RIGHTS

If you do not keep to your side of this agreement [but you have paid at least £x*]** the creditor may not take back the goods against your wishes unless he gets a court order. (In Scotland he may need to get a court order at any time.) If he does take the goods back without your consent or a court order, you have the right to get back all the money you have paid under this agreement.

The creditor must insert, in place of 'x*' the amount calculated in accordance with the provisions of CCA 1974, s.90.

The creditor must delete the wording in the square brackets followed by ** (i.e. 'but you have paid at least £x*') if the goods were protected at the time the modifying agreement was made.

Form 13: Pawn agreements subject to CCA 1974, s.114

If the agreement is subject to CCA 1974, s.114 and an article is taken in pawn then it must include a statement in the following form:

IMPORTANT – READ THIS CAREFULLY TO FIND OUT ABOUT YOUR RIGHTS

The Consumer Credit Act 1974 lays down certain requirements for your protection which should have been complied with when this agreement was made. If they were not, the creditor cannot enforce this agreement without getting a court order.

The Act also gives you a number of rights. In particular you should read the NOTICE TO DEBTOR [in this agreement]*[in your pawn receipt].**

If you would like to know more about your rights under the Act, contact either your local Trading Standards Department or your nearest Citizens' Advice Bureau.

If the agreement does not include a separate pawn-receipt, the third paragraph should read:

> The Act also gives you a number of rights. In particular you should read the NOTICE TO DEBTOR in this agreement.

If the debtor is given a separate pawn-receipt then the third paragraph should read:

> The Act also gives you a number of rights. In particular you should read the NOTICE TO DEBTOR in your pawn receipt.

Form 14: Debtor-creditor-supplier agreements falling within s.12(b) or (c), and multiple agreements not falling within para.15 of which at least one part is a debtor-creditor-supplier agreement falling within s.12(b) or (c)

For these types of agreements, the most obvious of which is a restricted-use loan for the purchase of goods or services, there must be a statement in the following form:

IMPORTANT – READ THIS CAREFULLY TO FIND OUT ABOUT YOUR RIGHTS

The Consumer Credit Act 1974 lays down certain requirements for your protection which should have been complied with when this agreement was made. If they were not, the creditor cannot enforce this agreement without getting a court order.

The Act also gives you a number of rights:

1) You can settle this agreement at any time by giving notice [in writing]* and paying off the amount you owe under the agreement [which may be reduced by a rebate]** [Examples indicating the amount you have to pay appear in the agreement.]***

[2) You can settle this agreement in part at any time by giving notice and paying off some of the amount you owe.]****

[3) If you received unsatisfactory goods or services paid for under this agreement [, apart from any bought with a cash loan,]***** you may have a right to sue the supplier, the creditor or both.

4) If the contract is not fulfilled, perhaps because the supplier has gone out of business, you may still be able to sue the creditor.]******

If you would like to know more about your rights under the Act, contact either your local Trading Standards Department or your nearest Citizens' Advice Bureau.

If the agreement is secured on land, the creditor must include the phrase 'in writing' immediately before '*' and delete the square brackets.

If the debtor is entitled to a rebate on early settlement under the Consumer Credit (Early Settlement) Regulations 2004, SI 2004/1483 then the creditor must include the phrase 'which may be reduced by a rebate' immediately before '**' and delete the square brackets.

If the agreement is for fixed-sum credit for a term of more than one month and secured on land, the creditor must include the phrase 'Examples indicating the amount you have to pay appear in the agreement' immediately before '***' and delete the square brackets. Otherwise, this phrase need not be included.

If the agreement is secured on land, the creditor must delete the phrase '(2) You can settle this agreement in part at any time by giving notice and paying off some of the amount you owe.' immediately before '****' and the square brackets.

If the agreement is a multiple agreement, of which at least one part is a debtor-creditor-supplier agreement falling within CCA 1974, s.12(b) or (c) and at least one part is a debtor-creditor agreement falling within CCA 1974, s.13(c), then the creditor must include the phrase ', apart from any bought with a cash loan,' immediately before '*****' and delete the square brackets. Otherwise, it should be deleted.

The creditor may delete the text in (3) and (4) where agreement is a debtor-creditor-supplier agreement for running-account credit:

- which provides for the making of payments by the debtor in relation to specified periods which, in the case of an agreement which is not secured on land, do not exceed three months; and
- which requires that the number of payments to be made by the debtor in repayments of the whole amount of credit provided in such period must not exceed.

Form 15: Multiple agreements where at least one part is an unregulated credit agreement

If the agreement is a multiple agreement where at least one part is an unregulated credit agreement then there must be a statement in the following form:

IMPORTANT – READ THIS CAREFULLY TO FIND OUT ABOUT YOUR RIGHTS

That part of this agreement which deals with [ ]* is a regulated agreement under the Consumer Credit Act 1974. As a result certain requirements for your protection should have been complied with when it was made. If they were not, the creditor cannot enforce this agreement without a court order.

The Act also gives you a number of rights. [You can settle the regulated agreement at any time by giving notice [in writing]** and paying off the amount you owe under this agreement [which may be reduced by a rebate]*** [Examples indicating the amount you have to pay appear in the agreement.]****]

[You can settle this agreement in part at any time by giving notice and paying off some of the amount you owe.]*****

If you would like to know more about your rights under the Act, contact either your local Trading Standards Department or your nearest Citizens' Advice Bureau.

The creditor must include, in place of the phrase '[ ]' immediately before '*', a description of the regulated agreement. For example, this may be 'the cash advance facility' or 'the hire-purchase agreement'.

If the agreement is secured on land, the creditor must include the phrase 'in writing' immediately before '**' and delete the square brackets.

If the debtor is entitled to a rebate on early settlement under the Consumer Credit (Early Settlement) Regulations 2004 then the creditor must include the phrase 'which may be reduced by a rebate' immediately before '***' and delete the square brackets.

If the agreement is for fixed-sum credit for a term of more than one month and secured on land, the creditor must include the phrase 'Examples indicating the amount you have to pay appear in the agreement' immediately before '****' and delete the square brackets. Otherwise, this phrase need not be included.

If the agreement is secured on land, the creditor must delete the phrase 'You can settle this agreement in part at any time by giving notice and paying off some of the amount you owe.' immediately before '*****' and the square brackets.

Form 16: All types of agreements not included in Forms 13 to 15

For all other agreements not included in Forms 13 to 15, the agreement must contain a statement in the following form:

IMPORTANT – READ THIS CAREFULLY TO FIND OUT ABOUT YOUR RIGHTS

The Consumer Credit Act 1974 lays down certain requirements for your protection which should have been complied with when this agreement was made. If they were not, the creditor cannot enforce this agreement without getting a court order.

The Act also gives you a number of rights. [You can settle this agreement at any time by giving notice [in writing]* and paying off the amount you owe under the agreement [which may be reduced by a rebate]**. [Examples indicating the amount you have to pay appear in the agreement.]***

[You can settle this agreement in part at any time by giving notice and paying off some of the amount you owe.]****

If you would like to know more about your rights under the Act, contact either your local Trading Standards Department or your nearest Citizens' Advice Bureau.

If the agreement is secured on land, the creditor must include the phrase 'in writing' immediately before '*' and delete the square brackets.

If the debtor is entitled to a rebate on early settlement under the Consumer Credit (Early Settlement) Regulations 2004, then the creditor must include the phrase 'which may be reduced by a rebate' immediately before '**' and delete the square brackets.

If the agreement is for fixed-sum credit for a term of more than one month and secured on land, the creditor must include the phrase 'Examples indicating the amount you have to pay appear in the agreement' immediately before '***' and delete the square brackets. Otherwise, this phrase need not be included.

If the agreement is secured on land, the creditor must delete the phrase 'You can settle this agreement in part at any time by giving notice and paying off some of the amount you owe.' immediately before '****' and the square brackets.

Form 17: Credit-token agreements

If the agreement is for a credit-token (like a credit card) which makes the debtor liable for the creditor's loss resulting from misuse of the credit-token by other persons then it must include a statement in the following form:

THEFT, LOSS OR MISUSE OF CREDIT-TOKEN*

If your credit-token* is lost, stolen or misused by someone without your permission, you may have to pay up to £x** of any loss to the creditor. If it is misused with your permission you will probably be liable for ALL losses. You will not be liable to the creditor for losses which take place after you have told the creditor about the theft, etc [as long as you confirm this in writing within seven days].***

[However, the credit-token* can also be used under an agreement to which this protection does not apply. As a result, there may be circumstances under which you may have to pay for all the losses to the creditor.]****

Instead of using the phrase 'credit-token', the creditor may insert (in place of credit-token*) the specific designation or trade name of the credit-token. This is often done by credit card providers as they use the phrase 'credit card' in place of 'credit-token'. If the creditor uses 'credit-token' it must still delete the '*' which immediately follows it.

The creditor must insert, in place of 'x**', the extent of the debtor's liability as set out in CCA 1974, s.84(1) or the credit limit (if lower) or such lower figure as the creditor decides.

If written notification is not required, the creditor must delete the phrase 'as long as you confirm this in writing within seven days' immediately before '***' and the square brackets. If written notice is required, the creditor need only delete the square brackets.

If the passage immediately before '****' is inapplicable, the creditor must delete it together with the square brackets.

Form 18: Pawn agreements with no separate pawn-receipt

If the agreement is subject to CCA 1974, s.114, and an article is taken in pawn where no separate pawn-receipt is given, then the agreement must include a statement in the following form:

NOTICE TO THE DEBTOR IMPORTANT – YOU SHOULD READ THIS CAREFULLY

Right to Redeem Articles

If you hand in this agreement (which is also your pawn-receipt) and pay the amount you owe, you may redeem the article(s) in pawn at any time within 6 months of the date of this agreement or any longer time agreed with the creditor ('the redemption period').

IF YOU DO NOT REDEEM THE ARTICLE(S) ON OR BEFORE * YOU MAY LOSE YOUR RIGHT TO REDEEM IT (THEM).

Loss of Receipt

If you lose your receipt you may provide either a statutory declaration or, if the credit (or credit limit) is not more than £x** and the creditor agrees a signed statement instead. The creditor may provide the form to be used and may charge for doing so.

Unredeemed Articles

An article not redeemed within the redemption period becomes the creditor's property if the credit (or credit limit) is not more than £x*** and the redemption period is 6 months. In any other case it may be sold by the creditor, but it continues to be redeemable until it is sold. Interest is payable until the actual date of redemption. Where the credit (or credit limit) is more than £x**** the creditor must give you 14 days' notice of his intention to sell. When an article has been sold you will receive information about the sale. If the proceeds (less expenses) are more that the amount that would have been payable to redeem the article on the date of the sale you will be entitled to receive the extra amount. If the proceeds are less than the amount you will owe the creditor the shortfall.

Your goods will not be insured by the creditor while they are in pawn.*****

In place of '*' the creditor must insert the date at the end of the redemption period. Instead of 'x**', the creditor must insert the amount specified in CCA 1974, s.118(1)(b). Instead of 'x***', the creditor must insert the amount specified in CCA 1974, s.120(1)(a). Instead of 'x****', the creditor must insert the amount specified in the Consumer Credit (Realisation of Pawn) Regulations 1983, SI 1983/1568. The creditor must delete the phrase 'Your goods will not be insured by the creditor while they are in pawn' immediately before '*****' if it is inapplicable.

5.6.6 Signature boxes

A regulated consumer credit agreement must also include, by CC(A)R 1983, reg.2(7), a signature box in the Form numbered in column 1 of Part I of CC(A)R 1983, Sched.5 and set out in column 3 in so far as it relates to the type of agreement referred to in column 2 and must:

- if the documents embody a principal agreement and subsidiary agreement to which CC(A)R 1983, reg.2(9) applies, or at the time of entering into the agreement the debtor is also purchasing an optional contract of insurance which will be financed by credit advanced under that agreement, contain a form of consent in the Form set out in Part III of Sched.5 immediately below the signature box; and
- if the agreement is: (i) one to which CCA 1974, s.58(1) applies; (ii) a cancellable agreement; or (iii) an agreement under which a person takes any article in pawn and under which the pawn-receipt is not separate from the document embodying the agreement, then it must contain a separate box (immediately above, below or next to the signature box) containing the statements (where relevant) in Forms 1 and 4 to 6 of Part I, and in Part II, of CC(A)R 1983, Sched.2.

Form 1: Hire-purchase agreements

Hire-purchase agreements must include the following signature box:

> This is a Hire-Purchase Agreement regulated by the Consumer Credit Act 1974. Sign it only if you want to be legally bound by its terms.
>
> Signature(s)
> of Debtor(s)
> Date(s) of signature(s)
>
> The goods will not become your property until you have made all the payments. You must not sell them before then.

The note to this Form makes it clear that the creditor may delete the wording 'Date(s) of signature(s)' where the date is not required by virtue of CC(A)R 1983, reg.6(3)(c).

Form 2: Conditional sale agreements relating to land

Conditional sale agreements relating to land must include the following signature box:

> This is a Conditional Sale Agreement regulated by the Consumer Credit Act 1974. Sign it only if you want to be legally bound by its terms.

Signature(s)
of Debtor(s)
Date(s) of signature(s)

The land will not become your property until you have made * payments. You must not sell it before then.

The note to this Form again makes it clear that the creditor may delete the wording 'Date(s) of signature(s)' where the date is not required by virtue of CC(A)R 1983, reg.6(3)(c). The creditor must also insert, in place of '*', the phrase 'all the' or the number of payments (as appropriate).

Form 3: Conditional sale agreements relating to goods

Conditional sale agreements relating to goods must include the following signature box:

This is a Conditional Sale Agreement regulated by the Consumer Credit Act 1974. Sign it only if you want to be legally bound by its terms.

Signature(s)
of Debtor(s)
Date(s) of signature(s)

The goods will not become your property until you have made * payments. You must not sell them before then.

The note to this Form again makes it clear that the creditor may delete the wording 'Date(s) of signature(s)' where the date is not required by virtue of CC(A)R 1983, reg.6(3)(c). The creditor must also insert, in place of '*', the phrase 'all the' or the number of payments (as appropriate).

Form 4: Pawn agreements where agreement not separate from the pawn-receipt

Agreements under which an article is taken in pawn and where the agreement is not separate from the pawn-receipt must include the following signature box:

This is a Credit Agreement regulated by the Consumer Credit Act 1974. Sign it only if you want to be legally bound by its terms.

Signature(s)
of Debtor(s)
Date(s) of signature(s)

This document is also your PAWN-RECEIPT. Keep it safely.

The note to this Form again makes it clear that the creditor may delete the wording 'Date(s) of signature(s)' where the date is not required by virtue of CC(A)R 1983, reg.6(3)(c).

Form 5: Multiple agreements where one part is not regulated

If there is a multiple agreement where at least one part is not regulated, it must include the following signature box:

> This is a Credit Agreement partly regulated by the Consumer Credit Act 1974. Sign it only if you want to be legally bound by its terms.
>
> Signature(s)
> of Debtor(s)
> Date(s) of signature(s)

The note to this Form again makes it clear that the creditor may delete the wording 'Date(s) of signature(s)' where the date is not required by virtue of CC(A)R 1983, reg.6(3)(c).

Form 6: Other agreements

Agreements not subject to Forms 1 to 5 or 7 and 8 must include the following signature box:

> This is a Credit Agreement regulated by the Consumer Credit Act 1974. Sign it only if you want to be legally bound by its terms.
>
> Signature(s)
> of Debtor(s)
> Date(s) of signature(s)

The note to this Form again makes it clear that the creditor may delete the wording 'Date(s) of signature(s)' where the date is not required by virtue of CC(A)R 1983, reg.6(3)(c).

Form 7: Modifying agreements varying or supplementing earlier agreements of which at least one part was not regulated and where at least one part of modified agreement is not regulated

Modifying agreements varying or supplementing earlier agreements of which at least one part was not regulated by CCA 1974, and where at least one part of the modified agreement is not regulated by CCA 1974, must include the following signature box:

This Agreement varies and/or supplements a Credit Agreement and is partly regulated by the Consumer Credit Act 1974. Sign it only if you want to be legally bound by the new terms.

Signature(s)
of Debtor(s)
Date(s) of signature(s)

The note to this Form again makes it clear that the creditor may delete the wording 'Date(s) of signature(s)' where the date is not required by virtue of CC(A)R 1983, reg.6(3)(c).

Form 8: Other modifying agreements

Modifying agreements other than those included in Form 7 must include the following signature box:

This Agreement varies and/or supplements a * Agreement regulated by the Consumer Credit Act 1974. Sign it only if you want to be legally bound by the new terms.

Signature(s)
of Debtor(s)
Date(s) of signature(s)

The note to this Form again makes it clear that the creditor may delete the wording 'Date(s) of signature(s)' where the date is not required by virtue of CC(A)R 1983, reg.6(3)(c). The creditor must also insert, in place of '*', the phrase 'Hire-Purchase' or 'Conditional Sale' or 'Credit' depending on the nature of the modified agreement.

5.6.7   Further signature box: separate form of consent

It is, once again, notable that the requirement for agreements to contain a form of consent in the Form set out in CC(A)R 1983, Sched.5, Part III only came into force on 31 May 2005. It is a fairly common consent box, particularly where payment protection insurance is sold, and is set out below:

I wish to purchase [creditor to list the product(s) being offered] [ ] (please tick)

I understand that I am purchasing the product(s) ticked above on credit provided by you and that the terms relating to the credit for the products can be found [creditor to insert the cross-references to the terms of the agreement containing the terms relating to the credit for the products being purchased] in this agreement.

Your signature(s):

5.7   FORM AND CONTENT OF PAWN-RECEIPTS UNDER CC(A)R 1983

If a pawn-receipt is given under CCA 1974, s.114(1) by a person taking an article in pawn under:

- a regulated consumer credit agreement; or
- a modifying agreement varying or supplementing an earlier credit agreement which is, or is treated under CCA 1974, s.82(3) as being, a regulated agreement,

then, where the pawn-receipt is not separate from any document embodying such an agreement, it must contain (in addition to the relevant matters discussed at **5.6** above):

- the information set out in CC(A)R 1983, Sched.1, paras.1, 2 and 20 (which are discussed at **5.6.4** above) or, in the case of a modifying agreement, CC(A)R 1983, Sched.8, paras.1, 2 and 20; and
- a notice in Form 18 of CC(A)R 1983, Sched.2 (as set at **5.6.5** above).

5.8   FORM AND CONTENT OF CONSUMER HIRE AGREEMENTS UNDER CC(A)R 1983

5.8.1   Introduction

The provisions of CC(A)R 1983 for consumer hire agreements have been untouched by the CCD. Owners therefore providing goods under regulated consumer hire agreements need only be concerned with CC(A)R 1983. By CC(A)R 1983, reg.3(1) (and subject to reg.3(2)), a document embodying a regulated consumer hire agreement must include the information set out in CC(A)R 1983, Sched.3.

5.8.2   Layout of agreement

Much like consumer credit agreements subject to CC(A)R 1983, consumer hire agreements are subject to the straightjacket of layout imposed by the Consumer Credit (Agreements) (Amendment) Regulations 2004, SI 2004/1482, which came into force on 31 May 2005. The effect of the change is found in CC(A)R 1983, reg.3(4) which states that the document embodying a regulated consumer hire agreement must be set out in the following order and, where applicable, under the headings specified below:

- the nature of the agreement as set out in CC(A)R 1983, Sched.3, para.1;
- the parties to the agreement as set out in Sched.3, para.2;
- under the heading 'Key Financial Information', the financial and related particulars set out in Sched.3, paras.3–8;
- under the heading 'Key Information':

157

     –   the information set out in Sched.3, para.9–11; and
     –   the statements of protection and remedies set out in Sched.4; and

- the signature box and, where applicable, the separate box required by CC(A)R 1983, reg.3(6),

and such information, statements of protection and remedies, signature and separate boxes must be shown together as a whole and must not be preceded by any information apart from trade names, logos or the reference number of the agreement or interspersed with any other information or wording apart from subtotals of total amounts and cross-references to the terms of the agreement.

5.8.3 Prescribed information

The information prescribed by CC(A)R 1983, reg.3(1) is as follows:

Nature of agreement: Sched.3, para.1

For all agreements, there must be a heading in the following words: 'Hire Agreement regulated by the Consumer Credit Act 1974'. If the hire agreement is secured on land, this heading must be followed by the words 'secured on' and then the address. For a hire agreement secured on land, an example of the heading would be 'Hire Agreement regulated by the Consumer Credit Act 1974 secured on 2 Park Lane, Leeds, LS3 1ES'.

Parties to agreement: Sched.3, para.2

For all agreements, the owner's and hirer's names, postal addresses and, where appropriate, any other address must be recorded on the agreement.

Description of the goods: Sched.3, para.3

For all agreements, there must be a description of the goods bailed or hired under the agreement. Taking an example of a motor vehicle, the goods may be described as a 'Vauxhall Astra 1.8 SXi motor car with registration No. CC06 CCA'.

Advance payments: Sched.3, para.4

If an advance payment is made by a hirer (whether under the agreement or as a condition precedent to making of the agreement) before he takes possession of the goods to be bailed or hired or, as the case may be, before entering into the agreement, the agreement must record the amount of the advance payment and, if the agreement is cancellable, the nature of such payment.

Hire payments: Sched.3, para.5

All agreements must state:

- the amount of each hire payment, other than an advance payment shown under para.4 (Sched.3, para.5(1));
- the timing of such payments to be made under the agreement expressed by reference to one or more of the following (Sched.3, para.5(2)):
  - the dates on which each payment is to be made;
  - the frequency and number of the payments and the date of the first payment or a statement indicating the manner in which that date will be determined;
  - a statement indicating the manner in which the dates of the payments will be determined.

By CC(A)R 1983, reg.3(2), if any information about financial and related particulars as set out in Sched.3, paras.5 and 6 cannot be exactly found out by the owner, estimated information based on such assumptions as the owner may reasonably make in all the circumstances of the case and an indication of the assumptions made must be included in documents embodying regulated consumer hire agreements. These provisions are similar to those contained in Sched.6, paras.5 and 6 and, therefore, readers are referred to the discussion under 'Repayments' at **5.6.3** above.

Other payments: Sched.3, para.6

All agreements that require payments other than hire or advance payments must state:

- the amount (or a statement indicating the manner in which the amount will be determined) of each of the following descriptions of payments:
  - any payment under arrangements for the installation, care, maintenance or protection of any goods;
  - any premium under a contract of insurance; or
  - any payment payable on termination of the agreement (other than a payment on default to be shown under para.10).
- the timing of such payments expressed by reference to one or more of the following:
  - the dates on which each payment is to be made;
  - the frequency and number of the payments and the date of the first payment or a statement indicating the manner in which that date will be determined;
  - a statement indicating the manner in which the dates of the payments will be determined.

The same ability to provide estimated information, which is explained under 'Hire payments' above, also applies to the information required by CC(A)R 1983, Sched.3, para.6.

Variable payments: Sched.3, para.7

For all agreements including provisions for variation of hire or other payments, where the amount of any such payment following any variation cannot be calculated at the time of the making of the agreement, then:

- there must be a statement (subject to Sched.3, para.7(2)) indicating the circumstances in which any hire payment under para.5 or any other payment under para.6 may be varied under the agreement and, where that information can be calculated at the time at which the document referred to in CCA 1974, s.61(1) is presented or sent to the hirer for signature, the time at which any such variation may occur (Sched.3, para.7(1));
- para.7(1) does not apply to a variation under the agreement which takes account only of a change in value added tax (Sched.3, para.7(2)); and
- reference in para.7(2) to a change in value added tax include references to a change to, or from, no tax being charged.

Duration of hire: Sched.3, para.8

For all agreements that contain a provision for goods to be bailed or hired for a fixed or minimum period, there must be a statement indicating that goods are to be bailed or hired under the agreement for a fixed or minimum period, as the case may be, and the duration of that period.

Security provided by hirer: Sched.3, para.9

For all agreements where any security is provided by the hirer to secure his carrying out of the obligations under the agreement, there must be a description of the security to be provided by the hirer under the agreement sufficient to identify it and a description of the subject matter to which it relates.

Charges: Sched.3, para.10

All agreements must contain:

- a list of any charges payable under the agreement to the owner upon failure by the hirer or a relative of his to do, or not do, anything which he is required to do or not do under the agreement (Sched.3, para.10(1)); and
- a statement indicating any term of the agreement which provides for charges not required to be shown under para.10(1) (Sched.3, para.10(2)).

These provisions are similar to those contained in Sched.1, para.22 – see **5.6.4** under 'Charges'.

Cancellation rights: Sched.3, para.11

For all agreements that are not cancellable, a statement that the agreement is not cancellable should be included.

5.8.4 Statements of protection and remedies

Under CC(A)R 1983, reg.3(3), documents embodying regulated consumer hire agreements must contain statements of the protection and remedies available to hirers under CCA 1974, as set out in CC(A)R 1983, Sched.4, to the extent that they relate to the type of agreement.

The statements are set out in turn below.

Form 1: Statement of your rights

If the agreement is subject to CCA 1974, s.58(1) then it must include a statement in the following form:

YOUR RIGHTS

Under the Consumer Credit Act 1974, you should have been given a copy of this agreement at least seven days ago so you could consider whether to go ahead. If the owner did not give you a copy this agreement can only be enforced with a court order.

Form 2: Missing payments

All agreements must include a statement in the following form:

MISSING PAYMENTS

Missing payments could have severe consequences and make obtaining credit more difficult.

Form 3: Agreements secured on property

If the agreement is secured on property then it must include a statement in the following form:

YOUR HOME MAY BE REPOSSESSED

Your home may be repossessed if you do not keep up repayments on a hire agreement secured by a mortgage or other security on your home.

Form 4: Cancellable agreement not included in Form 5

If the agreement is a cancellable agreement not included in Form 5 then it must include a statement in the following form:

YOUR RIGHT TO CANCEL

Once you have signed this agreement you have a short time in which you can cancel it. Details of how to cancel it will be sent to you by the owner.

Form 5: Modifying agreement treated as a cancellable agreement under s.82(5)

If the agreement is a modifying agreement, which by CCA 1974, s.82(5) is treated as a cancellable agreement, it must include a statement in the following form:

YOUR RIGHT TO CANCEL

This agreement modifies an earlier agreement. Once you have signed it, your right to cancel the earlier agreement will cover this modified agreement. The cancellation period itself is unchanged. Details of how you can cancel can be found in the copy of this agreement.

Form 6: Agreements where hirer has the right to terminate under CCA 1974, s.101(1) and the bailment or hiring lasts for at least 18 months

If the hirer has a right to terminate the agreement under CCA 1974, s.101(1) (which is discussed at **7.6.3**) and the bailment or hiring lasts for at least 18 months after making the agreement, the agreement must include a statement in the following form:

IMPORTANT – READ THIS CAREFULLY TO FIND OUT ABOUT YOUR RIGHTS

The Consumer Credit Act 1974 lays down certain requirements for your protection which should have been complied with when this agreement was made. If they were not, the owner cannot enforce this agreement without getting a court order.

The Act also gives you a number of rights. You can end this agreement by writing to the person you make your payments to and giving at least * notice. In order to do this the agreement must have been allowed to run for at least 18 months [from the date of the original agreement]** though this may include the period of notice.

You will have to make all payments and pay any amounts you owe until the date the agreement comes to an end.

If you would like to know more about your rights under the Act, contact either your local Trading Standards Department or your nearest Citizens' Advice Bureau.

The owner must replace '*' with the minimum period of notice as determined by CCA 1974, s.101. The owner must delete the phrase 'from the date of the original agreement' and the square brackets immediately before '**' unless this notice appears in a modifying agreement.

Form 7: Agreements not subject to Form 6

All agreements, except those subject to Form 6, must include a statement in the following form:

IMPORTANT – READ THIS CAREFULLY TO FIND OUT ABOUT YOUR RIGHTS

The Consumer Credit Act 1974 covers this agreement and lays down certain requirements for your protection which should have been complied with when this agreement was made. If they were not, the owner cannot enforce this agreement against you without getting a court order.

If you would like to know more about your rights under the Act, contact either your local Trading Standards Department or your nearest Citizens' Advice Bureau.

5.8.5 Signature boxes

CC(A)R 1983, reg.3(6) provides that a regulated consumer hire agreement must also include:

- a signature box in the Form numbered in column 1 of CC(A)R 1983, Sched.5, Part II and set out in column 3 in so far as it relates to the type of agreement referred to in column 2; and
- if the agreement is: (i) one to which CCA 1974, s.58(1) applies; (ii) a cancellable agreement, then it must contain a separate box (immediately above, below or next to the signature box) containing the statements (where relevant) in Forms 1, 4 and 5 of CC(A)R 1983, Sched.4 (which are set out at **5.8.4** above).

The signature boxes for regulated consumer hire agreements are therefore as listed below.

Form 9: All consumer hire agreements except modifying agreements

All consumer hire agreements, except for modifying agreements, must include the following signature box:

> This is a Hire Agreement regulated by the Consumer Credit Act 1974. Sign it only if you want to be legally bound by its terms.
>
> Signature(s)
> of Hirer(s)
> Date(s) of signature(s)
>
> Under this agreement the goods do not become your property and you must not sell them.

The note to this Form makes it clear that the owner may delete the wording 'Date(s) of signature(s)' where the date is not required by virtue of CC(A)R 1983, reg.6(3)(c).

Form 10: Agreements modifying regulated consumer hire agreements

Agreements modifying regulated consumer hire agreements must include the following signature box:

> This Agreement varies and/or supplements a Hire Agreement regulated by the Consumer Credit Act 1974. Sign it only if you want to be legally bound by the new terms.
>
> Signature(s)
> of Hirer(s)
> Date(s) of signature(s)

The note to this Form makes it clear that the owner may delete the wording 'Date(s) of signature(s)' where the date is not required by virtue of CC(A)R 1983, reg.6(3)(c).

5.9 STATUTORY FORMS, PERMITTED DIVERGENCES AND TOLERANCES FOR APR UNDER CC(A)R 1983

5.9.1 Statutory forms and permitted divergences

Regulation 5 of CC(A)R 1983 allows a creditor or owner some flexibility for agreements under the regulations. The rules are:

- the wording in any Form in CC(A)R 1983, Scheds.2, 4 and 5 must be reproduced exactly without any alteration or addition except that:

  - the words 'the creditor' may be replaced by the creditor's name, the expression by which the creditor is referred to in the agreement or by an

appropriate pronoun and any consequential changes to pronouns or verbs or other consequential grammatical changes that may be necessary;
- the word 'debtor' may be replaced by 'borrower' or 'customer' and the word 'debtor(s)' may be replaced by 'borrower(s)' or 'customer(s)'; and
- any notes to a Form must be completed;

- the notes may be reproduced in addition to the Form;
- if a note requires words to be deleted, then they must be deleted;
- if words in a Form set out in CC(A)R 1983, Scheds.2, 4 and 5 are shown in capital letters and must be included in an agreement then they must be given:

- more prominence (whether by capital letters, underlining, larger or bold print or otherwise) than any other lettering in that Form except any lettering inserted in accordance with any note; and
- no less prominence than any other information in the document apart from the heading to the document, trade names, names or parties to the agreement or lettering in the document inserted in handwriting.

5.9.2 Tolerances for the APR

CC(A)R 1983 takes on the complexity of the APR and allows some tolerances when displaying the APR on the credit or hire agreement. The APR must be rounded to one decimal place. The general rule on tolerances is set out in CC(A)R 1983, Sched.7, para.1A. This allows (unless para.2 or para.3 applies) the rate stated on the agreement:

- to exceed the actual APR by no more than 1 per cent; and
- to fall below the actual APR by no more than 0.1 per cent.

If, therefore, the actual APR is 15.12753 per cent, it can be recorded on the agreement as high as 16.1 per cent or as low as 15.0 per cent.

There are other more detailed provisions dealing with tolerances in Sched.4, paras.2 and 3. These cover tolerances where repayments are nearly equal and where the interval between the relevant date and the first repayment is greater than the interval between repayments.

5.10 FORM AND CONTENT OF CONSUMER CREDIT AGREEMENTS UNDER CC(A)R 2010

5.10.1 Introduction

For many creditors, the passing of 1 February 2011 marked a significant change from compliance with CC(A)R 1983 to compliance with CC(A)R 2010. It is important to remember that CC(A)R 2010 does not apply to all consumer credit agreements from 1 February 2011: it is limited to certain types of agreements that have been discussed at **5.4** and **5.5** above.

5.10.2 Layout of agreement

Unlike CC(A)R 1983, CC(A)R 2010 does not prescribe a format for the layout of the agreement: this is a significant change and removes a considerable straight-jacket which appeared in CC(A)R 1983. It therefore gives the creditor a consider-able amount of latitude in how such agreements are presented.

5.10.3 Content of consumer credit agreement

Consumer credit agreements subject to CC(A)R 2010 must, however:

- contain the information set out in column 2 of CC(A)R 2010, Sched.1 to the extent that the information relates to the type of agreement in column 1 (CC(A)R 2010, reg.3(1));
- contain (unless it is an 'exempted agreement') statements of the protection and remedies available to a debtor under CCA 1974, in the form numbered in column 1 of CC(A)R 2010, Sched.2 and set out in column 3, to the extent that those statements relate to the type of agreement referred to in column 2 (CC(A)R 2010, reg.3(4));
- contain details of any security provided by the debtor under the agreement (CC(A)R 2010, reg.3(5));
- if the agreement is a debtor-creditor-supplier agreement falling within CCA 1974, s.12(a) (this includes, for example, hire-purchase agreements) (called the 'principal agreement') and also contains, or includes the option of, a debtor-creditor-supplier agreement falling within s.12(b) (called the 'subsidiary agreement') which finances the premium under one or more of:

    (a) a contract of insurance to pay an amount in the event of the death of the debtor or in the event of the debtor suffering an accident, sickness, or unemployment, at any time before the credit under both agreements (i.e. the principal and the subsidiary agreement) has been repaid where:

     – the sum payable does not exceed the amount sufficient to settle the sums payable to the creditor in respect of that credit and of the total charge for credit; and
     – the policy monies payable under the contract of insurance are to be used for a repayment under the principal agreement and the subsidiary agreement (CC(A)R 2010, reg.3(6)(a));

    (b) a contract of shortfall insurance (CC(A)R 2010, reg.3(6)(b));
    (c) a contract of insurance to guarantee goods (CC(A)R 2010, reg.3(6)(c)),

then instead of the headings specified in CC(A)R 2010, Sched.1, para.1 and any applicable statements of protection and remedies available to debtors under CCA 1974 that would otherwise apply, the agreement may contain:

- a heading in so far as it relates to the principal agreement; and
- if applicable, statements of the protection and remedies available to debtors under CCA 1974 to the extent that they relate to the principal agreement.

The information to be included by virtue of CC(A)R 2010, Sched.1 must be presented in a 'clear and concise manner' (CC(A)R 2010, reg.3(2)). This includes a requirement for the wording, apart from any signature, to be easily legible and of a colour that is readily distinguishable from the background (whether that be paper or on a computer screen) ((CC(A)R 2010, reg.3(3)).

5.10.4 Prescribed information

Much like the requirements of reg.2(1) of CC(A)R 1983, a regulated consumer credit agreement subject to CC(A)R 2010 must, by CC(A)R 2010, reg.3(1), contain the information set out in column 2 of CC(A)R 2010, Sched.1. This requirement does not mean that all of the information in column 2 should be set out: it is only the information that is relevant to the agreement in question. Those readers who have experience with CC(A)R 1983 will note a significant amount of similarity between the prescribed information under both sets of regulations. It is therefore submitted that, to ensure consistency, they should be interpreted in the same, or broadly the same, way unless there is some good reason not to.

The information required by CC(A)R 2010, Sched.1 is summarised below.

Nature of the agreement (Sched.1, para.1)

Each agreement must include a description of the nature of the agreement. The phrases are stated in CC(A)R 2010, Sched.1, para.1 and are (depending on the exact nature of the agreement):

Hire Purchase Agreement regulated by the Consumer Credit Act 1974

Conditional Sale Agreement regulated by the Consumer Credit Act 1974

Fixed Sum Loan Agreement regulated by the Consumer Credit Act 1974

Credit Card Agreement regulated by the Consumer Credit Act 1974

Agreement modifying a Credit Agreement regulated by the Consumer Credit Act 1974

If none of these are relevant or appropriate then the following heading must be used: 'Credit Agreement regulated by the Consumer Credit Act 1974' and the agreement must describe the type of credit.

If the agreement also includes a pawn-receipt then the words 'and Pawn-Receipt' must immediately follow the word 'Agreement' (Sched.1, para.1(3)). For example, a fixed-sum loan agreement including a pawn-receipt would state 'Fixed-Sum Loan Agreement and Pawn-Receipt regulated by the Consumer Credit Act 1974'.

If the agreement is a multiple agreement (within the meaning of CCA 1974, s.18) where at least part of it is not regulated by CCA 1974, then the word 'partly' must be added before 'regulated' unless the regulated and unregulated parts of the agreements are clearly separate. For example, a hire-purchase agreement partly regulated by CCA 1974 would state 'Hire-Purchase Agreement partly regulated by the Consumer Credit Act 1974'.

Finally, if the agreement is being secured on land (and it is worth remembering that, as a general rule, CC(A)R 2010 does not apply to consumer credit agreements secured on land) then the words 'secured on' followed by the property's address must be added to the end of the heading. For example, 'Fixed-Sum Loan Agreement regulated by the Consumer Credit Act 1974 secured on 2 Park Lane, Leeds, LS3 1ES.'

Parties to the agreement (Sched.1, para.2)

There is a notable change under CC(A)R 2010, Sched.1, para.2 from CC(A)R 1983. Paragraph 2 of CC(A)R 2010, Sched.1 requires every agreement to state the identity and geographical address for:

- the creditor;
- the debtor; and
- if relevant, any credit intermediary.

The new requirement to state the credit intermediary's name and geographical address is, perhaps, to ensure complete transparency in the arrangement.

Duration of the agreement: fixed duration (Sched.1, para.3)

If an agreement is for a fixed duration then the agreement must state that duration.

Duration of the agreement: open ended duration (Sched.1, para.4)

If an agreement is open ended (the most obvious example is a running-account credit agreement like a credit card), then there must be a statement saying that the agreement has no fixed duration. The statement must also include details of the minimum duration of the agreement, if such a period is stated under the agreement.

Amount of credit (Sched.1, para.5 or para.6)

If the agreement falls within CC(A)R 2010, Sched.1, para.9 but is not an agreement where the total amount payable by the debtor is not greater than the total cash price required to be stated by CC(A)R 2010, Sched.1, para.10, and there is no advance payment, then it must (by CC(A)R 2010, Sched.1, para.5) state the amount of credit to be provided under the agreement which is the difference between the cash price under CC(A)R 2010, Sched.1, para.10 and the total of any advance payments.

Agreements for fixed-sum credit that do not fall within Sched.1, para.9 must state the amount of credit to be provided under the agreement.

The issue of what is 'credit' has already been discussed at **5.6.3** above.

Credit limit (Sched.1, para.7)

If an agreement is for running-account credit then it must state the credit limit expressed as:

- a sum of money (CC(A)R 2010, Sched.1, para.7(a)); or
- a statement that the credit limit will be determined by the creditor from time to time under the agreement and that notice of it will be given by the creditor to the debtor (para.7(b));
- a sum of money together with a statement that the creditor may vary the credit limit to such sum as the creditor may from time to time determine under the agreement and that notice of it will be given by the creditor to the debtor (para.7(c)); or
- in a case not falling within para.7(a)–(c), either a statement indicating the manner in which the credit limit will be determined and that notice of it will be given by the creditor to the debtor or a statement indicating that there is no credit limit.

The issue of the credit limit has already been discussed at **5.6.3** above. Because there is no real difference between CC(A)R 2010, Sched.1, para.7 and CC(A)R 1983, Sched.1, para.8, readers are referred to the discussions under 'Credit limit' at **5.6.3** above.

How and when credit will be provided (Sched.1, para.8)

By CC(A)R 2010, Sched.1, para.8 there must be a statement indicating how and when the credit to be advanced under the agreement is to be drawn down.

Description of goods, services, land, etc. (Sched.1, para.9)

For restricted-use debtor-creditor-supplier agreements for fixed-sum credit to finance a transaction which includes the debtor obtaining goods, services, land or other things stated in the agreement and agreed at the time the agreement is made, there must be a list or other description of those goods, services, or other things. In the case of land, there must be a general description of the land to be financed by the transaction.

Whilst the wording of CC(A)R 2010, Sched.1, para.9 is slightly different from the wording of CC(A)R 1983, Sched.1, para.3, it is submitted that there is no real difference between the two provisions. Readers are therefore referred to the discussion under 'Description of goods, services, land, etc.' at **5.6.4** above.

Cash price (Sched.1, para.10)

If an agreement falls within Sched.1, para.9, the agreement must also state the cash price of each of the goods, services, land or other thing and, where applicable, the total cash price. There is, once again, no real difference from the provisions of CC(A)R 1983, Sched.1, para.4 and therefore readers are referred to the discussion under 'Cash price' at **5.6.4** above.

Rate of interest (Sched.1, para.11)

All agreements subject to CC(A)R 2010 must state:

- the rate or rates of interest; and
- where available, any reference rate on which that rate is based.

The following additional information must be given in relation to each rate that applies:

- the conditions governing the application of the rate;
- the period during which the rate will apply;
- the conditions and procedure for changing the rate.

It is notable that CC(A)R 2010, Sched.1, para.11 goes much further than CC(A)R 1983, Sched.1, para.9. The requirement to state the conditions governing the application of the rate and the conditions and procedure for changing the rate are presumably imposed to ensure clarity. Under CC(A)R 1983, and following the Court of Appeal's decision in *Lombard Tricity Finance Ltd* v. *Paton* [1989] 1 All ER 918, it will be interesting to see whether the court adopts a similar approach. It is submitted that the purpose of the legislation is not to give the debtor too much information but to merely inform the debtor. Creditors may, however, wish to err on the side of caution until clarification is provided by the court.

Total amount payable (Sched.1, para.12)

All agreements subject to CC(A)R 2010 must state the total amount payable by the debtor (being the sum of the total amount of credit and the total charge for credit payable under the agreement as well as any advance payment) (CC(A)R 2010, Sched.1, para.12(1)).

In the case of running-account credit, where the credit limit is not known at the time the credit agreement is made, the total amount of credit referred to in para.12(1) will be assumed to be £1,200 or, in a case where credit is to be provided subject to a maximum credit limit of less than £1,200, an amount equal to that maximum limit (CC(A)R 2010, Sched.1, para.12(2)).

APR (Sched.1, para.13)

All agreements subject to CC(A)R 2010 must:

- state the APR in relation to the agreement calculated at the time the credit agreement is made, and all of the assumptions used to calculate that rate; or
- include, where applicable, a statement indicating that the total amount payable under the agreement is not greater than the total cash price of the goods, services, land or other things the acquisition of which is to be financed by credit under the agreement.

The APR is subject to some tolerances and these are discussed at **5.15** below. It is notable that the method by which the APR is calculated, now under the Consumer Credit (Total Charge for Credit) Regulations 2010, SI 2010/1011, is different from that under the Consumer Credit (Total Charge for Credit) Regulations 1980, SI 1980/51. There are already steps being taken to try to iron out these differences, which require specialist actuarial knowledge to explain, so it may be that the differing methods are regularised. Shortly before publication of this text, the European Union clarified its stance, which has led to the Department for Business Innovations & Skills (BIS) deciding to revise its guidance. At the time of writing, trade associations are lobbying BIS.

Repayments (Sched.1, para.14)

All agreements subject to CC(A)R 2010 must state the number (if applicable) and frequency of repayments to be made by the debtor.

This seems, on the face of it, a fairly straightforward provision. It is submitted, however, that a creditor should try and give as much information as reasonably possible. It is likely that the following will satisfy CC(A)R 2010, Sched.1, para.14:

> You must make [60] monthly payments of £[500], the first of which is due within 1 month of the date that [we/you] sign this agreement.

There are, of course, many variations that can be used. It is submitted that using the words:

> You must make [60] monthly payments of £[500]. We will write to you after we have completed this agreement to tell you when your first payment is due.

will also satisfy Sched.1, para.14 as similar phrases were approved by the Court of Appeal in *HSBC Bank plc* v. *Brophy* [2011] EWCA Civ 67 (adopting the High Court decision of *Brophy* v. *HFC Bank Ltd* [2010] EWHC 819 (QB)) and *Brooks* v. *Northern Rock (Asset Management) plc (formerly Northern Rock plc)* [2009] GCCR 9901.

Allocation of payments (Sched.1, para.14A)

If any agreement subject to CC(A)R 2010 applies (or will apply at any time during the period of the agreement) different rates of interest for:

- credit provided under the agreement for different purposes; or
- credit provided under each of the different parts of the agreement,

whether or not the agreement is a multiple agreement within CCA 1974, s.18, then it must include a statement explaining the order or proportions in which any payment which does not discharge the total debt then due under the agreement will be applied or appropriated: (i) for the amounts of credit provided for different purposes or (ii) in respect of different parts of the agreement, as the case may be. It is perhaps better to explain this provision by the use of an example.

Example

Mr Miller enters into a consumer credit agreement subject to CC(A)R 2010. There is a loan agreement, which is restricted to use for the purchase of goods, and some form of optional insurance. The rate of interest on the loan is 10 per cent fixed and the rate of interest for the insurance is 15 per cent fixed. The combined monthly payment is £250 (split between £100 for the loan and £150 for the insurance). After making some payments, Mr Miller can no longer afford the £250 monthly instalment. Instead, he pays £150. Paragraph 14A steps in at this stage and explains to Mr Miller how the creditor will allocate or apply his payment. In this case, the agreement states that any partial payments will be first applied to the more expensive credit (i.e. the insurance) with any surplus being applied to the loan.

Amount of repayments (Sched.1, para.15)

All agreements subject to CC(A)R 2010 must state the amount of each repayment expressed as:

1. a sum of money;
2. a specified proportion of a specified amount (including the amount outstanding from time to time);
3. a combination of the first and second options; or
4. if the amount cannot be expressed by any of the other options, a statement indicating the manner in which the amount will be determined.

If the repayments can be stated as a sum of money, this requirement is easily satisfied by stating the amount of the repayment. The more difficult question comes, of course, in running-account credit agreements where the creditor cannot say the amount of the repayment as it does not know how much of the credit the debtor will drawdown. Creditors faced with this situation must therefore rely on the fourth option and provide a statement indicating how the amount will be determined. For example, it may say that the repayment will be a specified percentage of the outstanding balance but subject to a minimum payment.

Statement of account (Sched.1, para.16)

For agreements subject to CC(A)R 2010 and for a fixed duration then, if a repayment results in an immediate reduction in the total amount of credit owed other than:

- agreements referred to in CC(A)R 2010, reg.2(2); or
- agreements where the total amount payable by the debtor does not exceed the total amount of credit,

then the agreement must include a statement of the debtor's right to receive, on request and free of charge at any time throughout the duration of the agreement under CCA 1974, s.77B (which is discussed at **6.6**), a statement in the form of a table showing:

- the details of each instalment owing under the agreement;
- the date on which each instalment is due, the amount and any conditions relating to the payment of the instalment; and
- a breakdown of each instalment showing how much comprises: (i) capital repayment; (ii) interest repayment; and (iii) if applicable, any other charges.

If the interest rate is variable or the other charges may be varied then the statement must clearly and concisely state that the information contained in the statement is valid only until the rates of interest or charges are varied.

Statement of account (no credit reduction) (Sched.1, para.17 or para.17A)

If payment of interest and charges made by the debtor does not result in a reduction in the total amount of credit owed under the agreement then the agreement must include a statement indicating the periods and conditions for the payment of the interest and of any associated recurrent or non-recurrent charges (CC(A)R 2010, Sched.1, para.17).

If payments by the debtor do not give rise to an immediate corresponding reduction in the total amount of credit owed but are used to constitute capital during periods and under conditions laid down in the credit agreement or in an ancillary agreement then the agreement must include a statement indicating that:

- the debtor's regular payments will not repay the capital advanced; and

173

- at the agreement's termination, the debtor must repay the capital advanced unless the agreement provides a guarantee that any capital constituted by the debtor's payments will repay the total amount of credit.

Charges (Sched.1, para.18)

Where applicable (and it may be that none of them are applicable), all agreements must state:

- the charges for maintaining an account recording both payment transactions and drawdowns, unless the opening of the account is optional;
- any charge payable as a result of using a method of payment for repayment transactions or drawdown;
- any other charges deriving from the credit agreements (other than those referred to in CC(A)R 2010, Sched.1, para.19(3)) and the conditions under which those charges may be changed.

Interest for late payment (Sched.1, para.19)

Where applicable (and it may be that none of them are applicable), all agreements must state:

- the rate of interest which applies in the case of late payments applicable at the time of the making of the credit agreement (CC(A)R 2010, Sched.1, para.19(1));
- the arrangements for its adjustment (CC(A)R 2010, Sched.1, para.19(2)); and
- any charges payable for late payment.

Missing payments warning (Sched.1, para.20)

All agreements which require a periodic payment to be made (other than pawn agreements) must include a statement warning about the consequences of missing payments including, for example, a reference to possible legal proceedings, the possibility that the debtor's home may be repossessed and the possibility of missing payments making it more difficult to obtain credit.

There has been much concern amongst the lending industry about the extent of this warning. It is, however, submitted that it should not state every action that a lender may take if payments are missed. Instead, it should simply explain the most obvious ones. If it went into every possibility, there would be a real prospect that the warning would take up more space than the rest of the agreement!

Notarial fees (Sched.1, para.21)

If applicable, the agreement must include a statement that notarial fees will be payable.

Security provided by the debtor (Sched.1, paras.22 and 23)

If the agreement is a pawn agreement to which CCA 1974, s.114 applies (discussed at **9.7**), and no separate pawn-receipt is given, then the agreement must include a statement indicating that an article has been taken in pawn under the agreement and a description of that article sufficient to identify it (CC(A)R 2010, Sched.1, paras.22 and 23).

For all other agreements where security or a guarantee is provided by the debtor (excluding those falling within Sched.1, para.22), the agreement must include a description of the security or guarantee (CC(A)R 2010, Sched.1, para.23). The most obvious example is land where the address should be sufficient. If known, it is submitted that any title number from the Land Registry should also be included.

Compulsory insurance (Sched.1, para.24)

If the agreement includes compulsory insurance, it must also include a description of that insurance.

Right of withdrawal (Sched.1, para.25 or para.25A)

For all agreements except:

- an agreement secured on land;
- a restricted-use credit agreement to finance the purchase of land;
- an agreement for a bridging loan connected to the purchase of land;
- for credit which exceeds £60,260; or
- a cancellable agreement,

there must be a statement providing details of the debtor's right under CCA 1974, s.66A to withdraw from the regulated consumer credit agreement including:

- the right to withdraw within 14 days without the debtor having to give any reason (CC(A)R 2010, Sched.1, para.25(1));
- when the period of withdrawal begins and ends (para.25(2));
- the requirement on the debtor to give the creditor notice, either orally or written, of his intention to withdraw (para.25(3));
- contact details explaining how the debtor can give this notification (para.25(4));
- the requirement for the debtor to repay the credit without delay and no later than 30 calendar days after giving notice of withdrawal (para.25(5));
- the requirement to pay, without delay and no later than 30 calendar days after giving notice of withdrawal, the interest accrued from the date the credit was provided to the date of repaying it (para.25(6));
- the amount of interest payable each day expressed as a sum of money (para.25(7)); and

- details of how and to whom the debtor must pay the credit and interest (para.25(8)).

The creditor does not need to give the information required by Sched.1, para.25(7) where the agreement is for running-account credit and it is not practicable for the creditor to state the amount of interest payable each day. Instead, the agreement must state that if credit is drawn down during the withdrawal period, the creditor must inform the debtor, on request and without delay, of the amount of interest payable each day.

For an agreement excluded by CC(A)R 2010, Sched.1, para.25, it must:

- include a statement that there is no right of withdrawal under CCA 1974, s.66A (para.25A(1)); and
- indicate any other right to cancel the credit agreement whether under CCA 1974 or otherwise, including appropriate details of that right to cancel (para.25A(2)).

Linked credit agreements (Sched.1, para.26 or para.27)

Under CC(A)R 2010, Sched.1, para.26, linked credit agreements to which CCA 1974, s.75A applies must include a statement explaining that:

- the credit agreement finances the supply of specific goods or services; and
- if the goods or services are not supplied, or are supplied only in part, or do not conform with the contract, then the debtor has the right to seek redress from the creditor if he cannot obtain redress from the supplier of the goods or services.

Under CC(A)R 2010, Sched.1, para.27, all agreements falling within CCA 1974, s.12(b) or (c) (meaning that CCA 1974, s.75 also applies) must include a statement explaining that the debtor may have a right to sue the supplier, the creditor or both if he has received unsatisfactory goods or services paid for under the agreement costing more than £100 and not more than £30,000.

Early repayment (Sched.1, para.28)

All agreements must include a statement providing details of the debtor's right of early repayment under CCA 1974, s.94 including:

- the fact that the debtor has a right to repay early in full or (except where the agreement is secured on land) in part (CC(A)R 2010, Sched.1, para.28(1));
- the procedure for early repayment (para.28(2)); and
- where applicable, details of the creditor's right to compensation under CCA 1974, s.95A and the manner in which that compensation will be determined (para.28(2)).

Debtor termination (Sched.1, paras.29 and 30)

If the agreement is open-ended then, by CC(A)R 2010, Sched.1, para.29, it must include a statement explaining how and when the debtor can terminate the agreement.

If the agreement is for hire purchase or conditional sale then, by CC(A)R 2010, Sched.1, para.30, it must include a statement explaining:

- how and when the debtor can terminate the agreement under CCA 1974, s.99 (para.30(1)); and
- the debtor's maximum liability under CCA 1974, s.100 (para.30(2)).

It is likely that this provision can be satisfied by including Form 9 from CC(A)R 2010, Sched.2.

Ombudsman scheme (Sched.1, para.31)

For all agreements, there must be a statement explaining that:

- a debtor who is not a business debtor has the right to complain to the Financial Ombudsman Service; and
- a debtor who is a business debtor may have a right to complain to the Financial Ombudsman Service.

Contractual terms and conditions (Sched.1, para.32)

All agreements must include, where applicable, the other contractual terms and conditions.

Supervisory authority (Sched.1, para.33)

All agreements must include a statement saying that the Office of Fair Trading (OFT) is the creditor's supervisory body under CCA 1974. The statement must also include the OFT's geographical address. This may, of course, change once the OFT has been dissolved.

5.10.5 Statements of protection and remedies

Under CC(A)R 2010, reg.3(4), a regulated consumer credit agreement (other than an exempt agreement) must contain statements of protection and remedies available to debtors under CCA 1974 as set out in CC(A)R 2010, Sched.2. Much like the prescribed information, the forms that need to be included on the agreement are only those that are relevant to the agreement in question. For example, a fixed-sum loan agreement does not need to include Form 9 because this is only relevant to a hire-purchase or conditional sale agreement.

The forms are explained in turn below.

Form 1: Statement of your rights

If the agreement is subject to CCA 1974, s.58(1) it must include a statement in the following form:

YOUR RIGHTS

Under the Consumer Credit Act 1974, you should have been given a copy of this agreement at least seven days ago so you could consider whether you wanted to go ahead. If the creditor did not give you a copy of this agreement he can only enforce it with a court order.

Form 2: Agreements secured on land

If the agreement is secured on land then it must include a statement in the following form:

YOUR HOME MAY BE REPOSSESSED

Your home may be repossessed if you do not keep up repayments on a mortgage or other debt secured on it.

Form 3: Cancellable agreement subject to CCA 1974, s.68(b)

If the agreement is a cancellable agreement subject to CCA 1974, s.68(b) it must include a statement in the following form:

YOUR RIGHT TO CANCEL

You can cancel this agreement within FOURTEEN days (starting the day after you signed it) by giving WRITTEN notice to *. If you intend to cancel you should not use any goods you have under the agreement and you should keep them safe. You can wait for them to be collected and you do not need to hand them over until you receive a written request for them.

The creditor must, in place of the '*', insert:

- the name and address of the person to whom the notice may be given; or
- an indication of the person to whom a notice may be given with clear reference to the place in the agreement where its name and address appears.

Form 4: Cancellable agreement not subject to Form 3 or 5

If the agreement is cancellable but is not caught by Form 3 or Form 5 then it must include a statement in the following form:

YOUR RIGHT TO CANCEL

Once you have signed this agreement you will have a short time in which you can cancel [it]*[that part of this agreement which is regulated by the Consumer Credit Act 1974]*. The creditor will send you exact details of how and when you can do this.

The creditor must delete the passage in square brackets which does not apply to the agreement. For example, if the agreement is partly regulated, the word '[it]' and the other square brackets must be deleted so it reads:

Once you have signed this agreement you will have a short time in which you can cancel that part of this agreement which is regulated by the Consumer Credit Act 1974. The creditor will send you exact details of how and when you can do this.

Alternatively, if the agreement is fully regulated by CCA 1974, the creditor must delete the words '[that part of this agreement which is regulated by the Consumer Credit Act 1974]' and also remove the remaining square brackets so it reads:

Once you have signed this agreement you will have a short time in which you can cancel it. The creditor will send you exact details of how and when you can do this.

Form 5: Cancellable modifying agreement under s.82(5)

If the agreement is a modifying agreement and is treated as being cancellable by virtue of CCA 1974, s.82(5) it must include a statement in the following form:

YOUR RIGHT TO CANCEL

This agreement modifies an earlier agreement. Once you have signed this agreement your right to cancel [that part of]* the earlier agreement [which was regulated by the Consumer Credit Act 1974]* will be widened to cover the [regulated]* agreement as modified. The cancellation period itself will be unchanged. Details of how to cancel are given in your copy of this agreement.

The creditor must delete the passages in square brackets unless the modifying agreement is partly unregulated by CCA 1974. If the modifying agreement is wholly regulated by CCA 1974, it will therefore read:

This agreement modifies an earlier agreement. Once you have signed this agreement your right to cancel the earlier agreement will be widened to cover the agreement as modified. The cancellation period itself will be unchanged. Details of how to cancel are given in your copy of this agreement.

Form 6: Pawn agreements subject to s.114

If the agreement is a pawn agreement within CCA 1974, s.114 it must include a statement in the following form:

IMPORTANT – READ THIS CAREFULLY TO FIND OUT ABOUT YOUR RIGHTS

The Consumer Credit Act 1974 ('the Act') lays down certain requirements for your protection which should have been complied with when this agreement was made. If they were not, the creditor cannot enforce this agreement without getting a court order.

The Act also gives you a number of rights. In particular, you should read the NOTICE TO DEBTOR [in this agreement]* [in your pawn-receipt].**

If you would like to know more about your rights under the Act, contact Consumer Direct, your local Trading Standards Department or your nearest Citizens' Advice Bureau.

If the pawn-receipt and agreement are combined then the creditor must keep the wording in square brackets (but delete the square brackets only) followed by * (i.e. 'in this agreement') but must then delete the wording in square brackets followed by ** (i.e. 'in your pawn-receipt').

If the creditor gives the debtor a separate pawn-receipt then the creditor must delete the wording in square brackets followed by * (i.e. 'in this agreement') but must keep the wording in square brackets (but delete the square brackets only) followed by ** (i.e. 'in your pawn-receipt').

Form 7: Conditional sale agreement secured on land

If the agreement is a conditional sale agreement secured on land then it must include a statement in the following form:

TERMINATION: YOUR RIGHTS

Until the title to the land has passed to you, you have a right to end this agreement. To do so write to the person you make your payments to. They will then be entitled to the return of the land and to [half the total amount payable under this agreement, that is]* £x**. If, at the time you end this agreement, you have already paid at least this amount plus any overdue instalments and you have taken reasonable care of the land, you will not have to pay any more.

If the amount is calculated in accordance with CCA 1974, s.100 then the creditor must keep the wording in the square brackets (but delete the square brackets only) followed by * (i.e. 'half the total amount payable under this agreement, that is'). If the agreement provides for an amount below the minimum prescribed by CCA 1974, s.100 then the passage in the square brackets followed by * is to be deleted.

The creditor must insert, in place of 'x**' the amount calculated in accordance with the provisions of CCA 1974, s.100 or such lower sum as the agreement may provide.

Form 8: Agreements modifying conditional sale agreements relating to land

If the agreement modifies a conditional sale agreement relating to land then it must include a statement in the following form:

> **TERMINATION: YOUR RIGHTS**
>
> Until the title to the land has passed to you, you have a right to end this agreement. To do so write to the person you make your payments to. They will then be entitled to the return of the land and to [half the total amount payable under this agreement, that is]* [£[–**]. If at the time you end this agreement, you have already paid at least this amount plus any overdue instalments and you have taken reasonable care of the land, you will not have to pay any more.

If the amount is calculated in accordance with CCA 1974, s.100 the creditor must keep the wording in the square brackets (but delete the square brackets only) followed by * (i.e. 'half the total amount payable under this agreement, that is'). If the agreement provides for an amount below the minimum prescribed by CCA 1974, s.100 then the passage in the square brackets followed by * is to be deleted.

The creditor must insert, in place of '–**' the amount calculated in accordance with the provisions of CCA 1974, s.100 or such lower sum as the agreement may provide.

Form 9: Agreements for hire purchase or conditional sale of goods

For hire-purchase or conditional sale agreements relating to goods (and not land) that do not fall within Form 10, there must be a statement in the following form:

> **TERMINATION: YOUR RIGHTS**
>
> You have a right to end this agreement. To do so, you should write to the person you make your payments to. They will then be entitled to the return of the goods and to [the cost of installing the goods plus half the rest of the total amount payable under this agreement, that is][half the total amount payable under this agreement, that is]* £x**. If you have already paid at least this amount plus any overdue instalments and have taken reasonable care of the goods, you will not have to pay any more.

If the amount is calculated in accordance with CCA 1974, s.100 the creditor must select the appropriate wording in the square brackets (but delete the square brackets only) followed by * (i.e. 'the cost of installing the goods plus half the rest of the total amount payable under this agreement, that is' if there is an installation charge under the agreement or 'half the total amount payable under this agreement, that is' if there is not). If the agreement provides for an amount below the minimum prescribed by CCA 1974, s.100 then both the passages in the square brackets followed by * must be deleted.

The creditor must insert, in place of 'x**' the amount calculated in accordance with the provisions of CCA 1974, s.100 or such lower sum as the agreement may provide.

Form 10: Agreements modifying an agreement for hire purchase or conditional sale of goods

If the agreement modifies a hire-purchase or conditional sale agreement relating to goods (and not land) then it must include a statement in the following form:

TERMINATION: YOUR RIGHTS

You have the right to end this agreement. To do so, write to the person you make your payments to. They will then be entitled to the return of the goods and to [the cost of installing the goods plus half the total amount yet to be paid under the earlier agreement as modified by this agreement, that is][half the total amount payable under the earlier agreement as modified by this agreement, that is]* £x**. If you have already paid at least this amount, plus any overdue instalments and have taken reasonable care of the goods, you will not have to pay any more.

If the amount is calculated in accordance with CCA 1974, s.100 then the creditor must select the appropriate wording in the square brackets (but delete the square brackets only) followed by * (i.e. 'the cost of installing the goods plus half the total amount yet to be paid under the earlier agreement as modified by this agreement, that is' if there is an installation charge under the agreement or 'half the total amount payable under the earlier agreement as modified by this agreement, that is' if there is not). If the modified agreement provides for an amount below the minimum prescribed by CCA 1974, s.100 then both the passages in the square brackets followed by * must be deleted.

The creditor must insert, in place of 'x**' the amount calculated in accordance with the provisions of CCA 1974, s.100 or such lower sum as the modified agreement may provide.

Form 11: Agreements for hire purchase or conditional sale of goods

For hire-purchase or conditional sale agreements relating to goods (and not land) that do not fall within Form 12, there must be a statement in the following form:

REPOSSESSION: YOUR RIGHTS

If you do not keep your side of the agreement but you have paid at least [the cost of installing the goods plus one third of the rest of the total amount payable under this agreement, that is][one third of the total amount payable under this agreement, that is]* £x** the creditor may not take back the goods against your wishes unless he gets a court order. (In Scotland he may need to get a court order at any time). If he does take the goods without your consent or a court order, you have the right to get back any money that you have paid under this agreement.

The creditor must select the appropriate wording in the square brackets (but delete the square brackets only) followed by * (i.e. either 'the cost of installing the goods plus one third of the rest of the total amount payable under this agreement, that is' or 'one third of the total amount payable under this agreement, that is').

The creditor must insert, in place of 'x**' the amount calculated in accordance with the provisions of CCA 1974, s.90.

Form 12: Agreements modifying an agreement for hire purchase or conditional sale of goods

If the agreement modifies a hire-purchase or conditional sale agreement relating to goods (and not land) then it must include a statement in the following form:

REPOSSESSION: YOUR RIGHTS

If you do not keep your side of this agreement [but you have paid at least £x*]** the creditor may not take back the goods against your wishes unless he gets a court order. (In Scotland he may need to get a court order at any time). If he does take the goods back without your consent or a court order, you have the right to get back all the money you have paid under this agreement.

The creditor must insert, in place of 'x*' the amount calculated in accordance with the provisions of CCA 1974, s.90.

The creditor must delete the wording in the square brackets followed by ** (i.e. 'but you have paid at least £x*') if the goods were protected at the time the modifying agreement was made.

Precedent

For a precedent of an unrestricted-use fixed-sum loan agreement drafted in accordance with CC(A)R 2010, see **Precedent 6**.

5.11   FORM AND CONTENT OF MODIFYING AGREEMENTS UNDER CC(A)R 2010

If the modifying agreement supplements or varies an earlier agreement which is, or is treated by CCA 1974, s.82(3) as being, a regulated agreement, then CC(A)R 2010 applies, by virtue of CC(A)R 2010, reg.5(1). The rules for modifying agreements are that:

- the heading for the agreement must say 'Agreement modifying a Credit Agreement regulated by the Consumer Credit Act 1974' (CC(A)R 2010, Sched.1, para.1(e));
- it must include the information required by CC(A)R 2010, reg.3(1) for a credit agreement (explained at **5.10.3** above) or CC(A)R 2010, reg.8(1) for an authorised overdraft agreement (explained at **5.13** below) but, if it is unchanged, then the modifying agreement may simply say that the information remains unchanged (CC(A)R 2010, reg.5(2));
- if the modifying agreement is an authorised business overdraft agreement or an authorised non-business overdraft agreement then the statement saying that the information remains unchanged does not need to be in the document signed by the debtor (CC(A)R 2010, reg.5(3A));
- if the modifying agreement is not caught by reg.5(3A) then the statement saying that the information remains unchanged does need to be in the document signed by the debtor (CC(A)R 2010, reg.5(3));
- the information required by CC(A)R 2010, Sched.1. paras.5–7, 11 and 14 to be contained in a regulated consumer credit agreement does not constitute prescribed terms for the purposes of the modifying agreement if the information in the earlier agreement has not been varied or supplemented by the modifying agreement (CC(A)R 2010, reg.5(4));
- it must include (where relevant) the forms of statements of protection and remedies set out in CC(A)R 2010, Sched.2 (explained at **5.10.5** above);
- for the purposes of CC(A)R 2010, Sched.1, when calculating:

  - the amount of repayments of credit or of any capital outstanding under an earlier agreement; or
  - the total charge for credit (or any items included in it) in relation to the credit provided under the modified agreement; or
  - the APR in relation to the modified agreement,

  the relevant date is determined by reference to the date of the modifying agreement (CC(A)R 2010, reg.5(5)).

The provisions of CC(A)R 2010, reg.5 do not apply to modifying agreements which are distance contracts unless the agreement is entered into by the debtor wholly or predominantly for the purposes of a business carried on, or intended to be carried on, by him (CC(A)R 2010, reg.2(5)).

5.12   FORM AND CONTENT OF PAWN AGREEMENTS UNDER CC(A)R 2010

By CCA(A)R 2010, reg.6, if a pawn-receipt is given under CCA 1974, s.114(1) (which is discussed at **9.7**) by someone who takes any article in pawn under a regulated consumer credit agreement or a modifying agreement varying or supplementing an earlier credit agreement which is, or is treated to be by CCA 1974, s.82(3) as a regulated agreement, then where the pawn-receipt is not separate from such an agreement it must contain:

- the information set out in CC(A)R 2010, Sched.1, paras.1, 2 and 22 (discussed at **5.10.4** above); and
- a notice in the following form (CC(A)R 2010, Sched.3):

NOTICE TO DEBTOR

IMPORTANT – YOU SHOULD READ THIS CAREFULLY

Right to Redeem Articles

If you hand in this agreement (which is also your pawn receipt) and pay the amount you owe, you may redeem the article(s) in pawn at any time within 6 months of the date of this agreement or any longer time agreed with the creditor ('the redemption period').

IF YOU DO NOT REDEEM THE ARTICLE(S) ON OR BEFORE[1] YOU MAY LOSE YOUR RIGHT TO REDEEM IT (THEM).

Loss of Receipt

If you lose your receipt you may provide either a statutory declaration or, if the credit (or credit limit) is not more than £x[2] and the creditor agrees, a signed statement instead. The creditor may provide the form to be used and may charge for doing so.

Unredeemed Articles

An article not redeemed within the redemption period becomes the creditor's property if the credit (or credit limit) is not more than £x[3] and the redemption period is 6 months. In any other case it may be sold by the creditor, but it continues to be redeemable until it is sold. Interest is payable until the actual date of redemption. Where the credit (or credit limit) is more than £x[4] the creditor must give you 14 days notice of his intention to sell. When an article has been sold you will receive information about the sale. If the proceeds (less expenses) are more that the amount that would have been payable to redeem the article on the date of the sale you will be entitled to receive the extra amount. If the proceeds are less than the amount you will owe the creditor the shortfall.

Your goods will not be insured by the creditor while they are in pawn.[5]

To complete this form, the creditor must:

- replace '[1]' with the date at the end of the redemption period;
- replace 'x[2]' with the amount specified in CCA 1974, s.118(1)(b);
- replace 'x[3]' with the amount specified in CCA 1974, s.120(1)(a);
- replace 'x[4]' with the amount specified in the Consumer Credit (Realisation of Pawn) Regulations 1983; and
- delete the sentence immediately before '[5]' (i.e. 'Your goods will not be insured by the creditor while they are in pawn.') if it is inapplicable.

5.13 FORM AND CONTENT OF AUTHORISED OVERDRAFT AGREEMENTS UNDER CC(A)R 2010

For an authorised non-business overdraft agreement or an authorised business overdraft agreement, the following information must be set out in writing in a clear and concise manner (CC(A)R 2010, reg.8(1)):

(a)   the type of credit,

(b)   the identities and geographical addresses of the creditor, debtor and, where relevant, of any credit intermediary involved,

(c)   the duration of the agreement,

(d)   the credit limit and the conditions governing its drawdown,

(e)   the rate of interest charged, any conditions applicable to that rate, any reference rate on which that rate is based and any information on changes to the rate of interest (including the periods that the rate applies, and any conditions or procedure applicable to changing the rate),

(f)   where different rates of interest are charged in different circumstances the creditor must provide the information in paragraph (e) in respect of each rate,

(g)   the total charge for credit, calculated at the time the agreement is made, mentioning all the assumptions used in order to calculate it,

(h)   an indication that the debtor may be requested to repay the amount of credit in full on demand at any time, and

(i)   the charges payable by the debtor under the agreement (and the conditions under which those charges may be varied).

As in CC(A)R 1983, the requirement for information to be 'clear' includes a requirement for the wording to be easily legible and of a colour which is readily distinguishable from the background medium upon which it is displayed (reg.8(2)). It is likely that black standard font text on a white background will satisfy this requirement.

If the agreement is an authorised business overdraft agreement or an authorised non-business overdraft agreement that is also an agreement secured on land then, by reg.8(3), the requirement to include the information required by reg.8(1)(g) does not apply.

By virtue of CC(A)R 2010, reg.2(4), the following regulations of CC(A)R 2010 do not apply to an authorised non-business overdraft agreement or an authorised business overdraft agreement: regs.2(2), 3, 4, 6 and 7.

5.14 SIGNATURE BOXES UNDER CC(A)R 2010

Unlike CC(A)R 1983, CC(A)R 2010 does not prescribe the format of the signature box. Instead, CC(A)R 2010, reg.4(2) simply states that the document containing the prescribed terms of a regulated consumer credit agreement must contain a 'space indicated for the purpose of the debtor's signature'. In practice, this is likely to be satisfied by including a signature box that would have been used if the agreement had been subject to CC(A)R 1983. Examples of these signature blocks are discussed at **5.6.6** above.

In terms of signing the agreement, CC(A)R 2010, reg.4(3) sets out the following rules:

- the agreement must be signed by the debtor or, if the debtor is a partnership or an unincorporated body of persons, for the debtor and, subject to reg.4(3)(c), the date of the signature must be added (reg.4(3)(a));
- the agreement must be signed by the creditor or for the creditor and, subject to reg.4(3)(c), the date of the signature must be added (reg.4(3)(b));
- except where the agreement is cancellable, the date that the unexecuted agreement becomes executed may be added to the agreement and, if it is, there is no need for dates to be added to the debtor's or creditor's signature (reg.4(3)(c)); and
- nothing in reg.4 prevents the inclusion in the agreement, or near to any signature, a signature by a witness (reg.4(3)(d)).

If the parties intend to conclude the agreement by electronic communication (normally the internet), reg.4(5) makes it clear that nothing in CC(A)R 2010, reg.4 prevents including in the agreement information about the process or means of providing, communicating or verifying the debtor's signature.

5.15 TOLERANCES FOR THE APR UNDER CC(A)R 2010

The APR is a complex calculation and often requires specialist advice from an actuary. Fortunately, CC(A)R 2010 (like CC(A)R 1983) takes this on board and allows some tolerances when displaying the APR on the credit agreement. The APR must be rounded to one decimal place. The general rule on tolerances is set out in CC(A)R 2010, Sched.4, para.2. This allows (unless para.3 or para.4 applies) the rate stated on the agreement:

- to exceed the actual APR by no more than 1 per cent; and
- to fall below the actual APR by no more than 0.1 per cent.

If, therefore, the actual APR is 15.12753 per cent, it can be recorded on the agreement as high as 16.1 per cent or as low as 15.0 per cent.

There are other more detailed provisions dealing with tolerances in Sched.4, paras.3 and 4. These cover tolerances where repayments are nearly equal and where the interval between the relevant date and the first repayment is greater than the interval between repayments.

5.16 STATUTORY FORMS AND PERMITTED DIVERGENCES UNDER CC(A)R 2010

Like CC(A)R 1983, CC(A)R 2010, reg.7 allows a creditor some flexibility. The rules are as follows:

- the wording in any Form in CC(A)R 2010, Sched.2 or 3 must be reproduced exactly without any alteration except that:

    - the words 'the creditor' may be replaced by the creditor's name, the expression by which the creditor is referred to in the agreement or by an appropriate pronoun and with any consequential changes to pronouns or verbs or other consequential grammatical changes that may be necessary;
    - the word 'debtor' may be replaced by 'borrower' or 'customer' and the word 'debtor(s)' may be replaced by 'borrower(s)' or 'customer(s)'; and
    - any notes to a Form must be completed;

- the notes may be reproduced in addition to the Form;
- if a note requires words to be deleted, then they must be deleted;
- if words in a Form set out in CC(A)R 2010, Sched.2 or 3 are shown in capital letters and must be included in an agreement then they must be given:

    - more prominence (whether by capital letters, underlining, larger or bold print or otherwise) than any other lettering in that Form except any lettering inserted in accordance with any note; and
    - no less prominence than any other information in the document apart from the heading to the document, trade names, names or parties to the agreement or lettering in the document inserted in handwriting.

5.17   DUTY TO SUPPLY COPIES

5.17.1   Introduction

CCA 1974 also sets out rules dealing with the supply of copies of the executed and unexecuted agreements. Until 1 February 2011, these were contained in CCA 1974, ss.62 and 63. From 1 February 2011, however, they are now found in ss.61A–63.

5.17.2   Duty to supply copy of executed consumer credit agreement

Duty

Where a regulated consumer credit agreement (other than an 'excluded agreement') has been made, the creditor must give the debtor a copy of the executed agreement and any other document referred to in it (CCA 1974, s.61A(1)). By CCA 1974, s.61A(2), this does not apply if:

- a copy of the unexecuted agreement and of any other document referred to in it has already been given to the debtor; and
- the unexecuted agreement is in the same terms as the executed agreement.

If CCA 1974, s.61A(2) applies then the creditor must, by s.61A(3), tell the debtor in writing that:

- the agreement has been executed;
- the executed agreement is in the same terms as the unexecuted agreement that has already been given to the debtor; and
- the debtor has the right to receive a copy of the executed agreement if the debtor asks for it at any time before the end of the withdrawal period under s.66A(2) (discussed at **4.13**).

If the debtor asks for a copy during the withdrawal period, the creditor must provide a copy 'without delay' (CCA 1974, s.66A(4)). This is not defined in CCA 1974 and may be a ground for defaulting debtors to argue. It is, however, submitted that the court is likely to adopt a sensible approach to this phrase and interpret it to mean 'without undue delay' so that a creditor satisfies this requirement if it can show that it took reasonable steps to provide the executed copy.

Exclusions

Under CCA 1974, s.61A(6), the following agreements are excluded from the requirements of s.61A:

- a cancellable agreement; or
- unless the creditor or a credit intermediary has complied with (or purported to comply with) the Consumer Credit (Disclosure of Information) Regulations 2010, reg.3(2), an agreement:
  - secured on land;
  - which provides credit of more than £60,260; or
  - entered into by a debtor wholly or predominantly for the purposes of a business carried on, or intended to be carried on, by him.

Consequences of non-compliance

If the creditor fails to comply with CCA 1974, s.61A then the agreement is, by s.61A(5), improperly executed. By virtue of CCA 1974, s.65, the creditor will need to apply to the court for an enforcement order under CCA 1974, s.127(1).

5.17.3 Duty to supply copy of overdraft agreement

Duty

If an authorised business overdraft agreement or an authorised non-business overdraft agreement has been made, then, by CCA 1974, s.61B(1), a document containing the terms of the agreement must be given to the debtor. By CCA 1974, s.61B(2), this must be done before or at the time the agreement is made unless:

- the creditor has provided the debtor with the information referred to in the Consumer Credit (Disclosure of Information) Regulations 2010 (CC(DI)R

189

2010), reg.10(3) (which is discussed at **4.4.11**), in which case it must be provided after the agreement is made;

- the creditor has provided the debtor with the information referred to in CC(DI)R 2010, reg.10(3)(c), (e), (f), (h) and (k), in which case it must be provided immediately after the agreement is made; or
- the agreement is an agreement of a description referred to in CC(DI)R 2010, reg.10(4)(b) (which is also discussed at **4.4.11**), in which case it must be provided immediately after the agreement is made.

Consequences of non-compliance

Under CCA 1974, s.61B, if the requirements of s.61B are not complied with then the agreement is only enforceable against the debtor with the court's permission. This is required before the creditor attempts to retake goods or land to which the agreement relates (CCA 1974, s.61A(3)).

5.17.4   Duty to supply copy of unexecuted agreement: excluded agreements

Duty

For regulated agreements that are excluded agreements (which are discussed at **5.17.2** above), if the unexecuted agreement is presented personally to the debtor or hirer for his signature, but when he signs it the document does not become an executed agreement (because it is not pre-signed by the creditor or owner), a copy of it, and of any other document referred to in it, must be there and then delivered to him (CCA 1974, s.62(1)).

If the unexecuted agreement is sent to the debtor or hirer for his signature then a copy of it, and of any other document referred to in it, must be sent to him at the same time (CCA 1974, s.62(2)).

Exclusions

By virtue of CCA 1974, s.62(4), an excluded agreement in CCA 1974, s.62 has the same meaning as in CCA 1974, s.61A (discussed under 'Exclusions' at **5.17.2** above).

Consequences of non-compliance

If the creditor or owner fails to comply with CCA 1974, s.62 then the regulated agreement is not properly executed. The creditor or owner may, however, apply for an enforcement order under CCA 1974, s.127(1) (CCA 1974, s.62(3)).

5.17.5 Duty to supply copy of executed agreement: excluded agreements

Duty

For regulated agreements that are excluded agreements, if the unexecuted agreement is presented personally to the debtor or hirer for his signature and, when he signs it the document becomes an executed agreement (because it is pre-signed by the creditor or owner), a copy of it, and of any other document referred to in it, must be there and then delivered to him (CCA 1974, s.63(1)).

By CCA 1974, s.63(2), a copy of the executed agreement, and of any other document referred to in it, must be given to the debtor or hirer within the seven days following the making of the agreement unless:

- section 63(1) applies (CCA 1974, s.63(2)(a)); or
- the unexecuted agreement was sent to the debtor or hirer for his signature and, on the occasion of his signing it, the document became an executed agreement (CCA 1974, s.63(2)(b)).

For a cancellable agreement, a copy under s.63(2) must be sent by an appropriate method (CCA 1974, s.63(3)). Service by an 'appropriate method' is discussed at **7.4**, but, in short, includes sending by post.

For a credit-token agreement, a copy under s.63(2) need not be given within the seven days following the making of the agreement if it is given before or at the time when the credit-token is given to the debtor (CCA 1974, s.63(4)). This allows credit card providers to send a copy of the executed agreement to the debtor with the credit card.

Exclusions

By CCA 1974, s.63(6), an excluded agreement in CCA 1974, s.63 has the same meaning as in CCA 1974, s.61A (discussed at **5.17.2** above).

Consequences of non-compliance

If the creditor or owner fails to comply with CCA 1974, s.63 then the regulated agreement is not properly executed. The creditor or owner may, however, apply for an enforcement order under CCA 1974, s.127(1) (CCA 1974, s.63(5)).

5.18 DUTY TO GIVE NOTICE OF CANCELLATION RIGHTS

5.18.1 Duty

For cancellable agreements, and by CCA 1974, s.64(1), a notice in the prescribed form stating the debtor's or hirer's right to cancel the agreement, how and when that right is exercisable, and the name and address of a person to whom notice of cancellation may be given:

- must be included in every copy given to the debtor or hirer under CCA 1974, s.62 or s.63 (CCA 1974, s.64(1)(a)); and
- except where CCA 1974, s.63(2) applies, must also be sent by an appropriate method to the debtor or hirer within the seven-day period after the making of the agreement (CCA 1974, s.64(1)(b)).

5.18.2 Exceptions

For credit-token agreements, a notice under CCA 1974, s.64(1)(b) need not be sent by an appropriate method within the seven days after the making of the agreement if either:

- it is sent by an appropriate method to the debtor or hirer before the credit-token is given to him; or
- it is sent by an appropriate method to him with the credit-token.

By virtue of CCA 1974, s.64(4) and the Consumer Credit (Notice of Cancellation Rights) (Exemptions) Regulations 1983, SI 1983/1558 (CC(NCR)(E)R 1983), certain agreements may be exempt from the requirement under CCA 1974, s.64(1)(b). To be exempt, (a) the agreement must satisfy the requirements of the Schedule to the CC(NCR)(E)R 1983 (which is essentially mail order credit) and (b) the OFT must have made a determination, following an application, in favour of a particular creditor.

5.18.3 Consequences of non-compliance

Under CCA 1974, s.64(5), a cancellable agreement is not properly executed if the requirements of s.64 are not complied with. If the agreement pre-dates 6 April 2007, it is irredeemably unenforceable by virtue of CCA 1974, s.127(4)(b).

CHAPTER 6

Obligations during the lifetime of a regulated agreement

6.1 INTRODUCTION

In this chapter, we look at the obligations that both parties have during the existence of an agreement regulated by the Consumer Credit Act 1974 (CCA 1974). These obligations have created a substantial amount of litigation over the last few years with a number of claims management companies and their solicitors attempting to use the statutory provisions either to obtain a declaration that the agreement is unenforceable or to obtain a signed copy of the agreement before assessing whether that agreement complies with the Consumer Credit (Agreements) Regulations 1983 (CC(A)R 1983). Whilst many of those claims have been unsuccessful, the provisions are extremely useful for both parties. We now turn to look at them.

6.2 CONNECTED LENDER LIABILITY: S.75

6.2.1 Introduction

Section 75(1) of CCA 1974 gives a debtor, if he has a particular agreement and where he has a claim against the supplier of goods for breach of contract or misrepresentation where the cash price of the goods is more than £100 but not more than £30,000, a 'like claim' against the creditor. This is an extremely powerful tool for a debtor: it gives him an additional claim (essentially for damages) against a creditor who has not supplied goods to the debtor.

6.2.2 When does it apply?

Under CCA 1974, s.75(1), if the debtor has:

- a debtor-creditor-supplier agreement falling within CCA 1974, s.12(b) or (c) entered into on or after 1 July 1977;
- any claim against the supplier of goods acquired under that agreement for misrepresentation or breach of contract,

then he has a 'like' claim against the creditor (which is jointly and severally liable with the supplier).

6.2.3 When does s.75(1) not apply?

By virtue of CCA 1974, s.75(3), subsection (1) does not apply to a claim under a non-commercial agreement or relating to a single item which has a cash price of £100 or less or more than £30,000.

6.2.4 Debtor-creditor-supplier agreement within s.12(b) or (c)

The effect of the limitation of CCA 1974, s.75(1) to debtor-creditor-supplier agreements is that it only applies to agreements where the creditor and the supplier are different entities. It does not, therefore, apply to a hire-purchase agreement (which is a debtor-creditor-supplier agreement within CCA 1974, s.12(a) because it is the finance company who is both supplying the goods (having bought them from a third party) and the supplier of credit). It is, however, submitted that the need for the potential claim under CCA 1974, s.75(1) is irrelevant for agreements within CCA 1974, s.12(a) because the debtor will have the benefit of the statutory implied terms under the Supply of Goods (Implied Terms) Act 1973.

Section 12(b) of CCA 1974 states that a debtor-creditor-supplier agreement is a regulated consumer credit agreement if it is for restricted-use credit to finance a transaction between the debtor and the supplier (where the supplier is not also the creditor) and made by the creditor under pre-existing arrangements, or in contemplation of future arrangements, between it and the supplier.

Section 12(c) of the Act states that a debtor-creditor-supplier agreement is a regulated consumer credit agreement if it is for unrestricted-use credit made by the creditor under pre-existing arrangements between it and a person other than the debtor (called the supplier) in the knowledge that the credit will be used to finance a transaction between the debtor and the supplier.

We discuss typical examples of debtor-creditor-supplier agreements at **1.4.5**.

Example

Mrs Lodge applies for, and obtains, a debtor-creditor-supplier running-account credit agreement (otherwise known as a credit card) with Credit Card For Debtors Ltd (CCFDL). CCFDL is a finance company and has a consumer credit licence. Mrs Lodge's credit limit is £5,000 but she is free to use the credit as she wishes. In this case, the agreement will fall within CCA 1974, s.12(c) meaning that if she uses the card to make a purchase and she has any claim against the supplier for misrepresentation or breach of contract, then she will have a 'like claim' against CCFDL.

6.2.5 What is a 'like claim'?

There has been much discussion over the years about what a 'like claim' is. It seems clear that a claim for damages for breach of contract or misrepresentation (including fraudulent misrepresentation or a claim under the Misrepresentation Act 1967, s.2(1)) falls within the meaning of a 'like claim'. The creditor is, however, entitled to rely upon any defence that the supplier may have which should include any exclusion or limitation clause appearing in the supplier's standards terms and conditions. Any attempt to rely upon an exclusion or limitation of liability clause will, of course, be subject to incorporation of that term and the provisions of the Unfair Contract Terms Act 1977 and the Unfair Terms in Consumer Contracts Regulations 1999, SI 1999/2083.

The more difficult issue is whether any other claim or remedy, perhaps an injunction or rescission, can be properly classified as a 'like claim'. Until recently, the answer following the Scottish decision of *United Dominions Trust Ltd* v. *Taylor* 1980 SLT (Sh Ct) 28 was that CCA 1974, s.75(1) was wide enough to cover injunctions or rescission. The practical effect of this decision was that if a debtor had acquired goods, he or she could rescind the contract of sale and (at the same time) also rescind the credit agreement. Despite this decision being subject to considerable academic criticism, it was followed in another Scottish decision of *Forward Trust Ltd* v. *Hornsby and another* 1995 SCLR 574.

The issue has, however, recently put beyond doubt by another Scottish decision of *Durkin* v. *DSG Retail Ltd & HFC Bank plc* [2010] CSIH 49. Mr Durkin agreed to buy a laptop from DSG Retail Ltd (otherwise known as PC World). Because the box was sealed, PC World's employee said that if, after opening the box, the laptop did not have an inbuilt modem, Mr Durkin could return it. On the same day, Mr Durkin entered into a debtor-creditor-supplier credit agreement under which HFC Bank plc provided credit for Mr Durkin to buy the laptop. Upon returning home and unsealing the box, Mr Durkin discovered that the laptop did not have an inbuilt modem. He then returned the laptop to PC World and purported to reject it. Mr Durkin refused to make the payments due under the credit agreement. HFC Bank plc later served a default notice and registered adverse entries on his credit file.

Mr Durkin issued proceedings against PC World, for a declaration that he had validly rescinded the sale contract, and against HFC Bank plc, for a declaration that he had validly rescinded the credit agreement. He also sought damages of £250,000. The court, after considering the authorities including *Taylor*, decided that:

- the earlier decisions of *Taylor* and *Hornsby* were wrongly decided;
- the contract of sale and the loan contract were separate agreements;
- since the right to rescind a contract can only be exercised by one contracting party against the other contracting party, there is no joint and several liability relating to rescission;
- the words 'like claim' should be given their ordinary contextual meaning leading to the term being construed as entitling a debtor to pursue against his

creditor claims he could have pursued against his supplier for the supplier's misrepresentation or breach of contract;

- the declaration sought against HFC Bank plc did not fall within 'like claim';
- the factual circumstances which entitled Mr Durkin to rescind his contract of sale did not provide a factual basis which also enabled him to invoke the provisions of CCA 1974, s.75(1) and rescind his credit agreement with HFC Bank plc.

It is notable that no claim was made by Mr Durkin for misrepresentation. It is submitted that if such a claim had been made, it would have fallen within CCA 1974, s.56 meaning it was made by the creditor's deemed agent. This could have given Mr Durkin a defence to the claim under the credit agreement.

6.2.6 Is the creditor entitled to an indemnity from the supplier?

By CCA 1974, s.75(2) and subject to any other agreement between the creditor and supplier, the creditor is entitled to an indemnity from the supplier for any amount paid by the creditor to the debtor in satisfaction of a claim and any costs incurred by the creditor in defending the debtor's claim. This is supplemented by s.75(5) which states that, subject to the Civil Procedure Rules 1998, if a debtor issues a claim only against the creditor, the creditor is entitled to make the supplier a party to the proceedings.

It is important to remember that the statutory right to an indemnity is contained in an Act of Parliament. Interesting questions therefore arise when a creditor is included in proceedings by a debtor together with the supplier. If the debtor is unsuccessful, and the matter is allocated to the small claims track, is the creditor still entitled to an indemnity for its costs from the supplier? The county court recently decided in *Kim Patricia Parker* v. *Black Horse Ltd & Browne & Sons (Loddon) Ltd t/a ESS Scooters* (unreported, Dartford County Court, 17 December 2010) that the creditor was entitled to an indemnity. After receiving detailed submissions, Deputy District Judge Austin decided that:

- the key question was the meaning of the word 'liability' in CCA 1974, s.75(2) and, in particular, whether this just gives an indemnity where a debtor succeeds in her claim;
- Black Horse's argument that its costs were 'costs reasonably incurred by [Black Horse] in defending proceedings instituted by' Mrs Parker was 'unimpeachable';
- the argument, despite the restriction on costs under CPR rule 27.14, that an Act of Parliament giving an indemnity for those costs must prevail was accepted 'as valid';
- the effect of CCA 1974, s.75(2) was that 'liability' refers to 'the creditor's inclusion as a party to the action' as it would otherwise lead to the odd result that only an unsuccessful creditor could obtain an indemnity under s.75(2);

- there was abundant evidence to show that Mrs Parker was a party to the transaction because she paid part of the deposit and entered into the agreement.

It therefore follows that in proceedings under CCA 1974, s.75(1), it is good practice for a creditor to seek an indemnity under s.75(2). If it does so, suppliers will be well advised to try and resolve the dispute because even if the claim fails, the supplier will still be responsible for the lender's costs.

6.2.7 Purchases by card holders

Currently, there is an interesting issue arising in CCA 1974, s.75 claims which involve purchases made by a card holder who is not the debtor under the debtor-creditor-supplier credit agreement. This typically happens where a debtor applies for, and obtains, a credit card with a creditor. The debtor then adds a third party, perhaps a family member, to the account as an authorised card holder yet they do not become a debtor under the agreement. In such a situation, does CCA 1974, s.75(1) apply to any purchases made by the card holder (and not the debtor)? It is submitted that it does not: s.75(1) applies where the 'debtor under a debtor-creditor-supplier agreement ... has ... any claim against the supplier.' Plainly, in such a case, it is the card holder and not the debtor who has the claim. Similarly, any argument that the card holder acts as the debtor's agent is unlikely to succeed: the contract is plainly to benefit the third party and not the debtor meaning nothing is done for the debtor.

6.2.8 Payment of deposit

It is debatable whether CCA 1974, s.75(1) applies where the debtor under a debtor-creditor-supplier agreement falling within CCA 1974, s.12(b) or (c) simply pays a deposit towards goods with a cash price of more than £100 but not more than £30,000. The OFT's view in 'Connected Lender Liability' (First Report – March 1994; Second Report – May 1995) is, however, that CCA 1974, s.75(1) applies to such transactions given that the wording of s.75(1) does not explicitly require the credit agreement to be solely used by the debtor.

6.2.9 Charge cards

Section 75(1) of CCA 1974 does not apply to a charge card which, whilst advancing sums to the debtor under a debtor-creditor-supplier agreement, requires payment in full at the end of each month. In such a case, no credit is advanced to the debtor meaning CCA 1974, s.75(1) does not come into play.

6.2.10 Foreign purchases

Until recently, there was much debate between creditors, borrowers and the OFT over whether CCA 1974, s.75(1) applied to contracts made abroad. Creditors often argued that for there to be a claim under s.75(1), there needed to be a contract between a customer and supplier subject to UK law. If it applied to contracts made abroad, it would give CCA 1974 extraterritorial effect and there was nothing within CCA 1974 which suggested this was the intention. This argument has now been resolved after being considered by the House of Lords (now, of course, the Supreme Court) in *Office of Fair Trading* v. *Lloyds TSB Bank plc and others* [2007] UKHL 48. In short, the House of Lords decided that CCA 1974, s.75(1) does apply to transactions under a debtor-creditor-supplier agreement, falling within s.75(1), that are entered into abroad. This does, of course, often leave creditors with difficulties enforcing claims for an indemnity or contribution under CCA 1974, s.75(2).

6.3 FURTHER CONNECTED LENDER LIABILITY: S.75A

6.3.1 Introduction

For many creditors, one of the main concerns with CCA 1974, s.75(1) is that it does not require the debtor to enforce his claim against the supplier first. It is therefore entirely possible for the supplier to be completely unaware of the debtor's complaint at the time that a claim against the creditor is made. Debtors also faced problems where the goods bought were outside the ambit of CCA 1974, s.75(1): typically when the cash price is £100 or less or more than £30,000. Some of these issues have been addressed by CCA 1974, s.75A but, given it results from amendments by the Consumer Credit (EU Directive) Regulations 2010, SI 2010/1010, (CC(EUD)R 2010) it does not apply to all agreements.

6.3.2 When it applies

CCA 1974, s.75A states that if a debtor under a 'linked credit agreement' has a claim against the supplier for breach of contract (but not, unlike CCA 1974, s.75(1), misrepresentation) then the debtor may pursue that claim where any of the conditions in s.75A(2) are met. These are:

- the supplier cannot be traced;
- the debtor has contacted the supplier but the supplier has not responded;
- the supplier is insolvent; or
- the debtor has taken reasonable steps to pursue his claim against the supplier but has not obtained satisfaction for his claim.

Section 75A(3) makes it clear that 'reasonable steps' in s.75A(2) need not include litigation. It is therefore arguable that one letter to the supplier, which has not been responded to, will bring s.75A(1) into play. Debtors seeking to enforce such a claim would, however, be well advised to take all reasonable steps to secure satisfaction from the supplier. By doing so, it gives a creditor less room for attempting to avoid a claim.

If a debtor has accepted a replacement product or service or other compensation from the supplier then he is, by CCA 1974, s.75A(4), deemed to have obtained satisfaction from the supplier.

Section 75A(1) only applies where the debtor has a 'linked credit agreement'. By s.75A(5), this is defined as a regulated consumer credit agreement which serves exclusively to finance an agreement for the supply of specific goods or the provision of a specific service and where:

- the creditor uses the services of the supplier in connection with the preparation or making of the credit agreement; or
- the specific goods or provision of a specific service are explicitly specified in the credit agreement.

6.3.3   When it does not apply

By virtue of CCA 1974, s.75A(6), s.75A does not apply where:

- the cash value of the goods or service is £30,000 or less (because such a claim (assuming it was over £100, would fall within CCA 1974, s.75(1));
- the linked credit agreement is for credit which exceeds £60,260; or
- the linked credit agreement is entered into by the debtor wholly or predominantly for the purposes of a business carried on, or intended to be carried on, by him.

In this latter case, if the debtor has made a declaration of business use for the purposes of CCA 1974, s.16B. then this declaration may be taken into account for the purposes of s.75A (CCA 1974, s.75A(7)).

6.3.4   Date in force

Section 75A is forward-looking and applies to linked credit agreements entered into on or after 1 February 2011. It may also apply to some of these agreements before that date but dated on or after 30 April 2010 where the conditions contained in CC(EUD)R 2010, reg.101 are satisfied.

6.4   DUTY TO GIVE INFORMATION UNDER A FIXED-SUM CREDIT AGREEMENT

6.4.1   Introduction

CCA 1974, s.77 (together with s.78) has created a considerable amount of litigation in recent years (much of it unsuccessful from a debtor's point of view). It does, however, play an important role in informing the debtor about the status of his account.

6.4.2 Duty

By CCA 1974, s.77(1), if a creditor receives a written request from the debtor under a regulated agreement for fixed-sum credit and the statutory fee (£1 since 1 May 1998) it must provide, within the 'prescribed period', a copy of the executed agreement (if any) and a signed statement (according to the information to which it is practicable for him to refer) showing:

- the total amount paid under the agreement by the debtor;
- the total amount which has become payable under the agreement by the debtor but remains unpaid, and the various amounts comprised in that total sum, with the date when each became due; and
- the total amount which is to become payable under the agreement by the debtor, and the various amounts comprised in that total sum, with the date, or method of calculating the date, when each becomes due.

The statement in response to a request under CCA 1974, s.77(1) must be accurate. If it is not, the creditor will be bound by it subject to the court's power to grant relief under CCA 1974, s.172(1). Section 113(1) of CCA 1974 is also likely to give a surety the right to rely upon the statement.

Precedent

For a precedent response to a request under CCA 1974, s.77(1), see **Precedent 7**.

6.4.3 Prescribed period

The prescribed period is, by reg.2 of the Consumer Credit (Prescribed Periods for Giving Information) Regulations 1983, SI 1983/1569, 12 working days. The date on which the debtor's request is received by the creditor does not count: *Goldsmith's Co* v. *West Metropolitan Railway Co* [1904] 1 KB 1.

6.4.4 'Copy' of the executed agreement

The recent increase in litigation under CCA 1974, s.77(1) was, in part, based upon the allegation that, to comply with s.77(1), the creditor must provide a copy of the original (and signed) agreement. This allegation came before His Honour Judge Waksman QC, sitting in the High Court, in *Carey and others* v. *HSBC Bank plc and others* [2009] EWHC 3417 (QB). In a robust judgment, he decided (in the context of CCA 1974, s.78(1) but, as both ss.77 and 78 rely upon the Consumer Credit (Cancellation Notices and Copies of Documents) Regulations 1983, SI 1983/1557 for the definition of 'copy', it equally applies to s.77(1)) that:

- there is no need to keep the original signed agreement: creditors can satisfy s.78 (and, it follows, s.77) by providing a reconstituted version of the executed agreement which may be from sources other than the actual signed agreement;
- creditors need not, when responding to a s.78 or s.77 request, provide a document which would comply (if signed) with the requirements of CC(A)R 1983 as to the form of the agreement;
- the copy provided must contain the debtor's name and address at the time of entering into the agreement. Creditors can, however, insert this information from sources other than the actual signed agreement.

6.4.5 'From the debtor'

There is also an interesting point raised by the wording of CCA 1974, s.77(1) where it says that the request must be received 'from the debtor'. Creditors have argued, with some force, that the request must therefore be made by the debtor and not a claims management company or his solicitors. There is no authority on this point so we must look to other areas of law for some help.

The most obvious is landlord and tenant law. It is fairly well established that notice can be served by a party's agent so long as it has express or implied authority to send the notice. Recently, in *Procter & Gamble Technical Centres Ltd* v. *Brixton plc* [2003] 2 EGLR 24, Mr Justice Neuberger said that 'the giving of a notice can be delegated, provided it was delegated by the person who was required to give the notice'. It therefore follows that creditors receiving a request under CCA 1974, s.77(1) should ensure it has been sent by the debtor or someone acting for him. Where a request comes from a third party, it is entirely reasonable for the creditor to ask for a form of authority. Indeed, it is good practice for anyone acting for a debtor to provide one at the same time as the request. This is now reflected in the OFT's 'Guidance on sections 77, 78 and 79 of the Consumer Credit Act 1974', October 2010 (OFT 1272) which is available at **www.oft.gov.uk/shared_oft/business_ leaflets/consumer_credit/OFT1272.pdf**.

6.4.6 Missing information

If the creditor does not have sufficient information to provide a statement showing the information required by CCA 1974, s.77(1)(c) then it can comply by giving the basis on which, under the regulated agreement, these sums would be calculated. In short, this makes it easier for a creditor, perhaps where the rate of interest is variable, to comply with s.77(1). It does not allow a creditor to avoid compliance with CCA 1974, s.77(1)(c) where it should have the information but does not.

6.4.7 When the duty does not apply

The requirement to provide information under CCA 1974, s.77(1) does not apply, by s.77(3), to:

- an agreement where no sum is, or will or may become, payable by the debtor (i.e. where the agreement has been paid off); or
- a request made by the debtor less than one month after a previous request under s.77(1) and relating to the same agreement.

Section 77 does not apply to non-commercial agreements (CCA 1974, s.77(5)).

6.4.8   Consequences of non-compliance

If the creditor does not comply with CCA 1974, s.77(1) then it is not entitled, whilst the default continues, to 'enforce' the agreement. Until the introduction of the Consumer Protection from Unfair Trading Regulations 2008, SI 2008/1277 (CPUTR 2008) on 26 May 2008, non-compliance was also a criminal offence. However, the criminal sanction in s.77(4)(b) has now been repealed. Creditors not complying with s.77(1) still, however, risk a criminal prosecution under CPUTR 2008.

The meaning of the word 'enforce', contained in CCA 1974, s.77(4)(a), was recently considered by Mr Justice Flaux, sitting as a judge of the High Court, in *McGuffick v. Royal Bank of Scotland plc* [2009] EWHC 2386 (Comm). In this case, Mr McGuffick argued that his agreement was unenforceable as the creditor had failed to comply with CCA 1974, s.77(1). He therefore sought a declaration of unenforceability and various injunctions and mandatory orders either preventing the creditor from referring Mr McGuffick's default to credit reference agencies (CRAs) or requiring the creditor to either remove or amend the data provided.

In an emphatic judgment, the court decided that:

- reporting Mr McGuffick's default to CRAs did not amount to enforcement, nor did:

    - reporting to CRAs without telling them that the agreement was unenforceable;
    - publishing or threatening to publish Mr McGuffick's personal data concerning his conduct of the agreement to third parties;
    - demanding payment from Mr McGuffick;
    - issuing a default notice;
    - threatening legal proceedings;
    - instructing a third party to demand or seek payment; or
    - bringing proceedings;

- the claim for injunctive relief and mandatory orders failed in light of the court's finding on the word 'enforcement'.

It therefore seems fairly settled law that the only thing that a creditor may not do where it has failed to comply with CCA 1974, s.77(1) is to obtain and enforce a judgment against a debtor. Indeed, this was the conclusion that the Court of Appeal appeared to reach in *Phoenix Recoveries Ltd* v. *Kotecha* [2011] EWCA Civ 105 (which dealt with CCA 1974, s.78).

If the creditor complies with a CCA 1974, s.77(1) request, but out of time, then the only consequence is that it cannot 'enforce' the agreement during the period of non-compliance. By virtue of CCA 1974, s.170(1) there is no other sanction. If, therefore, a s.77(1) reply is served after proceedings are issued but before judgment, it is not a defence to say that at the time proceedings were issued, the creditor was in breach. After *McGuffick*, a creditor is entitled to issue proceedings during a period of non-compliance.

Non-compliance with CCA 1974, s.77(1) therefore gives a debtor a limited remedy which is, in essence, that the creditor cannot obtain judgment against him during the period of non-compliance. What happens if the debtor wrongfully, and in breach of the fixed-sum credit agreement, sells goods let under that agreement to a third party? Is the creditor prevented from bringing proceedings against the third party (subject, of course, to Part III of the Hire Purchase Act 1964 and other exceptions to the nemo dat rule) for wrongful interference? It seems the answer is no following *Bowmakers Ltd* v. *Barnet Instruments Ltd* [1945] KB 65, [1944] 2 All ER 579.

6.4.9 OFT guidance

Creditors may, however, wish to review their enforcement strategies where there is an unenforceable credit agreement, as it may be conduct that the OFT can take into account when considering a creditor's fitness to hold a licence. Fitness to hold a licence is discussed in detail at **2.10.5**. The OFT's 'Guidance on sections 77, 78 and 79 of the Consumer Credit Act 1974' (see **6.4.5** above) explains the OFT's view on the impact of CCA 1974, ss.77–79. Whilst it is respectfully submitted that the OFT's view goes beyond the legal framework, however, well-advised creditors and owners need to be aware of the guidance and, to avoid any regulatory issues, should comply with it.

6.5 DUTY TO GIVE PERIODIC STATEMENTS FOR FIXED-SUM CREDIT

6.5.1 Introduction

For many years, there was no requirement under CCA 1974 to serve a periodic statement for fixed-sum credit. It was, of course, open to a creditor to provide such a statement and some creditors decided to do so. Under the Consumer Credit Act 2006 (CCA 2006), s.6 there is now a statutory requirement from 1 October 2008 (contained in CCA 1974, s.77A) to provide such a statement for all agreements that have not completed by 1 October 2008.

6.5.2 Duty

By CCA 1974, s.77A, a creditor under a regulated agreement for fixed-sum credit must:

- within the period of one year beginning on the day after the date of the completed agreement or when the first movement takes place on the debtor's account, give the debtor a statement; and
- after the giving of this first statement, give further statements to the debtor at intervals of not more than a year.

If the period of one year expires on a non-working day then the period is extended to the next working day. The notice must be served (by CCA 1974, s.77A(1E)) within 30 days beginning with the day after the end of the period to which the statement relates.

Example

A creditor enters into a regulated fixed-sum agreement with a debtor on 5 January 2010. On the same day, the loan is advanced to the debtor. By CCA 1974, s.77(1C), the first notice must relate to the period from 5 January 2010 to 5 January 2011 (if, however, this day fell on a non-working day then the creditor could cover the period up to the next working day). It would then have 30 days after 5 January 2011 (or 30 days after the next working day after 5 January if it fell on a non-working day) to send the notice to the debtor.

6.5.3 When the duty does not apply

The creditor is not, however, required to serve a periodic notice, by virtue of CCA 1974, s.77A(4), if:

- there is no sum payable under the agreement by the debtor; and
- there is no such sum which will or may become payable under the agreement by the debtor.

CCA 1974, s.77A also does not apply to non-commercial agreements by virtue of s.77A(8). Similarly, it does not apply where the holder of a current overdraft overdraws on the account without a pre-arranged overdraft or exceeds the pre-arranged overdraft limit (CCA 1974, s.77A(9)).

6.5.4 Prescribed form

The Secretary of State was given power to make regulations about the form and content of this periodic statement under CCA 1974, s.77A(2). So far, no such regulations have been made. By CCA 1974, s.77A(3), the creditor cannot charge the debtor for the preparation or service of a periodic notice under s.77A.

6.5.5 Consequences of non-compliance

By virtue of CCA 1974, s.77A(6), if, before s.77A(4) is satisfied, the creditor fails to send the debtor a periodic statement within the timescale contained in s.77A(1E) then:

- the creditor is not entitled to 'enforce' the agreement during the period of non-compliance;
- the debtor has no liability to pay any sum of interest calculated during the period of non-compliance or any part of it; and
- the debtor has no liability to pay any default sum which would have become payable during the period of non-compliance or would have been payable after the end of that period but which relates to a breach that took place during the period of non-compliance.

It is likely, given the similarity and interrelationship between CCA 1974, s.77 and s.77A, that the High Court's decision in *McGuffick* v. *Royal Bank of Scotland plc* [2009] EWHC 2386 (Comm) on the meaning of the word 'enforce' will apply to CCA 1974, s.77A as it does to s.77.

The 'period of non-compliance' is defined in CCA 1974, s.77A(7) as being the period which:

- begins immediately after the end of the timescale contained in s.77A(1E); and
- ends at the end of the day on which the statement is given to the debtor or s.77A(4) is satisfied, whichever is the sooner.

6.6 DUTY TO GIVE STATEMENT OF ACCOUNT FOR FIXED-SUM CREDIT ON REQUEST

6.6.1 Duty

From 1 February 2011, and by CCA 1974, s.77B, a debtor under a regulated consumer credit agreement:

- for fixed-sum credit;
- for a fixed duration or term;
- where the credit is repayable by the debtor in instalments; and
- where the credit agreement is not an 'excluded agreement',

may request the creditor to, as soon as reasonably practical, provide a statement in writing which complies with CCA 1974, s.77B(3)–(5). By s.77B(6), a debtor may make a request at any time that the agreement is in force unless a previous request has been made less than one month before and has been complied with.

It is important to remember that CCA 1974, s.77B is forward-looking: it applies to agreements entered into on or after 1 February 2011 that fall within s.77B(1) and are not excluded agreements. It may also apply to some of these agreements dated on or after 30 April 2010 where the conditions contained in CC(EUD)R 2010, reg.101 are satisfied.

6.6.2   When the duty does not apply

Under CCA 1974, s.77B(9), an excluded agreement for the purposes of s.77B is an agreement:

- secured on land;
- under which a person takes an article in pawn;
- under which the creditor provides the debtor with credit exceeding £60,260; or
- entered into by the debtor wholly or predominately for the purpose of business carried on, or intended to be carried on, by him.

In this last category, a creditor may rely upon a declaration given by the debtor at the time of entry into an agreement under CCA 1974, s.16B.

6.6.3   Form of statement

CCA 1974, s.77B(3)–(5) requires the following details to be included in the statement to be given to the debtor:

- a table showing the details of each instalment owing under the agreement at the date of the request and for each instalment:
    - the date on which the instalment is due;
    - the amount of the instalment;
    - any conditions relating to the payment of the instalment; and
    - a breakdown of the instalment showing how much is made up of capital repayment, interest payment and other charges;
- where the rate of interest is variable or the charges under the agreement may be varied, a clear and concise indication that the table is valid only until the rate of interest or charges are varied.

The creditor cannot charge the debtor for the preparation or service of the statement (CCA 1974, s.77B(7)).

6.6.4   Consequences of non-compliance

If the creditor fails to comply with CCA 1974, s.77B, the debtor may by s.77B(8) bring a claim for breach of statutory duty although it is difficult to see how, in many cases, there would be any claim for damages given the requirement to prove loss.

6.7 DUTY TO GIVE INFORMATION UNDER A RUNNING-ACCOUNT CREDIT AGREEMENT

6.7.1 Introduction

As noted in **6.4.1** above, s.78 (together with s.77) of CCA 1974 has created a considerable amount of litigation in recent years (much of it unsuccessful from a debtor's point of view). It does, however, play an important role in informing the debtor about the status of his account.

6.7.2 Duty

By CCA 1974, s.78(1), if a creditor receives a written request from the debtor under a regulated agreement for running-account credit and the statutory fee (£1 since 1 May 1998) it must provide, within the 'prescribed period':

- a copy of the executed agreement (if any) and of any other document referred to in it; and
- a signed statement (according to the information to which it is practicable for him to refer) showing:

    - the state of the account;
    - the amount (if any) currently payable under the agreement; and
    the amounts and the due dates of any payments which, if the debtor does not draw further on the account, will later become payable under the agreement by the debtor.

The statement in response to a request under CCA 1974, s.78(1) must be accurate. If it is not, the creditor will be bound by it subject to the court's power to grant relief under CCA 1974, s.172(1). Section 113(1) of CCA 1974 is also likely to give a surety the right to rely upon the statement.

Precedent

For a precedent response to a request under CCA 1974, s.78(1), see **Precedent 8**.

6.7.3 Prescribed period

The 'prescribed period' is the same as it is for CCA 1974, s.77(1) (discussed at **6.4.3** above): 12 working days excluding the date of receipt.

6.7.4 'Copy' of the executed agreement

The requirement to provide a 'copy' is also the same as it is under CCA 1974, s.77(1) (discussed at **6.4.4** above): it can simply be a reconstituted version of the agreement. It does not need to be in the format required by CC(A)R 1983 (although as a matter of good practice it should be) and should give the debtor's name and address at the date of the agreement.

6.7.5 'From the debtor'

The requirement for a written request 'from the debtor' is the same as it is under CCA 1974, s.77(1) (discussed at **6.4.5** above).

6.7.6 When the duty does not apply

By CCA 1974, s.78(3), the duty under s.78(1) does not apply to:

- an agreement under which no sum is, or will or may become, payable by the debtor; or
- a request made less than one month after a previous request relating to the same agreement was complied with.

His Honour Judge Simon Brown QC, sitting in the High Court, decided in *Rankine* v. *American Express Services Europe Ltd* [2008] GCCR 7701 that the duty also does not apply where the agreement has been terminated. Finally, the duty does not apply to non-commercial agreements (CCA 1974, s.78(7)).

6.7.7 Consequences of non-compliance

The consequences of failing to comply with CCA 1974, s.78(1) are, by virtue of s.78(6), the same as failing to comply with CCA 1974, s.77(1) (discussed at **6.4.8** above).

6.7.8 OFT guidance

The OFT's Guidance, see further at **6.4.9** above, also applies to CCA 1974, s.78(1).

6.8 DUTY TO GIVE PERIODIC STATEMENTS FOR RUNNING-ACCOUNT CREDIT

6.8.1 Introduction

Unlike CCA 1974, s.77, s.78 always contained a requirement for a creditor to give a periodic statement where running-account credit is provided under a regulated agreement.

6.8.2   Duty

Under CCA 1974, s.78(4) the creditor is required to serve on the debtor a statement in the prescribed form and with the prescribed contents:

(a)   showing according to the information to which it is practicable for him to refer, the state of the account at regular intervals of not more than twelve months, and

(b)   where the agreement provides, in relation to specified periods, for the making of payments by the debtor, or the charging against him of interest or any other sum, showing according to the information to which it is practicable for him to refer the state of the account at the end of each of those periods during which there is any movement in the account.

By CCA 1974, s.78(4A), regulations may require such a statement to contain information in the prescribed terms about the consequences of the debtor failing to make payments as required by the agreement or only making payments of a prescribed description in prescribed circumstances.

6.8.3   Prescribed form

The form of the statement under CCA 1974, s.78(4) is prescribed by reg.2 of the Consumer Credit (Running-Account Credit Information) Regulations 1983, SI 1983/1570 (CC(RACI)R 1983). By reg.2(1), the statement must be in writing and comply with the Schedule to CC(RACI)R 1983. By the Schedule, the prescribed contents are:

1   Any opening balance standing on the account at the beginning of the period to which the statement relates and the balance at the end of that period.

1A   In the case of –

(a)   an authorised non-business overdraft agreement, or

(b)   an agreement which would be an authorised non-business overdraft agreement but for the fact that the credit is not repayable on demand or within three months,

the date of the previous statement.

2   The date of any movement in the account shown on the statement during the period to which the statement relates and the date of the end of that period.

3   The amount of any payment made into the account by, or to the credit of, the debtor during the period to which the statement relates.

4   The amount of any drawing on the account by the debtor during the period to which the statement relates, with sufficient information to enable the debtor to identify the drawing.

5   The amount of any interest or other charges payable by the debtor and applied to the account during the period to which the statement relates, whether or not the interest or other charges relate only to the said period.

6   Subject to paragraph 7 where the statement shows that interest has been applied to the account during the period to which the statement relates –

(a)   sufficient information to enable the debtor to check the calculation of the amount of the interest so applied; or

(b)   the rate of interest which has been used to calculate the amount of the interest so applied or, if the rate was varied, each rate of interest which has been so used and the time during which each rate applied; or

(c) a statement that the rate, or each rate, of interest which has been used to calculate the amount of the interest so applied will be provided by the creditor on request, together with a clear explanation of the manner in which the amount of the interest so applied has been calculated.

7 In the case of an authorised non-business overdraft agreement, only sub-paragraph (b) of paragraph 6 shall apply.

6.8.4 Prescribed period

By CCA 1974, s.78(5), a statement under s.78(4) must be given within the prescribed period after the end of the period to which the statement relates. Section 78(5) is supplemented by CC(RACI)R 1983, reg.3 and provides for the following prescribed periods:

- one month from the end of the period to which the statement relates if it includes a demand for payment; or
- 12 months from the end of the period to which the statement relates if there is no credit or debit balance at the end of that period; or
- 12 months from the date of the next credit or debit balance on the account where there has been no credit or debit balance on the account at any time to which the statement relates; or
- in any other case, six months from the end of the period to which the statement relates.

6.8.5 Consequences of non-compliance

Unlike a statement given under CCA 1974, s.78(1), a statement given under s.78(4) is not binding on the creditor because it is not specifically stated in s.172(1). Indeed, there is no sanction for non-compliance with CCA 1974, s.78(4) (as s.78(6) only applies to non-compliance with s.78(1)) and any further sanction is prohibited by CCA 1974, s.170(1). Creditors, should, however ensure that such notices are sent and are accurate. If a creditor fails to do so it is likely that the OFT, with its regulatory role, will consider it relevant when assessing the creditor's fitness to hold a consumer credit licence.

6.9 DUTY TO GIVE INFORMATION ON CHANGE OF RATE OF INTEREST

6.9.1 Duty

From 1 February 2011, and by CCA 1974, s.78A(1), a debtor under a regulated consumer credit agreement (other than an 'excluded agreement') with a variable rate of interest must be given written notice of the variation before it can take effect.

It is important to remember that s.78A is forward-looking: it applies to agreements entered into on or after 1 February 2011 that fall within s.78A(1) and are not excluded agreements. It may also apply to some of these agreements dated on or after 30 April 2010 where the conditions contained in CC(EUD)R 2010, reg.101 are satisfied.

6.9.2 When the duty does not apply

CCA 1974, s.78A(1) does not apply where:

- the agreement provides that the creditor must periodically tell the debtor in writing (at times provided in the agreement) of the matters set out in s.78A(3) in relation to any variation;
- the agreement provides that the rate of interest is to vary according to a reference rate;
- the reference rate is publicly available;
- information about the reference rate is available on the creditor's premises; and
- the variation of the rate of interest results from a change to the reference rate.

6.9.3 Excluded agreements

By virtue of CCA 1974, s.78A(6), an excluded agreement for the purposes of s.78A is:

(a) a debtor-creditor agreement arising where the holder of a current account overdraws on the account without a pre-arranged overdraft or exceeds a pre-arranged overdraft limit, or

(b) an agreement secured on land.

6.9.4 Information to be provided

If CCA 1974, s.78A(1) does apply, and the agreement is not excluded, then the information given to the debtor is (by s.78(3)):

(a) the variation in the rate of interest,

(b) the amount of any payments that are to be made after the variation has effect, if different, expressed as a sum of money where practicable, and

(c) if the number or frequency of payments changes as a result of the variation, the new number or frequency.

By s.78A(4) and (5), if the agreement is:

- an authorised business overdraft agreement;
- an authorised non-business overdraft agreement; or
- an agreement which would be an authorised non-business overdraft agreement but for the fact that the credit is not repayable on demand or within three months,

then the obligation to provide information under s.78A(1) only applies if the rate of interest increases and the only information required to be provided is the variation in the rate of interest.

6.10 DUTY TO GIVE HIRER INFORMATION

6.10.1 Duty

If an owner receives a written request from the hirer under a regulated consumer hire agreement and the statutory fee (£1 since 1 May 1998), under CCA 1974, s.79(1), it must provide, within the 'prescribed period':

- a copy of the executed agreement; and
- a signed statement (according to the information to which it is practicable for him to refer) showing:
  - the total sum which has become payable under the agreement but which remains unpaid; and
  - the various amounts comprised in this total sum with the date when each sum became due.

The statement in response to a request under s.79(1) must be accurate. If it is not, the creditor will be bound by it subject to the court's power to grant relief under CCA 1974, s.172(1). Section 113(1) of CCA 1974 is also likely to give a surety the right to rely upon the statement.

Precedent

For a precedent response to a request under CCA 1974, s.79(1), see **Precedent 9**.

6.10.2 Prescribed period

The 'prescribed period' is the same as it is for CCA 1974, s.77(1) (discussed at **6.4.3** above): 12 working days excluding the date of receipt.

6.10.3 'Copy' of the executed agreement

The requirement to provide a 'copy' is also the same as it is under CCA 1974, s.77(1) (discussed at **6.4.4** above): it can simply be a reconstituted version of the agreement. It does not need to be in the format required by CC(A)R 1983 (although as a matter of good practice it should be) and it should give the hirer's name and address at the date of the agreement.

6.10.4 'From the hirer'

The requirement for a written request 'from the hirer' is the same (in this context, there is no difference between the 'debtor' and the 'hirer') as it is under CCA 1974, s.77(1) (discussed at **6.4.5** above).

6.10.5 When the duty does not apply

By CCA 1974, s.79(2), the duty under s.79(1) does not apply to:

- an agreement under which no sum is, or will or may become, payable by the hirer; or
- a request made less than one month after a previous request under s.79(1) relating to the same agreement was complied with.

His Honour Judge Simon Brown QC's decision in *Rankine* v. *American Express Services Europe Ltd* [2008] GCCR 7701 (discussed at **6.7.6** above) is likely to apply to s.79(1). The effect of this is that there is no duty once the agreement has been terminated. The duty does not apply to non-commercial agreements (CCA 1974, s.79(4)).

6.10.6 Consequences of non-compliance

The consequences of failing to comply with CCA 1974, s.79(1) are, by virtue of s.79(3), the same as failing to comply with CCA 1974, s.77(1) (discussed at **6.4.8** above).

6.10.7 OFT guidance

The OFT's Guidance, see further at **6.4.9** above, also applies to CCA 1974, s.79(1).

6.11 DEBTOR'S DUTY TO GIVE INFORMATION ABOUT GOODS

6.11.1 Introduction

If a creditor or owner allows a debtor or hirer to have possession of goods under an agreement (regulated or otherwise), it is likely to have one eye on recovering possession of those goods in the event of default. Whilst the agreement will typically have provisions requiring the goods to remain in the debtor's or hirer's control at all times, defaulting debtors or hirers sometimes overlook these provisions and dispose of the goods. Creditors or owners therefore need some mechanism to find out where the goods are. This is contained in CCA 1974, s.80.

6.11.2 Duty

By CCA 1974, s.80(1), if the creditor or owner under a regulated agreement requires the goods to be kept in the debtor's or hirer's control, it may write to the debtor or hirer and ask him to tell the creditor, within seven working days, where the goods are. Section 80 does not, however, apply to non-commercial agreements.

Precedent

For a precedent request under CCA 1974, s.80(1), see **Precedent 10**.

6.11.3 Consequences of non-compliance

If the debtor or hirer fails to comply with a notice served under CCA 1974, s.80(1) within seven working days and continues to breach this provision for another 14 days then he commits a criminal offence (CCA 1974, s.80(2)). It is submitted that the offence is also committed if the debtor or hirer gives false or misleading information.

6.11.4 Joint debtors

By CCA 1974, s.185(1)(b), if there is more than one debtor or hirer then compliance with CCA 1974, s.80(1) by one of them will be compliance by both of them.

6.12 ALLOCATION OF PAYMENTS

Creditors or owners who have more than one agreement with their customers can run into an issue of how those payments are allocated. If the agreement is unregulated, the creditor or owner may (depending on the terms and conditions) allocate monies paid towards one agreement to another agreement. This is often the case in first charge mortgages, which are generally unregulated by CCA 1974. There is often a provision allowing the creditor to take money out of the debtor's current account with the same creditor and use it to pay off mortgage arrears.

In the case of a regulated agreement, the common law or contractual right to appropriate payments is restricted by CCA 1974, s.81. Section 81(1) gives the debtor or hirer the right to ask, where a payment is made towards two or more regulated agreements which is not enough to pay the total amount due under those agreements, that:

- the whole of the payment is appropriated to one of the agreements; or
- the payment is split, and appropriated in such proportion as he thinks fit.

If the debtor or hirer does not ask for the funds to be allocated in a certain way at the time of payment then, by CCA 1974, s.81(2), if the agreements include a hire-purchase, conditional sale, consumer hire or a secured agreement, the payment will be split in the same proportions as the sums due under those agreements bear to one another.

Example

Mr Taylor has two regulated agreements with a creditor: a fixed-sum loan agreement and a hire-purchase agreement. The monthly instalments are £100 for the loan agreement and £200 for the hire-purchase agreement. He sends a cheque to the lender for £30 but does not ask for it to be split in any particular way. Because one of the agreements falls within the list in CCA 1974, s.81(2), the creditor does not have a choice: the payment must be split £10 towards the loan and £20 towards the hire-purchase agreement.

If the debtor or hirer does not make the apportionment when making payment and none of his regulated agreements falls within CCA 1974, s.81(2) then the creditor is free to allocate the payment as it sees fit. Taking Mr Taylor's example, if both agreements were loan agreements then the creditor could apply the whole payment to one agreement, split it equally or split it in any other way as it thinks fit.

By CCA 1974, s.173(1), the parties cannot agree (either in the terms of the agreement or otherwise) to remove the debtor's or hirer's right under CCA 1974, s.81. It therefore follows that any such provision in a regulated agreement is void and unenforceable.

The position is, therefore, fairly straightforward where a debtor has two or more regulated agreements. What happens if, for example, one agreement is regulated and one is not? Does CCA 1974, s.81 apply either in part or at all? It seems the answer (although there is no authority on this point) is:

- the provisions of CCA 1974, s.81 do not apply where only one of the two agreements is regulated by CCA 1974. In these circumstances, a term in the agreement allowing the creditor or owner to apply the payments to a separate debt, not due under the regulated agreement, will be enforceable;
- if there are three or more agreements and at least two of them are regulated, a provision in the unregulated agreement allowing the creditor or owner to apply the payments to a separate debt (which, in many cases, will be the unregulated agreement) will be enforceable. If the payment exceeds the amount due under the unregulated agreement, then the balance will be subject to CCA 1974, s.81.

Example

Mr Holland has two regulated agreements, a fixed-sum loan agreement and a hire-purchase agreement, and an unregulated agreement with a creditor. The monthly instalments are

£100 for the loan agreement, £200 for the hire-purchase agreement and £500 for the unregulated agreement. He sends a cheque to the lender for £560 but does not ask for it to be split in any particular way. The unregulated agreement includes a term allowing the creditor to allocate a payment as it thinks fit. The creditor therefore applies £500 towards the unregulated agreement leaving a balance of £60. Because one of the agreements falls within the list in CCA 1974, s.81(2), it must be split £20 towards the loan and £40 towards the hire-purchase agreement.

6.13 VARIATION OF AGREEMENTS

6.13.1 Introduction

It is not unusual for parties (or one of the parties) to a regulated consumer credit or hire agreement to want to vary the terms. Those wishing to do so should remember that there are formal steps to take before a regulated agreement can be varied, which are found in CCA 1974, s.82.

Section 82 deals with two situations:

- where the variation is made by one of the parties in accordance with a power under the existing regulated agreement (this is when CCA 1974, s.82(1) applies); or
- where the parties agree together that they want to modify or change the terms of an existing regulated agreement (this is when CCA 1974, s.82(2)–(6) applies).

These provisions do not apply to non-commercial agreements (CCA 1974, s.82(7)).

6.13.2 Unilateral variation

By CCA 1974, s.82(1), if the parties wish to vary the agreement under a power or provision contained in that agreement then the variation does not take effect until written notice is given to the debtor or hirer in the 'prescribed manner'. This provision often applies where a regulated agreement contains a provision allowing the creditor or owner to vary the rate of interest. If it does so, it must give written notice to the debtor or owner.

The 'prescribed manner' is found in the Consumer Credit (Notice of Variation of Agreements) Regulations 1977, SI 1977/328 (CC(NVA)R 1977). For many variations, these regulations simply require particulars of the variation to be served on the debtor or hirer before the variation takes effect (CC(NVA)R 1977, reg.2). More unusual variations are dealt with by CC(NVA)R 1977, regs.3 and 4 which (amongst other things) require notice to be given in the *London Gazette* or at the property.

If written notice in the prescribed manner is not provided, the variation does not take effect. By CCA 1974, s.170, there is no further sanction for breach of CCA 1974, s.82(1). The creditor is therefore entitled to enforce the terms of the unvaried agreement assuming, of course, that there are no other issues preventing enforcement.

6.13.3 Exceptions to s.82(1)

By virtue of CCA 1974, s.82(1A)–(1E), there are some exceptions to s.82(1) for agreements entered into on or after 1 February 2011. The exceptions also apply to prospective consumer credit agreements entered into on or after 30 April 2010 but before 1 February 2011 where the conditions contained in CC(EUD)R 2010, reg.101 are satisfied.

The exceptions to CCA 1974, s.82(1) are where:

- there is a variation to the rate of interest charged under an agreement not secured on land as this is caught by CCA 1974, s.78A (s.82(1A));
- there is a variation to the rate of interest charged under an agreement secured on land if (a) the agreement falls within CCA 1974, s.82(1D) and (b) the variation is a reduction in rate (s.82(1B));
- there is a variation in any other charge under an agreement if (a) the agreement falls within CCA 1974, s.82(1D) and (b) the variation is a reduction in the charge (s.82(1C));
- the agreement is a debtor-creditor-supplier agreement arising where the holder of a current account overdraws on the account without a pre-arranged overdraft or exceeds a pre-arranged overdraft limit (s.82(1E)).

Section 82(1D) of CCA 1974 says that the agreements mentioned in s.82(1B) and (1C) are:

- an authorised business overdraft agreement;
- an authorised non-business overdraft agreement; or
- an agreement which would be an authorised non-business overdraft agreement but for the fact that the credit is not repayable on demand or within three months.

6.13.4 Variation by agreement

Section 82(2)–(6B) of CCA 1974 deals with variations or supplements to a regulated agreement agreed by both parties. The effect of such an agreement is, by s.82(2), that it is treated (for the purposes of CCA 1974) as:

- revoking the earlier agreement; and
- containing provisions reproducing the combined effect of the two agreements,

and obligations outstanding under the first agreement are treated as being outstanding under the modifying agreement.

6.13.5 When does s.82(2) not apply?

By virtue of CCA 1974, s.82(2A) and (2B), there are some exceptions to s.82(2) for agreements entered into on or after 1 February 2011. These exceptions also apply to prospective consumer credit agreements entered into on or after 30 April 2010 but before 1 February 2011 where the conditions contained in CC(EUD)R 2010, reg.101 are satisfied. The exceptions are where:

- the earlier or the modifying agreements are exempt agreements within the meaning of CCA 1974, s.16(6C) or s.16C;
- the modifying agreement varies (a) the amount of the repayments made under the earlier agreement or (b) the duration of the agreement as a result of the debtor's decision to partially repay his indebtedness under the agreement using the provisions of CCA 1974, s.94(3) (discussed at **7.7**).

6.13.6 Earlier agreement regulated but modifying agreement is not: effect

There is often a problem where the earlier agreement is a regulated agreement but the modifying agreement is not. In such a case then, unless the modifying agreement is for running-account credit or an exempt agreement as a result of CCA 1974, s.16(6C) or s.16C, it is, by CCA 1974, s.82(3), treated as a regulated agreement.

6.13.7 Temporary extension of credit under modifying agreement: effect

If the earlier agreement is a regulated agreement for running-account credit and, under the terms of the modifying agreement, the creditor allows the debtor to temporarily exceed the credit limit, then Part V of CCA 1974 (except s.56) does not apply to the modifying agreement (CCA 1974, s.82(4)).

6.13.8 Earlier agreement regulated and cancellable: effect of modification

If the earlier agreement is a cancellable agreement and the modification is made within the statutory period under CCA 1974, s.68 then, whether or not the modifying agreement would be a cancellable agreement, it will be treated as a cancellable agreement. It also follows, by CCA 1974, s.82(5), that a notice may be served under CCA 1974, s.68 not later than the end of the statutory period for the earlier agreement.

Example

Mrs Twist enters into a regulated debtor-creditor fixed-sum regulated credit agreement which is cancellable. She therefore has a statutory cancellation period or a cooling-off period, by CCA 1974, s.68, between her signing the unexecuted agreement and:

- the end of the fifth day following the day on which she received a copy of the executed agreement or a notice by s.64(1)(b); or
- if s.64(1)(b) does not apply, the end of the 14th day following the day on which she signed the unexecuted agreement.

If, before the end of the cooling-off period, she and the creditor agree to modify the terms, then the effect of CCA 1974, s.82(5) is to simply say that the cooling-off period is not extended.

Under CCA 1974, s.82(6), a modifying agreement is not treated as a cancellable agreement unless the provisions of s.82(5) apply. It therefore follows that the only time a modifying agreement will be a cancellable agreement is if it is entered into during the cancellation period of the initial agreement. Even in that case, the cancellation period is not extended.

Finally, by CCA 1974, s.82(5A), the provisions of s.82(5) do not apply where the modifying agreement is an exempt agreement as a result of CCA 1974, s.16(6C) or s.16C.

6.13.9 Earlier agreement regulated with right to withdraw: effect of modification

If the earlier agreement is an agreement subject to CCA 1974, s.66A and the modifying agreement is made within the period that the debtor may give written notice of his withdrawal, then, whether or not the modifying agreement would be an agreement to which CCA 1974, s.66A applies, it will be treated as such an agreement but the period for giving the withdrawal notice is not extended (CCA 1974, s.82(6A)).

Under CCA 1974, s.82(6B), the provisions relating to withdrawal contained in CCA 1974, s.66A do not apply to a modifying agreement except to the extent provided in s.82(6A). It therefore follows that the only time a modifying agreement will be treated as containing a right of withdrawal is if it is entered into during the period of the right to withdraw from the initial agreement. Even in that case, the withdrawal period is not extended.

6.13.10 Non-commercial agreements

Section 82 of CCA 1974 does not apply to a non-commercial agreement (CCA 1974, s.82(7)).

6.13.11 Form and content of modifying agreements

The form and content of modifying agreements under CCA 1974, s.82(2) is discussed at **5.11**.

6.14 ASSIGNMENT OF RIGHTS

Under CCA 1974, s.82A(1), where the creditor's rights under a regulated consumer credit agreement are assigned to a third party, the assignee must arrange for notice of the assignment to be given to the debtor:

- as soon as reasonably possible; or
- if, after the assignment, the arrangements for servicing the credit under the agreement do not change as far as the debtor is concerned, on or before the first occasion that they do.

By virtue of CCA 1974, s.82A(2), this section does not apply to an agreement secured on land.

It is suggested that there is nothing new in these provisions. Third parties who have acquired a debt from a creditor should, to ensure the assignment is lawful and complies with the Law of Property Act 1925, s.136, serve notice of the assignment on the debtor. It is therefore submitted that creditors having rights assigned to them under consumer hire agreements, which are not caught by CCA 1974, s.82A, should still serve a notice of assignment to avoid issues recovering the debt.

It is important to remember that CCA 1974, s.82A is, once again, forward-looking: it applies to agreements entered into on or after 1 February 2011. It may also apply to some agreements entered into on or after 30 April 2010 but before 1 February 2011 where the conditions contained in CC(EUD)R 2010, reg.101 are satisfied.

6.15 MISUSE OF CREDIT AND CREDIT-TOKENS

6.15.1 Introduction

There are some relatively short provisions dealing with misuse: CCA 1974, ss.83 and 84. Section 83 deals with liability for misuse of credit facilities whilst s.84 deals with liability for misuse of credit-tokens.

6.15.2 Misuse of credit facilities

Section 83(1) of CCA 1974 makes it clear that the debtor under a regulated credit agreement will not be liable for any loss resulting from the use of a credit facility by another person that does not act, and is not treated as acting, as his agent. There is a saving provision in CCA 1974, s.83(2) which makes it clear that the provisions of s.83(1) do not apply where the agreement is non-commercial or where loss results from misuse of an instrument to which the Cheques Act 1957, s.4 applies.

It is clear that credit facilities include not only running-account credit (for example, credit cards) but also fixed-sum credit because of the wording of CCA 1974, s.10(1). The provisions are also likely to apply to a debit card (but not a charge card as this is exempt) but only where the account becomes overdrawn. It is only at that stage that the creditor advances 'credit' to the debtor and, by doing so, creates a regulated consumer credit agreement.

The issue of agency is, once again, relevant in CCA 1974, s.83. In particular, it looks at whether a person misusing credit facilities is 'treated as acting' as the debtor's agent. There is no definition in CCA 1974 of when a third party acts as the debtor's agent, unlike the position for creditors where CCA 1974, s.56 or s.102 apply, meaning common law of agency applies. In short, this should mean that a debtor is not liable unless he authorises the third party's use of the credit facilities or is aware that the third party is using it.

6.15.3 Misuse of credit-tokens

The purpose of CCA 1974, s.84 is to provide two exceptions to CCA 1974, s.83, namely:

- a debtor under a credit-token agreement will be liable up to £50 (or the credit limit, if lower) for loss arising following misuse of the credit-token by third parties during any time when the credit-token is not in the debtor's (or any other authorised person's) hands (CCA 1974, s.84(1)); and
- a debtor under a credit-token agreement will be liable for any loss to the creditor resulting from use of the credit-token by any person who obtained possession of it with the debtor's consent (CCA 1974, s.84(2)).

There are also carve-out provisions in CCA 1974, s.84(3) and (4). This makes it clear that s.84(1) and (2) does not apply:

- to any use of a credit-token after the creditor has been given oral or written notice that it is lost or stolen or is for any other reason liable to misuse (CCA 1974, s.84(3)); or
- unless contained in the credit-token agreement in the 'prescribed manner' are particulars of the name, address and telephone number of the person who must be given notice under s.84(3) (CCA 1974, s.84(4)).

The 'prescribed manner' is given in reg.2 of the Consumer Credit (Credit-Token Agreements) Regulations 1983, SI 1983/1555.

If a debtor gives notice under CCA 1974, s.84(3) then it takes effect when it is received. If, however, the notice was given orally but the agreement requires it in writing then it is treated as not being given if it is not confirmed in writing within seven days (CCA 1974, s.84(5)). To maximise the benefit of CCA 1974, s.84, creditors should therefore ensure their terms and conditions require written notice to be given and then have procedures in place to ensure any notice received is logged. Debtors, on the other hand, would be well advised to give both oral and written notice.

If, under one credit-token agreement, more than one credit-token is issued then the provisions of CCA 1974, s.84 apply to each credit-token separately (CCA 1974, s.84(8)). This is a particularly important issue for debtors who obtain a further credit card for another person (perhaps their partner). If this happens, and both credit-tokens are misused, the provisions of s.84 apply separately to both credit-tokens.

6.16 ISSUE OF NEW CREDIT-TOKENS

If a creditor issues a new credit-token (which they often do before a credit card expires) then it must, at the same time, give the debtor a 'copy' of the executed agreement (if any) and any other document referred to in it (CCA 1974, s.85(1)). If it fails to do so, the creditor is not entitled (whilst the default continues) to enforce the agreement (CCA 1974, s.85(2)(a)).

The use of the word 'copy' will, of course, bring the Consumer Credit (Cancellation Notices and Copies of Documents) Regulations 1983 into play. In short, and following the High Court's recent judgment in *Carey and others* v. *HSBC Bank plc and others* [2009] EWHC 3417 (QB), this will mean that a reconstituted copy of the agreement may be provided. This is discussed in more detail at **6.4.4** above.

It is submitted that the consequences of failing to comply with CCA 1974, s.85(1) will be exactly the same as the consequences of the creditor failing to comply with CCA 1974, ss.77–79. For a fuller consideration of the consequences of failing to comply and the meaning of 'enforce' in this context, see **6.4.8** above.

If there are joint debtors, the effect of CCA 1974, s.185(1)(a) appears to be that each debtor will need a copy of the documents mentioned in CCA 1974, s.85(1) even where a token is only given to one of them. By virtue of CCA 1974, s.85(3), s.85 does not apply to small agreements.

6.17 DEATH OF DEBTOR OR HIRER

The debtor's or hirer's death often causes practical problems for creditors. In short:

- a creditor or owner is not entitled, because of the debtor's or hirer's death, to do any of the acts mentioned in CCA 1974, s.87(1)(a)–(e) where the agreement is fully secured at the date of death (CCA 1974, s.86(1));
- if the agreement is only partly secured or is unsecured at the date of death, the creditor or owner is entitled to do any of the acts mentioned in CCA 1974, s.87(1)(a)–(e) but only with the court's permission (CCA 1974, s.86(2)).

The debtor's or hirer's death, however, does not:

- prevent an agreement which is not for a fixed duration being terminated (CCA 1974, s.86(3)); or
- prevent the creditor from taking steps to treat the debtor's or owner's right to draw on any credit as restricted or deferred (CCA 1974, s.86(4));

- affect the operation of any agreement providing for payment of sums out of the proceeds of a life assurance policy towards monies due under a regulated agreement or becoming due on the debtor's or hirer's death (CCA 1974, s.86(5)).

If there are joint debtors then, by virtue of CCA 1974, s.185(4), the provisions of CCA 1974, s.86 apply when only one of the debtors has died. The creditor or owner may, however, take the steps in CCA 1974, s.87(1)(a)–(e) if the personal representatives give their 'informed consent'. The problems of 'informed consent' are discussed under 'Consent to repossession' at **7.3.5**.

CHAPTER 7

Termination

7.1 INTRODUCTION

The formalities for ending a regulated agreement are complex and prescribed by the Consumer Credit Act 1974 (CCA 1974) and the Consumer Credit (Enforcement, Default and Termination Notices) Regulations 1983, SI 1983/1561 (CC(EDTN)R 1983). Proper termination is particularly important for lenders in the market of providing finance to acquire goods. For example, if a vehicle is repossessed following the service of a defective default notice, the agreement will probably end and the debtor may be entitled to repayment of the sums made under the agreement. We therefore turn to the various ways in which a regulated agreement may be terminated.

7.2 ARREARS AND DEFAULT SUMS NOTICES

7.2.1 Notice of sums in arrears – fixed-sum credit

When does s.86B apply?

Section 86B of CCA 1974 applies where the following conditions are satisfied:

- the debtor or hirer under a regulated agreement for fixed-sum credit or a regulated consumer hire agreement which is neither a non-commercial agreement nor a small agreement is required to have made at least two payments under the agreement before that time;
- the total sum paid under the agreement by the debtor or hirer is less than the total sum which he is required to have paid before that time;
- the amount of the shortfall is no less than the sum of the last two payments which he is required to have made before that time;
- the creditor or owner is not already under a duty to give the debtor or hirer notices under CCA 1974, s.86B for the agreement; and
- if a judgment has been given under the agreement before that time, there is no sum still to be paid under the judgment by the debtor or hirer.

If the debtor or hirer must make all payments at intervals of one week or less then, by CCA 1974, s.86B(9), the phrase 'four payments' replaces the phrase 'two payments' in CCA 1974, s.86(1)(a) and (c). For such agreements made before the beginning of the 'relevant period', only amounts resulting from failures by the debtor or hirer to make payments he is required to have made during that period are be taken into account in determining any shortfall for the purposes of s.86B(1)(c) (CCA 1974, s.86B(10)). The 'relevant period' means the period of 20 weeks ending with the day on which the debtor or hirer is required to have made the most recent payment under the agreement.

Duty

If the above conditions are satisfied then, by CCA 1974, s.86B(2), the creditor or owner:

- must, within 14 days beginning with the day on which the conditions mentioned in s.86B(1) are satisfied, give the debtor or hirer a notice under this section (CCA 1974, s.86B(2)(a)); and
- after the giving of that notice, must give the debtor or hirer further notices at intervals of not more than six months (CCA 1974, s.86B(2)(b)).

By virtue of CCA 1974, s.86B(6), an arrears sums notice must include a copy of the current arrears information sheet. The latest arrears information sheets are published by the OFT and are available from the OFT's website (at **www.oft.gov.uk/about-the-oft/legal-powers/legal/cca/CCA2006/information/**). By s.86B(7), the creditor or owner cannot charge the debtor or hirer for the preparation or service of an arrears sums notice.

When does the duty come to an end?

The creditor or owner's duty to give notices under CCA 1974, s.86B(2) ends when:

- the debtor or hirer is no longer in arrears; or
- a judgment is given on the agreement under which a sum is required to be paid by the debtor or hirer.

By CCA 1974, s.86B(5), a debtor or hirer is no longer in arrears when:

- no payments, which the debtor or hirer has ever failed to make under the agreement when required, are still owing;
- no default sum, which has ever become payable under the agreement for his failure to pay any sum under the agreement when required, is still owing;
- no sum of interest, which has ever become payable under the agreement for such a default sum, is still owing; and

- no other sum of interest, which has ever become payable under the agreement in connection with his failure to pay any sum under the agreement when required, is still owing.

By CCA 1974, s.86B(3), if either of the conditions bringing the duty under s.86B(2) to an end happens before the notice under s.86B(2)(a) is given, the duty does not end until after that notice is given.

Prescribed form

The Secretary of State was given the power under CCA 1974, s.86B(8) to make regulations about the form and content of an arrears sums notice. Such a power was exercised when the Secretary of State made the Consumer Credit (Information Requirements and Duration of Licences and Charges) Regulations 2007, SI 2007/1167 (CC(IRDLC)R 2007). By CC(IRDLC)R 2007, reg.19(1), and subject to regs.20 to 23, the notice must contain:

- a form of wording to the effect that the notice is given in compliance with CCA 1974 because the debtor or hirer is behind with the sums payable under the agreement;
- a form of wording encouraging the debtor or the hirer to discuss the state of his account with the creditor or owner;
- the information required by Sched.3, paras.1–3;
- statements in the form specified in Sched.3, paras.4 and 5 as applicable; and
- a statement in the form specified in Part 5 of Sched.3.

If the notice is given under CCA 1974, s.86B(2)(a) then by CC(IRDLC)R 2007, reg.19(2):

- it must include the information set out in Part 2 of Sched.3;
- the creditor or owner must within 15 working days of receiving the debtor's or hirer's request for further information about the shortfall which gave rise to the duty to give the notice, give the debtor or hirer in relation to each of the sums which comprise the shortfall, notice of:
  - the amount of the sums due which comprise the shortfall;
  - the date on which the sums became due; and
  - the amounts the debtor or hirer paid in respect of the sums due and the dates of those payments;
- it must, except where it contains all the information specified in CC(IRDLC)R 2007, reg.19(2)(b), include a statement in the following form:

  If you want more information about which payments you failed to make please get in touch with us. We are required to give you this information within fifteen working days of receiving your request for it.

- where the creditor or owner and the debtor or hirer have entered into an agreement to aggregate, the references to sums due and the reference to amounts paid in CC(IRDLC)R 2007, reg.19(2)(b) may be construed as a reference to the aggregated sums due to the creditor or owner and the aggregated amounts paid by the debtor or hirer in accordance with the terms of that agreement.

If the notice is given under CCA 1974, s.86B(2)(a) then by CC(IRDLC)R 2007, reg.19(3), subject to reg.19(3A), it must also include the information set out in Part 3 of Sched.3 and the statement in Sched.3, para.4(1) must be amended as specified in para.13 of that Schedule. By reg.19(3A), if the rate or rates of interest provided for under the agreement are not applicable on an annual basis, Sched.3, para.9 does not require amounts and dates of interest which became due during the period to which the notice relates to be set out separately in the notice.

By CC(IRDLC)R 2007, reg.19(4), if the notice includes a form of wording to the effect that it is not a demand for immediate payment, the creditor or owner must include wording explaining why it is not such a demand.

Failure to give notice

If the creditor or owner fails to give notice within the prescribed period, it is not entitled to enforce the agreement during the period of non-compliance (CCA 1974, s.86D(3)). This period of non-compliance begins the day after the last date for the notice and ends on the date that the notice is given. By CCA 1974, s.86D(4), the debtor or hirer has no liability to pay:

- any sum of interest to the extent calculated by reference to the period of non-compliance or to any part of it; or
- any default sum which (apart from s.86D(4)):
  - would have become payable during the period of non-compliance; or
  - would have become payable after the end of that period in connection with a breach of the agreement which occurs during that period (whether or not the breach continues after the end of that period).

It is submitted that the word 'enforce' means the same as it does in the context of CCA 1974, ss.74–79. We have already discussed this concept at **6.4.8**.

7.2.2 Notice of sums in arrears – running-account credit

When does s.86C apply?

Section 86C of CCA 1974 applies at any time when the following conditions are satisfied:

- the debtor under a regulated agreement for running-account credit which is neither a non-commercial agreement nor a small agreement is required to have made at least two payments under the agreement before that time;
- the last two payments which he is required to have made before that time have not been made;
- the creditor has not already been required to give a notice under s.86C for either of those payments; and
- if a judgment has been given on the agreement before that time, there is no sum still to be paid under the judgment by the debtor.

Duty

If those conditions are satisfied then, by CCA 1974, s.86C(2), the creditor must, no later than the end of the period within which it is next required to give a statement under CCA 1974, s.78(4) for the agreement, give the debtor a notice under CCA 1974, s.86C. By s.86C(3), an arrears sums notice must include a copy of the current arrears information sheet. The latest arrears information sheets are published by the OFT and are available from the OFT's website (at **www.oft.gov.uk/about-the-oft/ legal-powers/legal/cca/CCA2006/information/**). Under CCA 1974, s.86C(5), the creditor or owner cannot charge the debtor or hirer for the preparation or service of an arrears sums notice.

Prescribed form

The Secretary of State was given the power to make regulations under CCA 1974, s.86C(6) about the form and content of an arrears sums notice. Such a power was exercised when the Secretary of State made CC(IRDLC)R 2007. By CC(IRDLC)R 2007, reg.24(1), and subject to regs.25 and 26, the notice must contain:

- a form of wording to the effect that it is given in compliance with CCA 1974 because the debtor is behind with his payments under the agreement;
- a form of wording encouraging the debtor to discuss the state of his account with the creditor;
- the information required by Sched.3, paras.14–17;
- a statement in the form set out in Sched.3, para.18 and the appropriate statement specified in Sched.3, para.19; and
- a statement in the form specified in Part 5 of Sched.3.

By CC(IRDLC)R 2007, reg.24(2), where the notice includes wording to the effect that it is not a demand for immediate payment the creditor must include wording explaining why it is not such a demand. Under CCA 1974, s.86C(4), the notice may be incorporated in a statement or other notice which the creditor gives the debtor in relation to the agreement by virtue of another provision of CCA 1974.

Failure to give notice

If the creditor or owner fails to give notice within the prescribed period, it is not entitled to enforce the agreement during the period of non-compliance (CCA 1974, s.86D(3)). This period of non-compliance begins the day after the last date for the notice and ends on the date that the notice is given. By virtue of s.86D(4), the debtor or hirer has no liability to pay:

- any sum of interest to the extent calculated by reference to the period of non-compliance or to any part of it; or
- any default sum which (apart from s.86D(4)):
  - would have become payable during the period of non-compliance; or
  - would have become payable after the end of that period in connection with a breach of the agreement which occurs during that period (whether or not the breach continues after the end of that period).

It is submitted that the word 'enforce' means the same as it does in the context of CCA 1974, ss.74–79. We have already discussed this concept at **6.4.8**.

7.2.3 Notice of default sums

Section 86E of CCA 1974 applies where a default sum becomes payable under a regulated agreement by the debtor or hirer (CCA 1974, s.86E(1)). It does not, by s.86E(8), apply to non-commercial or small agreements. Under s.86E(2), the creditor or owner is under a duty, within the prescribed period after the default sum becomes payable, to give the debtor or hirer a notice. By s.86E(3), a notice of default sums may be incorporated in a statement or other notice which the creditor or owner gives the debtor or hirer for the agreement by virtue of another provision of CCA 1974. By s.86E(4), the debtor or hirer has no liability to pay interest on the default sum to the extent that the interest is calculated by reference to a period starting before the 29th day after the day on which the debtor or hirer is given the notice under CCA 1974, s.86E.

If the creditor or owner fails to give the debtor or hirer the notice within the prescribed period then it is not entitled to enforce the agreement until the notice is given to the debtor or hirer (CCA 1974, s.86(5)). It is submitted that the word 'enforce' means the same as it does in the context of CCA 1974, ss.77–79. We have already discussed this concept at **6.4.8**. By virtue of CCA 1974, s.86E(6), the creditor or owner cannot charge the debtor or hirer for the preparation or service of a default sums notice. By CCA 1974, s.86F(2), the debtor or hirer is only liable to pay simple interest on the default sum.

Under CC(IRDLC)R 2007:

- a default sums notice must be given to the debtor or hirer by the creditor or owner within 35 days of a default sum becoming payable by the debtor or hirer (reg.28);

- a default sums notice must contain a form of wording to the effect that it relates to default sums and is given in compliance with CCA 1974 (reg.29);
- a default sums notice must contain the information and the form of wording set out in Part 1 of Sched.4 (reg.30);
- if a default sums notice is given for an agreement which provides that interest is payable on default sums it must contain the appropriate form of wording set out in Part 2 of Sched.4 (reg.31);
- if a default sums notice is incorporated into another notice or statement which the creditor gives the debtor in relation to the agreement by virtue of another provision of CCA 1974 (the 'other notice'), the default sums notice need not contain such of the information required under Sched.4, paras.1–3 as is required to be included in the other notice by the provision of CCA 1974 under which the other notice is given (reg.32).

7.3   TERMINATION BY THE CREDITOR OR OWNER

7.3.1   Default notice

Introduction

Like the name suggests, a default notice is required where the debtor or hirer has defaulted on his obligations under a regulated consumer credit or hire agreement. It should, however, be remembered that a default notice is not required (nor, indeed, is any other notice under CCA 1974) to bring proceeding against the debtor or hirer for instalments that have fallen due. Similarly, there is no requirement to serve a default notice before the creditor can become entitled to treat the debtor's right to draw upon any credit as restricted or deferred (CCA 1974, s.87(2)). What this means in practice is that creditors providing credit cards need not serve a default notice to prevent a debtor using the card where he has exceeded the credit limit. Instead, a default notice is required only to bring forward the debtor's or hirer's obligations and to:

- terminate the agreement (s.87(1)(a)); or
- demand earlier payment of any sum (s.87(1)(b)); or
- recover possession of any goods or land (s.87(1)(c)); or
- treat any right conferred on the debtor or hirer by the agreement as terminated, restricted or deferred (s.87(1)(d)); or
- enforce any security (s.87(1)(e)).

Form and content

Under CCA 1974, s.88(1), the default notice must contain the following information:

- the nature of the alleged breach (s.88(1)(a));

230

- if the default is capable of remedy (the most common default is non-payment which is, of course, capable of being remedied), what the debtor or hirer must do and the date by which the debtor must do it (s.88(1)(b));
- if the default is not capable of remedy (the most common of which is where the debtor or hirer wrongfully sells the goods to a third party or they are destroyed), what compensation (if any) is required and the date by which the debtor or hirer must pay it (s.88(1)(c));
- a date of not less than 14 days (7 days if the notice pre-dates 1 October 2006) after service of the notice by which time the debtor or hirer must comply (s.88(2));
- the consequences if the debtor or hirer fails to comply with the default notice (s.88(4));
- a copy of the OFT's default information sheet (s.88(4A)).

Section 88 is also supplemented by CC(EDTN)R 1983, reg.2(2). This surprisingly adds very little to the requirements of CCA 1974, ss.87 and 88 but requires the creditor or owner to:

- state that the notice is a 'default notice served under section 87(1) of the Consumer Credit Act 1974' (CC(EDTN)R 1983, reg.2(2)(a));
- include the following information:

  - a description of the agreement sufficient to identify it (CC(EDTN)R 1983, Sched.2, para.1);
  - the name and a postal address of the creditor or owner (Sched.2, para.2(a));
  - the name and a postal address of the debtor or hirer (Sched.2, para.2(b));
  - a specification of the provision alleged to have been breached (Sched.2, para.3(a));
  - a specification of the nature of the alleged breach (Sched.2, para.3(b));
  - if the breach is capable of remedy, what action is required to remedy it and the date (being a date not less than 14 days after the date of service of the notice) before that action is to be taken (Sched.2, para.3(c)); or
  - if the breach is not capable of remedy, the sum (if any) required to be paid as compensation for the breach and the date (being a date not less than 14 days after the date of service of the notice) before that sum is to be paid (Sched.2, para.3(d));
  - a clear and unambiguous statement indicating that, if any action required to be specified by Sched.2, para.3(c) or (d) is to be taken or if no such action is to be taken, the relevant action or actions (specified in CCA 1974, s.87(1)) which the creditor or owner intends to take after the date on the notice expires (Sched.2, para.6);
  - if a sum of money is required to be paid, the amount of the sum before any rebate on early settlement and, if a rebate is allowable, the amount of the rebate calculated on the assumption that early settlement takes place on

the date specified in the notice and the difference between the rebated and unrebated sum (Sched.2, para.8);

- include statements in the following form:

    – for all agreements where any action under Sched.2, para.3(c) or (d) is required, the following statement immediately after the statement of that action (Sched.2, para.4):

    > IF THE ACTION REQUIRED BY THIS NOTICE IS TAKEN BEFORE THE DATE SHOWN NO FURTHER ENFORCEMENT ACTION WILL BE TAKEN IN RESPECT OF THE BREACH

    – for all agreements where any action under Sched.2, para.3(c) or (d) is required, the following statement immediately before the statement required by Sched.2, para.6 (Sched.2, para.5):

    > IF YOU DO NOT TAKE THE ACTION REQUIRED BY THIS NOTICE BEFORE THE DATE SHOWN THEN THE FURTHER ACTION SET OUT BELOW MAY BE TAKEN AGAINST YOU [OR A SURETY]

    – for hire-purchase or conditional sale agreements made on or after 19 May 1985 where title to the goods remains in the creditor, the following statement immediately after the statement required by Sched.2, para.6 and immediately before a statement recording either the total amount payable under the agreement or, where there is an installation charge, separately, the amount of the installation charge and the rest of the total amount payable under the agreement and (in either case) the total amount that the debtor has paid to the creditor by the date of the giving of the notice (Sched.2, para.7):

    > BUT IF YOU HAVE PAID AT LEAST ONE-THIRD OF THE TOTAL AMOUNT PAYABLE UNDER THE AGREEMENT SET OUT BELOW (OR ANY INSTALLATION CHARGE PLUS ONE-THIRD OF THE REST OF THE AMOUNT PAYABLE), THE CREDITOR MAY NOT TAKE BACK THE GOODS AGAINST YOUR WISHES UNLESS HE GETS A COURT ORDER. (IN SCOTLAND, HE MAY NEED TO GET A COURT ORDER AT ANY TIME.) IF HE DOES TAKE THEM WITHOUT YOUR CONSENT OR A COURT ORDER, YOU HAVE THE RIGHT TO GET BACK ALL THE MONEY YOU HAVE PAID UNDER THE AGREEMENT SET OUT BELOW.

    – for hire-purchase or conditional sale agreements, a statement in the following form (Sched.2, para.8A):

    > You [may]* have the right to end this agreement at any time before the final payment falls due.

    > Note that this right may be lost if you do not act before the date shown (after which we may take action).

If the date for final payment has not passed and you wish to end this agreement, you should write to the person to whom you make your payments. [You will need to pay £[amount]** if you wish to end this agreement by the date shown and we will be entitled to the return of the goods. You will also be liable for costs if you have not taken reasonable care of the goods.]***

Note that if you end this agreement, this will not necessarily terminate any insurance finance agreements that are linked to this agreement.

The creditor may, if the agreement is a hire-purchase agreement, delete the words '[may]' appearing before '*'. In place of '[amount]**', the creditor must insert the amount to be paid by the debtor calculated in accordance with the provisions of CCA 1974, ss.99(2) and 100 and on the assumption that the debtor terminates the agreement on the date shown in the notice. The creditor must insert the words in square brackets immediately before '***' if (and only if) the debtor's right to terminate under CCA 1974, s.99 exists.

– a statement in the following form (Sched.2, para.9):

> IF YOU HAVE DIFFICULTY IN PAYING ANY SUM OWING UNDER THE AGREEMENT OR TAKING ANY OTHER ACTION REQUIRED BY THIS NOTICE, YOU CAN APPLY TO THE COURT WHICH MAY MAKE AN ORDER ALLOWING YOU OR ANY SURETY MORE TIME.

– if interest is payable under the terms of the agreement on any judgment of the court, a statement in the following form (Sched.2, para.9A):

> You should be aware that if we take you to court and get a judgment against you requiring you to pay us the money you owe us under the agreement, you may have to pay us both the amount of the judgment and interest under the agreement on all the sums owed by you at the date of the judgment until you have paid these in full. This means that even if you pay off the whole amount of the judgment, you may still have a further sum to pay.

– a statement in the following form (Sched.2, para.10):

> IF YOU ARE NOT SURE WHAT TO DO, YOU SHOULD GET HELP AS SOON AS POSSIBLE. FOR EXAMPLE YOU SHOULD CONTACT A SOLICITOR, YOUR LOCAL TRADING STANDARDS DEPARTMENT OR YOUR NEAREST CITIZENS' ADVICE BUREAU.

– a statement in the following words (Sched.2, para.10A):

> This notice should include a copy of the current Office of Fair Trading information sheet on default. This contains important information about your rights and where to go for support and advice. If it is not included, you should contact us to get one.

– a statement in the following words (Sched.2, para.11):

> IMPORTANT – YOU SHOULD READ THIS CAREFULLY.

The lettering in the default notice must, apart from any signature, be easily legible and of a colour which is readily distinguishable from the colour of the paper (reg.2(4)). It should also be given in writing and in paper form: it cannot, therefore, be sent by email (reg.2(4A)). Other style requirements include:

- any statement to be given more prominence than any other lettering in the notice (reg.2(5): it is often easier to simply copy the style and format of statements used in CC(EDTN)R 1983);
- the wording of such a statement being reproduced without any alteration or addition except that 'the creditor' may be replaced with the creditor's name or by the expression used in the agreement together with any necessary changes to pronouns and verbs (reg.2(6)); and
- where a note requires any words to be omitted, for those words to be omitted or deleted (reg.2(7)).

It is often the case that lenders serve a default notice in the form of a letter. Other lenders, by contrast, serve a covering letter enclosing a statutory form. So long as the letter or notice complies with the statutory requirements, there is no harm in serving a default notice in either way.

Time for compliance

The debtor should be given 'not less than 14 days after the date of service of the default notice' by CCA 1974, s.88(2) to remedy the alleged breach. The 14-day time frame was introduced by s.14(1) of the Consumer Credit Act 2006 (CCA 2006) which extended the time frame from seven days for all default notices issued on or after 1 October 2006. If a creditor or owner relies upon a default notice pre-dating 1 October 2006, it only needs to give not less than seven days for remedy of the breach after the date of service of the default notice.

Whilst we look at the way in which service can be effected at **7.4** below, the simple point is that time does not begin to run until after service has been effected. If the time limit is 14 days from the date of the default notice then clearly not enough time will be given for the debtor or hirer to remedy his breach. It is also interesting that in CC(EDTN)R 1983, Sched.2, para.3(c) and (d), both sub-paragraphs simply say that the notice must specify 'the date, being a date not less than fourteen days after the date of service of the notice'. It is submitted that these requirements can be satisfied by either stating a particular date or using wording like: 'You must comply with this notice within 14 days after the date of the service of this notice.'

Information sheets

Another new requirement introduced by CCA 2006 is the obligation to provide an information sheet produced by the OFT. The default notice must include a copy of the current information sheet (CCA 1974, s.88(4A). If it fails to do so, the notice is likely to be invalid. One trap for the unwary is the fact that the OFT regularly updates its information sheets. Creditors or owners should therefore regularly check the OFT's website (at **www.oft.gov.uk/about-the-oft/legal-powers/legal/ cca/CCA2006/information/**) to see if the information sheet has been updated.

Inaccuracies

Creditors or owners should ensure that a default notice is clear and unambiguous. They should also ensure that a notice is accurate. The important Court of Appeal decision of *Woodchester Lease Management Services Ltd* v. *Swain & Co* [1999] 1 WLR 263 shows just how important this factor is. A default notice was served but it substantially overstated the amount of the arrears which the debtor needed to pay to remedy its breach. The Court of Appeal placed reliance upon CCA 1974 being a consumer protection measure and said that the lender is in a much better position to state, with certainty, the arrears. Because it failed to do so, and the error was more than minor or de minimis, the default notice was invalid. The court refused to give judgment for the sums which had yet to fall due but, instead, gave judgment for the arrears accrued by the time of trial. Whilst this was not ideal, it was not disastrous. Take, however, the following example: a creditor serves a default notice (which is invalid) and later recovers a motor car which is let under a hire-purchase agreement. In such a case, the creditor will have wrongfully interfered with the debtor's interest in the goods and the debtor will be entitled to either return of the goods or damages limited to its interest in the goods: *Eshun* v. *Moorgate Mercantile Co Ltd* [1971] 1 WLR 722. If the goods were protected by CCA 1974, s.90, the agreement may also be terminated and the debtor would be entitled to a refund.

The High Court has (more recently) considered the issue of default notices in *American Express Services Europe PE Ltd* v. *Brandon* [2010] GCCR 10301. The facts were relatively straightforward: Mr Brandon obtained a credit card with American Express Services Europe PE Ltd (AMEX) on 28 March 1998. By June 2007, the outstanding balance was around £6,500. Mr Brandon failed to make his payments so on 19 June 2007 AMEX served a default notice under CCA 1974, s.87(1). It required Mr Brandon to make a minimum payment of £275.80 'within 14 calendar days from the date of this default notice'. Mr Brandon failed to make any further payment so AMEX wrote to him on 11 July 2007 ending the agreement and demanding the unpaid balance. If it was not paid within 28 days, AMEX said it would register the default with credit reference agencies.

His Honour Judge Denyer QC decided that the period of notice was too short but, because AMEX did not take any steps until 11 July 2007 (when it wrote terminating the agreement) and Mr Brandon was not prejudiced by a technical breach of CCA 1974, s.88(2), he decided that the default notice was valid and the agreement was therefore properly terminated. The Court of Appeal considered Mr Brandon's appeal in *Brandon* v. *American Express Services Europe PE Ltd* [2011] EWCA Civ 1187. Lord Justice Gross made it clear that the Court of Appeal was dealing with summary judgment under CPR rule 24.2. AMEX had successfully argued before the county court and the High Court that the inaccuracy failed to disclose a real prospect of success. The inaccuracy point *was* arguable, meaning the appeal on that point was allowed. It is therefore open to a creditor or owner to argue a 'no prejudice' point but there is now no authority supporting that principle.

Consequences of non-compliance

If the breach is remediable and, before the deadline stated in the default notice, the debtor or hirer remedies his breach then it is treated as not having happened by CCA 1974, s.89. If the debtor or hirer partially complies with the notice then, unless the outstanding breach is minor, the creditor or owner is entitled to treat the partial compliance as non-compliance.

Joint debtors and sureties

If there are joint debtors who are not partners or an unincorporated body of persons then, by CCA 1974, s.185(1), anything required to be done (including the service of a notice) must be done to both of them. The only exception to this requirement is where a periodic statement is required by CCA 1974, s.77A or s.78(4) and the debtors give a 'dispensing notice' giving the creditor permission to serve the statement on one party. If the agreement is with joint debtors then a notice must be served on each debtor. Similarly, if there is a surety then a copy of the notice must also be sent to that person by CCA 1974, s.111.

Precedents

For a precedent default notice under CCA 1974, s.87(1) for a fixed-sum loan agreement, see **Precedent 11A**. For a precedent default notice under CCA 1974, s.87(1) for a hire-purchase agreement, see **Precedent 11B**.

7.3.2   Enforcement notice

Introduction

Unlike default notices, an enforcement notice is used in a non-default case by virtue of CCA 1974, s.76(6). Without wishing to stress the position too much, if the debtor has defaulted in any way, then a default notice must be used. Enforcement notices are, however, often combined with a termination notice (which, confusingly, is not a notice sent following a default notice). It is easier to deal with an example: a debtor enters into a regulated hire-purchase agreement for plant and machinery. The term is for five years. He maintains his payments but sells the asset to a third party. If this is not a breach of the agreement (which would be surprising) then the creditor cannot serve a default notice. Instead, in order to call in the balance, the creditor's option is to serve an enforcement and termination notice because the creditor will want to (a) terminate the agreement and call in the balance and (b) potentially consider pursuing the third party who now has possession of the asset.

Section 76(1) of CCA 1974 says that the creditor or owner is not entitled, in a non-default case, to enforce a term of a regulated agreement by:

- demanding earlier payment of any sum (s.76(1)(a)); or
- recovering possession of any goods or land (s.76(1)(b)); or
- treating any right conferred on the debtor or hirer by the agreement as terminated, restricted or deferred (s.76(1)(c)),

unless it first serves an enforcement notice on the debtor or hirer. It is important to remember, however, that s.76 only applies where the agreement is for a fixed period (CCA 1974, s.76(2)(a)) and that period has not yet expired when the creditor intends to do any of the acts mentioned in s.76(1) (CCA 1974, s.76(2)(b)). It does not apply, therefore, to an agreement which is open-ended (like a credit card).

Form and content

Under CCA 1974, s.76(3) an enforcement notice is ineffective if it is not in the prescribed form. Section 76(3) is supplemented by CC(EDTN)R 1983, reg.2(1). This requires the creditor or owner to:

- state that the notice is 'served under section 76(1) of the Consumer Credit Act 1974' (reg.2(1)(a));
- include the following information (reg.2(1)(b)):
    - a description of the agreement sufficient to identify it (CC(EDTN)R 1983, Sched.1, para.1);
    - the name and a postal address of the creditor or owner (Sched.1, para.2(a));
    - the name and a postal address of the debtor or hirer (Sched.1, para.2(b));
    - the term of the agreement to be enforced, or a reference to, and a short description of, that term (Sched.1, para.3);
    - a clear and unambiguous statement by the creditor or owner indicating which (one or more) of the following types of action it intends to take to enforce the term of the agreement: (a) demanding earlier payment of any sum; (b) recovering possession of any goods or land; and/or (c) treating any right conferred on the debtor or hirer by the agreement as terminated, restricted or deferred (Sched.1, para.4(a));
    - a clear and unambiguous statement by the creditor or owner indicating the manner and circumstances in which it intends to take such action (Sched.1, para.4(b));
    - a clear and unambiguous statement by the creditor or owner indicating the date, being a date not less than seven days after giving of the notice, on or after which it intends to take such action (Sched.1, para.4(c));
    - if the creditor intends to demand earlier repayment of any sum, the amount of the sum before any rebate on early settlement and, if a rebate is

allowable, the amount of the rebate calculated on the assumption that early settlement takes place on the date specified in the notice and the difference between the rebated and unrebated sum (Sched.1, para.5);

- include certain specified statements (reg.2(1)(c)):

    - a statement in the following form (Sched.1, para.6):

        IF YOU HAVE DIFFICULTY IN PAYING ANY SUM OWING UNDER THE AGREEMENT YOU CAN APPLY TO THE COURT WHICH MAY MAKE AN ORDER ALLOWING YOU OR ANY SURETY MORE TIME.

    - a statement in the following form (Sched.1, para.7):

        IF YOU ARE NOT SURE WHAT TO DO, YOU SHOULD GET HELP AS SOON AS POSSIBLE. FOR EXAMPLE YOU SHOULD CONTACT A SOLICITOR, YOUR LOCAL TRADING STANDARDS DEPARTMENT OR YOUR NEAREST CITIZENS' ADVICE BUREAU.

    - a statement in the following form (Sched.1, para.8):

        IMPORTANT – YOU SHOULD READ THIS CAREFULLY.

The notice must also include the content, and be in the form, required by reg.2(4)–(7). These provisions have, of course, already been discussed at **7.3.1** above.

Interaction with s.98(1) of CCA 1974

It will be seen later in this chapter that CCA 1974, s.76(1) often works together with CCA 1974, s.98(1). For example, a creditor or owner in a non-default case may wish to demand earlier payment of any sum, meaning a s.76(1) notice will be required, and may also wish to terminate the agreement, meaning a s.98(1) notice is required. To avoid unnecessary copies of notices being served on an unassuming debtor or hirer, CC(EDTN)R 1983, reg.2(8) allows a creditor or owner to combine a s.76(1) notice with a s.98(1) notice. Indeed, it is submitted that creditors or owners should always look at rolling up notices together where they are allowed to do so.

Time for compliance

The creditor or owner should give to the debtor or hirer 'not less than seven days' notice of his intention to do' any of the acts envisaged by CCA 1974, s.76(1). This is a somewhat curious phrase and, on first reading, differs from the requirement under CCA 1974, s.88(2) which provides for 'not less than 14 days after the date of service of the default notice'. However, the most sensible way to read the wording in CCA 1974, s.76(1) is to consider there is no difference from CCA 1974, s.87(1) and proceed on the basis that it means seven days after service.

Inaccuracies

Just like default notices, creditors or owners should ensure that an enforcement notice is clear, unambiguous and accurate. If it is not, and for the reasons set out at **7.3.1** above (under 'Inaccuracies'), the court may, unless the error is minor, consider the enforcement notice is defective.

Consequences of non-compliance

If an enforcement notice is not in the prescribed form then it is likely to be ineffective by CCA 1974, s.76(3). Put simply, this prevents the creditor or owner doing any of the things it wishes to do so by serving the notice. Great care must therefore be taken. If the notice is in the prescribed form then unless it is withdrawn, the notice will come into effect on the expiry of the period specified in it. After this time, the creditor or owner will be able to do the acts envisaged by CCA 1974, s.76(1).

Joint debtors and sureties

We have already discussed the issue of joint debtors and sureties in the context of a default notice at **7.3.1** above. These provisions are exactly the same for service of enforcement notices.

7.3.3 Termination notice

Introduction

Unlike default notices but like enforcement notices, a termination notice is used in a non-default case by virtue of CCA 1974, s.98(6). It should be remembered that a termination notice is not the same as a termination letter (often known as a formal demand) which follows non-compliance with a default notice. Section 98 has no relevance where the debtor or hirer has defaulted. Termination notices are, however, often combined with an enforcement notice.

Section 98(1) says that the creditor or owner is not entitled, in a non-default case, to terminate a regulated agreement except by or after giving the debtor or hirer not less than seven days' notice of the termination. It is important to remember, however, that s.98 only applies (like CCA 1974, s.76) where the agreement is for a fixed period (CCA 1974, s.98(2)(a)) and that period has not yet expired when the creditor intends to do any of the acts mentioned in s.98(1) (CCA 1974, s.98(2)(b)).

Form and content

By CCA 1974, s.98(3) a termination notice is ineffective if it is not in the prescribed form. Section 98(3) is supplemented by CC(EDTN)R 1983, reg.2(3). CC(EDTN)R 1983 requires the creditor to:

- state that the notice is a 'served under section 98(1) of the Consumer Credit Act 1974' (reg.2(3)(a));
- include the following information (reg.2(3)(b)):
  - a description of the agreement sufficient to identify it (Sched.3, para.1);
  - the name and a postal address of the creditor or owner (Sched.3, para.2(a));
  - the name and a postal address of the debtor or hirer (Sched.3, para.2(b));
  - the term of the agreement giving the creditor to right to terminate the agreement or a reference to and a short description of that term (Sched.3, para.3);
  - a clear and unambiguous statement by the creditor or owner indicating that by giving the notice, it is terminating the agreement and indicating any steps that it intends to take to effect termination or, as the case may be, indicating the manner and circumstances in which it intends to take action to terminate the agreement (Sched.3, para.4(a));
  - a clear and unambiguous statement by the creditor or owner indicating the date, being a date not less than seven days after the giving of the notice, of the termination of, as the case may be, the date on or after which it intends to take action to terminate the agreement (Sched.3, para.4(b));
  - any right or liability that will arise on termination of the agreement and the date by which that right will arise including the amount of the sum before any rebate on early settlement and, if a rebate is allowable, the amount of the rebate calculated on the assumption that early settlement takes place on the date specified in the notice and the difference between the rebated and unrebated sum (Sched.3, para.5);
- include certain specified statements (reg.2(3)(c)):
  - a statement in the following form (Sched.3, para.6):

    IF YOU HAVE DIFFICULTY IN PAYING ANY SUM OWING UNDER THE AGREEMENT, YOU CAN APPLY TO THE COURT WHICH MAY MAKE AN ORDER ALLOWING YOU OR ANY SURETY MORE TIME.

  - a statement in the following form (Sched.3, para.7):

    IF YOU ARE NOT SURE WHAT TO DO, YOU SHOULD GET HELP AS SOON AS POSSIBLE. FOR EXAMPLE YOU SHOULD CONTACT A SOLICITOR, YOUR LOCAL TRADING STANDARDS DEPARTMENT OR YOUR NEAREST CITIZENS' ADVICE BUREAU.

  - a statement in the following form (Sched.3, para.8):

    IMPORTANT – YOU SHOULD READ THIS CAREFULLY.

The notice must also include the content, and be in the form, required by reg.2(4)–(7). These provisions have, of course, already been discussed at **7.3.1** above.

Interaction with s.78(1) of CCA 1974

It has already been suggested that CCA 1974, s.98(1) often works together with CCA 1974, s.76(1). A more detailed explanation of the interaction has been discussed at **7.3.2** above.

Time for compliance

The creditor or owner should give to the debtor or hirer 'not less than seven days' notice of the termination' (CCA 1974, s.98(1)). Keen readers will note that this period is exactly the same as under CCA 1974, s.76(1). A more detailed explanation has been given at **7.3.2** above. In short, the time period is likely to be seven days after service.

Inaccuracies

Just like default notices, creditors or owners should ensure that a termination notice is clear, unambiguous and accurate. If it is not, and for the reasons set out at **7.3.1** above, the court may, unless the error is minor, consider the termination notice is defective.

Consequences of non-compliance

If a notice is not in the prescribed form then it is ineffective by CCA 1974, s.98(3). Put simply, this prevents the creditor or owner doing any of the things it wishes to do so by serving the notice. Great care must therefore be taken. If the notice is in the prescribed form then unless it is withdrawn, the notice will come into effect on the expiry of the period specified in it. After this time, the creditor or owner will be able to do the acts envisaged by CCA 1974, s.98(1).

Joint debtors and sureties

We have already discussed the issue of joint debtors and sureties in the context of a default notice at **7.3.1** above. These provisions are exactly the same for service of termination notices.

7.3.4 Termination of open-end consumer credit agreements

Introduction

The Consumer Credit Directive (87/102/EEC) (CCD) brought in a concept of 'open-end consumer credit agreements' on 1 February 2011. Given the lead-in time from publication of the various regulations, creditors could enter into agreements complying with the CCD on or after 30 April 2010 but before 1 February 2011 so long as the conditions contained in CC(EUD)R 2010, reg.101 are satisfied. The introduction of open-end agreements meant that specific provisions were needed to deal with termination. These are contained in CCA 1974, s.98A.

Debtor termination

Under CCA 1974, s.98A(1), a debtor under a regulated open-end consumer credit agreement may by notice terminate the agreement, free of charge, at any time, subject to any period of notice not exceeding one month provided for by the agreement. This does not apply, by s.98A(8), if the agreement (called 'an excluded agreement') is:

(a)   an authorised non-business overdraft agreement,
(b)   an authorised business overdraft agreement,
(c)   a debtor-creditor agreement arising where the holder of a current account overdraws on the account without a pre-arranged overdraft or exceeds a pre-arranged overdraft limit, or
(d)   an agreement secured on land.

By s.98A(2), notice of termination does not need to be in writing unless the creditor requires it to be in writing. It is submitted that creditors wishing to ensure a proper paper trail should require written notice to be given by the debtor.

Creditor termination

Under CCA 1974, s.98A(3), if a regulated open-end consumer credit agreement, other than an excluded agreement, allows for termination of the agreement by the creditor:

(a)   the termination must be by notice served on the debtor, and
(b)   the termination may not take effect until after the end of the period of two months, or such longer period as the agreement may provide, beginning with the day after the day on which notice is served.

Suspension of debtor's right to draw on credit

Under CCA 1974, s.98A(4), if a regulated open-end consumer credit agreement, other than an excluded agreement, provides for termination or suspension by the creditor of the debtor's right to draw on credit:

- to terminate or suspend the right to draw on credit the creditor must serve a notice on the debtor before the termination or suspension or, if that is not practicable, immediately afterwards;
- the notice must give reasons for the termination or suspension; and
- the reasons must be 'objectively justified'.

This is supplemented by CCA 1974, s.98A(5) which states that the first two limbs of the test in s.98A(4) does not apply where giving the notice:

- is prohibited by an EU obligation; or
- would, or would be likely to, prejudice the prevention or detection of crime, the apprehension or prosecution of offenders or the administration of justice.

It is likely that the requirement for the reasons to be 'objectively justified' will cause some issues given the imprecise phraseology. Some examples are given in CCA 1974, s.98A(6). These are:

(a) the unauthorised or fraudulent use of credit, or
(b) a significantly increased risk of the debtor being unable to fulfil his obligation to repay the credit.

It is submitted that the courts are likely to take a commonsense approach to the interpretation of the phrase 'objectively justified' and, so long as the reasons appear sensible and rationale (or have been made for good commercial reasons), the court is unlikely to interfere.

Termination for breach of contract

By CCA 1974, s.98A(7), the debtor's right to terminate under s.98A(1) and the creditor's right to terminate under s.98A(3) do not affect any right to terminate an agreement for breach of contract.

7.3.5 Restrictions on remedies following termination: repossession of goods under hire purchase or conditional sale

Introduction

For many creditors, the provisions in CCA 1974, ss.90 and 91 have a significant impact. Where a debtor has paid one-third of the total amount payable, the creditor has a further restriction (even after terminating the agreement following service of a notice and a formal demand) on the recovery of goods let under a hire-purchase or conditional sale agreement. We now turn to look at those provisions.

Prohibition on recovery of goods

By CCA 1974, s.90(1), at any time when:

(a)   the debtor is in breach of a regulated hire-purchase or a regulated conditional sale agreement relating to goods, and

(b)   the debtor has paid to the creditor one-third or more of the total price of the goods, and

(c)   the property in the goods remains in the creditor,

the creditor is not entitled to recover possession of the goods from the debtor except on an order of the court.

Such goods become 'protected' from repossession and are often called 'protected goods' (a phrase coined by CCA 1974, s.90(7)).

One-third or more of the total price of the goods

If the creditor is required to carry out any installation and the agreement specifies, as part of the total price, the amount to be paid in respect of the installation (the 'installation charge') the reference in CCA 1974, s.90(1)(b) to one-third of the total price means the aggregate of the installation charge and one-third of the remainder of the total price (CCA 1974, s.90(2)).

Later agreements

By CCA 1974, s.90(3), in a case where:

(a)   subsection (1)(a) is satisfied, but not subsection (1)(b), and

(b)   subsection (1)(b) was satisfied on a previous occasion in relation to an earlier agreement, being a regulated hire-purchase or regulated conditional sale agreement, between the same parties, and relating to any of the goods comprised in the later agreement (whether or not other goods were also included),

subsection (1) shall apply to the later agreement with the omission of paragraph (b).

If the later agreement is a modifying agreement under CCA 1974, s.82(2) then s.90(3) applies with the substitution, for the second reference to the later agreement, of a reference to the modifying agreement (CCA 1974, s.90(4)).

Debtor termination

If the debtor terminates the agreement (discussed at **7.6** below), CCA 1974, s.90(5) makes it clear that s.90(1) does not apply, or no longer applies, to the agreement. This resolves any doubt over whether the creditor still needs to obtain a court order where a debtor terminates the agreement but has paid over one-third of the total price for the goods.

Death of debtor

If goods became protected at the death of the debtor, they continue to be protected until the grant of probate or administration under CCA 1974, s.90(6). The only person who can give consent to repossession is therefore the person who is (or will be) the debtor's personal representative. If, however, the breach of the agreement only happens after the debtor's death, s.90(1) does not apply because s.90(1)(a) is not engaged.

Abandoned goods

Section 90(1) of CCA 1974 prevents the creditor from retaking possession of the goods 'from the debtor'. It does not prevent the recovery of protected goods from a third party. Great care must, however, be taken before a creditor recovers possession of goods from persons who are not the debtor. The phrase 'from the debtor' prevents repossession from third parties holding the goods as the debtor's agent or bailee: *Bentinck Ltd* v. *Cromwell Engineering Co* [1971] 1 QB 324 and *Kassam* v. *Chartered Trust plc* [1998] RTR 220.

If, however, the debtor has obviously abandoned the goods by leaving the vehicle in need of repair in a public place (like the debtor did in *Lombank Ltd* v. *Dowdall* (1973) 118 Sol Jo 96) or in a third party's hands with no intention of recovering them, then the creditor may recover them. In such a case, the goods have not been repossessed from the debtor (or his agent) meaning CCA 1974, s.90(1) does not come into play. Given, however, the speed and relative low cost of obtaining a court order, it is respectfully suggested that if there is any doubt, a court order should be obtained.

Consent to repossession

Section 173(3) of CCA 1974 makes it clear that a creditor may recover protected goods if it obtains the debtor's informed and voluntary consent to the repossession at the time of the repossession. Even if the consent is reluctant, as long as the creditor can show it was informed and voluntary, the repossession will be lawful: *Mercantile Credit Co Ltd* v. *Cross* [1965] 2 QB 205. The more difficult question is what 'informed' consent means. It is submitted, however, that the more information given to the debtor before the repossession takes place, the more likely it is that the debtor gives his informed consent. For example, a creditor may use a standard letter which explains the impact of CCA 1974, s.90 and makes it clear that the creditor, if the debtor does not wish to give up possession of the goods, will need to get a court order (with the additional costs). Creditors instructing recovery agents must therefore use great care so they can evidence an 'informed' consent if the repossession is later challenged by the debtor.

Consequences of breaching s.90

If goods are recovered by the creditor in breach of CCA 1974, s.90 then, by s.91:

• the regulated agreement, if not previous terminated, will terminate; and

- the debtor is released from all liability under the agreement, and is entitled to recover from the creditor all sums paid by the debtor under the agreement.

It has been suggested by some debtors that they are also entitled to the goods' return. It is respectfully submitted that such an analysis is wrong: CCA 1974, s.91 does not mention the goods. By virtue of CCA 1974, s.170(1), there is no further sanction for breach of CCA 1974, s.90. It therefore follows that the creditor must be entitled to keep the goods (or their sale proceeds).

7.3.6 Restrictions on remedies following termination: recovery of possession of goods or land

CCA 1974, s.92 provides further restrictions on the recovery of possession of goods or land:

- By CCA 1974, s.92(1), the creditor or owner is not entitled to enter any premises to take possession of goods subject to a regulated hire-purchase agreement, regulated conditional sale agreement or regulated consumer hire agreement without a court order. Any contractual right allowing the creditor or owner to enter premises is likely to be void (CCA 1974, s.173(1)) but may be overcome if the debtor or hirer gives his informed consent at the time of the repossession (CCA 1974, s.173(3)).
- By CCA 1974, s.92(2), at any time when the debtor is in breach of a regulated conditional sale agreement relating to land, the creditor is entitled to recover possession of the land from the debtor, or any person claiming under him, only with a court order.
- By CCA 1974, s.92(3), if the creditor or owner breaches s.92(1) or (2), the debtor or hirer has a claim for breach of statutory duty.

7.4 SERVICE OF NOTICES

7.4.1 Statutory framework

By CCA 1974, s.176(1), a document to be served under CCA 1974 is treated as being properly served on the other party if the method of service is envisaged by CCA 1974, s.176. A document may (by CCA 1974, s.176(2)) be:

- delivered; or
- sent by an 'appropriate method'; or
- addressed to the recipient by name and left at his proper address.

The effect of these provisions appears to be relatively straightforward because it brings into play the Interpretation Act 1978. If a creditor or owner therefore properly addresses, pre-pays and posts a notice, deemed service will take place at the time when the letter would be ordinarily delivered in the post. Debtors have tried, unsuccessfully, to argue that a notice is not deemed served if it does not come to the debtor's attention. For example, the county court decided in *Lombard North Central plc* v. *Power-Hines* [1995] CCLR 24 that the service provisions under CCA 1974, s.176 were designed to apply where, through no fault of the creditor or owner, the notice was not brought to the debtor's attention. The court was also entitled to assume, where the notice had not been returned undelivered, that it had been delivered.

It should be remembered that a creditor or owner may not serve a default, termination or enforcement notice by email. Under CC(EDTN)R 1983, reg.2(4A), such a notice must be in 'paper' form.

7.4.2 Common problems

Problems may arise if a creditor or owner, instead of saying a specific date, uses a number of days. Take the following example: a default notice is posted on Tuesday 1 January 2011 by first-class post. In the normal course of post (and without a postal strike!), it should be received by Wednesday 2 January 2011. The debtor must have at least 14 days after the date of service (i.e. until 17 January 2011). If the notice specifically says 17 January 2011 or any later date, it validly states the time for compliance. Instead, the notice says 'you are required to remedy your breach within 17 days of the date of this notice.'

Does the notice, in these circumstances, comply with CCA 1974, s.88(2) and CC(EDTN)R 1983, Sched.2, para.3(c) and (d)? There is no clear decision on this issue in consumer credit cases so we must borrow from another area where notices, and their validity, are more often changed: landlord and tenant law. In *W Davies (Spitalfields) Ltd* v. *Huntley and others* [1947] 1 All ER 246 a notice was served saying that 'we regret that we must give you 3 months' notice' and it did not, like our example, say a specific date. The recipient unsuccessfully argued that the notice was invalid because it failed to identify the date on which it would expire. Henn Collins J said: 'Does not the [recipient] know perfectly well when the notice expires, namely, in three months from the moment it meets his eye?'

More recently, the House of Lords decided in *Mannai Investment Co Ltd* v. *Eagle Star Life Assurance Co Ltd* [1997] AC 749 that a notice is valid even if it is defective as long as the 'reasonable recipient' can understand it and its impact. It is therefore arguable that a reasonable recipient of the notice would add 17 days to the date of the notice and believe he has to comply by 18 January 2010. Creditors or owners would, however, be well advised to say a specific date to avoid such arguments.

7.5   DEBTOR LIABILITY ON TERMINATION

7.5.1   Liquidated damages

It is common practice for creditors and owners to specifically spell out the debtor's or hirer's liability on termination in their terms and conditions. The most obvious way to deal with it is by a liquidated damages clause saying that, upon termination, the debtor or hirer must pay to the creditor or owner the balance due under the agreement minus a deduction (if any) for the net sale proceeds of any goods let under the regulated agreement and the appropriate rebate on early settlement. If goods are let under a regulated agreement and no credit is given for their early return (either, in the case of a hire agreement, the difference between the sale proceeds and the estimated value at the end of the term (often called a 'residual value') or, in the case of lease agreements including hire purchase and conditional sale, the net sale proceeds), then such a clause is often successfully challenged as a penalty clause: *Volkswagen Financial Services (UK) Ltd* v. *Ramage* [2008] CCLR 3. If there is a successful challenge, a prudent creditor (and its advisers) should try to explain the creditor's actual loss as a result of the debtor's breach of the agreement.

It is also important to consider the relevant terms and conditions of business. In *Lombard North Central plc* v. *Butterworth* [1987] 1 QB 527, the Court of Appeal considered the debtor's argument that trivial breaches of the agreement should not entitle a creditor to terminate and seek payment of the unpaid balance. The Court of Appeal decided that the parties were free to make payment a condition of the agreement (which they did) and, where they did so, a failure to make any one payment entitled the creditor to terminate the agreement and seek payment of the unpaid balance under the agreement.

7.5.2   Is there a 'cap' on liability on termination of hire-purchase or conditional sale agreements?

Further problems have arisen in the context of hire-purchase and conditional sale agreements in two conflicting decisions of the county court. The issue is whether the debtor's liability should be limited to his liability under CCA 1974, s.100 (discussed at **7.6.2** below). In *Rover Finance Ltd* v. *Siddons* (unreported, Leicester County Court, 19 July 2002), the court decided that the amount recoverable by a creditor on termination should be limited to the debtor's liability under s.100 and the recovery of a greater sum amounts to a penalty. By contrast, the county court more recently decided in *First Response Finance* v. *Donnelly* [2007] CCLR 4 that an amount recoverable by a creditor should not be limited to the debtor's liability under s.100. Until we have a decision from a higher court, the issue will remain unresolved. It is, however, submitted that the decision in *Donnelly* is perhaps the better view and one which should be followed by the courts: the creditor gives the debtor notice of his right to terminate under CCA 1974, s.99(1) both on the face of the agreement and in the default notice (CC(EDTN)R 1983, Sched.2, para.8A). If the debtor fails to act upon this, and simply ignores the default notice and its warnings, the creditor should not be prejudiced by such action. It would, of course, have recovered the full amount under the agreement had the debtor made all of the payments due.

7.5.3 Amount of judgment

Tricky problems can sometimes arise where a judgment is entered against the debtor or hirer for the balance due under a regulated agreement before all of those sums would have fallen due (but for the debtor's or hirer's default). In such a case, if the judgment is paid in full on entry of it, the creditor will receive a substantial windfall. If judgment was entered for the sum due including the rebate payable under the Consumer Credit (Early Settlement) Regulations 2004, SI 2004/1483, the creditor may miss out on interest if the judgment is not paid because interest is not payable on county court judgments based on regulated agreements.

To overcome this problem, the Court of Appeal decided in *Forward Trust Ltd* v. *Whymark* [1990] 2 QB 670 that judgment should be entered for the full and unrebated sum but the judgment should record the fact that the debtor or hirer may be entitled to a rebate. The Court of Appeal's suggested wording was as follows:

> The judgment debtor can satisfy his obligations under this judgment by paying the full amount adjudged due from him less any rebate for early settlement to which he may be entitled under the Consumer Credit Act 1974, and regulations made thereunder.
>
> The judgment debtor can find out whether any rebate is applicable and, if so, the amount of the rebate by inquiry from the judgment creditor. In the event of dispute, the judgment debtor should apply to the court for a determination of whether he is entitled to any rebate and, if so, its amount.

7.6 TERMINATION BY THE DEBTOR OR OWNER

7.6.1 Introduction

CCA 1974 gives the debtor or hirer, in certain circumstances, the right to terminate a regulated agreement. Such provisions are often missing from non-regulated agreements (for obvious reasons on the creditor's part) and provide a powerful mechanism for the debtor or hirer to end the agreement early. The right of early termination (which is different from the right to pay ahead of time either in full or part) only arises with:

- regulated hire-purchase or conditional sale agreements by CCA 1974, s.99; or
- regulated hire agreements by CCA 1974, s.101.

We now turn to look at those provisions in some more detail.

7.6.2 Regulated hire-purchase and conditional sale agreements

Introduction

Whilst there are a number of advantages of regulated hire-purchase or conditional sale agreements from a creditor's point of view, particularly the fact that the goods or land are security for the debt, CCA 1974 gives the debtor a right to end such an agreement early under s.99. It should be remembered, however, that the debtor must return the goods: he does not get to keep the goods and terminate the agreement under CCA 1974, s.99(1).

When does it apply?

Under CCA 1974, s.99(1), the debtor has the right to terminate a regulated hire-purchase or conditional sale agreement before the final payment under the agreement falls due by giving written notice to the creditor or any person authorised to receive the sums payable under the agreement. This right does not, therefore, arise after the date the final payment has fallen due even if the debtor is in arrears.

When does it not apply?

The right under CCA 1974, s.99(1) is not exercisable if:

- under a regulated conditional sale agreement for land, title to the land has passed to the debtor (CCA 1974, s.99(3)); or
- under a regulated conditional sale agreement for goods, property to the goods has vested in the debtor and is, in turn, transferred to a third party (CCA 1974, s.99(4)).

Effect of termination

Section 99(2) of CCA 1974 makes it clear that termination under CCA 1974, s.99(1) does not affect any liability incurred by the debtor before termination takes place. If, therefore, the debtor is in arrears before termination under s.99(1) takes place, the creditor is still entitled to recover those arrears. If, under a regulated conditional sale agreement, title to the goods is vested in the debtor at the date of termination then, upon termination it will immediately re-vest in the previous owner (i.e. the creditor) (CCA 1974, s.99(5)).

Liability on termination

If a debtor has validly exercised his right to terminate a regulated hire-purchase or conditional sale agreement under CCA 1974, s.99(1) then, upon termination, the creditor is entitled to:

- where the debtor has paid less than one-half of the total amount payable and unless the agreement says otherwise, the difference between what the debtor has paid and one-half of the total amount payable (CCA 1974, s.100(1)); or
- where the debtor has paid more than one-half of the total amount payable and unless the agreement says otherwise, payment of any arrears due under the agreement (s.99(2)).

If the debtor has failed to take reasonable care of the goods then the creditor is also entitled to compensation for the creditor's loss (CCA 1974, s.100(4)). This will usually require the creditor to, first, prove that the debtor has failed to take reasonable care of the goods and, secondly, provide evidence to prove on the balance of probabilities the goods' market value in a reasonable condition and the goods' value in their current condition. If the creditor provides such evidence, it will be entitled to the difference between those two valuations.

There may be times where the creditor, in addition to supplying the goods under a regulated hire-purchase or conditional sale agreement, also agrees to install the goods. The cost of doing so is often added to the monies advanced. In such a case, does the installation cost need to be taken into account when considering the debtor's liability under CCA 1974, s.100(1)? The short answer is yes it does: s.100(2) says that in such a case, the amount to be paid for the installation is added to one-half of the remaining total amount payable.

Example

Mr Thomas agrees to acquire a motor car under a regulated hire-purchase agreement. There is no part-exchange. The cash price is £10,000 and the charges total £5,000 making the total amount payable under the agreement to be £15,000. The monthly instalments are £300. Mr Thomas pays £10,000 before missing three payments. He then terminates the agreement under CCA 1974, s.99(1). In such a case, the debtor's liability is £900 (he has paid more than one half of the total amount payable so only needs to pay the arrears of £900) plus compensation (if any) for failure to take reasonable care of the car.

If, however, Mr Thomas only makes 10 monthly instalments totalling £3,000 and then terminates the agreement under CCA 1974, s.99(1), the situation is entirely different. In such a situation, the debtor's liability is £4,500 (i.e. the difference between one-half of the total price of £15,000 (i.e. £7,500 minus the payments already made) plus compensation (if any) for failure to take reasonable care of the car.

So how does the situation change if there is an installation charge? Mrs Smith acquires a kitchen under a conditional sale agreement for £8,000. The creditor agrees to advance further credit to pay the installation charge of £2,000. The charge for credit is £4,000 making the total amount payable as £14,000 or £12,000 excluding the installation charge. Mrs Smith pays £5,000 before terminating the agreement under CCA 1974, s.99(1). In this situation, the debtor's liability is likely to be £1,000 (i.e. the difference between half of £12,000 and the amount already paid) plus the installation charge of £2,000. Mrs Smith will also need to pay compensation (if any) for failure to take reasonable care of the kitchen.

Retention of goods by debtor

Creditors sometimes have problems with debtors who terminate the agreement under s.99(1) and then fail or refuse to return the goods. In such a case, the creditor may attempt to recover possession of them but, if it is unable to do so and needs to issue proceedings for a return of goods order, the court must (unless in the circumstances it is just not to do so) order the goods to be returned without giving the debtor an option to pay the value of the goods (CCA 1974, s.100(5)).

7.6.3 Regulated consumer hire agreements

When does it apply?

Under CCA 1974, s.101(1):

> The hirer under a regulated consumer hire agreement is entitled to terminate the agreement by giving written notice to any person entitled or authorised to receive the sums payable under the agreement.

When does it not apply?

Under CCA 1974, s.101(7), the hirer's right to terminate the agreement does not apply to any agreement:

- which provides for the making by the hirer of payments which in total (and without breach of the agreement) exceed £1,500 in any year; or
- where:
  - goods are bailed to the hirer for the purposes of a business carried on by him, or the hirer holds himself out as requiring the goods for those purposes; and
  - the goods are selected by the hirer, and acquired by the owner for the purposes of the agreement at the request of the hirer from any person other than the owner's associate; or
- where the hirer requires, or holds himself out as requiring, the goods for the purpose of bailing or hiring them to other persons in the course of a business carried on by him.

Effect of termination

By s.101(2), termination of an agreement under s.101(1) does not affect the liability under the agreement which has accrued before the termination. The hirer is therefore liable to the owner for any arrears or other sums that had fallen due by the date of termination.

Time period for notice

By CCA 1974, s.101(3), a notice under s.101(1) cannot expire earlier than 18 months after the making of the agreement. This absolute bar is supplemented by further rules (unless the agreement allows for a shorter period):

- if the hirer is required to make payments at equal intervals, the minimum period of notice (which cannot expire before 18 months after the date of the agreement) is the length of one interval or three months, whichever is less (CCA 1974, s.101(4));
- if the hirer is required to make payments at differing intervals, the minimum period of notice (which cannot expire before 18 months after the date of the agreement) is the length of the shortest interval or three months, whichever is less (CCA 1974, s.101(5)); or
- in any other case, the minimum notice period is three months (CCA 1974, s.101(6)).

7.7 EARLY PAYMENT BY DEBTORS

7.7.1 Introduction

For many years, a creditor under a regulated consumer credit agreement was entitled to end his agreement early by repaying the balance due under the agreement (minus a rebate). Following the introduction of the CCD, a debtor under any regulated consumer credit agreement (other than an agreement secured on land) dated on or after 1 February 2011 has a right to make early partial repayments. This provision may also apply to some agreements entered into on or after 30 April 2010 but before 1 February 2011 where the conditions contained in CC(EUD)R 2010, reg.101 are satisfied. These provisions do not apply to regulated consumer hire agreements. We now turn to look at those provisions.

7.7.2 Full early settlement

Under CCA 1974, s.94(1), the debtor under a regulated consumer credit agreement is entitled, by giving notice and paying the outstanding balance (minus any rebate under CCA 1974, s.95), to end the agreement early. If the agreement is not secured on land and is dated on or after 1 February 2011 (or it falls within the transitional provisions discussed at **7.7.1** above), the debtor may also need to pay any compensation that the creditor is entitled to under CCA 1974, s.95A(2). The debtor's notice may, by CCA 1974, s.94(2), include the exercise by the debtor of any option to purchase goods let under a regulated consumer credit agreement or deal with any other matter relating to the termination of the agreement. By CCA 1974, s.94(6), and unless the consumer credit agreement is secured on land, the notice may be given orally or in writing.

7.7.3 Partial early settlement

By CCA 1974, s.94(3), a debtor under a regulated consumer credit agreement dated on or after 1 February 2011 (unless it falls within the transitional provisions which are discussed at **7.7.1** above) which is not secured on land is entitled, at any time, to discharge part of his indebtedness. To do so, the debtor must follow the steps set out in CCA 1974, s.94(4). These are:

- notice must be given to the creditor (which can be done orally);
- the debtor must pay to the creditor some of the amount payable by him under the agreement before the time for its payment under the agreement (i.e. make an early payment); and
- the payment must be made: (i) before the end of 28 days beginning with the day following that on which notice of an early payment was received by the creditor; or (ii) on or before any later date stated in the notice.

If the debtor takes the steps in s.94(4), his indebtedness is discharged by an amount equal to the sum of the amount paid and any rebate allowable under CCA 1974, s.95 minus any amount which the creditor is entitled to claim as compensation under s.95A(2). This right is likely to cause significant issues for creditors. For example, if a debtor pays weekly and, because he is going on holiday, decides to pay a week's payment in advance, is s.94(3) engaged? The most sensible answer, it is submitted, is that the right only applies when the debtor gives notice of an intention to repay earlier, rather than to make an earlier payment for his convenience.

7.7.4 Compensatory amount

CCA 1974, s.95A applies where (s.95A(1)):

- a regulated credit agreement (which is not secured on land) provides for the rate of interest on the credit to be fixed for a period of time; and
- the creditor discharges (under CCA 1974, s.94) all or part of his indebtedness during that period.

If CCA 1974, s.95A applies then the creditor may claim an amount equal to the cost which the creditor has incurred as a result only of the debtor's indebtedness being discharged during that period if:

- the amount of the payment under s.94 exceeds £8,000 or, where the debtor makes more than one payment in a 12-month period, the total of those payments exceed £8,000 (s.95A(2)(a));
- the agreement is not a debtor-creditor agreement allowing the debtor to overdraw on a current account (s.95A(2)(b)); and
- the amount of payment under s.94 is not paid from a contract of payment protection insurance (s.95A(2)(c)).

If CCA 1974, s.95A(2) is satisfied then the amount claimed by the creditor as compensation must be fair, objectively justified and must not exceed whichever is the lower of:

- the relevant percentage of the amount of the payment under s.94, i.e.
    - if the period between the date of payment under s.94 and the date on which that payment was due under the agreement is more than one year, 1 per cent of the amount of the payment under s.94; or
    - if the period between the date of payment under s.94 and the date on which that payment was due under the agreement is equal to or less than one year, 0.5 per cent of the amount of the payment under s.94; and
- the total amount of interest that would have been paid by the debtor under the agreement from the date of the payment until the date when that payment fell due.

7.7.5 Rebate

Section 95(1) of CCA 1974 brings into play the Consumer Credit (Early Settlement) Regulations 2004, SI 2004/1483 (or, for agreements before 31 May 2005, the Consumer Credit (Rebate on Early Settlement) Regulations 1983, SI 1983/1562. These regulations have the effect that the debtor is, in certain circumstances, entitled to a rebate if the agreement is settled earlier than the end of the term. There has been much criticism over the years over the way in which the rebate is calculated. Such a calculation is beyond the scope of this work but, it is submitted, the Consumer Credit (Early Settlement) Regulations 2004 give a 'fairer' rebate than the earlier regulations (which introduced the concept of the 'Rule of 78').

7.7.6 Effect of early payment on linked transactions

By virtue of CCA 1974, s.96:

- Where for any reason the indebtedness of the debtor under a regulated consumer credit agreement is discharged before the time fixed by the agreement, the debtor, and any relative of his, is at the same time discharged from any liability under a linked transaction, other than a debt which has already become payable (s.96(1)).
- The release in s.96(1) does not apply to a linked transaction which is an agreement providing the debtor or his relative with credit (s.96(2)).
- Regulations may exclude linked transactions from the operation of s.96(1) (s.96(3)). Under the Consumer Credit (Linked Transactions) (Exemptions) Regulations 1983, SI 1983/1560, reg.2, the same categories of linked transaction that are prescribed for the purposes of exemption under CCA 1974, ss.19(3) and 69(1) are excluded from s.96(1).

7.7.7 Creditor's duty to give settlement statement

Duty

By CCA 1974, s.97(1), the creditor under a regulated consumer credit agreement must, within the prescribed period after he has received a request from the debtor, give the debtor a statement in the prescribed form indicating, according to the information to which it is practicable for him to refer, the amount of the payment required to discharge the debtor's indebtedness under the agreement, together with the prescribed particulars showing how the amount is arrived at. By s.97(2A), the debtor's request does not need to be in writing unless the regulated consumer credit agreement is secured on land. This provision was introduced on 1 February 2011: before then, the request needed to be in writing for all consumer credit agreements.

When does the duty not apply?

By CCA 1974, s.97(2), the duty under s.97(1) does not apply to a request made less than one month after a previous request for the same agreement was complied with.

Prescribed period

By reg.4 of the Consumer Credit (Settlement Information) Regulations 1983, SI 1983/1564, the prescribed period is seven days. The date on which the debtor's request is received by the creditor does not count: *Goldsmith's Co* v. *West Metropolitan Railway Co* [1904] 1 KB 1.

Consequences of non-compliance

If a creditor does not comply with CCA 1974, s.97(1) then, by s.97(3), it is not entitled, while the default continues, to enforce the agreement. For a more detailed consideration of the consequences of non-compliance in the context of CCA 1974, s.77(1) (and it is submitted the effect of non-compliance with s.97(1) is the same), see further **6.4.8**.

7.7.8 Creditor's duty on partial repayment

By CCA 1974, s.97A(1), if a debtor under a regulated consumer credit agreement:

- makes a payment by virtue of which part of his indebtedness is discharged under CCA 1974, s.94; and
- at the same time or later requests the creditor to give him a statement concerning the effect of the payment on the debtor's indebtedness,

the creditor must give the statement to the debtor before the end of the period of seven working days beginning with the day following that on which the creditor receives the request. The statement must, by CCA 1974, s.97A(2), be in writing and must contain the following particulars:

- a description of the agreement sufficient to identify it;
- the name, postal address and, where appropriate, any other address of the creditor and the debtor;
- where the creditor is claiming an amount under CCA 1974, s.95A(2), that amount and the method used to determine it;
- the amount of any rebate to which the debtor is entitled:

  - under the agreement; or
  - by virtue of CCA 1974, s.95 (where that is higher);

- where the amount of the rebate is given, a statement indicating that this amount has been calculated having regard to the Consumer Credit (Early Settlement) Regulations 2004;
- where the debtor is not entitled to any rebate, a statement to this effect;
- any change to the number, timing or amount of repayments to be made under the agreement, or the duration of the agreement, which results from the partial discharge of the indebtedness of the debtor; and
- the amount of the debtor's indebtedness remaining under the agreement at the date the creditor gives the statement.

7.8 INTEREST ON DEFAULT

By CCA 1974, s.93, the debtor under a regulated consumer credit agreement must not be required to pay interest on sums which, in breach of the agreement, are unpaid by him at a rate:

- where the total charge for credit includes an item for interest, exceeding the rate of that interest; or
- in any other case, exceeding what would be the rate of the total charge for credit if any items included in the total charge for credit by virtue of CCA 1974, s.20(2) were disregarded.

7.9 AGENCY FOR RECEIVING NOTICE OF RESCISSION

If the debtor or hirer under a regulated agreement claims to have a right to rescind the agreement, under CCA 1974, s.102(1) each of the following is deemed to be the creditor or owner's agent for the purpose of receiving any written notice rescinding the agreement which is served by the debtor or hirer:

- a credit-broker or supplier who was the negotiator in antecedent negotiations; and

- any person who, in the course of a business carried on by him, acted for the debtor or hirer in any negotiations for the agreement.

By s.102(2), the entitlement for the debtor or hirer to serve notice on someone who is not the creditor or owner does not apply to:

- service of a notice of cancellation; or
- termination of an agreement under CCA 1974, s.99 or s.101 or the exercise of a right or power expressly conferred by the agreement.

Section 102 of CCA 1974 is of significant practical importance. It allows, in effect, a debtor or hirer under a regulated agreement to serve a notice of rescission on a third party (who may or may not send it on to the creditor or owner despite its obligation to do so under CCA 1974, s.175). This is particularly problematic for motor finance providers where a debtor will often consider he has 'bought' the goods from the dealer (and not the creditor). If there are any problems, he will generally approach the dealer. If, during one of those approaches, the debtor purports to reject the goods as being (for example) unsatisfactory by sending a letter or email, the dealer is the creditor's deemed agent. Creditors should therefore put in place procedures with dealers to ensure notices are immediately sent on following receipt.

7.10 TERMINATION STATEMENTS

7.10.1 Duty

By CCA 1974, s.103(1):

If an individual (the 'customer') serves on any person (the 'trader') a notice –

(a) stating that –

    (i) the customer was the debtor or hirer under a regulated agreement described in the notice, and the trader was the creditor or owner under the agreement, and

    (ii) the customer has discharged his indebtedness to the trader under the agreement, and

    (iii) the agreement has ceased to have any operation; and

(b) requiring the trader to give the customer a notice, signed by or on behalf of the trader, confirming that those statements are correct,

the trader shall, within the prescribed period after receiving the notice, either comply with it or serve on the customer a counter-notice stating that, as the case may be, he disputes the correctness of the notice or asserts that the customer is not indebted to him under the agreement.

By CCA 1974, s.103(2), if the trader disputes the correctness of the notice he must give particulars of the way in which he alleges it to be wrong.

7.10.2 When does the duty not apply?

The duty under CCA 1974, s.103(1) does not apply to:

- any agreement if the trader has previously complied with s.103(1) following the service of a notice for that agreement (s.103(3)); and
- a non-commercial agreement (s.103(4)).

7.10.3 Prescribed period

By virtue of the Consumer Credit (Prescribed Periods for Giving Information) Regulations 1983, SI 1983/1569, reg.2 the prescribed period is 12 working days. The date on which the debtor's request is received does not count: *Goldsmith's Co* v. *West Metropolitan Railway Co* [1904] 1 KB 1.

7.10.4 Consequence of non-compliance

If the trader fails to comply with the duty under CCA 1974, s.103(1), the individual is entitled to bring a claim for breach of statutory duty (s.103(6)). It is difficult, however, to see what loss would be suffered by non-compliance.

CHAPTER 8

Enforcing an agreement

8.1 INTRODUCTION

For many creditors or owners, how they go about enforcing the agreement is a key aspect to their business. They must, of course, have an enforceable agreement in the first place. We have discussed these requirements in earlier chapters. We have also discussed how a creditor or owner terminates the agreement. In this chapter, we look at the practical steps that the creditor or owner can take to enforce an agreement.

8.2 COUNTY OR HIGH COURT?

In England and Wales, the county court has jurisdiction under the Consumer Credit Act 1974 (CCA 1974) by s.141(1) to hear and determine:

- the creditor's or owner's claim to enforce a regulated agreement or any security;
- any claim to enforce any linked transaction against the debtor or hirer or his relative;

and such a claim must not be brought in any other court.

By s.141(2), if any such claim is brought in the High Court then it is not treated as improperly brought (and therefore liable to be struck out under rule 3.4 of the Civil Procedure Rules 1998, SI 1998/3132 (CPR)) but will be transferred to the county court.

Unless otherwise provided by the CPR, all the parties to a regulated agreement (including any surety) must be made parties to any proceedings relating to the agreement (CCA 1974, s.141(5)).

8.3 CONSUMER CREDIT ACT PROCEDURE

8.3.1 Introduction

Section 141 of CCA 1974 is supplemented by Practice Direction (PD) 7B to the CPR. This is known as the 'Consumer Credit Act procedure'. Under PD 7B, para.2.1, a claimant must use this procedure where any claim is made under a provision stated in PD 7B, para.3. These are:

- a claim under CCA 1974, s.141 by the creditor to enforce a regulated agreement or any security;
- an application by the debtor or hirer for a time order under CCA 1974, s.129;
- a claim by the creditor for recovery of goods protected by CCA 1974, s.90;
- a claim by the creditor or owner to enter premises to recover possession of goods under CCA 1974, s.92(1);
- a debtor's or surety's application under CCA 1974, s.140B(2)(a) for an order that the credit agreement is an unfair relationship;
- a claim by the creditor to enforce a regulated agreement where a court order is required because:
  - the agreement is improperly executed within CCA 1974, s.65(1);
  - the hirer or debtor has died and the agreement is partly secured or wholly unsecured as envisaged by CCA 1974, s.86(2);
  - a default notice has not been served on a surety (CCA 1974, s.111(2));
  - a negotiable instrument has been taken in breach of CCA 1974, s.123 (CCA 1974, s.124(1) or (2));
  - security has not been expressed in writing or is improperly executed (CCA 1974, s.105(7)(a) or (b)).

By PD 7B, para.3.2, any claim relating to the recovery of land is not subject to the Consumer Credit Act procedure. Plainly, this includes a claim for repossession of property subject to a charge in favour of a lender. In these cases, the proceedings are subject to CPR Part 55.

8.3.2 Which county court?

If the claim includes a claim to recover goods let under a regulated hire-purchase agreement or conditional sale agreement, it may only be started in the county court for the district in which the debtor, or one of the debtors:

- lives or carries on business; or
- lived or carried on business at the date when the defendant last made a payment under the agreement.

For any other claim to recover goods, the claim may only be started in the court for the district in which the defendant, or one of the defendants, lives or carries on business, or in which the goods are situated.

If a debtor or hirer makes a claim for a time order under CCA 1974, s.129, it must be started in the court where the claimant lives or carries on business.

8.3.3 Consequences

If the claim is subject to the Consumer Credit Act procedure under PD 7B then the court will fix a hearing date when it issues the claim (PD 7B, para.5.1). The date of this hearing must be not less than 28 days after service of the notice of the hearing (PD 7B, para.5.6). The particulars of claim must be served with the claim form (PD 7B, para.5.2).

There is no requirement for the defendant to file an acknowledgement of service or defence (PD 7B, para.5.3) but someone wishing to dispute the claim would be well advised to do so. By PD 7B, para.5.4, if a defendant wants to file a defence then he should do so within 14 days of service of the particulars of claim. In the author's experience, the court will often overlook late service as long as the defence is served before the fixed-date hearing. The court may, however, take into account any late service when exercising its discretion on costs.

Importantly, CPR Part 12 does not apply to claims subject to the Consumer Credit Act procedure meaning judgment in default cannot be obtained. If default judgment is entered then it is an irregular judgment for the purposes of CPR rule 13.2 meaning a defendant is entitled to have it set aside.

By PD 7B, para.6.1, the court may dispose of the claim at the fixed-date hearing. The court will often do so for return of goods claims, where the purpose of the fixed-date hearing is to decide whether the goods should be returned to the creditor or owner. If, however, a defence is filed, the court will usually allocate it to a track and give directions (including an order for the claim to proceed under CPR Part 7) in accordance with PD 7B, para.6.2.

8.3.4 Content of particulars of claim

There are various requirements as to the content of the particulars of claim, depending on the nature of the claim. For all Consumer Credit Act procedure cases the particulars of claim must state that it is subject to the Consumer Credit Act procedure (PD 7B, para.7.1). Specific requirements are as follows:

1.   If the claimant's claim is for return of goods let under a regulated hire-purchase agreement or regulated conditional sale agreement against a person other than a company or other corporation then the particulars of claim must, by PD 7B, para.7.2 state in the following order:

    (a)   the date of the agreement,
    (b)   the parties to the agreement,
    (c)   the number or other identification of the agreement (with enough information to allow the debtor to identify the agreement),
    (d)   where the claimant was not one of the original parties to the agreement, the means by which the rights and duties of the creditor passed to him,
    (e)   the place where the agreement was signed by the defendant (if known),
    (f)   the goods claimed,
    (g)   the total price of the goods,

(h)   the paid up sum,

(i)   the unpaid balance of the total price,

(j)   whether a default notice or a notice under section 76(1) or section 88(1) of the Act has been served on the defendant, and, if it has, the date and the method of service,

(k)   the date on which the right to demand delivery of the goods accrued,

(l)   the amount (if any) claimed as an alternative to the delivery of goods, and

(m)   the amount (if any) claimed in addition to –

    (i)   the delivery of the goods, or

    (ii) any claim under sub paragraph (l) above with the grounds of each such claim.

2.   If a claimant is a debtor or hirer making a claim for a time order under CCA 1974, s.129, he must attach a copy of the notice served on the creditor or owner under CCA 1974, s.129A(1)(a) and state (by PD 7B, para.7.3) in the following order:

    (1)   the date of the agreement,

    (2)   the parties to the agreement,

    (3)   the number or other means of identifying the agreement,

    (4)   details of any sureties,

    (5)   if the defendant is not one of the original parties to the agreement then the name of the original party to the agreement,

    (6)   the names and addresses of the persons intended to be served with the claim form,

    (7)   the place where the claimant signed the agreement,

    (8)   details of the notice served by the creditor or owner giving rise to the claim for the time order,

    (9)   the total unpaid balance the claimant admits is due under the agreement, and –

      (a)   the amount of any arrears (if known), and

      (b)   the amount and frequency of the payments specified in the agreement,

    (10)   the claimant's proposals for payments of any arrears and of future instalments together with details of his means;

    (11)   where the claim relates to a breach of the agreement other than for the payment of money the claimant's proposals for remedying it.

3.   If the claimant is seeking an enforcement order under CCA 1974, s.127, the particulars of claim must state why the claimant needs one (PD 7B, para.7.4).

8.3.5 Admissions

In claims to recover goods under CCA 1974, s.90, the defendant can admit the claim and offer terms on which a court order should be suspended. This is known as a 'suspended return of goods order'. If granted, it allows the debtor to retain the goods unless he fails to comply with the terms of the suspension. Upon receipt, the court will serve a copy of the admission on the claimant who may then either accept those terms by filing Form N228 (and obtain a judgment) or reject those terms. If rejected, the court can use the admissions as evidence.

8.3.6 Miscellaneous provisions

The court may dispense with the requirement in CCA 1974, s.141(5) that all the parties to a regulated agreement and any surety must be made party to any proceedings relating to the agreement so long as the claim form has not been served on the debtor or surety and the claimant either before or at the hearing makes an application (with or without notice) for the court to make such an order. The requirement under CCA 1974, s.141(5) does not apply to a former creditor, unless the court orders otherwise, if the claimant was not one of the original parties to the agreement and the former creditor's rights and duties under the agreement have passed to him by operation of law or assignment.

Where a claimant who is a creditor or owner makes a claim for a court order under CCA 1974, s.86(2), the personal representatives of a deceased debtor or hirer must be a party to the proceedings unless no grant of representation has been made to the estate (PD 7B, para.9.3). If no grant has been made, the claimant must make an application in accordance with CPR Part 23 for directions about which persons (if any) should be made parties to the claim (PD 7B, para.9.4).

By PD 7B, paras.10.1 and 10.2, a debtor or surety must serve written notice of intention on the court and every other party to the claim within 14 days of service of the claim form if:

- he seeks an order relating to an unfair relationship between a creditor and the debtor arising out of a credit agreement;
- a claim relating to that agreement or any related agreement has already begun; and
- CCA 1974, s.140B(2)(b) or (c) applies.

8.4 OTHER CLAIMS

If the Consumer Credit Act procedure does not apply (and it will not do if the debtor or hirer is a corporate body or if the creditor or owner is pursuing the debtor or hirer simply for money outstanding under the agreement) then it is important to remember that CPR Part 16 still includes details of what must be included in the particulars of claim. By CPR rule 16.4, the general rules for particulars of claim are as follows:

(1)   Particulars of claim must include –

       (a)   a concise statement of the facts on which the claimant relies;
       (b)   if the claimant is seeking interest, a statement to that effect and the details set out in paragraph (2);
       (c)   if the claimant is seeking aggravated damages or exemplary damages, a statement to that effect and his grounds for claiming them;

    (d)   if the claimant is seeking provisional damages, a statement to that effect and his grounds for claiming them; and

    (e)   such other matters as may be set out in a practice direction.

(2)   If the claimant is seeking interest he must –

    (a)   state whether he is doing so –

        (i)   under the terms of a contract;

        (ii)   under an enactment and if so which; or

        (iii)   on some other basis and if so what that basis is; and

    (b)   if the claim is for a specified amount of money, state –

        (i)   the percentage rate at which interest is claimed;

        (ii)   the date from which it is claimed;

        (iii)   the date to which it is calculated, which must not be later than the date on which the claim form is issued;

        (iv)   the total amount of interest claimed to the date of calculation; and

        (v)   the daily rate at which interest accrues after that date.

If, however, the claim is made under a hire-purchase or conditional sale agreement then by CPR PD 16, para.6:

- where the claim is for the delivery of goods let under a hire-purchase agreement or conditional sale agreement to a person other than a company or other corporation (but is not a claim subject to PD 7B), the claimant must state in the particulars of claim (by PD 16, para.6.1).

    (1)   the date of the agreement,

    (2)   the parties to the agreement,

    (3)   the number or other identification of the agreement,

    (4)   where the claimant was not one of the original parties to the agreement, the means by which the rights and duties of the creditor passed to him,

    (5)   whether the agreement is a regulated agreement, and if it is not a regulated agreement, the reason why,

    (6)   the place where the agreement was signed by the defendant,

    (7)   the goods claimed,

    (8)   the total price of the goods,

    (9)   the paid-up sum,

    (10)   the unpaid balance of the total price,

    (11)   whether a default notice or a notice under section 76(1) or 98(1) of the Consumer Credit Act 1974 has been served on the defendant, and if it has, the date and method of service,

    (12)   the date when the right to demand delivery of the goods accrued,

    (13)   the amount (if any) claimed as an alternative to the delivery of goods, and

    (14)   the amount (if any) claimed in addition to –

        (a) the delivery of the goods, or

        (b) any claim under (13) above,

        with the grounds of each claim.

- where the claim is not for the delivery of goods, the claimant must state in the particulars of claim (by PD 16, para.6.2):

(1)   the matters set out in paragraph 6.1(1) to (6) above,
(2)   the goods let under the agreement,
(3)   the amount of the total price,
(4)   the paid-up sum,
(5)   the amount (if any) claimed as being due and unpaid in respect of any instalment or instalments of the total price, and
(6)   the nature and amount of any other claim and how it arises.

For any other claim to recover possession of goods, the particulars of claim must, by CPR PD 16, para.7.2, contain a statement showing the value of the goods. By PD 16, para.7.3 if a claim is based upon a written agreement:

(1)   a copy of the contract or documents constituting the agreement should be attached to or served with the particulars of claim and the original(s) should be available at the hearing, and
(2)   any general conditions of sale incorporated in the contract should also be attached (but where the contract is or the documents constituting the agreement are bulky this practice direction is complied with by attaching or serving only the relevant parts of the contract or documents).

Under PD 16, para.7.6, for a claim issued in the High Court relating to a regulated consumer credit agreement, the particulars of claim must contain a statement that the claim is not one to which CCA 1974, s.141 applies.

8.5   CLAIMS FOR COSTS

Many creditors or owners will have a contractual right to claim costs incurred in pursuing a debt from the debtor or hirer. If proceedings are issued, it is important that a claim for contractual costs is included in the particulars of claim. The Court of Appeal in *Gomba Holdings (UK) Ltd and others* v. *Minories Finance Ltd and others (No.2)* [1993] Ch 171 decided that a mortgagee (and, it is submitted that it must follow, a creditor or owner) is entitled to recover, under the terms of the mortgage deed (or agreement), the actual costs, charges and expenses incurred, except for any costs that have not been reasonably incurred or were unreasonable in amount. The court's discretion as to the basis of assessment of a mortgagee's costs will normally be exercised so it corresponds with the contractual entitlement. In a consumer credit context, this decision was approved and applied by the county court on a return of goods hearing in *BMW Financial Services (GB) Ltd* v. *Taylor* [2006] CLY 698. Instead of awarding fixed costs, District Judge Newman decided that the term relating to payment of the lender's fees was clear and the court had no reason to interfere with that term.

If there is such a clause in the agreement, costs can be sought under CPR rule 48.3 which has the effect of presuming that the costs incurred have been reasonably incurred and are reasonable in amount.

8.6 INTEREST ON JUDGMENTS

Practitioners will be aware that interest on a judgment cannot be recovered as a result of art.2(3)(a) of the County Courts (Interest on Judgment Debts) Order 1991, SI 1991/1184. To overcome this problem, many creditors or owners have included terms and conditions allowing interest to be charged both before and after judgment. Until recently, there was no restriction on such a provision under CCA 1974. However, from 1 October 2008, any creditor or owner under a regulated agreement wanting to recover interest from the debtor or hirer after judgment has been entered will, under CCA 1974, s.130A(1), after the entering of judgment, need to give the debtor written notice of its intention to charge interest, and after giving the first notice, give further notices at intervals of not more than six months.

Interest from the date of the judgment cannot be recovered until the first notice is sent out (CCA 1974, s.130A(2)).

8.7 PRECEDENTS

- For a precedent particulars of claim for the unpaid balance under a regulated fixed-sum credit agreement following termination for non-payment, see **Precedent 12**.
- For a precedent defence and counterclaim responding to Precedent 12 and seeking a declaration that the agreement is unenforceable, see **Precedent 13**.
- For a precedent reply and defence to counterclaim responding to Precedent 13, see **Precedent 14**.
- For a precedent particulars of claim for return of goods let under a regulated hire-purchase agreement and/or the balance due under the agreement, see **Precedent 15**.
- For a precedent defence and counterclaim responding to Precedent 15 and seeking a declaration that that vehicle was rejected as being of unsatisfactory quality and/or damages for breach of warranty, see **Precedent 16**.
- For a precedent reply and defence to counterclaim responding to Precedent 16, see **Precedent 17**.
- For a precedent particulars of claim alleging breach of contract by the supplier, and a claim against the creditor under CCA 1974, s.75(1), see **Precedent 18**.
- For a precedent defence and additional claim responding to Precedent 18 by the creditor, and seeking an indemnity from the supplier, see **Precedent 19**.

CHAPTER 9

Security

9.1 INTRODUCTION

Part VIII of the Consumer Credit Act 1974 (CCA 1974) deals with the security aspects of consumer credit and consumer hire agreements. Security often plays a significant role and, without it, the availability of credit may be reduced. In this chapter, we look at the various rules on security, when the availability to enforce against the security is restricted or destroyed and some of the key steps which must be followed before enforcing that security.

9.2 GENERAL POSITION FOR SECURITY INSTRUMENTS

By s.105(1) of CCA 1974, any security provided for a regulated agreement must be in writing. This does not apply if the security is given by the debtor or hirer (s.105(6)). It therefore only applies where security is given by a third party. The obligation in s.105(1) is supplemented by s.105(2), which gives a power to pre-scribe the form and content of documents to be made under s.105(1) (called a 'security instrument'). By s.105(4), a security instrument is not properly executed unless:

- a document in the prescribed form, containing all the prescribed terms and conforming to regulations under s.105(2), is signed in the prescribed manner by, or for, the surety; and
- the document embodies all the terms of the security, other than implied terms; and
- the document, when presented or sent for the purpose of being signed by, or for, the surety, is in such state that its terms are readily legible; and
- when the document is presented or sent for the purpose of being signed by or for the surety there is also presented or sent a copy of the document.

Section 105(5) supplements s.105(4) by ensuring that a security instrument is not properly executed unless:

- where the security is provided after, or at the time when, the regulated agreement is made, a copy of the executed agreement, together with a copy of any other document referred to in it, is given to the surety at the time the security is provided; or
- where the security is provided before the regulated agreement is made, a copy of the executed agreement, together with a copy of any other document referred to in it, is given to the surety within seven days after the regulated agreement is made.

By s.105(7), if:

- in breach of s.105(1), a security is not expressed in writing; or
- a security instrument is improperly executed,

then the security, so far as provided in relation to a regulated agreement, is enforceable against the surety only on an order from the court. If an application for such an order is dismissed (except on technical grounds only), CCA 1974, s.106 applies to the security.

9.3 INEFFECTIVE SECURITIES

If, under any provision of CCA 1974 (most notably s.105), s.106 is applied to any security provided in relation to a regulated agreement then (subject to CCA 1974, s.177):

- the security, so far as it is provided, is be treated as never having effect;
- any property lodged with the creditor or owner solely for the purposes of such security must be immediately returned;
- the creditor or owner must take any necessary action to remove or cancel an entry in any register, so far as the entry relates to the security as so provided; and
- any amount received by the creditor or owner on realisation of the security will, so far as it is referable to the agreement, be repaid to the surety.

This section has a significant practical effect as it requires a creditor to remove entries in any registers. The most obvious examples are land provided as security, where entries at the Land Registry must be removed or cancelled, or where motor vehicles are provided as security, where it seems to follow that entries with bodies like HPI Limited will need to be removed.

9.4 DUTY TO GIVE INFORMATION

9.4.1 Introduction

Readers will be aware that there is a duty to give information to debtors or hirers elsewhere in CCA 1974, most obviously in CCA 1974, ss.77–79 (which has caused a substantial amount of litigation in recent years). We discussed these provisions at **6.4**, **6.7** and **6.10**. There are very similar obligations where security has been provided by third parties. These are contained in CCA 1974, ss.107–111. We now consider those provisions.

9.4.2 Duty to give information to surety under fixed-sum credit agreements

Duty

By CCA 1974, s.107(1), the creditor under a regulated agreement for fixed-sum credit under which security is provided must, within the prescribed period after receiving a request in writing from the surety and payment of a fee of £1, give the surety (if a different person from the debtor):

(a) a copy of the executed agreement (if any) and of any other document referred to in it;

(b) a copy of the security instrument (if any); and

(c) a statement signed by or on behalf of the creditor showing, according to the information to which it is practicable for him to refer, –

   (i) the total sum paid under the agreement by the debtor,

   (ii) the total sum which has become payable under the agreement by the debtor but remains unpaid, and the various amounts comprised in that total sum, with the date when each became due, and

   (iii) the total sum which is to become payable under the agreement by the debtor, and the various amounts comprised in that total sum, with the date, or mode of determining the date, when each becomes due.

If the creditor has insufficient information to allow it to work out the amounts and dates mentioned in CCA 1974, s.107(1)(c)(iii), then it is taken to comply with that sub-paragraph if the statement under s.107(1)(c) gives the basis on which, under the regulated agreement, they would fall to be worked out (CCA 1974, s.107(2)).

Prescribed period

The prescribed period, by reg.2 of the Consumer Credit (Prescribed Periods for Giving Information) Regulations 1983, SI 1983/1569, is 12 working days. The date on which the surety's request is received by the creditor or owner does not count: *Goldsmith's Co* v. *West Metropolitan Railway Co* [1904] 1 KB 1.

Exception

By CCA 1974, s.107(3), the duty under s.107(1) does not apply to:

• an agreement under which no sum is, or will or may become, payable by the debtor (i.e. where the agreement has been paid off); or

• a request made less than one month after a previous request under that subsection relating to the same agreement was complied with.

270

Consequences of non-compliance

By CCA 1974, s.107(4), if the creditor fails to comply with s.107(1) then it is not entitled, while the default continues, to enforce the security, so far as provided in relation to the agreement. Because the wording replicates CCA 1974, s.77(4), readers are referred to **6.4.8** for an analysis of the effect of non-compliance. In addition, it is submitted that it only creates temporary unenforceability preventing enforcement against the security. It does not follow that non-compliance with CCA 1974, s.107(1) means the creditor cannot enforce the agreement against the debtor.

Non-commercial agreements

Section 107 of CCA 1974, does not apply to non-commercial agreements (CCA 1974, s.107(5)).

9.4.3 Duty to give information to surety under running-account credit agreements

Duty

Under CCA 1974, s.108(1), the creditor under a regulated agreement for running-account credit under which security is provided must, within the prescribed period after receiving a request in writing from the surety and payment of a fee of £1, give to the surety (if a different person from the debtor):

(a) a copy of the executed agreement (if any) and of any other document referred to in it;

(b) a copy of the security instrument (if any); and

(c) a statement signed by or on behalf of the creditor showing, according to the information to which it is practicable for him to refer, –

    (i) the state of the account, and

    (ii) the amount, if any, currently payable under the agreement by the debtor to the creditor, and

    (iii) the amounts and due dates of any payments which, if the debtor does not draw further on the account, will later become payable under the agreement by the debtor to the creditor.

If the creditor has insufficient information to enable it to work out the amounts and dates mentioned in CCA 1974, s.108(1)(c)(iii), it will be taken to comply with that sub-paragraph if its statement under s.108(1)(c) gives the basis on which, under the regulated agreement, they would fall to be worked out (CCA 1974, s.108(2)).

Prescribed period

The prescribed period, by reg.2 of the Consumer Credit (Prescribed Periods for Giving Information) Regulations 1983, is 12 working days. The date on which the surety's request is received by the creditor does not count: *Goldsmith's Co* v. *West Metropolitan Railway Co* [1904] 1 KB 1.

Exception

By virtue of CCA 1974, s.108(3), the duty under s.108(1) does not apply to:

- an agreement under which no sum is, or will or may become, payable by the debtor (i.e. where the agreement has been paid off); or
- a request made less than one month after a previous request under that subsection relating to the same agreement was complied with.

Consequences of non-compliance

Under CCA 1974, s.108(4), if the creditor fails to comply with s.108(1) then it is not entitled, while the default continues, to enforce the security, so far as provided in relation to the agreement. Because the wording replicates CCA 1974, s.77(4), readers are referred to **6.4.8** for an analysis of the effect of non-compliance. In addition, it is submitted that it only creates temporary unenforceability preventing enforcement against the security. It does not follow that non-compliance with CCA 1974, s.108(1) means the creditor cannot enforce the agreement against the debtor.

Non-commercial agreements

Section 108 of CCA 1974, does not apply to non-commercial agreements (CCA 1974, s.108(5)).

9.4.4 Duty to give information to surety under consumer hire agreements

Duty

Under CCA 1974, s.109(1), the owner under a regulated consumer hire agreement under which security is provided must, within the prescribed period after receiving a request in writing from the surety and payment of a fee of £1, give to the surety (if a different person from the hirer):

(a) a copy of the executed agreement and of any other document referred to in it;
(b) a copy of the security instrument (if any); and
(c) a statement signed by or on behalf of the owner showing, according to the information to which it is practicable for him to refer, the total sum which has become payable under the agreement by the hirer but remains unpaid and the various amounts comprised in that total sum, with the date when each became due.

Prescribed period

The prescribed period, by reg.2 of the Consumer Credit (Prescribed Periods for Giving Information) Regulations 1983, is 12 working days. The date on which the surety's request is received by the owner does not count: *Goldsmith's Co* v. *West Metropolitan Railway Co* [1904] 1 KB 1.

Exception

By virtue of CCA 1974, s.109(2), the duty under s.109(1) does not apply to:

- an agreement under which no sum is, or will or may become, payable by the hirer (i.e. where the agreement has been paid off); or
- a request made less than one month after a previous request under that subsection relating to the same agreement was complied with.

Consequences of non-compliance

Under CCA 1974, s.109(3), if the owner fails to comply with s.109(1) then it is not entitled, while the default continues, to enforce the security, so far as provided in relation to the agreement. Because the wording replicates CCA 1974, s.79(3), readers are referred to **6.4.8** for an analysis of the effect of non-compliance. In addition, it is submitted that it only creates temporary unenforceability preventing enforcement against the security. It does not follow that non-compliance with CCA 1974, s.109(1) means the owner cannot enforce the agreement against the hirer.

Non-commercial agreements

Section 109 of CCA 1974, does not apply to non-commercial agreements (CCA 1974, s.109(4)).

9.4.5 Duty to give information to debtor or hirer

Duty

Under CCA 1974, s.110(1), the creditor or owner under a regulated agreement must, within the prescribed period after receiving a request in writing from the debtor or hirer and payment of a fee of £1, give to the debtor or hirer a copy of any security instrument executed as security in relation to that agreement after the making of the agreement.

Prescribed period

The prescribed period, by reg.2 of the Consumer Credit (Prescribed Periods for Giving Information) Regulations 1983, is 12 working days. The date on which the debtor's or hirer's request is received by the creditor or owner does not count: *Goldsmith's Co* v. *West Metropolitan Railway Co* [1904] 1 KB 1.

Exception

By virtue of CCA 1974, s.110(2), the duty under s.110(1) does not apply to:

- a non-commercial agreement;
- an agreement under which no sum is, or will or may become, payable by the debtor or hirer (i.e. where the agreement has been paid off); or
- a request made less than one month after a previous request under that subsection relating to the same agreement was complied with.

Consequences of non-compliance

Under CCA 1974, s.110(3), if the creditor or owner fails to comply with s.110(1) then it is not entitled, while the default continues, to enforce the security, so far as provided in relation to the agreement. Because the wording replicates CCA 1974, s.77(4), readers are referred to **6.4.8** for an analysis of the effect of non-compliance. It is also submitted that it only creates temporary unenforceability preventing enforcement against the security. It does not follow that non-compliance with CCA 1974, s.110(1) means the creditor or owner cannot enforce the agreement against the debtor or hirer.

9.4.6 Duty to give surety a copy of default, enforcement or termination notices

Duty

Under CCA 1974, s.111(1), if a default notice is served under CCA 1974, s.87(1), or an enforcement notice is served under CCA 1974, s.76(1), or a termination notice is served under CCA 1974, s.98(1) on the debtor or hirer, a copy of that notice must also be served by the creditor or owner on the surety (if he is a different person from the debtor or hirer).

Consequences of non-compliance

If the creditor or owner fails to comply with s.111(1) by serving a notice on the surety then the security is only enforceable against the surety (for the breach or other matter to which the notices relates) with the court's permission (CCA 1974, s.111(2)).

9.5 REALISATION OF SECURITIES

Under s.112 of CCA 1974, and subject to s.121, regulations may provide for any matters relating to the sale or other realisation by the creditor or owner, of property over which any right has been provided by way of security in relation to an actual or prospective regulated agreement, other than a non-commercial agreement. So far, there have been no such regulations.

9.6 AVOIDANCE OF CCA 1974 BY USE OF SECURITIES

CCA 1974 states, on many occasions, that the parties cannot contract out of its provisions. Given the aim of consumer protection, the draftsman of CCA 1974 was aware that creditors or owners may try to avoid CCA 1974 by using securities. CCA 1974, s.113(1) therefore states that where security is provided in relation to an actual or prospective regulated agreement the security must not be enforced so as to benefit the creditor or owner, directly or indirectly, to an extent greater (whether in terms of the amount of any payment or the time or manner of its being made) than would be the case if the security were not provided and any of the debtor's or hirer's obligations (or those of his relative) under or in relation to the agreement were carried out to the extent (if any) to which they would be enforced under CCA 1974.

By CCA 1974, s.113(2), where a regulated agreement is enforceable only with a court order or with an order from the OFT, any security provided in relation to the agreement is enforceable (so far as provided in relation to the agreement) where such an order has been made in relation to the agreement, but not otherwise. This prevents the creditor or owner from enforcing against the security where it is unable to enforce against the debtor or hirer without a court order or the OFT's permission. This ensures that the security is safeguarded against enforcement until after the creditor or owner has obtained a court order or the OFT's permission.

By CCA 1974, s.113(3), where:

- a regulated agreement is cancelled under CCA 1974, s.69(1) (discussed at **4.12**) or becomes subject to s.69(2); or
- a regulated agreement is terminated under CCA 1974, s.91 (discussed at **7.3.5**); or
- for any agreement, an application for an order under CCA 1974, ss.40(2), 65(1), 124(1) or 149(2) is dismissed (except on technical grounds only); or
- a declaration is made by the court under CCA 1974, s.142(1) (discussed at **10.12**) for any regulated agreement,

then CCA 1974, s.106 applies to any security provided in relation to the agreement (see **9.3** above).

If CCA 1974, s.113(3)(d) applies (i.e. where an application for an order under CCA 1974, ss.40(2), 65(1), 124(1) or 149(2) is dismissed (except on technical grounds only)) and the declaration relates to a part only of the regulated agreement, CCA 1974, s.106 only applies to the security provided for that part (s.113(4)). This provision is important for multiple agreements where different parts make up the agreement: if security is split for the different parts and part of the agreement is unenforceable, it only destroys the security for that part.

For a cancelled agreement, the duty imposed on the debtor or hirer by CCA 1974, s.71 or s.72 is not enforceable until the creditor or hirer has discharged any duty imposed on it by CCA 1974, s.106 (as applied by s.113(3)(a)) (CCA 1974, s.113(5)).

By CCA 1974, s.113(6), if the security is provided for a prospective agreement or transaction, the security will be enforceable for the agreement or transaction only after the time (if any) when the agreement is made. Until that time, the person providing the security is entitled, by notice to the creditor or owner, to require that CCA 1974, s.106 will from that point apply to the security.

For many creditors or owners, a guarantee and indemnity forms an important part of the security. If a guarantee or indemnity is given where the debtor or hirer is a minor, or an indemnity is given in a case where the debtor or hirer is otherwise not of full capacity (for example, there is mental incapacity), the reference in CCA 1974, s.113(1) to the extent to which his obligations would be enforced must be read in relation to the indemnity or guarantee as a reference to the extent to which those obligations would be enforced if he were of full capacity (CCA 1974, s.113(7)).

Finally, it is important to remember that CCA 1974, s.113(1)–(3) also applies when security is provided for an actual or prospective linked transaction (discussed at **1.3.6**). In these cases then (by s.113(8)):

- references to the agreement should be read as references to the linked transaction;
- references to the creditor or owner should be read as references to any person (other than the debtor or hirer, or his relative) who is a party, or a prospective party, to the linked transaction.

9.7 PLEDGES

9.7.1 Pawn-receipts

If a person receives an article in pawn under a regulated agreement then he must (at the time he receives the article) give to the person from whom he receives the article a pawn-receipt in the prescribed form (CCA 1974, s.114(1)).

If a person takes an article in pawn from an individual that he knows to be, or who appears to be, a minor then he commits an offence (CCA 1974, s.114(2)). It does not appear to be the case, given the wording of CCA 1974, s.170, that such an agreement is (as a result) rendered unenforceable.

By virtue of s.114(3), ss.114–122 of CCA 1974 do not apply to:

- a pledge of documents or title or bearer bonds; or
- a non-commercial agreement.

9.7.2   Failure to supply copies of pledge agreement, etc.

If a creditor under a regulated agreement takes any item in pawn and fails to comply with CCA 1974, ss.62–64 or 114(1) then he commits an offence (CCA 1974, s.115). The requirements of ss.62 to 64 are discussed at **5.17.4**, **5.17.5** and **5.18**. The requirements of s.114(1) are discussed at **9.7.1** above.

9.7.3   Redemption period

The basic position is set out in CCA 1974, s.116(1) which states that a pawn is redeemable at any time within six months after it was taken. Subject to that requirement, the period within which a pawn is redeemable will be the same as the period fixed by the parties for the duration of the credit secured by the pledge, or such longer period as they may agree (CCA 1974, s.116(2)). There is therefore a six-month minimum redemption period but, if the credit agreement is for (say) 12 months then the redemption period will be the same unless agreed otherwise.

If the pawn is not redeemed by the end of the redemption period, by CCA 1974, s.116(3) it remains redeemable until it is realised by the pawnee under CCA 1974, s.121 except where, under CCA 1974, s.120(1)(a), the property in it passes to the pawnee. By CCA 1974, s.116(4), no special charge may be made for redemption of a pawn after the end of the redemption period, and charges for its safe keeping must not be at a higher rate after the end of the redemption period than before.

9.7.4   Redemption procedure

If a pawn-receipt is surrendered and the amount owing is paid then, so long as the pawn is redeemable under CCA 1974, s.116, the pawnee must deliver the pawn to the bearer of the pawn-receipt (CCA 1974, s.117(1)). In fraudulent situations, this can cause problems as, if a pawn-receipt has been stolen, CCA 1974 would require the pawn to be handed over to a thief. Section 117(2) therefore steps in and makes it clear that s.117(1) does not apply if the pawnee knows or has reasonable cause to suspect that the bearer of the pawn-receipt is neither the owner of the pawn nor authorised by the owner to redeem it. Whilst this goes some way to protecting owners of pawn, it is not a complete answer.

The normal position for an owner who has had his goods handed over to another person is to bring a claim for wrongful interference with goods, i.e. a claim for conversion, reversionary damage, negligence or trespass. CCA 1974, s.117(3) significantly cuts down that right by stating that the pawnee is not liable to any person in tort or delict for delivering the pawn where s.117(1) applies, or refusing to deliver it where the person demanding delivery does not comply with s.117(1) or where s.117(1) does not apply (because of s.117(2)).

9.7.5   Importance of pawn-receipts

The importance of a pawn-receipt is therefore fundamental: if it is lost or stolen, it would cause significant difficulties in the recovery of pawned goods. Section 118(1) of CCA 1974 deals with this potential issue. It allows a person (called the 'claimant') who is not in possession of the pawn-receipt but claims to be the owner of the pawn, or to be otherwise entitled or authorised to redeem it, to recover the pawn when it is redeemable by tendering to the pawnee in place of the pawn-receipt:

- a statutory declaration made by the claimant in the prescribed form and with the prescribed contents; or
- where the pawn is security for fixed-sum credit not exceeding £75 or for running-account credit where the credit limit does not exceed £75, and the pawnee agrees, a statement in writing in the prescribed form, and with the prescribed contents, signed by the claimant.

The form is prescribed by the Consumer Credit (Loss of Pawn-Receipt) Regulations 1983, SI 1983/1567. The form of statutory declarations appear at Scheds.1 and 2 to those regulations.

If a claimant complies with CCA 1974, s.118(1) then, by s.118(2), s.117 applies as if the declaration or statement were the pawn-receipt, and the original pawn-receipt becomes inoperative for the purposes of CCA 1974, s.117.

9.7.6   Unreasonable refusal to deliver pawn

By CCA 1974, s.119(1), if a person has taken a pawn under a regulated agreement and refuses, without reasonable cause, to allow the pawn to be redeemed, he commits a criminal offence. The standard of proof is, once again, beyond reasonable doubt. Section 119(2) provides some further guidance: if a person is convicted of an offence under s.119(1) in England and Wales, which does not amount to theft, s.148 of the Powers of Criminal Courts (Sentencing) Act 2000 (which deals with restitution orders) applies as if the pawnee had been convicted of stealing the pawn.

9.7.7   Failing to redeem pawn

By CCA 1974, s.120(1), if at the end of the redemption period the pawn has not been redeemed then:

- despite the provisions of CCA 1974, s.113, property in the pawn passes to the pawnee where all of the following apply:
    - the redemption period is six months;
    - the pawn is security for fixed-sum credit not exceeding £75 or running-account credit under which the credit limit does not exceed £75; and
    - the pawn was not immediately before the making of the regulated consumer credit agreement a pawn under another regulated consumer credit

agreement for which the debtor has discharged his indebtedness in part under CCA 1974, s.94(3); or

- in any other case, the pawn becomes realisable by the pawnee.

If the debtor or hirer is entitled to apply to the court for a time order under CCA 1974, s.129 (discussed at **10.4**), then CCA 1974, s.120(1) is varied so that 'at the end of the redemption period' is replaced by 'after the expiry of five days following the end of the redemption period'.

9.7.8 Realisation of pawn

If a pawn has become realisable by a person then, by CCA 1974, s.121(1), he may sell it after giving the pawnor (except in prescribed cases) not less than the prescribed period of notice of the intention to sell. The notice must indicate the asking price and such other particulars as may be prescribed.

After the sale takes place, the pawnee must (within the prescribed period) give the pawnor, in writing, the prescribed information about the sale, its proceeds and expenses (CCA 1974, s.121(2)). If the net sale proceeds exceed the amount which, if the pawn had been redeemed on the date of sale, would have been payable for its redemption, the debt secured by the pawn is discharged (CCA 1974, s.121(3)). Any surplus must also be paid by the pawnee to the pawnor.

The period is prescribed by reg.2 of the Consumer Credit (Realisation of Pawn) Regulations 1983, SI 1983/1568 (CC(RP)R 1983). This prescribes a period of 14 days for CCA 1974, s.121(1) and a period of 20 working days for s.121(2). The information to be included in the notice of intention to sell under s.121(1) is prescribed by CC(RP)R 1983, reg.4 and Sched.1. The information to be given following the sale under s.121(2) is prescribed by CC(RP)R 1983, reg.5 and Sched.2.

If the net sale proceeds do not exceed the amount payable for the pawn's redemption on the date of sale, the debt is treated as the difference between the amount payable and the net sale proceeds (CCA 1974, s.121(4)).

The position under CCA 1974 is no different from that under other legal principles: the pawnor may argue that the gross amount is less than the pawn's true market value on the date of sale (i.e. the pawnee failed to mitigate its loss by selling at an undervalue). If he does so then, by CCA 1974, s.121(6), the onus is on the pawnee to prove that he (and any agents employed by him) used reasonable care to ensure that the true market value was obtained. If he fails to do so, the net sale proceeds will be increased (and the balance decreased) by the difference between the sale price and the true market value. It must be remembered, however, that the obligation to mitigate loss is not a high one. Recently, the Court of Appeal decided in *Lombard North Central plc* v. *Automobile World (UK) Ltd* [2010] EWCA Civ 20 that:

[I]t is well recognised that the duty to mitigate is not a demanding one. Ex hypothesi, it is the party in breach which has placed the other party in a difficult situation. The burden of proof is therefore on the party in breach to demonstrate a failure to mitigate. The other party only has to do what is reasonable in the circumstances.

The pawnor may also allege that the expenses of sale were unreasonable high. If he does so then, by CCA 1974, s.121(7), the onus is (once again) on the pawnee to prove that they were reasonable. If he fails to do so, the net sale proceeds will be increased (and the balance decreased) by the difference between the costs incurred and the notional amount of reasonable costs.

9.8   NEGOTIABLE INSTRUMENTS

9.8.1   Restrictions on taking and negotiating instruments

Under CCA 1974, s.123(1), a creditor or owner must not take a negotiable instrument, other than a bank note or cheque, in discharge of any sum payable:

- by the debtor or hirer under a regulated agreement; or
- by any person as surety for the agreement.

The ban in CCA 1974, s.123(1) is supplemented by s.123(2) which prevents the creditor or owner from negotiating a cheque taken by it in discharge of a sum payable within s.123(1) to anyone other than a banker (within the meaning of the Bills of Exchange Act 1882). This provision is unlikely to concern most creditors or owners.

There is also a ban on a creditor or owner taking a negotiable instrument as security for the discharge of any sum payable within s.123(1) (CCA 1974, s.123(3)). What constitutes taking a negotiating instrument as security for such discharge is explained by s.123(4): it is where the sum is intended to be paid in some other way, and the negotiable instrument is to be presented for payment only if the sum is not paid in that way. For example, this covers situations where the creditor or owner requires payment to be made by direct debit but holds on to a cheque in case there is any default. The effect of s.123(3) and (4) is to ban such a practice.

By CCA 1974, s.123(5), the provisions of s.123 do not apply to non-commercial agreements. By s.123(6), the Secretary of State may make an order providing that s.123 does not apply where the regulated agreement has a connection with a country outside the UK. To date, the only order made is the Consumer Credit (Negotiable Instruments) (Exemption) Order 1984, SI 1984/435. The general effect of this order is to remove the application of s.123 to certain consumer hire agreements.

9.8.2   Consequences of breaching the restrictions on taking and negotiating instruments

If a creditor or owner breaches CCA 1974, s.123:

- for any sum payable by the debtor or hirer under a regulated agreement then, by CCA 1974, s.124(1), the agreement under which the sum is payable is only enforceable against the debtor or hirer with a court order;
- for any sum payable by any surety then, by s.124(2), the security is only enforceable with a court order.

If a court order under s.124(2) is sought but dismissed (except on technical grounds only), then CCA 1974, s.106 applies to that security. The provisions of s.106 are discussed at **9.3** above.

9.8.3   Holders in due course

Under CCA 1974, s.125(1), a person who takes a negotiable instrument in breach of CCA 1974, s.123(1) or (3) is not a holder in due course, and is not entitled to enforce the instrument. Similarly, by s.125(2), where a person negotiates a cheque in breach of s.123(2), his doing so constitutes a defect in his title within the meaning of the Bills of Exchange Act 1882. By s.125(3), if a person mentioned in s.123(1)(a) or (b) ('the protected person') becomes liable to a holder in due course of an instrument taken from the protected person in breach of s.123(1) or (3), or taken from the protected person and negotiated in breach of s.123(2), the creditor or owner must indemnify the protected person in respect of that liability. Finally, s.125(4) makes it clear that nothing in CCA 1974 affects the rights of the holder in due course of any negotiable instrument.

9.9   LAND MORTGAGES

A land mortgage securing a regulated agreement is enforceable (so far as provided under the agreement) only with a court order (CCA 1974, s.126). Creditors or owners must therefore obtain a court order for repossession before recovering possession of the land.

CHAPTER 10

Judicial control of agreements

10.1 INTRODUCTION

Given that the Consumer Credit Act 1974 (CCA 1974) is, to a large extent, a consumer protection mechanism, the judiciary have considerable powers to ensure that creditors or owners are complying with CCA 1974 and its associated regulations. In this chapter, we look at how the court exercises that control. For example, in certain circumstances a creditor must obtain the court's permission before enforcing the agreement. In other cases, a debtor may apply to the court for a time order or allege that the relationship between him and the creditor is unfair.

10.2 ENFORCEMENT ORDERS: INFRINGEMENT

10.2.1 When can an enforcement order be made?

The court is given the power, by virtue of CCA 1974, s.127(1), to make an enforcement order where there has been infringement by:

- failing to provide pre-contract information in accordance with CCA 1974, s.55(2);
- failing to provide a copy of the overdraft agreement in accordance with CCA 1974, s.61B(3);
- having an improperly executed agreement by CCA 1974, s.65(1);
- having an improperly executed security instrument by CCA 1974, s.105(7)(a) or (b);
- failing to serve a copy of a notice on a surety by CCA 1974, s.111(2); or
- by taking a negotiable instrument in contravention of CCA 1974, s.123 by s.124(1) or (2).

If an enforcement order is available, the creditor is entitled to make an application to the court under CCA 1974, s.127(1) for the court's permission to enforce the agreement. If the court gives permission, this is called an enforcement order.

10.2.2 Failure to include prescribed terms/cancellation notices

Until the repeal of CCA 1974, s.127(3)–(5) on 6 April 2007, the court was unable to make an enforcement order:

- where the agreement failed to include the terms prescribed by Sched.6 to the Consumer Credit (Agreements) Regulations 1983 (CC(A)R 1983); or
- where the agreement was cancellable:

  - either s.62 or s.63 of CCA 1974 (dealing with the provision of copy documents) were not complied with and the creditor or owner did not give a copy of the executed agreement (and any document referred to in it) to the debtor or hirer before beginning proceedings; or
  - CCA 1974, s.64(1) (dealing with the duty to give notice of cancellation rights) was not complied with.

Following the repeal of s.127(3)–(5), the court will be able to make an enforcement order for agreements dated on or after 6 April 2007 which fail to include this information. The danger of irredeemable unenforceability is therefore alive and kicking for pre-6 April 2007 agreements.

10.2.3 The test

The effect of CCA 1974, s.127(1) is that the court may refuse to make an enforcement order where it would be 'just to do so' but it must bear in mind the prejudice caused to the debtor and the culpability for the non-compliance. It is submitted that the proper approach to be taken by the court is to make an enforcement order unless (and only unless) the debtor or hirer can show:

- he has been prejudiced; or
- the creditor or owner is culpable for the non-compliance.

This approach was adopted in *Nissan Finance UK Ltd* v. *Lockhart* [1993] CCLR 39 where the court concluded, in the absence of any evidence put forward by the debtor, that there was no prejudice or culpability meaning an enforcement order should be made. It also follows from this decision that where the non-compliance is a technical one falling within CCA 1974, s.65, a debtor has to show he would have acted differently if the agreement had been compliant before a finding of prejudice will be made. In terms of culpability, it seems arguable that if a creditor under a regulated credit agreement, perhaps with a variable rate of interest, decides for purely commercial reasons not to include the rate of interest (perhaps because it is, at first blush, rather high), the court may make a finding of culpability. In such a case, the debtor is likely to attractively argue that he has been prejudiced by the failure to include the rate of interest or the APR and the reason for that was the creditor or owner's commercial decision to exclude this information.

Precedent

For a precedent particulars of claim including a claim for an enforcement order under CCA 1974, s.127(1), see **Precedent 20**.

10.3 ENFORCEMENT ORDERS: DEATH OF HIRER OR DEBTOR

If the hirer or debtor dies, and the agreement is partially secured or unsecured on death (which is dealt with in CCA 1974, s.86(2) and discussed at **6.17**), the creditor or owner is entitled to make an application to the court under CCA 1974, s.128 for permission to enforce the agreement. If it does so, the court will make an enforcement order if (but only if) the creditor or owner proves that it has been unable to establish that the present or future obligations of the debtor or hirer under the agreement are likely to be discharged.

10.4 TIME ORDERS

10.4.1 Introduction

For many debtors or hirers, the provisions in CCA 1974, s.129 provide a valuable tool to give them extra time and avoid repossession of goods and land or termination of the regulated agreement. These rights have been strengthened following the Consumer Credit Act 2006, which amended CCA 1974 to allow a debtor to make an application after receiving an arrears sums notice (which often arrives on a debtor's or hirer's doormat before a default notice).

10.4.2 When can the court make a time order?

By virtue of CCA 1974, s.129(1) and subject to s.129(3), the court may make a time order if it is just to do so:

- on the creditor's or owner's application for an enforcement order;
- on the debtor's or hirer's application following service upon him of:
  - a default notice under CCA 1974, s.87(1);
  - an enforcement notice under CCA 1974, s.76(1); or
  - a termination notice under CCA 1974, s.98(1);

- on the debtor's or hirer's application following service upon him of an arrears sums notice under CCA 1974, s.86B or s.86C; or

- in any claim brought by the creditor or owner to enforce a regulated agreement or any security, or recover possession of any goods or land let under a regulated agreement.

10.4.3 What order can the court make?

Under CCA 1974, s.129(2), the court can order one or both of the following (whichever it considers just):

- the payment by the debtor or hirer or any surety of any sum owed under a regulated agreement or a security by instalments payable at such times (after considering the debtor's, hirer's or surety's means) as the court thinks reasonable; or
- the remedying by the debtor or hirer of any breach of a regulated agreement (but not non-payment of money) within such a period as the court may say.

This is an extremely wide power which the court can exercise and do what it thinks is 'just' or fair.

10.4.4 Future payments

It is notable, however, that as a general rule this power does not extend to sums that have yet to fall due at the date of the court hearing to determine the application for a time order. If the agreement has yet to be terminated then the court does not generally have the power to reorganise future payments. There are three exceptions to this basic principle:

- if the terms of the agreement say that upon default, all of the sums become due and payable (an accelerated payment clause) then the court does have the power to reorganise those payments as they have fallen due: *First National Bank plc* v. *Syed* [1991] 2 All ER 250;
- if the agreement is secured on land and, after termination, the creditor seeks repossession. Following the Court of Appeal's decision in *Southern and District Finance plc* v. *Barnes* [1995] CCLR 62, the consequence of proceedings for repossession is that the whole of the loan becomes due, meaning the court can reorganise those payments;
- if the agreement is one of conditional sale or hire purchase then the court has, by CCA 1974, s.130(2), the power to make a time order for instalments that have fallen due or will fall due even if there is no accelerated payment clause.

10.4.5 Exercise of the court's powers

It is submitted that, following the Court of Appeal's decision in *Southern and District Finance plc* v. *Barnes* [1995] CCLR 62, the court should exercise its powers in the following way:

285

- When a time order is applied for, or a possession order sought of land subject to a regulated agreement, the court must first consider whether it is just to make a time order. This involves consideration of all the circumstances of the case, including the creditor's position as well as the debtor's.
- A time order should normally be made for a stated period to cover the debtor's temporary financial difficulty. If the debtor is unlikely to be able to resume payment of the total indebtedness by at least the amount of the agreed contractual instalments, no order should be made and the agreement should be enforced.
- When a time order relates to non-payment the court must consider what instalments would be reasonable, in terms of both amount and timing, having regard to the debtor's means. The time order may include an amendment to the agreement. For example, if the rate of interest is amended, it is relevant that smaller instalments will result in a liability to pay interest on accumulated arrears.
- If a time order is made when the whole outstanding balance is owed, there will inevitably be consequences for the term of the loan or the rate of interest, or both. The court has power to alter these, said the Court of Appeal in *Barnes*, under s.136.
- The court should, when making a time order, suspend any possession order that it also makes, as long as the terms of the time order are complied with.

10.4.6 Offers to settle in litigation

If an application for a time order has been issued by a debtor or hirer, he is entitled to make an offer (either under CPR Part 36 or otherwise) to pay by instalments. If such an offer is accepted by the creditor or owner, the court is entitled by CCA 1974, s.130(1) to make an order under CCA 1974, s.129(2)(a) giving effect to the offer without hearing evidence of means from the debtor or hirer.

10.4.7 Are any agreements excluded from s.129?

Under CCA 1974, s.130(3), the court is unable to make a time order under CCA 1974, s.129(2)(a) where the regulated agreement is secured by a pledge if, as a result of regulations made under CCA 1974, ss.76(5), 87(4) or 98(5), service of a notice is not necessary for the enforcement of a pledge. To date, no such regulations have been made.

10.4.8 Nature of debtor's or hirer's interest in goods following a time order

What happens if an agreement has been terminated but the debtor or hirer is entitled to keep the goods let under a regulated hire-purchase, conditional sale or hire agreement? By CCA 1974, s.130(4) the answer appears straightforward: the debtor or hirer is treated (except in cases where title has already passed to him) as a bailee.

10.4.9   Effect of a time order

If a time order is made, the effect by CCA 1974, s.130(5) is as follows:

- the creditor or owner is not entitled to take any of the steps mentioned in CCA 1974, s.87(1);
- if any provision of the agreement takes effect (the 'secondary provision') upon breach of another provision of the agreement (the 'primary provision') and the time order provides for remedying of such a breach of the primary provision, the creditor or owner is not entitled to treat the secondary provision as operative within the relevant period; or
- if a breach to which the order relates happens during the period of the time order but is remedied, it is treated as not happening.

10.4.10   Variation or revocation of time orders

Under CCA 1974, s.130(6), any person affected by a time order (often only the creditor or owner) may apply to the court for an order revoking or varying the order.

10.4.11   Debtor's notice of intention to apply after service of default sums or arrears sums notice

If a debtor or hirer intends to apply for a time order following service of a notice under CCA 1974, s.86B or s.86C he must;

- give written notice under CCA 1974, s.129A(2); and
- make his application no earlier than 14 days after giving that notice to the creditor or owner.

Section 129A(2) requires the written notice to include:

- a statement that the debtor or hirer wishes to make an application for a time order;
- a statement that he wants to make a proposal to the creditor or owner towards his repayments; and
- details of his proposal.

10.4.12   Form of application

Debtors or hirers wishing to make an application for a time order should apply to their local court using Form N440. This is available from HM Courts and Tribunals Service's website (at **www.justice.gov.uk/about/hmcts/index.htm**).

Precedent

For a precedent application for a time order, see **Precedent 21**.

10.5   PROTECTION ORDERS

If a creditor or owner is concerned that goods let under a regulated agreement may be damaged or destroyed, it can apply to the court under CCA 1974, s.131 for a 'protection order'. The court may make such an order where it thinks it is 'just' to do so and may make an order restricting or stopping the debtor or hirer's use of the property or even require the debtor or owner to hand it over to a nominated person. It is submitted that the burden is upon the creditor or owner to prove that the damage or depreciation is likely and it would be just to make a protection order.

10.6   SPECIAL POWERS FOR HIRE-PURCHASE OR CONDITIONAL SALE AGREEMENTS: RETURN OR TRANSFER ORDERS

Hire-purchase and conditional sale agreements are given significant consideration by CCA 1974. If the court considers it just to do so:

- on an application for an enforcement order or a time order; or
- in the creditor's claim for return of the goods let under the agreement,

the court may:

- make an order (called a 'return order') returning the goods let under the agreement to the creditor (CCA 1974, s.133(1)(i)); or
- make an order (called a 'transfer order') for transfer to the debtor of the creditor's title to certain goods let under the agreement (these are called the 'transferred goods') and the return to the creditor of the remainder of the goods (CCA 1974, s.133(1)(ii)).

10.7   CONDITIONS OR SUSPENSION OF ORDERS

Under CCA 1974, s.135(1), the court has the power (if it considers it just to do so) to include provisions:

- putting conditions on the operation of any order; or
- suspending any order either (a) until such time as the court decides or (b) until a certain event has taken place.

The court is unable, however, to suspend the operation of any term unless it is satisfied that the goods are in the debtor's or hirer's control (CCA 1974, s.135(2)). The court's powers for consumer hire agreements are further restricted by s.135(3) as it cannot, by virtue of the suspension, allow the hirer to keep the goods for longer than the term of the agreement. Finally, any party affected by a court order under s.135(1) is entitled, by s.135(4), to apply to the court to vary the order. CCA 1974 does not specifically say that the court has the power to revoke such an order but it is likely that the court has such a power.

10.8 POWER TO VARY AGREEMENTS AND SECURITIES

The court has a very wide power in CCA 1974, s.136 to amend agreements or securities as it thinks fit. Such a power can only, however, be used where it is necessary as a consequence of any term of an order under CCA 1974, ss.127–135. It is not, therefore, a wide-ranging power for the court to do whatever it thinks is just: such a power for consumer credit agreements (and not hire agreements) is, of course, now contained in the unfair relationship provisions in CCA 1974, ss.140A–140D.

10.9 FINANCIAL RELIEF FOR HIRERS

It is notable that where a debtor has goods let under a hire-purchase or conditional sale agreement and pays more than one-third of the total amount payable, those goods become 'protected' from repossession. In short, this means that the creditor must obtain a court order or the debtor's informed consent before obtaining possession of the goods (CCA 1974, s.90). This is, of course, discussed in more detail at **7.3.5**.

Hirers, on the other hand, who have acquired goods under a regulated consumer hire agreement (and not consumer credit agreements like hire-purchase or conditional sale agreements) are not protected by s.90. There is, therefore, no requirement to obtain a court order before repossessing the goods. Hirers also have no right to a postponed order under CCA 1974, s.133 and are unable to invoke the extortionate credit bargain provisions in CCA 1974, s.139 (before their repeal) or the unfair relationship provisions in CCA 1974, s.140A–140D.

If, however, goods let under a consumer hire agreement are repossessed without a court order, the hirer may apply to the court under CCA 1974, s.132(1) for an order that:

- the whole or part of the sums paid by the hirer to the owner should be repaid; and
- the obligation to pay the whole or part of any sum owed under the agreement no longer exists.

If such an application is made, and the court considers it 'just' to do so after considering the extent of the hirer's enjoyment of the goods, it can grant the application either in full or in part. If the owner has issued proceedings for return of the goods let under the regulated hire agreement, it may also make an order under s.132(1) (CCA 1974, s.132(2)).

At first blush, this seems like an extremely powerful right for a hirer under a regulated hire agreement. There is, however, very little reported case law on the provisions. Indeed, there is only one reported case: the Scottish decision of *Automotive Financial Services Ltd* v. *Henderson & Henderson* 1992 SLT (Sh Ct) 63. In this case, a motor vehicle was let under a regulated consumer hire agreement for 36 months. After six months, the hirers returned the motor vehicle to the owners and stopped paying the rentals. The owners, in turn, terminated the agreement for non-payment and sought recovery of the balance outstanding under the agreement. The hirers sought relief under CCA 1974, s.132 but the sheriff dismissed the application. The hirers appealed to the sheriff principal, who was satisfied that the sheriff had taken all relevant matters into account when exercising his discretion (which should rarely be disturbed on appeal), and dismissed the appeal. It is therefore submitted that the use of CCA 1974, s.132(1) will be limited to very rare cases; perhaps where the hirer has had no, or little, enjoyment from the goods.

10.10 EXTORTIONATE CREDIT BARGAINS

10.10.1 Introduction

Until the introduction of the unfair relationship test (subject, of course, to transitional provisions), debtors (but not hirers) were entitled to argue that the credit agreement was an 'extortionate credit bargain' within the meaning of CCA 1974, ss.137–140. It was hoped, at the time of their inception, that the courts would readily use these powers to intervene, where appropriate, to protect consumers. It is commonly accepted that these expectations did not turn into decisions meaning there was considerable call by consumer groups for a review of the law. After much consultation, the unfair relationship provisions finally hit the statute book (for the most part) on 6 April 2007 subject to complex transitional provisions. The old extortionate credit bargain provisions will, however, continue to apply to agreements pre-dating 6 April 2007 that 'complete' (i.e. where there are no further sums to be paid), by the latest, before 6 April 2008.

10.10.2 Do the provisions apply to regulated agreements only?

The extortionate credit bargain provisions (like the unfair relationship provisions which replaced them) apply to both regulated and non-regulated agreements so long as the debtor is an 'individual' (as defined by CCA 1974, s.189(1)). It is therefore possible for any 'individual' under a credit agreement, whether it be regulated or unregulated, to argue (subject to the transitional provisions) that their credit agreement is an extortionate credit bargain.

10.10.3 Limitation

It is now fairly settled law, following the Court of Appeal's decision in *Rahman* v. *Sterling Credit Ltd* [2001] 1 WLR 496, that:

- if the debtor makes an application to the court, the limitation period is 12 years (unless there is a claim for repayment) from the date of the credit agreement; and
- if the debtor claims repayment of monies paid, the limitation period is six years.

What the Court of Appeal did not address is, first, the date that the six-year limitation period begins for repayments and, second, whether there is any limitation period if the extortionate credit bargain provisions are simply used as a defence to a claim (rather than a separate claim). It is respectfully submitted that the answers are as follows: first, the limitation period will run from the date of payment and, second, the position does not change where the extortionate credit bargain provisions are used as a defence and counterclaim meaning there is either a 12-year or a six-year limitation period depending on the nature of the relief sought (a position recently accepted by the High Court in *Peter Nolan* v *Graham Michael Wright* [2009] EWHC 305 (Ch)). The first point remains untested by the courts.

10.10.4 The test

The test is whether the credit agreement, or the credit agreement together with other transactions whose charges form part of the total charge for credit, requires the debtor or his relative to make payments which are 'grossly exorbitant, or otherwise [the credit bargain] grossly contravenes the ordinarily principles of fair dealing' (CCA 1974, s.138(1)).

The court must also, by CCA 1974, s.138, consider the following factors:

- the interest rates available at the time when the credit bargain was made (s.138(2)(a)). Following *Nash* and *Spencer* (discussed at **10.10.7** below, this means the annual percentage rate (i.e. the APR));
- factors affecting the debtor including his age, experience, business capacity, state of health and the degree of financial pressure on the debtor at the time of entering into the credit bargain (s.138(3));
- factors affecting the creditor including the risk it accepts, the value of any security provided to it, its relationship with the debtor and whether or not a 'colourable cash price' was quoted for any goods or services included in the credit bargain (s.138(4));

- general factors including how far any linked transaction was required to protect the debtor or creditor or was in the debtor's interest (s.138(5)); and
- any other relevant considerations (s.138(2)(c)).

The 'credit bargain' is, if there is no other transaction, the credit agreement but if there is more to the transaction than a credit agreement (for example, a legal charge or a contract of maintenance), the 'credit bargain' will be all of those documents.

10.10.5 The court's powers

The court is given a fairly wide power, in CCA 1974, s.137(1) and where it finds an extortionate credit bargain, to re-open the credit agreement so it can 'do justice' between the parties. This is supplemented by CCA 1974, s.139(2), which gives the court the power to relieve the debtor or surety from payment of any sum in excess of that fairly due by ordering:

- an account to be taken between any persons;
- the setting aside of any obligation on the debtor or surety under the credit bargain or any related agreement;
- the creditor to repay the whole or part of any sum paid under the credit bargain or any related agreement (regardless of who paid it);
- the return to the surety of any property provided as security.

The court may make an order under CCA 1974, s.139(2) even if the effect of it is to put a burden on the creditor for an advantage enjoyed by a third party who is a party to a linked agreement (s.139(3)). The making of such an order does not alter the effect of any judgment (s.139(4)).

The court can only exercise its powers to declare a credit bargain extortionate if an application is made by the debtor or any surety (s.139(1)). Given the potential potency of these powers, Parliament did not allow the court to make an order on its own initiative. The application can be made by the debtor or any surety to the county court (which has exclusive jurisdiction for regulated agreements or unregulated agreements where the creditor provides the debtor with fixed-sum credit or running-account credit) or the High Court (s.139(1)(a)) or as a counterclaim to any proceedings by the creditor in the county court to enforce the agreement, any security or a linked transaction (s.139(1)(b)). In any other proceedings where the amount under the agreement is relevant, the debtor or surety may also bring a counterclaim alleging an extortionate credit bargain (s.139(1)(c)).

10.10.6 Burden of proof

Somewhat curiously, the burden of proof is not stated in CCA 1974, ss.137–140. Instead, it is found in CCA 1974, s.171(7) which says, quite simply, where the debtor alleges that the credit bargain is extortionate, it is for the creditor to prove to the contrary.

10.10.7 Decisions

Given that the extortionate credit bargain provisions have been replaced and, therefore, have a limited impact going forward, we concentrate on the key decisions on the extortionate credit bargain provisions.

A Ketley Ltd v. Scott [1981] ICR 241

Mr and Mrs Scott were occupying a flat as protected tenants. They wished to buy it and exchanged contracts but failed to complete. The seller served a notice to complete, which required completion to take place on 6 November 1978. On the last day for completion, they approached A Ketley Ltd for a loan of the completion monies. They submitted an application form, which did not completely disclose all of their liabilities, and A Ketley Ltd agreed to lend them £20,500 at an interest rate of 48 per cent a year. As it was a lender of last resort, A Ketley Ltd required the loan to be repaid in three months (which Mr and Mrs Scott failed to do).

After considering the submissions on whether the agreement was an extortionate credit bargain, the High Court noted that:

- the lender was the only company that would advance monies to Mr and Mrs Scott for three months without the prospect of a permanent mortgage being granted by another lender at the end of that period to pay off the balance;
- the cost of the loan was clear to Mr and Mrs Scott: indeed, it was recorded in three separate documents;
- the lender acted very quickly in making the loan available on the same day;
- the lender did not have time to check Mr and Mrs Scott's financial position; and
- a solicitor was advising Mr Scott.

Given these factors, the court decided that the loan was not grossly exorbitant meaning there was no extortionate credit bargain.

Paragon Finance plc (formerly The National Home Loans Corporation) v. Nash; Paragon Finance plc v. Staunton [2001] EWCA Civ 1466

Mr and Mrs Nash obtained a loan of £45,000 secured against their property from Paragon Finance plc. Under the terms of its charge, they needed to repay the loan together with interest, initially at an annual rate of 12.75 per cent, which could later be varied. Mr and Mrs Nash argued that Paragon Finance plc failed, despite being under no contractual obligation to do so, to reduce the rate of interest in line with the Bank of England or prevailing rate. They therefore argued that the agreement was an extortionate credit bargain and there should be an implied term in the loan that Paragon Finance plc was required to vary its interest rates fairly, honestly and in good faith.

After considering submissions from both parties, the Court of Appeal decided that:

- the discretion to vary interest was not completely unfettered and was subject to the implied term suggested by Mr and Mrs Nash;
- the implied term was not, however, breached by Paragon Finance plc as it increased its rates because it was trying to avoid serious financial difficulties; and
- the claim that the rate of interest meant the agreement was an extortionate credit bargain was bound to fail as only the charges existing at the date of the agreement were relevant.

Broadwick Financial Services Ltd v. Spencer and another [2002] EWCA Civ 35

Mr and Mrs Spencer obtained a loan of £7,700 secured against their property from Argyll Financial Services Ltd (which, on the date of completion, transferred the benefit of the charge and the agreement to Broadwick Financial Services Ltd). Under the terms of its charge, they needed to repay the loan together with interest, initially at an annual rate of 29.78 per cent. Before the Court of Appeal, Mr and Mrs Spencer argued that the trial judge was wrong to only consider the APR and disregard how the creditor exercised its right to vary the rate of interest.

After considering submissions from both parties, the Court of Appeal decided that:

- the trial judge was right to only consider the APR and not other rates of interest because this was the rate used for comparison purposes;
- the trial judge correctly refused to compare the APR with evidence of APRs from banks and building societies because these were prime lenders: there was a requirement to compare like with like;
- non-compliance with the OFT's 'Non-Status Lending Guidelines for Lenders and Brokers' did not automatically mean that the credit bargain grossly contravened the principles of fair dealing;
- the Court of Appeal's decision in *Paragon Finance plc (formerly The National Home Loans Corporation) v. Nash; Paragon Finance plc v. Staunton* [2001] EWCA Civ 1466 was approved meaning that interest variations were not relevant to the consideration of whether the credit bargain was extortionate;
- if a creditor had a policy to vary interest rates in a certain way or not change them when the base rate changed, fair dealing required the creditor to tell the debtor about this before the bargain is made;
- the statutory test for an extortionate credit bargain was a high one.

10.11 UNFAIR RELATIONSHIPS

10.11.1 Introduction

One of the most contentious consequences of the Consumer Credit Act 2006 was the repeal of the extortionate credit bargain test contained in CCA 1974, ss.137–140 and its replacement with the 'unfair relationship test' now contained in CCA 1974, ss.140A–140D.

10.11.2 Do the provisions apply to regulated agreements only?

Section 140C(1) of CCA 1974 defines a 'credit agreement' (which is the phrasing used in CCA 1974, s.140A(1)) as 'any agreement between an individual (the 'debtor') and any other person (the 'creditor') by which the creditor provides the debtor with credit of any amount'. It therefore follows that the unfair relationship provisions are not limited to regulated agreements but apply to any credit agreement (as defined) with an 'individual' (as defined by CCA 1974, s.189(1)). It therefore follows that even unregulated credit agreements can be subject to these provisions and, indeed, many of the reported judgments have (so far) involved unregulated agreements.

10.11.3 Limitation

There is a significant difference between limitation for an extortionate credit bargain claim (discussed at **10.10.3** above) and limitation for a claim of unfair relationship. His Honour Judge George Leggatt QC, sitting as a judge of the High Court, recently considered the issue of limitation for an unfair relationship claim in *Upendra Rasiklal Patel* v. *Vithalbhai Bikabhai Patel* [2009] EWHC 3264 (QB).

The lender alleged that any claim of unfair relationship in relation to a loan from 1992 was statute barred by the Limitation Act 1980, s.8 and relied upon the Court of Appeal's decision in *Rahman* v. *Sterling Credit Ltd* [2001] 1 WLR 496 and the High Court's decision in *Nolan* v. *Wright* [2009] 3 All ER 823 (both of which, of course, were claims of extortionate credit bargain). The borrower accepted that a 12-year limitation period applied but argued that, in contrast to the extortionate credit bargain provisions, the unfair relationship provisions required the court to consider the relevant relationship throughout the course of the agreement and take into account matters arising after the date of the agreement as well as the terms of the agreement.

The court essentially accepted the borrower's argument and decided that:

- it would be 'an artificial and unsatisfactory exercise if, in determining what is fair to the debtor, the court were permitted to have regard only to matters which occurred in the 12 years before the debtor's application was made and was required to shut its eyes to agreements between the parties and other relevant matters which occurred before that time';

- under CCA 1974, s.140A(1), the 'court is required to have regard to certain matters specified in s.140(A)(1) and to all other matters it thinks relevant, whenever those matters occurred';
- an application 'under s.140B can be made at any time during the currency of the relationship arising out of a credit agreement, based on an allegation that the relationship is unfair to the debtor at the time when the application is made, or at any later time (as s.140A(4) expressly permits) until the expiration of the applicable period of limitation after the relationship has ended'; and
- the applicable limitations periods are six years for a claim for repayment of money (and, for the reasons set out at **10.10.3** above this six-year period is likely to begin from the date of payment) and 12 years for any other claim.

It therefore follows that a debtor who takes 20 years to repay sums due under a credit agreement potentially has up to a 26-year limitation period for the recovery of money and 32 years for any other claim. It is respectfully submitted that the court's decision is wrong. Section 140A(1)(c) refers to 'any other thing done (or not done) by, or on behalf of, the creditor'. For example, if a debtor argues that the creditor misled him about the terms of a related agreement and seeks damages for that act, it is submitted that such a claim is, in essence, a misrepresentation claim (which attracts, unless there is fraud or concealment, a six-year limitation period). It must therefore follow that the limitation period is six years from the date of the act, not six years from when each repayment was paid. If it is not, it would produce an odd position where the debtor can complain many years later when his other limitation periods have expired.

10.11.4 When do the provisions apply?

Whilst there are some complicated transitional provisions, it seems that (as a general rule) the unfair relationship provisions apply to all new consumer credit agreements made on or after 6 April 2007 and to all consumer credit agreements which have not completed before 6 April 2008: *Soulsby and Soulsby* v. *FirstPlus Financial Group plc and another* (unreported, Leeds Mercantile Court, 5 March 2010). By 'completed', it is submitted that this must mean paid off. It is likely that an agreement that has terminated before 6 April 2008 but has yet to be paid off will be subject to the unfair relationship provisions. If the unfair relationship provisions do not apply, the extortionate credit bargain test will.

10.11.5 Related agreement

Section 140C(4)–(8) of CCA 1974 defines a related agreement as any agreement that is consolidated by the main agreement, or is a linked transaction (within the meaning of CCA 1974, s.19), or is security provided for the main agreement or consolidated agreement or linked transaction. His Honour Judge Langan QC decided in *Soulsby and Soulsby* v. *FirstPlus Financial Group plc and another* (unreported, Leeds Mercantile Court, 5 March 2010) that an agreement that was completed before 6 April 2008 was not 'capable of attack' under the unfair relationship provisions. This decision has been refined (but not conclusively) by His Honour Judge Waksman QC's decision in *Barnes and another* v. *Black Horse Ltd* [2011] EWHC 1416 (QB) where he expressed the view that earlier agreements are capable of forming part of the court's consideration of whether a later agreement, which has not completed before 6 April 2008, is unfair but the court cannot (it seems) make any order for repayment of sums due under those earlier (and completed) agreements. Plainly, this is an unsatisfactory half-way house.

10.11.6 Associate

As defined in CCA 1974, ss.184 and 189(1) an 'associate' is:

- the individual's husband or wife or civil partner;
- a relative of:
  - the individual; or
  - the individual's husband or wife or civil partner; or
- the husband or wife or civil partner of a relative of:
  - the individual; or
  - the individual's husband or wife or civil partner.
- a person with whom he is in partnership, and of the husband or wife or civil partner or a relative of any individual with whom he is in partnership.

A body corporate is an associate of another body corporate if:

- the same person is a controller of both, or a person is a controller of one and persons who are his associates, or he and persons who are his associates, are controllers of the other; or
- a group of two or more persons is a controller of each company, and the groups either consist of the same persons or could be regarded as consisting of the same persons by treating (in one or more cases) a member of either group as replaced by a person of whom he is an associate.

A body corporate is an associate of another person if that person is a controller of it or if that person and persons who are his associates together are controllers of it.
    Section 184(5) of CCA 1974 defines the word 'relative' as follows:

> brother, sister, uncle, aunt, nephew, niece, lineal ancestor or lineal descendant, references to a husband or wife include a former husband or wife and a reputed husband or wife, references to a civil partner include a former civil partner and a reputed civil partner and for the purposes of this subsection a relationship shall be established as if any illegitimate child, step-child or adopted child of a person were the legitimate child of the relationship in question.

10.11.7 The test

The test for whether a credit agreement (and not a hire agreement) is unfair is contained in CCA 1974, s.140A(1). In short, it is whether the relationship between the creditor and the debtor arising out of the agreement (or the agreement taken with any related agreement) is unfair to the debtor because of one or more of the following:

(a)   any of the terms of the agreement or of any related agreement;

(b)   the way in which the creditor has exercised or enforced any of his rights under the agreement or any related agreement;

(c)   any other thing done (or not done) by, or on behalf of, the creditor (either before or after the making of the agreement or any related agreement).

By s.140A(2) the court must consider all matters it thinks are relevant including matters relating to the creditor and the debtor. The court is also able to consider anything done or not done by the creditor's 'associate' or former associate.

This is, at first blush, an extremely wide test and gives the court jurisdiction to consider the agreement and the dealings between the debtor and the creditor and its associates. This plainly leads to uncertainty for both debtors and creditors. Whilst creditors argued for an 'indicative list' (similar to the one in the Unfair Terms in Consumer Contracts Regulations 1999), this was rejected by Parliament. This is likely to lead, it is submitted, to conflicting decisions from the county court. The Court of Appeal recently considered the unfair relationship provisions in *Harrison and Harrison* v. *Black Horse Ltd* [2011] EWCA Civ 1128. Lord Justice Tomlinson, delivering the only judgment of the court, noted this was a 'test case to provide guidance'. For the reasons set out at **10.11.10**, the ambit of unfair relationships must be significantly narrowed.

10.11.8 The court's powers

Given the wide range of issues that the court can take into account when making an order under CCA 1974, s.140A, it is perhaps unsurprising that it also has wide powers contained in CCA 1974, s.140B. Such an order may do one or more of the following (s.140B(1)):

(a)   require the creditor, or any associate or former associate of his, to repay (in whole or in part) any sum paid by the debtor or by a surety by virtue of the agreement or any related agreement (whether paid to the creditor, the associate or the former associate or to any other person);

(b)   require the creditor, or any associate or former associate of his, to do or not to do (or to cease doing) anything specified in the order in connection with the agreement or any related agreement;

(c)   reduce or discharge any sum payable by the debtor or by a surety by virtue of the agreement or any related agreement;

(d)   direct the return to a surety of any property provided by him for the purposes of a security;

(e)   otherwise set aside (in whole or in part) any duty imposed on the debtor or on a surety by virtue of the agreement or any related agreement;

(f)   alter the terms of the agreement or of any related agreement;

(g)   direct accounts to be taken . . . between any persons.

The court's powers under CCA 1974, s.140B(1) may only be made (s.140B(2)):

(a)   on an application made by the debtor or by a surety;

(b)   at the instance of the debtor or a surety in any proceedings in any court to which the debtor and the creditor are parties, being proceedings to enforce the agreement or any related agreement; or

(c)   at the instance of the debtor or a surety in any other proceedings in any court where the amount paid or payable under the agreement or any related agreement is relevant.

If an order made under CCA 1974, s.140B places on the creditor, or any associate or former associate of his, a burden for an advantage enjoyed by another person, s.140B(3) makes it clear that this does not prevent the court from making such an order.

10.11.9   Burden of proof

If a debtor or surety alleges that the relationship is unfair then it is for the creditor to prove that the relationship is fair (CCA 1974, s.140B(9)). This essentially reverses the burden of proof. It is not enough, however, for a debtor to simply allege that there is an unfair relationship without putting forward some reasons why: His Honour Judge Waksman QC decided in *Carey and others* v. *HSBC Bank plc and others* [2009] EWHC 3417 (QB) that whilst the burden of proof remained with the creditor, it was for the debtor to put forward some reasons why there was an unfair relationship (and prove the factual allegations made).

10.11.10   Decisions

Whilst it is accepted that the unfair relationship provisions give the judiciary an amount of discretion, often meaning that other judgments are not necessarily binding, it is useful to set out the main decisions under these provisions so both debtors and creditors have an idea of the situations where the court has been willing to make an order under CCA 1974, s.140B.

Khodari v. Al Tamimi [2008] EWHC 3065 (QB)

Mr Khodari was a banker and issued a claim against Mr Tamimi (a businessman) for repayment of the balance outstanding under a number of loans made to him. Mr Tamimi often borrowed considerable sums of money from Mr Khodari (in his personal capacity) for gambling purposes. These loans were usually made outside normal banking hours. In his defence, Mr Tamimi argued that the money was 'forced' on to him but the court rejected this claim. Mr Tamimi also argued that Mr

Khodari's charge of 10 per cent of lending, when the loan could be repaid within a matter of days, was unfair.

After considering the arguments, the High Court decided that the agreement (which was not regulated by CCA 1974) was not unfair. Even though the charge was seemingly high, the credit risk was also high, meaning there was nothing in the agreement to justify it as unfair. The Court of Appeal dismissed the appeal.

Nine Regions (t/a Log Book Loans) v. Sadeer (unreported, Bromley County Court, 14 November 2008)

Mr Sadeer entered into a bill of sale and a loan agreement regulated by CCA 1974. The APR was 384.4 per cent. Under the terms of the bill of sale, title to Mr Sadeer's vehicle was transferred to Log Book Loans as security for the debt. Mr Sadeer fell into arrears and the loan was terminated. Upon termination, the vehicle was recovered by Log Book Loans and sold. The net sale proceeds were used to partially discharge the outstanding sum. Log Book Loans issued proceedings for the balance and Mr Sadeer argued there was an unfair relationship. After considering the evidence, the court decided that there was no unfair relationship because:

- whilst the APR was high, the risk to Log Book Loans was also high;
- Log Book Loans was a lender 'of last resort';
- Mr Sadeer had time to consider the documentation and fully understand the provisions of the agreement;
- Mr Sadeer did not even pay one instalment and avoided contact with Log Book Loans; and
- the APR was competitive with other similar lenders.

Maple Leaf Macro Volatility Master Fund and another v. Rouvroy [2009] EWHC 257 (Comm)

Maple Leaf entered into a number of complicated loan funding agreements with Mr Rouvroy. After Maple Leaf sought to recover sums due, Mr Rouvroy argued that the agreements (which were not regulated by CCA 1974) were unfair because:

- the return on funding was excessive;
- despite the level of collateral, personal guarantees were needed;
- the agreement was one-sided because if Mr Rouvroy defaulted, Maple Leaf could keep the collateral: it was not two-way; and
- the termination provisions were not reciprocal.

After considering the evidence, the court rejected the arguments that the agreement was unfair. It decided that Mr Rouvroy's own actions created the need for funding on expensive terms, he was an experienced businessman and there was considerable risk for Maple Leaf.

Patel v. Patel [2009] EWHC 3264 (QB)

There were a number of loan agreements between family members. This led to a lack of formality and the agreements were not regulated by CCA 1974. The lender sought repayment of the sums due under an agreement from 1992. After hearing evidence from the parties, the High Court decided that the 1992 agreement was unfair after taking into account:

- the terms of the agreement; and
- the way in which the lender exercised his rights under the agreement, particularly considering the lender's failure to provide any further calculation after 1992 or to keep any proper record of the outstanding amount.

It therefore reduced the amount claimed by the lender by significantly reducing the amount of interest on the capital (but not the capital).

MBNA Europe Bank Ltd v. Thorius (unreported, Newcastle upon-Tyne County Court, 21 September 2009)

This is a county court decision that is often wrongly cited by many debtors. The court's only decision was that the creditor had failed to comply with CCA 1974, s.78 meaning it could not obtain judgment for the balance due under the regulated running-account credit agreement (importantly, creditors and debtors must remember that this decision pre-dates *McGuffick* – see below). The other comments in Deputy District Judge Smart's judgment are therefore simply comments (or, to the lawyers amongst us, obiter) meaning they carry very little (if any) weight. In the context of the unfair relationship question, the learned judge's comments were that the failure by the creditor to tell the debtor that it would receive a commission from the insurer for selling payment protection insurance (PPI) may mean a debtor is entitled to a rebate of the premiums or for the commission to be off-set against the premiums. Plainly, this is now bad law following the Court of Appeal's decision in *Harrison and Harrison v. Blackhorse Ltd* [2011] EWCA Civ 1128 (see below).

McGuffick v. The Royal Bank of Scotland plc [2009] EWHC 2386 (Comm)

Mr McGuffick entered into a fixed-sum loan agreement on 3 October 2005. The agreement was regulated by CCA 1974. Mr McGuffick stopped paying the monthly payments and The Royal Bank of Scotland plc (the 'Bank') served a default notice under CCA 1974, s.87(1). Mr McGuffick did not remedy his breach so the Bank terminated the agreement and demanded the balance.

Following termination, Mr McGuffick's solicitors wrote to the Bank and made a request for information under CCA 1974, s.77 and enclosed the statutory fee of £1. The Bank could not find a copy of the agreement so wrote to Mr McGuffick's solicitors saying it would not enforce the agreement but added that Mr McGuffick should continue to make payments. If he failed to do so, the Bank said it would tell credit reference agencies.

Later, the Bank found a copy of the agreement and sent it to Mr McGuffick's solicitors but forgot to enclose a signed statement of account (required by CCA 1974, s.77(1)). To allow the issues to be determined by the court, the Bank did not remedy this breach before trial.

Despite the agreement being unenforceable, the High Court decided that a failure to comply with CCA 1974, s.77(1) and/or reporting to credit reference agencies (as a result of its finding on the meaning of the word 'enforcement') did not create an unfair relationship. It was entirely right and proper that credit reference agencies were told about any default, even where the agreement was unenforceable, to ensure responsible lending.

Carey and others v. HSBC Bank plc & Others [2009] EWHC 3417 (QB)

The court was asked to determine six preliminary issues, some of which were broken down into sub-issues, on matters arising out of CCA 1974, s.78. Much like in *McGuffick*, the debtor argued that a breach of s.78(1) gave, on its own, rise to an unfair relationship. The High Court disagreed and adopted the reasoning in *McGuffick* (given the similarity between CCA 1974, s.77 and s.78).

Barry Robinson Soulsby and Lynne Soulsby v. (1) FirstPlus Financial Group plc and (2) Loans.co.uk Ltd (unreported, Leeds District Registry (QB), 5 March 2010)

Mr and Mrs Soulsby were a married couple. They applied for, and obtained, three separate loan agreements with FirstPlus Financial Group plc ('FirstPlus') dated 26 February 2002, 21 July 2003 and 13 July 2005. The first agreement was repaid when Mr and Mrs Soulsby entered into the second agreement which, in turn, was repaid when Mr and Mrs Soulsby entered into the third agreement. At the same time as entering into each loan, Mr and Mrs Soulsby obtained further credit from FirstPlus to allow them to enter into contracts for PPI.

The High Court had to consider whether the first and second agreements, which completed before 6 April 2008, were 'related agreements' for the purposes of the unfair relationship provisions in CCA 1974, s.140A. If they were, they formed part of the court's consideration. FirstPlus argued they were not 'related agreements' and could not, therefore, be attacked by the unfair relationship provisions.

His Honour Judge Langan QC heard submissions from experienced consumer credit barristers for both parties and honed in on the wording of the Consumer Credit Act 2006, Sched.3, para.16(4) and (5) (which dealt with transition from an extortionate credit bargain to unfair relationships). He decided that:

- the court could make an order on the third agreement under CCA 1974, s.140B(1);

- the first and second agreements would otherwise have been related agreements as they were entered into before 6 April 2007 but they had become completed before 6 April 2008;
- the first and second agreements could not, therefore, be attacked under the unfair relationship provisions although they could (but in fact were not by Mr and Mrs Soulsby) be challenged as extortionate credit bargains under CCA 1974, ss.137–140.

Ian Wollerton v. Black Horse Ltd (unreported, Leicester County Court, 26 March 2010)

Mr Wollerton entered into a fixed-sum loan agreement for £17,385 to help him acquire a vehicle from a motor dealer on 27 September 2005. Mr Wollerton also signed a further box, appearing on the face of the agreement, opting to take further credit to pay the premium of £3,601.08 for a PPI policy. Mr Wollerton argued that there was no discussion over the policy and he thought it was a condition of advancing the loan. He also argued that he did not have time to properly read the documents, having signed them at a Lloyds TSB branch in Wakefield. He therefore argued that the amount of credit was wrongly stated and also argued, in the alternative, that there was an unfair relationship.

Mr Recorder Dawson, sitting as a judge in the Leicester County Court, decided (if he was wrong on the unenforceability point) that:

- the manner in which the policy came to be added to the agreement (i.e. without prior discussion);
- the size of the premium; and
- the lack of opportunity to consider the documentation,

meant there was an unfair relationship between the parties. In the learned judge's view, the proper order to make was to strike out the entirety of the premium and charges on this sum from the agreement and for the balance of the agreement to be repaid by instalments at the agreed monthly rate (after deducting the policy monthly payment).

Yates and Lorenzelli v. Nemo Personal Finance & Another [2010] GCCR 10351

Mr Yates and Miss Lorenzelli were a couple living together in a property in Manchester. They applied for, and obtained, a loan (secured by a second mortgage) with Nemo Personal Finance ('Nemo') after approaching a broker. The cash loan was £60,500 meaning the agreement was not regulated by CCA 1974. The debtors also opted to take further credit of £15,468.75 to pay the premium for a PPI policy and also agreed to pay a broker fee of £2,000.

Mr Yates and Miss Lorenzelli argued that there was an unfair relationship between the parties within the meaning of CCA 1974, s.140A. The court decided, after hearing evidence from Miss Lorenzelli and Nemo's managing director that:

- the policy was expensive;
- the amount of the commission was not disclosed to the debtors;
- Nemo could have told the debtors about the commission but did not;
- the commission affected the broker's independence; and
- Nemo's scripts failed to tell the debtors about the 30-day cooling-off period for the policy (although the documentation did tell the debtors about this).

After taking these factors into account, the court decided that there was an unfair relationship. It should be noted, following *Harrison and Harrison* v. *Black Horse Ltd* [2011] EWCA Civ 1128 (see below), that the Court of Appeal criticised this decision. It is submitted that it is now wrong.

Black Horse Ltd v. David Speak and Caroline Speak [2010] EWHC 1866 (QB)

Mr and Mrs Speak were a married couple. On 13 October 2006 they applied for, and obtained, a loan for £5,000 with Black Horse. They also applied for, and obtained, further credit from Black Horse to pay a premium of £2,012.39 for the policy. The agreement was documented in a fixed-sum loan agreement regulated by CCA 1974. The agreement separately documented the amount of the loan, the charges for the loan, the premium for the policy and the charges for the policy.

Mr and Mrs Speak argued that Black Horse told them that the policy was a condition of advancing the loan. They also argued that Black Horse had failed to comply with the FSA's Insurance: Conduct of Business Rules (ICOB), which applied to the sale of insurance products after 14 January 2005. These two arguments, said Mr and Mrs Speak, meant there was an unfair relationship.

After hearing evidence from Mr and Mrs Speak and Black Horse's employee, the High Court decided that there was no representation that the policy was compulsory and Black Horse had not failed to comply with ICOB. It therefore followed that there was no unfair relationship.

Joseph Sternlight and others v. Barclays Bank plc and others [2010] EWHC 1865 (QB)

Five test cases came before the High Court in July 2010 concerning credit card agreements. Because the rate of interest was variable, the creditors were required to state (as a prescribed term) the 'rate of interest on the credit to be provided under the agreement' by CC(A)R 1983, Sched.6, para.4. If they failed to do so then, because the agreements pre-dated the repeal of CCA 1974, s.127(3) on 6 April 2007, they would be irredeemably unenforceable. The debtors also argued that an improperly executed agreement created, on its own, an unfair relationship within the meaning of s.140A.

His Honour Judge Waksman QC, sitting in the High Court, decided that the agreements were wholly enforceable but, even if they were unenforceable, he re-affirmed his decision in *Carey and others* v. *HSBC Bank plc and others* [2009] EWHC 1681 that such a finding did not, on its own, create an unfair relationship.

Norman Vernalls and Ann Vernalls v. Black Horse Ltd (unreported, Oxford County Court, 4 November 2010)

Mr and Mrs Vernalls argued that the relationship was unfair because Black Horse paid a commission out of the premium and, if the policy was sold, the salesperson would receive a bonus. They also argued that the policy was expensive and that, instead of advancing around £11,000 to pay the premium, Black Horse should have offered to lend more money to Mr and Mrs Vernalls without selling the policy.

After hearing evidence and submissions, HHJ Harris QC decided that the agreement was fair because:

- commissions paid by the insurer to the lender were 'widespread' and 'because of them it is not necessary to charge borrowers for the provision of the service';
- it was clear that Mr and Mrs Vernalls 'knew what they were being asked to pay and decided to do so';
- a 'consumer is fully able to decide whether something is sufficiently attractive to make it an item that he wished to buy';
- the fact that the policy was expensive did not make the relationship unfair;
- the payment of the commission did not, unlike the decision in *Yates and Lorenzelli* v. *Nemo Personal Finance and another* [2010] GCCR 10351, cause the broker to give false information;
- the fact that the salesperson would receive a bonus did not make an agreement unfair. Indeed, such a bonus existed 'to incentivise her to carry out the procedures properly';
- a lender is under no obligation to tell prospective borrowers that, instead of using credit to pay for the premium, they could borrow more.

Harrison and Harrison v. Black Horse Ltd [2010] EWHC 3152 (QB)

His Honour Judge Waksman QC, sitting as a judge of the High Court in the Manchester Mercantile Court, considered the appeal of Mr and Mrs Harrison from District Judge Marston's decision. In short, they were a married couple. In 2003 they applied for, and obtained, a second mortgage with Black Horse. In 2006 they applied for, and obtained, further credit from Black Horse and repaid the first agreement. This later agreement was for £60,000. Mr and Mrs Harrison also opted to take further credit of £10,200 to pay the premium for the policy. They were provided with a 'demands and needs' statement, a key facts document and a copy of the policy's terms. Black Horse also completed a questionnaire recording Mr and Mrs Harrison's answers to Black Horse's questions. The loan was repaid in March 2009.

HHJ Waksman QC noted that District Judge Marston had adopted the correct approach and repeated that an appellate court should be 'most reluctant to interfere' where the discretion has been correctly exercised. Mr and Mrs Harrison argued that there was an unfair relationship and relied on three factors: a large commission, the limited length of the policy compared to the term of the loan and the policy's costs.

HHJ Waksman QC noted that District Judge Marston had rejected these allegations; saying that Mr and Mrs Harrison were aware of the policy's terms and, in particular, its cost. He then went on to decide that there was no unfair relationship because:

- Black Horse clearly set out that it only could advise on the policy and, if Mr and Mrs Harrison wanted to look at other policies, they should have either done so or consulted a broker that could advise on a variety of policies.
- It was not relevant whether Black Horse was responsible for the policy's terms: it is the terms (and not who drafted them) that are relevant.
- District Judge Marston failed to deal with the issue of a large commission and its non-disclosure to Mr and Mrs Harrison and, since her judgment, His Honour Judge Platts, sitting in the Manchester County Court, handed down judgment in *Yates and Lorenzelli* v. *Nemo Personal Finance and another* [2010] GCCR 10351 (see above).
- The commission did not, however, create an unfair relationship because:
  - there was no misrepresentation in this case about the policy, unlike the broker's misrepresentation in *Yates* that the policy was compulsory;
  - the facts of this case were very similar to those considered by His Honour Judge Harrison QC in *Norman Vernalls and Ann Vernalls* v. *Black Horse Ltd* (unreported, 4 November 2010) (see above) where he found no unfair relationship when an expensive policy was sold;
  - the cost of the policy was fully explained. Indeed, the figures were set out side by side to the loan;
  - the fact that there was no breach of ICOB 4.3 counts against there being any unfairness;
  - issues of causation were relevant to a claim of unfair relationship and, given HHJ Waksman QC's finding that there was no causation, it was a non-point;
  - there was no evidence that Mr and Mrs Harrison would have done anything differently had they known about the size of the commission;
  - there was no likelihood of the commission causing a conflict, particularly given HHJ Waksman QC's findings on ICOB 2.3.

The decision on the unfair relationship point was appealed to the Court of Appeal. We discuss that decision below.

David Woodward and Sarah Woodward v. Black Horse Ltd (unreported, Warrington County Court, 30 November 2010)

Mr and Mrs Woodward argued that a contract of PPI was wrongly recorded on the loan agreement as optional (when, according to the borrowers, it was a condition of advancing the loan) making the agreement unenforceable and that the lender failed to comply with the Insurance: Conduct of Business Rules. If they succeeded on either ground, Mr and Mrs Woodward argued that there was an unfair relationship.

After hearing evidence, District Judge Little decided that:

- there was (contrary to what Mr and Mrs Woodward said) a discussion about the policy before they entered into the agreement: this was shown by the questions and answers recorded on the demands and needs questionnaire;
- Mr and Mrs Woodward's solicitors also referred, before proceedings were issued, to 'some discussion about protection': this was consistent with the demands and needs questionnaire;
- the scripted procedure in place meant it would have been 'improbable' for Black Horse's employee to have deviated from it. In particular, it was relevant that the employee's annual assessment was carried out shortly before Mr and Mrs Woodward entered into their agreement;
- there were a number of references on the face of the agreement to PPI: it was therefore more likely than not that Mr and Mrs Woodward were, in fact, aware of the policy;
- the tick accepting the policy could not have been inserted digitally as the documents had been generated centrally;
- Mr and Mrs Woodward had a general awareness of PPI as they had obtained earlier loans with other lenders including PPI.

District Judge Little therefore decided that as discussions clearly took place concerning the policy, and it was clearly marked on the agreement, the policy was optional and the agreement was therefore enforceable. The judge also decided that, whilst the court had not heard from the representative as the court had done in *Black Horse Ltd* v. *David Speak and Caroline Speak* [2010] EWHC 1866 (QB) (see above), it was not prevented from reviewing the evidence and producing a result that was compatible with *Speak*. The claim on the first two issues failed, meaning the court did not decide the unfair relationship allegation.

Cudahy and Liburd v. Black Horse Ltd (unreported, Leeds County Court, 19 May 2011)

Mr Cudahy and Ms Liburd argued that the contract of PPI was unsuitable in breach of the Insurance: Conduct of Business Rules. They also argued that the lender's taking of a commission from the insurer, which was not disclosed to them, created an unfair relationship. After hearing the evidence, His Honour Judge Gosnell decided:

- Whilst Ms Liburd (who dealt with the lender's salesperson) and Ms Ingham (the lender's salesperson) were honest witnesses, Ms Liburd's recollection of the events was 'sketchy'. Whilst this was not her fault, given the passage of time, the learned judge expressed surprise that Ms Liburd could not remember her past loans or that there was a significant difference over her income stated in her sworn witness statement and the documents. By contrast, Ms Ingham was a 'very straightforward and clear woman and a business-like employee'. She was also praised for her 'mastery' of the documents and explanation of the logs.
- Ms Ingham followed the standard sales script which made it clear that the PPI was optional.
- Ms Liburd's decision to decline more expensive cover in favour of life cover (which was cheaper) was an instruction that she wanted PPI.
- Because the loan was secured, the lender had to comply with CCA 1974, s.58(1). This meant it had to post an advance copy of the documents and could not, for seven days after sending them, contact the borrowers. After this period finished, the lender sent signature copies of the documentation and could not, once again, contact the borrowers for another seven days after sending them. The mortgage deed was also witnessed by a third party, not the lender's employee. The borrowers therefore had a long time to consider all of the documentation before entering into the agreement.
- The lender was not required to assess the PPI's costs because the borrowers did not tell the lender that it was relevant to their demands and needs. Even if the borrowers did, the learned judge followed His Honour Judge Waksman QC's decision in *Harrison and Harrison* v. *Black Horse Ltd* [2010] EWHC 3152 (QB). The effect of this was that because the lender only sold one policy, it only needed to consider the PPI's costs against other policies that it sold (of which there were none) by virtue of ICOB 4.3.7(1)G. This would have been meaningless so there was no breach of ICOB.
- The borrowers had 'taken their eye off the ball' and may not 'with the benefit of hindsight' have taken the PPI but they did so. They were not told the PPI was compulsory and all of the documentation explained its cost, its cover and the fact it was optional. It was not, in the learned judge's view, Parliament's intention to 'protect people that did not exercise common sense'. It therefore followed that there was no unfair relationship.

Barnes and Barnes v. Black Horse Ltd [2011] EWHC 1416 (QB)

After hearing substantial argument, His Honour Judge Waksman QC decided that His Honour Judge Langan QC had correctly applied the transitional provisions in *Barry Robinson Soulsby and Lynne Soulsby* v. *(1) FirstPlus Financial Group plc and (2) Loans.co.uk Ltd* (unreported, Leeds District Registry, 5 March 2010) (see above). This meant that any agreement 'completed' before 6 April 2008 could not be attacked under the unfair relationship provisions. Those earlier agreements were, however, relevant for considering whether the relationship between the parties was fair although the court could not make an order requiring repayment of sums under those earlier (and completed) agreements.

Harrison and Harrison v. Black Horse Ltd [2011] EWCA Civ 1128

The facts of *Harrison* are set out earlier in this section when we looked at the High Court's decision. In short, the issue for the Court of Appeal to consider was supposed to be limited to whether the taking of an undisclosed commission, which amounted to 87 per cent of the premium for a PPI policy, amounted to an unfair relationship. After hearing submissions, and Mr and Mrs Harrison's legal team trying to extend the scope of the hearing even further, Lord Justice Tomlinson decided that:

- the county court decision of His Honour Judge Platts in *Yates and Lorenzelli* v. *Nemo Personal Finance and another* [2010] GCCR 10351 (see above), which is often cited by borrowers and their advisers, was wrong and of no assistance;
- if things done or not done by the creditor 'are in compliance with and involve no non-compliance with the statutorily prescribed regulatory regime, it is not easy to see from where unfairness in the relationship is to be derived';
- the legislative provisions in CCA 1974, ss.140A to 140D:
  - required the *relationship* between the parties to be determined as unfair, not the agreement between them;
  - required the court, when determining unfairness, to look at matters relating to the creditor *and* the debtor: it is not a one-sided consideration;
  - did not offer any guidance (unlike the Unfair Contract Terms Act 1977 or the Unfair Terms in Consumer Contracts Regulations 1999);
- the OFT's guidance on unfair relationships was 'significant in that it points one, not unnaturally, in the direction of the regulatory framework' (i.e. ICOB);
- there was 'no requirement for commission disclosure';
- the argument of Mr Doctor QC, counsel for the Harrisons, 'really resolves to a single point that, in the absence of an explanation, the commission is so egregious that it gives rise to a conflict of interest which it was the lender's duty to disclose. Only disclosure could give the borrowers the opportunity to decide whether they wished to purchase a product in the circumstances where the lender derived so significant a benefit from the purchase';
- while the 'commission here is on any view quite startling ... I struggle however to spell out of the mere size of the undisclosed commission an unfairness in the relationship between the lender and borrower';

- the 'touchstone must in my view be the standard imposed by the regulatory authorities pursuant to their statutory duties, not resort to a visceral instinct that the relevant conduct is beyond the Pale';
- it would 'be an anomalous result if a lender was obliged to disclose receipt of a commission in order to escape a finding of unfairness under s.140A of the Act but yet not obligated to disclose it pursuant to the statutorily imposed regulatory framework under which it operates. Mr Doctor had no answer to this point';
- the circle cannot be squared 'by arguing that a recommendation of suitability cannot be objective if given by a lender in receipt of a large commission. The judge rejected that submission on the facts of this case. There is also the obvious difficulty in deciding where the line is to be drawn';
- a 'seller is not ordinarily obliged to warn his buyer that his product is expensive when compared to other similar product and in my judgement it is telling that in this heavily regulated market no such obligation has been imposed'; and
- the 'non-disclosure of commission is not listed amongst the fifteen common failings which were said to result in detriment or poor outcomes for consumers. The FSA knew from its earlier work that the median average undisclosed commission … was 70%'.

The appeal was therefore dismissed by Lord Justice Tomlinson (and Lord Neuberger and Lord Justice Patten agreed). Given the clear and unanimous decision, it must be now beyond doubt that the taking of an undisclosed commission, no matter how big or small, does not create an unfair relationship. The Court of Appeal was at pains to explain the detailed (and thoughtful) history of insurance regulation and, in particular, the fact that commission disclosure is not required (and never has been) for retail customers. It was no accident that the decision was made to not require the disclosure of commission: it was clearly an issue on the FSA's radar but not one which warranted a rule. It should be noted that the loan was a secured second charge loan for £60,000. At the time the loan was made, the regulated financial limit was £25,000. The loan was not therefore regulated by CCA 1974. Although Black Horse has a consumer credit licence, it could have made this loan even if it did not have the licence. Neither was this lending regulated by the FSA because, in general, only first money purchase mortgages for residential property are regulated by the FSA.

The Court of Appeal has now, for the first time, clarified the impact of the unfair relationship provisions. As His Honour Judge Waksman QC decided in *Carey and others* v. *HSBC Bank plc and others* [2009] EWHC 3417 (QB), the evidential burden of proving the alleged facts giving rise to the unfairness is on the debtor and, once he has proved those facts (but only if he does), the legal burden of proof shifts onto the creditor to prove that the relationship is not unfair. The Court of Appeal came to a similar conclusion (and, it is suggested, tacitly approved *Carey*) by making two important points: first, it is the relationship (not the agreement) which must be considered; secondly, the relationship includes consideration of the creditor's position and the debtor's position. Equal weight must be given to both the creditor and the debtor. Similarly, if there is a technical or trivial breach of ICOB (or some other regulatory provision), that should not create an unfair relationship. The court must look at the relationship or relationships and see whether the breach causes that relationship or those relationships to be unfair as a whole: not the other way around.

Although the decision in *Patel* (discussed at **10.11.3** above) was referred to in the skeleton arguments and oral submissions of the Harrison's counsel in the Court of Appeal, it was not referred to at all by Lord Justice Tomlinson. The lower courts will now have to apply *Harrison* as it is a Court of Appeal decision (and a second appeal at that) and binds them. Although *Patel* is a High Court decision, it is only a first instance decision. While the trial judge in *Patel* reached a decision which was fair on its unusual facts, it is submitted that *Patel* can no longer be regarded as having much value for trial courts in establishing whether there was an unfair relationship or not. There is much outstanding litigation in this field, and it can only be a matter of time before the decision in *Patel* is expressly overruled.

10.12 POWER TO DECLARE RIGHTS

By virtue of CCA 1974, s.142(1), if under any provision in CCA 1974 something can be done by a creditor or owner only with the court's permission under CCA 1974, s.127(1) or s.128, and either:

- the court dismisses (except on technical grounds only) an application for an enforcement order; or
- where no such application has been made or such an application has been dismissed on technical grounds only, an interested party applies to the court for a declaration under s.142(1),

the court may, if it thinks just, make a declaration that the creditor or owner is not entitled to do that thing and, from that date, no application for an enforcement order for it will be entertained by the court.

By virtue of s.142(2), if:

- a regulated agreement or linked transaction is cancelled under CCA 1974, s.69(1), or becomes subject to s.69(2); or
- a regulated agreement is terminated under CCA 1974, s.91,

and an interested party applies to the court for a declaration under s.142(2), the court may make a declaration to that effect.

CHAPTER 11

Current issues in consumer credit litigation

Aamir Khan, Head of Legal – Dispute Resolution & Contentious Regulatory, Lloyds Banking Group

11.1 INTRODUCTION

The litigation landscape is always changing but recent developments have permanently changed how consumer credit claims and complaints are now instigated and how they will take shape in the future. In this chapter, we consider some of the current issues in consumer credit (and financial services) litigation from the viewpoint of an in-house lawyer. We also consider potential future issues, trends and challenges.

11.2 THE PAST

To properly consider the present and future litigation trends, we need to recall the past. The now infamous 'bank charges test case' (which led to the Supreme Court's decision on the nature of personal current account overdraft charges in *Office of Fair Trading* v. *Abbey National plc and others* [2010] 1 AC 696) was a genuine watershed in financial services litigation as defendant firms learned from their experience of settling claims to avoid an unhelpful legal precedent. The settlement of cases simply led to more claims being made and attracted claims management companies and law firms to this 'money spinner'. The bank charges litigation was also fuelled by the widespread use of the internet and consumer forums, where template letters of claim and claim forms could be downloaded by individuals. This has firmly brought the focus of consumer litigation in to the firms' minds meaning they are more likely to take on cases at the county court level to get clarity on issues.

Another significant development arising out of the bank charges litigation was the proliferation of claims management companies (CMCs). Despite the Supreme Court's decision, which firmly decided the bank charges litigation in the banks' favour, the number of CMCs has continued to grow. CMCs instead focused on new areas to challenge financial institutions, particularly technical breaches of CCA 1974, and enforceability of agreements. The CMCs have continued to adapt their business model after each legal setback (of which there have been many) and have made use of technology and the internet to continue to challenge financial institutions. Whilst often the approach taken by CMCs can be crude, we have to accept (whether we like it or not) that they are now a permanent part of the financial services legal community.

Financial institutions have had little choice but to adapt their approach to financial services litigation due to CMCs and a number of other important developments. In particular, the popularity of consumer forums and the rise of various consumer champion websites mean that any perceived 'weaknesses' or 'loopholes' in a firm's terms and conditions or paperwork become 'public knowledge' in a matter of hours and act as a conduit for complaints and claims. Before this massive growth of the internet, a confidential settlement or obscure county court judgment would not necessarily have become widely known or used as a 'template' for other claims. With the advances in technology comes a different kind of pressure and a new dimension to litigation strategy and risk management.

11.3 THE FUTURE

11.3.1 Group Litigation Orders

As technology has 'enabled' claimants to share information about settlements, legal cases, template documents and tactics, the current regime of group actions and the proposed changes at both a European and domestic level present a further challenge. The mechanics of the current Group Litigation Order (GLO) regime are governed by CPR Part 19 (and its Practice Direction) and contain a number of safeguards to ensure that the process is not abused or manipulated. There have been a number of consultation papers on collective proceedings and how to effect harmonisation across Europe and to ensure access to justice.

It is inevitable that there will be changes to the current regime. As a result, it is conceivable that we will see a range of consumer credit issues being brought as collective proceedings in the near future (much like we have where groups of consumers have combined for personal injury litigation: the recent litigation involving leather chairs is one that immediately springs to mind). The main challenge to such claims will be the individual nature of consumer credit cases, which may make bringing a collective action less straightforward. It is often the case that few consumers have the same complaint or, indeed, have entered into the same type of agreement. However, if the claimants are able to frame their claim on an appropriate basis (and within the current framework of GLOs) then it is conceivable that this will be a rich source of legal proceedings and challenges in the near future.

The GLO made for the Shared Appreciation Mortgages litigation is an example of where, in principle, a GLO was ordered by the Master but, in practice, the formulation for the claims around unfair relationship could not be worked due to the individual nature of the claims, which ultimately rendered them unsuitable for a class action.

11.3.2   Funding of litigation

The development of conditional fee agreements, and insurance providers willing to provide cover for cost orders made against the insured, has seen a rise in the number of cases brought with the benefit of conditional fee agreements and the corresponding 'success fee', which is usually 100 per cent. We have seen an increasing trend for law firms to issue proceedings on the basis of a conditional fee agreement with a 100 per cent success fee (with or without insurance cover for costs liabilities) in Consumer Credit Act-based litigation.

This usually results in a disproportionate costs order (relative to the sum recovered or claimed) being made where the claimant is successful. However, recent proposals by Lord Justice Jackson (many of which are, at the moment, being progressed by the Government) suggest that conditional fee arrangements may be replaced with US-style contingency fee arrangements. This would mean consumers agreeing to their legal representative taking a share of any sum that is recovered. At this stage it is unclear what impact this may have on consumer credit litigation but commentators have already expressed their concerns that, far from increasing access to justice, the proposed changes will alienate large proportions of the population and reduce access to justice. If these changes go through, then it is almost certain to impact on the business model of CMCs and associated law firms, which have relied heavily on conditional fee agreements. What remains to be seen is whether customers will be willing to forgo a large portion of their recoveries as part of the new costs regime.

11.3.3   New regulators

The dismantling of the Financial Services Authority (FSA), and its proposed replacement by the Financial Conduct Authority (FCA), may lead to a more powerful regulator. There is much speculation as to the extent of the additional powers that the new regulator may have and the scope of its jurisdiction. In particular, it is not clear at this time whether the FCA will extend its jurisdiction to the Consumer Credit Act 1974 (although it seems likely this will happen). The FSA already has wide-ranging powers and the creation of a new regulator may lead to further challenges for regulated entities.

11.3.4   New consumer credit landscape

The proposals to repeal CCA 1974, which has been well established for a number of years, and replace it with a sourcebook similar to the FSA's 'Conduct of Business Rules' will present, if it goes ahead, massive challenges. Many lenders are still coming to terms with the considerable amount of regulatory change that has happened over the past 10 years or so: further (and substantial) change may be too much.

11.4 THE FUTURE: LITIGATION

11.4.1 Introduction

The constant change in consumer credit is likely to lead to further litigation in the future. We now turn to look at some of the areas which may lead to litigation.

11.4.2 The Consumer Credit Directive

The Consumer Credit Directive (87/102/EEC) (CCD) came into force on 1 February 2011 and introduced wide-ranging changes to the existing consumer credit framework. The prescriptive requirements (which are discussed in more detail in earlier chapters) are likely to give rise to a number of challenges. Some of the key changes that may give rise to such challenges include the following:

- *Early repayment:* The existing right of a consumer to repay a loan early is extended to a right of partial early repayment on a similar basis. The calculation of the amount repayable on a partial repayment is to be made according to a new formula. The consumer will be told how the repayment will affect future payments and the outstanding balance. Where a fixed-rate loan is repaid early and the amount repaid exceeds £8,000 in a 12-month period, the lender is able to claim compensation of up to 1 per cent of the early repayment figure. This is discussed in detail at **7.7**.
- *Contractual information:* The Consumer Credit (Agreements) Regulations 2010 set out the information that must be provided to a consumer for certain types of consumer credit agreement. All information must be presented in a way that is 'clear and concise'. Lenders can, however, continue to rely on regulations that were applicable before 1 February 2011 where agreements fall outside the scope of the CCD. This is discussed in detail at **4.4**.
- *APR calculation:* There are new requirements (including a new formula) for the calculation of the annual percentage rate of charge.
- *Variation of interest rates:* There are minor changes to the way in which changes in interest rates must be notified to consumers, which apply to all regulated agreements. Changes to variable interest rates not linked to a reference rate must be notified to the consumer in advance. Under the new regime, the consumer must be notified personally, periodically and in durable form about changes to rates linked to reference rates. This is discussed in detail at **6.9**.
- *Credit intermediaries:* Credit intermediaries must now disclose their status to consumers in advertising and other materials. They must also disclose any fee

charged to the consumer and pass that fee information to the lender so it is able to calculate the APR.

The CCD also contains some requirements which are largely new to UK law. These include the following and may give rise to further challenges:

- *Adequate explanations:* Creditors under certain credit agreements must provide an 'adequate explanation' to a consumer about the credit offered to enable the consumer to decide whether the loan suits their needs and circumstances. The adequate explanation must be provided 'in good time' before the consumer becomes bound by the agreement, and in the form of the Pre-Contract Credit Information. This is also known as the Standard European Consumer Credit Information (SECCI) or, in the case of overdrafts, the European Consumer Credit Information. These forms are highly prescriptive and different in nature from previous requirements. This is discussed in detail at **4.5**.
- *Opting in:* For business loans and loans exceeding £60,260 or secured over land, the pre-CCD rules largely continue to apply, although lenders can choose to comply with the new rules if they prefer. The obligation to provide adequate explanations does not apply to loans above £60,260.
- *Assessment of creditworthiness:* Lenders are now required to assess a consumer's creditworthiness on the basis of 'sufficient information' before concluding a credit agreement. They also have to do this before there is any 'significant increase' in the total amount of credit. Previously, there was no specific requirement to check creditworthiness, though there were (and remain) provisions relating to irresponsible lending. The new regulations do not state what checks should be made, and lenders are left to determine the appropriate methods in each set of circumstances. This is discussed in detail at **4.6**.
- *Checks with credit reference agencies:* There is no obligation on lenders to carry out checks with credit reference agencies although in many cases this will be an appropriate part of checking creditworthiness. However, where a consumer's application is rejected as a result of a database search, lenders must advise them immediately of the search results and at no charge, providing details of the database consulted. This is discussed in detail in at **4.4.3**.

11.4.3 Unfair relationships

There have already been a number of successful claims arguing that the creditor's conduct has created an unfair relationship. As an unfair relationship includes anything done or not done before, during and after a credit agreement is entered into, the scope is potentially very wide. This is discussed in detail at at **10.11**.

11.4.4 Irresponsible lending

As with the provisions relating to unfair relationships, there is a wide scope for different interpretations as to what may be irresponsible. The recent OFT 'Irresponsible Lending – OFT guidance for creditors' (OFT 1107) (updated February 2011) concentrates on an assessment of affordability rather than simply whether the customer could repay the loan. As the OFT has stated that this is the standard that it expects, it leaves the question open as to whether this test would be applied retrospectively. It is, however, submitted that it should not be applied retrospectively.

On 15 December 2010, the FSA issued a Final Notice and fined DB Mortgages (DBM) £840,000 for irresponsible lending practices and unfair treatment of customers in arrears. The FSA found that:

- DBM's systems and controls were such that the firm was unable to show that some customers could afford mortgages sold where the term continued after their retirement;
- DBM failed to look at whether there were cheaper deals available for customers seeking self-certified mortgages, failed to show that customers could afford mortgages where the term continued into their retirement, and failed to make sure customers with an interest-only mortgage had thought about where they would live if they had to sell their house to pay off the loan,
- DBM had not considered customers' individual circumstances or told them about the range of options that were available to them, and applied charges that were unfair because they were charged repeatedly or did not accurately reflect the cost of administering an account in arrears.

The FSA did, however, take into account that DBM worked in an open and co-operative way with the FSA and that it agreed to a wide-ranging customer redress programme of approximately £1.5m and has made significant improvements to its arrears handling procedures.

DBM is the fourth lender referred to enforcement following the FSA's thematic project on mortgage arrears handling. Previously, penalties were imposed against GMAC-RFC (a £2.8m fine), Kensington Mortgages (a £1.2m fine) and Redstone Mortgages Ltd (a £630,000 fine).

There has already been an increase in litigation with an irresponsible lending angle. There are four potential areas of focus for litigation:

- High risk credit providers, including payday loan companies, may fall foul of the OFT guidelines. If they do, we may see CMCs partnering with/buying information from debt management companies to bring claims for debtors against these types of lenders.
- Providers of self-certified mortgages are likely to come under further scrutiny. In the new world, they will need to be able to show that correct questions were asked about the borrower's requirements and proper advice was provided.

- Borrowers lacking mental capacity – the risk of litigation proceedings may be low as it will come down to the circumstances of each case and whether there is anyone that will raise a claim for the borrower. However, given the new guidance on mental capacity, this may become a further area for new litigation.
- Handling of defaults and arrears – this ties in with issues around vulnerable borrowers and those lacking mental capacity. The OFT has made it clear it expects firms to take a view on each case and see whether any reasonable adjustments can be made to the loan/credit provision that could help the borrower. This may mean the measures used in financial hardship situations are given a wider application. Heavy rises in mortgage arrears were reported on 15 March 2011 and this could be a rich source for CMCs.

11.5 CONCLUSIONS

The world of consumer credit rarely stands still and it seems clear that the future will be very interesting. There are a number of potential areas for litigation but it is the wider changes in the litigation landscape that mean the nature of the challenges will be significant. In order for financial institutions to meet those challenges it will become necessary to consider the impact of legislation, not only in terms of operational changes, but also in terms of how those changes might be exploited by CMCs and lead to legal challenges.

This requires a more sophisticated approach to new legislation and legal decisions and a greater role for in-house counsel and legal advisers. It will no longer be sufficient to analyse current trends and deal with the issues as they arise. Going forwards it will be just as important to identify what is looming on the horizon and to be prepared with a strategy on how to deal with the consequences and potential challenges by CMCs.

Finally, the financial crisis of 2008 has led to a demand for greater protection for consumers, which is likely to lead to greater powers for regulators. Whilst the need for effective regulation remains paramount along with the need to protect consumers and to treat customers fairly, there is a risk that financial institutions could end up being held accountable for the poor decisions of customers. A balance needs to be struck between responsible behaviour by financial institutions, a more effective regulatory environment and consumers taking responsibility for their own decisions.

APPENDIX

Precedents

PRECEDENT 1
EXEMPTION: FORM OF DECLARATION OF HIGH NET WORTH BY THE DEBTOR OR HIRER

*[**Note:** Schedule 1 to the Consumer Credit (Exempt Agreements) Order 2007 (CC(EA)O 2007) sets out the form of this declaration. See 'High net worth debtors and hirers' at **1.3.3**.]*

DECLARATION BY HIGH NET WORTH DEBTOR OR HIRER

(section 16A(1)(b) Consumer Credit Act 1974)

I confirm that I have received a copy of the statement of high net worth made in relation to me for the purposes of section 16A(1)(c) of the Consumer Credit Act 1974.

I understand that by making this declaration I will not have the benefit of the protection and remedies that would be available to me under the Consumer Credit Act 1974 if this agreement were a regulated agreement under that Act.

I understand that this declaration does not affect the powers of the court to make an order under section 140B of the Consumer Credit Act 1974 in relation to a credit agreement where it determines that the relationship between the creditor and the debtor is unfair to the debtor.*

I am aware that if I am in any doubt as to the consequences of making this declaration I should seek independent legal advice.

Signed: . . . .
Dated: . . . .

* This sentence should be omitted in the case of a consumer hire agreement.

PRECEDENT 2
EXEMPTION: STATEMENT OF HIGH NET WORTH

*[**Note:** Schedule 2 to CC(EA)O 2007 sets out the form of this statement. See 'High net worth debtors and hirers' at **1.3.3**.]*

STATEMENT OF HIGH NET WORTH

(section 16A(1)(c) of the Consumer Credit Act 1974)

I/We* *[full name]* of *[address and postcode]* confirm that I am/we are* a person qualified to make a statement of high net worth under article 4 of the Consumer Credit (Exempt Agreements) Order 2007, by virtue of the fact that *[give the reason why the person making the statement is an appropriate person to make it – see the list under 'High net worth debtors and hirers' at **1.3.3**, e.g.* I am a member of the Institute of Chartered Accountants in England and Wales].

In my/our* opinion *[full name of debtor/hirer]* of *[address and postcode of debtor/hirer]* is an individual of high net worth because he/she* –

(a)   received during the previous financial year net income totalling an amount of not less than £150,000*; and/or*
(b)   had throughout that year net assets with a total value of not less than £500,000*.

[Insert one of the following declarations as appropriate:]

I/We* declare that I am/we are* not connected to *[name of creditor(s)/owner(s)]* [any person who is a creditor/owner offering consumer credit agreements/consumer hire agreements*].

I/We* declare that I am/we are* [connected to] *[name of creditor(s)/owner(s)]* as I am/we are* [the creditor(s)/owner(s)/an employee of/an agent of the creditor(s)/owner(s)/a person who otherwise acts on behalf of the creditor(s)/owner(s) in relation to the consumer credit agreement/consumer hire agreement/an associate of the creditor(s)/owner(s)].*

I/We* declare that I am/we are*/[a/an] creditor(s)/owner(s) offering consumer credit agreements/consumer hire agreements/an employee of/an agent of/a person who otherwise acts on behalf of/an associate of creditor(s)/owner(s) offering consumer credit agreements/consumer hire agreements.*

In this statement –

(a)   'associate' shall be construed in accordance with section 184 of the Consumer Credit Act 1974;
(b)   'financial year' means a period of one year ending with 31 March;
(c)   'net assets' shall not include –

(i)   the value of the debtor's or hirer's primary residence or any loan secured on that residence;
(ii)   any rights of the debtor or hirer under a qualifying contract of insurance within the meaning of the Financial Services and Markets Act 2000 (Regulated Activities) Order 2001 (SI 2001/544); and
(iii) any benefits (in the form of pensions or otherwise) which are payable on the termination of the service of the debtor or hirer or on his death or retirement and to which he is (or his dependents are), or may be, entitled;

(d)   'net income' means the total income of the debtor or hirer from all sources reduced by the amount of income tax and national insurance contributions payable in respect of it; and

(e) 'previous financial year' means the financial year immediately preceding the financial year during which the statement is made.

Signed: . . . .
Dated: . . . .

* Delete as appropriate.

PRECEDENT 3
EXEMPTION: FORM OF DECLARATION OF BUSINESS USE

*[**Note:** Schedule 3 to CC(EA)O 2007 sets out the form of this declaration. See 'Business exemption' at **1.3.3**.]*

DECLARATION FOR EXEMPTION RELATING TO BUSINESSES

(sections 16B and 189(1) and (2) of the Consumer Credit Act 1974)

I am/We are* entering this agreement wholly or predominantly for the purposes of a business carried on by me/us* or intended to be carried by me/us.*

I/We* understand that I/we* will not have the benefit of the protection and remedies that would be available to me/us* under the Consumer Credit Act 1974 if this agreement were a regulated agreement under that Act.

I/We* understand that this declaration does not affect the powers of the court to make an order under section 140B of the Consumer Credit Act 1974 in relation to a credit agreement where it determines that the relationship between the creditor and the debtor is unfair to the debtor.**

I am/We are* aware that if I am/we are* in any doubt as to the consequences of the agreement not being regulated by the Consumer Credit Act 1974 I/we should seek independent legal advice.

Signed: . . . .
Dated: . . . .

* *Delete as appropriate.*

** *This section should be omitted in the case of a consumer hire agreement.*

PRECEDENT 4
STANDARD EUROPEAN CONSUMER CREDIT INFORMATION (SECCI)

*[**Note:** Schedule 1 to the Consumer Credit (Disclosure of Information) Regulations 2010 (CC(DI)R 2010) sets out the form of the SECCI. It must be completed in accordance with CC(DI)R 2010, reg.8(3) (see **4.4.8**).]*

PRE-CONTRACT CREDIT INFORMATION

(Standard European Consumer Credit Information)

1. **Contact details**

Creditor	[Identity]
Address	[Geographical address of the creditor to be used by the debtor]
Telephone number(s)*	
E-mail address*	
Fax number*	
Web address*	
If applicable	
Credit intermediary	[Identity]
Address	[Geographical address of the credit intermediary to be used by the debtor]
Telephone number(s)*	
E-mail address*	
Fax number*	
Web address*	

* This information is optional for the creditor. The row may be deleted if the information is not provided.

Wherever 'if applicable' is indicated, the creditor must give the information relevant to the credit product or, if the information is not relevant for the type of credit considered, delete the respective information or the entire row, or indicate that the information is not applicable.

Indications between square brackets provide explanations for the creditor and must be replaced with the corresponding information.

2. Key features of the credit product

The type of credit	
The total amount of credit This means the amount of credit to be provided under the proposed credit agreement or the credit limit	[The amount is to be expressed as a sum of money. In the case of running-account credit, the total amount may be expressed as a statement indicating the manner in which the credit limit will be determined where it is not practicable to express the limit as a sum of money]
How and when credit would be provided	[Details of how and when any credit being advanced is to be drawn down]
The duration of the credit agreement	[The duration or minimum duration of the agreement or a statement that the agreement has no fixed or minimum duration]
Repayments	[The amount (expressed as a sum of money), number (if applicable) and frequency of repayments to be made by the debtor. In the case of an agreement for running-account credit, the amount may be expressed as a sum of money or a specified proportion of a specified amount or both, or in a case where the amount of any repayment cannot be expressed as a sum of money or a specified proportion, a statement indicating the manner in which the amount will be determined]
If applicable: Your repayments will pay off what you owe in the following order	[The order in which repayments will be allocated to different outstanding balances charged at different rates of interest]

The total amount you will have to pay This means the amount you have borrowed plus interest and other costs	[The amount payable by the debtor under the agreement (where necessary, illustrated by means of a representative example). The total amount payable will be the sum of the total amount of credit and the total charge for credit payable under the agreement as well as any advance payment where required. In the case of running-account credit, where it is not practicable to express the limit as a sum of money, a credit limit of £1200 should be assumed. In a case where credit is to be provided subject to a maximum credit limit of less than £1200, an amount equal to that maximum limit. The total charge for credit is to be calculated using the relevant APR assumptions set out in Schedule 2 to CC(DI)R 2010 and the Consumer Credit (Total Charge for Credit) Regulations 2010 (CC(TCC)R 2010), and where appropriate the relevant components of the debtor's preferred credit]
If applicable [The proposed credit will be granted in the form of a deferred payment for goods or service] or [The proposed credit will be linked to the supply of specific goods or the provision of a service] Description of goods/services/land (as applicable) Cash price	[A list or other description] [Cash price of goods or service] [Total cash price]
If applicable Security required This is a description of the security to be provided by you in relation to the credit agreement	[Description of any security to be provided by or on behalf of the debtor]

If applicable Repayments will not immediately reduce the amount you owe	[In the case of a credit agreement under which repayments do not give rise to an immediate reduction in the total amount of credit advanced but are used to constitute capital as provided by the agreement (or an ancillary agreement), a clear and concise statement, where applicable, that the agreement does not provide for a guarantee of the repayment of the total amount of credit drawn down under the credit agreement]

3.   Costs of the credit

The rates of interest which apply to the credit agreement	[Details of the rate of interest charged, any conditions applicable to that rate, where available, any reference rate on which that rate is based and any information on changes to the rate of interest (including the periods that the rate applies, and any conditions or procedure applicable to changing the rate). Where different rates of interest are charged in different circumstances, the creditor must provide the above information in respect of each rate]
Annual Percentage Rate of Charge (APR) This is the total cost expressed as an annual percentage of the total amount of credit The APR is there to help you compare different offers	[% if known. If the APR is not known a representative example (expressed as a %) mentioning all the necessary assumptions used for calculating the rate (as set out in Schedule 2 to CC(DI)R 2010, CC(TCC)R 2010 and, where appropriate, the relevant components of the debtor's preferred credit). Where the creditor uses the assumption set out in regulation 6(g) of CC(TCC)R 2010 the creditor shall indicate that other drawdown mechanisms for this type of agreement may result in a higher APR]

If applicable In order to obtain the credit or to obtain it on the terms and conditions marketed, you must take out: – an insurance policy securing the credit, or – another ancillary service contract If we do not know the costs of these services they are not included in the APR	[Nature and description of any insurance or other ancillary service contract required]
Related costs	
If applicable You must have a separate account for recording both payment transactions and drawdowns	[Details of any account or accounts that the creditor requires to be set up in order to obtain the credit together with the amount of any charge for this]
If applicable Charge for using a specific payment method	[Specify means of payment and the amount of charge]
If applicable Any other costs deriving from the credit agreement	[Description and amount of any other charges not otherwise referred to in this form]
If applicable Conditions under which the above charges can be changed	[Details of the conditions under which any of the charges mentioned above can be changed]
If applicable You will be required to pay notarial fees	[Description and amount of any fee]
Costs in the case of late payments	Either [A statement that there are no charges for late or missed payments] Or [Applicable rate of interest in the case of late payments and arrangements for its adjustment and, where applicable any charges payable for default]
Consequences of missing payments	[A statement warning about the consequences of missing payments, including: – a reference to possible legal proceedings and repossession of the debtor's home where this is a possibility; and – the possibility of missing payments making it more difficult to obtain credit in the future]

4. Other important legal aspects

Right of withdrawal	Either: [A statement that the debtor has the right to withdraw from the credit agreement before the end of 14 days beginning with the day after the day on which the agreement is made, or if information is provided after the agreement is made, the day on which the debtor receives a copy of the executed agreement under sections 61A or 63 of the Consumer Credit Act 1974, the day on which the debtor receives the information required in section 61A(3) of that Act or the day on which the creditor notifies the debtor of the credit limit, the first time it is provided, whichever is the latest] Or [There is no right to withdraw from this agreement – if there is a right to cancel the agreement this should be stated][1] [If the right to cancel is under the Financial Services (Distance Marketing) Regulations 2004 refer to section 5 of the form]
Early repayment If applicable Compensation payable in the case of early repayment	[A statement that the debtor has the right to repay the credit early at any time in full or partially][2] [Determination of the compensation (calculation method) in accordance with section 95A of the Consumer Credit Act 1974]
Consultation with a Credit Reference Agency[3]	[A statement that if the creditor decides not to proceed with a prospective regulated consumer credit agreement on the basis of information from a credit reference agency the creditor must, when informing the debtor of the decision, inform the debtor that it has been reached on the basis of information from a credit reference agency and of the particulars of that agency]

Right to a draft credit agreement[4]	[A statement that the debtor has the right, upon request, to obtain a copy of the draft credit agreement free of charge, unless the creditor is unwilling at the time of the request to proceed to the conclusion of the credit agreement]
If applicable The period of time during which the creditor is bound by the pre-contractual information	[This information is valid from [ ] until [ ]] or [Period of time during which the information on this form is valid]

If applicable:
5. Additional information in the case of distance marketing of financial services

(a) concerning the creditor	
If applicable The creditor's representative in your Member State of residence Address Telephone number(s) E-mail address* Fax number* Web address*	[i.e. where different from section 1] [Identity] [Geographical address to be used by the debtor]
If applicable Registration number	[Consumer credit licence number and any other relevant registration number of the creditor]
If applicable The supervisory authority	[The Office of Fair Trading or any other relevant supervisory authority or both]
(b) concerning the credit agreement	
If applicable[5] Right to cancel the credit agreement	[Practical instructions for exercising the right to cancel indicating, amongst other things, the period for exercising the right, the address to which notification of exercise of the right to cancel should be sent and the consequences of non-exercise of that right]
If applicable The law taken by the creditor as a basis for the establishment of relations with you before the conclusion of the credit agreement	[English/other law]

If applicable The law applicable to the credit agreement and/or the competent court	[A statement concerning the law which governs the contract and the courts to which disputes may be referred]
If applicable Language to be used in connection with the credit agreement	[Details of the language that the information and contractual terms will be supplied in and used, with your consent, for communication during the duration of the credit agreement]
(c) concerning redress	
Access to out-of-court complaint and redress mechanism	[Whether or not there is an out-of-court complaint and redress mechanism for the debtor and, if so, the methods of access to it]

* This information is optional for the creditor. The row may be deleted if the information is not provided.

Notes

[1]   i.e. if there is a cancellation right in respect of an agreement involving credit in excess of £60,260.
[2]   The words 'or partially' may be excluded in the case of agreements secured on land.
[3]   This requirement does not apply in the case of agreements secured on land.
[4]   This requirement does not apply in the case of agreements secured on land, agreements for credit agreements exceeding £60,260, pawn agreements and business purpose agreements.
[5]   If the right to withdraw referred to in section 4 does not apply.

PRECEDENT 5
EUROPEAN CONSUMER CREDIT INFORMATION (ECCI)

[*Note: Schedule 3 to CC(DI)R 2010 sets out the form of the ECCI. It must be completed in accordance with CC(DI)R 2010, reg.11(2) (see 4.4.12).*]

PRE-CONTRACT CREDIT INFORMATION FOR OVERDRAFTS

(European Consumer Credit Information)

1. Contact details

Creditor	[Identity]
Address	[Geographical address of the creditor to be used by the debtor]
Telephone number(s)*	
E-mail address*	
Fax number*	
Web address*	
If applicable	
Credit intermediary	[Identity]
Address	[Geographical address of the credit intermediary to be used by the debtor]
Telephone number(s)*	
E-mail address*	
Fax number*	
Web address*	

* This information is optional for the creditor. The row may be deleted if the information is not provided.

Wherever 'if applicable' is indicated, the creditor must give the information relevant to the credit product or, if the information is not relevant for the type of credit considered, delete the respective information or the entire row or indicate that the information is not applicable.

Indications between square brackets provide explanations for the creditor and must be replaced with the corresponding information.

2. **Description of the main features of the credit product**

The type of credit	
The total amount of credit This means the amount of credit to be provided under the agreement or the credit limit	[The amount is to be expressed as a sum of money. In the case of running-account credit, the total amount may be expressed as a statement indicating the manner in which the credit limit will be determined where it is not practicable to express the limit as a sum of money]
The duration of the credit agreement.	[The duration or minimum duration of the agreement or a statement that the agreement has no fixed or minimum duration]
If applicable Repayment of the credit	[A statement informing the debtor that the debtor may be required to repay the amount of credit in full on demand at any time]

3. **Costs of the credit**

The rates of interest which apply to the credit agreement	[Details of the rates of interest charged, any conditions applicable to that rate, where available any reference rate on which that rate is based and any information on changes to the rate of interest (including the periods that the rate applies and any conditions or procedure applicable to changing the rate). Where different rates of interest are charged in different circumstances, the creditor must provide the above information in respect of each rate]
If applicable Costs If applicable The conditions under which those costs may be changed	[The costs applicable from the time the credit agreement is concluded]

Costs in the case of late payments	Either [A statement that there are no charges for late or missed payments] Or [Applicable rate of interest, in the case of late payments and arrangements for its adjustment and, where applicable, any charges payable for default]

4. Other important legal aspects

Termination of the credit agreement	[The conditions and procedure for termination of the credit agreement]
Consultation with a credit reference agency	[A statement that if the creditor decides not to proceed with a prospective regulated consumer credit agreement on the basis of information from a credit reference agency the creditor must, when informing the debtor of that decision, inform the debtor that it has been reached on the basis of information from a credit reference agency and of the particulars of that agency]
If applicable The period of time during which the creditor is bound by the pre-contractual information	[This information is valid from [ ] until [ ]] or [Period of time during which the information on this form is valid]

If applicable
5. Additional information to be given in the case of distance marketing of financial services

(a) concerning the creditor	
If applicable	[i.e. where different from section 1]
The creditor's representative in [the UK] [your Member State of residence]	[Identity]
Address	[Geographical address to be used by the debtor]
Telephone number*	
E-mail address*	
Fax number*	
Web address*	

333

If applicable Registration number	[Consumer credit licence number and any other relevant registration number of the creditor]
If applicable The supervisory authority	[The Office of Fair Trading or any other relevant supervisory authority or both]
(b) concerning the credit agreement	
If applicable The law taken by the creditor as a basis for the establishment of relations with you before the conclusion of the credit contract.	[English/other law]
If applicable The law applicable to the credit agreement and/or the competent court	[A statement concerning the law which governs the contract and the courts to which disputes may be referred]
If applicable Language to be used in connection your agreement	[Details of the language that the information and contractual terms will be supplied in and used, with the debtor's consent, for communication during the duration of the credit agreement]
(c) concerning redress	
Access to out-of-court complaint and redress mechanism	[Whether or not there is an out-of-court complaint and redress mechanism for the debtor who is party to the distance contract and, if so, the methods of access to it]

* This information is optional for the creditor. The row may be deleted if the information is not provided.

PRECEDENT 6
UNRESTRICTED-CREDIT FIXED-SUM LOAN AGREEMENT

Fixed-Sum Loan Agreement regulated by the Consumer Credit Act 1974

Between:

(1)   SSH Finance plc of 2 Park Lane, Leeds, LS3 1ES (**'us'** or **'we'** or **'SSH'**); and

(2)   Mr Joseph Bloggs of 1 Park Lane, Leeds, LS3 1ES (**'you'** or the **'Borrower'**)

The credit intermediary (if any) is [*name*] of [*address*].

Financial information

Duration of this Agreement:	[ ] months from the date of this Agreement (the **'Term'**).
Amount of Credit (the **'Loan'**):	£[ ]. We will advance the Loan on the date of this Agreement by cheque or bank transfer.
Total Charge for Credit (Interest):	£[ ].
Total Amount Payable:	£[ ].
Rate of Interest:	[ ]% a year fixed. Interest is calculated and charged on the Loan on the date, and for the Term, of this Agreement. The Rate of Interest is not variable.
APR:	[ ]%. The APR is calculated on the assumption that this Agreement will continue for the Term and that you will perform your obligations promptly and in accordance with the terms of this Agreement.
Repayments:	£[ ] equal consecutive monthly instalments (the **'Monthly Repayment'**), the first of which is payable on or before [*date*], the second of which is due on or before [*date*], and so on.
Other Charges:	If you have asked us to transfer the Loan to you by bank transfer, we will charge you £30.

Default charges

We may debit your account with reasonable charges for your breaches of this Agreement. These are covered in more detail in Clause 5 of the terms and conditions of this Agreement.

Periodic statements of account

You have the right to receive under Section 77B of the Consumer Credit Act 1974 (the 'CCA 1974'), on request and free of charge and at any time throughout the Term of this Agreement, a statement of account showing (a) the details of each Monthly Repayment owing under this Agreement; (b) the date on which each Monthly Repayment is due, the amount and any conditions relating to the payment of that Monthly Repayment; and (c) a breakdown of each Monthly Repayment showing how much comprises capital repayment, interest and any other charges.

Missing payments

Missing payments could have severe consequences. For example, we may terminate the Agreement, report your default to credit reference agencies and bring legal proceedings to recover the balance. If we do so, there is a possibility that your home may be repossessed. It may also make it more difficult for you to obtain credit.

Your right to withdraw

By Section 66A of the CCA 1974, you have the right to withdraw from this Agreement without having to give any reason within 14 days beginning with the day after you receive a copy of the executed agreement.

You may give us notice of withdrawal orally, by telephoning us on 0113 123 4567, or by writing to us at 2 Park Lane, Leeds, LS3 1ES, or by emailing us at withdrawal@sshfinance.co.uk. If you withdraw from this Agreement, you must repay the Loan without delay and no later than 30 calendar days after giving notice of withdrawal together with interest at the Rate of Interest from the date the Loan was provided until the date it was repaid. Interest accrues at £[ ] a day. You may repay the Loan and interest by sending a cheque to us (quoting your agreement number) at SSH Finance plc, 2 Park Lane, Leeds, LS3 1ES or by electronic transfer to [*bank details*].

Your right to repay early

By Section 94 of the CCA 1974, you have the right to repay early, in whole or part. To do so, you must write to us at Early Repayments, SSH Finance plc, 2 Park Lane, Leeds, LS3 1ES and enclose a cheque for the amount you wish to repay. We may be entitled to claim compensation for early repayment under Section 95A of the CCA 1974 for the cost incurred as a result of your early repayment if this exceeds £8,000.00 or, where you have made more than one early repayment, the total of early repayments in any twelve month period exceeds £8,000.00. The compensation will not exceed the lower of 1% of the early repayment where the outstanding period of this Agreement exceeds one year, 0.5% where it is equal to or less than one year, or the total amount of interest that would have been payable under this Agreement if you had not repaid early.

Financial Ombudsman Service

If you are not a business debtor, you have the right to complain to the Financial Ombudsman Service, South Quay Plaza, 183 Marsh Wall, London, E14 9SR. If you are a business debtor, you may have the right to complain to the Financial Ombudsman Service.

Supervisory authority

Our supervisory body under the CCA 1974 is the Office of Fair Trading, Fleetbank House, 2–6 Salisbury Square, London, EC4Y 8JX.

Data protection

Please read the data protection notice and the Agreement's terms and conditions before signing this Agreement.

This is a Credit Agreement regulated by the Consumer Credit Act 1974. Sign only if you want to be legally bound by its terms.

Signature(s) of Borrower(s)   . . . .

Date(s) of Signature(s)   . . . .

Signed for SSH Finance plc: . . . .
On . . . ., which is the date of this Agreement.

Terms and conditions

1 Pre-contract information

1.1 You confirm that you have received and understood the pre-contract information provided to you before entering into this Agreement.
1.2 If you are in any doubt about your liability or responsibilities under this Agreement, or need to ask any questions, please contact us immediately and DO NOT enter into this Agreement. You are entitled to take independent legal advice if you wish.

2 Loan

2.1 On the date of this Agreement, we will send the Loan to you by bank transfer or by cheque.
2.2 If, before the date of this Agreement, you have not asked us to send the Loan by bank transfer, we will send it by cheque to your address stated on this Agreement.

3 Repayment

3.1 You agree to repay the Total Amount Payable (together with any charges or interest) by the Monthly Repayments on or before their due dates stated in this Agreement. Prompt payment of these sums is an essential condition of this Agreement.
3.2 We will allocate Monthly Repayments first towards any default charges under clause 5 of these terms and conditions, secondly to interest accrued and thirdly to the balance outstanding of the Loan.
3.3 Unless we agree otherwise, you must repay the Monthly Repayments and any other sums due under this Agreement by direct debit.
3.4 If you pay by any other method, you are responsible for any payment lost in the post or not made on time and in accordance with the terms of this Agreement.

4 Default

4.1 You are in default of this Agreement if:

    (a) any of the Monthly Repayments remain unpaid for more than 7 days after their due dates;
    (b) you break any of the other terms of this Agreement;
    (c) you in any way perpetrate, attempt or are involved in any act of fraud or other criminal activity;
    (d) you made any statement when applying for this Agreement which is false or misleading in a relevant way;
    (e) you die;

(f) a bankruptcy petition is presented against you or you are declared bankrupt;

(g) you make arrangements with your creditors for a compromise about how much you will pay them (which includes applying for, or entering into, an individual voluntary arrangement).

4.2 If you are in default of this Agreement we may (either by letter or, where required, in accordance with the Consumer Credit Act 1974) end this Agreement and require you immediately to pay to us the outstanding balance under this Agreement minus any rebate to which you may be entitled at the date you pay off everything due under this Agreement.

5 Default charges

5.1 If you fail to pay us any amount you owe under this Agreement by the date it is due, we may (in addition to our other rights under this Agreement) charge you interest on that amount at the Rate of Interest until you pay it in full and in cleared funds. We will charge interest at the Rate of Interest for each day you still owe us the payment. We can charge this interest even after we have received a judgment against you.

5.2 You are responsible for any and all reasonable legal and other costs and expenses incurred by us in attempting to obtain repayment of any money you owe us under this Agreement.

5.3 We may debit your account with reasonable charges if you breach this Agreement. Our standard costs are currently:

(a) Late payment or failure to pay charge: £20;

(b) Returned payment charge: £20;

(c) Letter notifying non-payment: £7; and

(d) Visits to your home to collect payments: £100.

5.4 We have the right to vary these costs and charges to reflect any change in the cost incurred by us in carrying out the work. We will give you at least 30 days' notice in writing of any charge variations.

5.5 Charges will be debited to your account when incurred and form part of the outstanding balance.

6 Joint borrowers

6.1 If two or more of you entered into this Agreement as the debtor, you will be jointly and severally liable for the debtor's obligations under this Agreement. That means that each of you can be held fully liable for the debtor's obligations, including payment, under this Agreement.

7 Data protection and use of your information

7.1 **Use of your information:** Before entering into this Agreement we may search your records at credit reference agencies. They will add to their record about you details of our search which will be seen by other organisations making searches. Details about you and your payment record under this Agreement will be used to help make credit and insurance related decisions about you and members of your household and occasionally for fraud prevention or to trace debtors. You can contact us for details of the credit reference agencies used by us. You have a legal right to these details and can receive a copy of the information held about you on payment of a fee.

7.2 Information held about you by credit reference agencies may be linked to records relating to any person with whom you are linked financially and other members of your household. We may give information about you and your payment record under this Agreement to credit reference agencies, debt collecting agents and any proposed assignee, transferee or chargee of this Agreement or of our interest in this Agreement, their insurers or advisers.

7.3 We may use a credit scoring or other automated decision-making system.

7.4 We may monitor and record telephone calls for the purpose of security and training.

8 Your obligation to keep us informed

8.1 We will send all notices, information and statements to your address shown on this form or your last known address. Some notifications may also be sent to you by email, SMS and may be delivered verbally by telephone.

8.2 To make sure we are able to keep you informed, you MUST tell us within 7 days if you change your home address, your name, email address or any telephone number which we use to contact you.

8.3 You can tell us in writing at our normal address, by telephone, or by email to changeofdetails@sshfinance.co.uk.

9 General terms

9.1 If any single part of this Agreement is found to be invalid or unenforceable, it will not affect any other condition.

9.2 You agree that we will not be liable if we are unable to meet our responsibilities under this Agreement because of a problem with a computer system or third party supplier, such as the postal service, or because of an industrial dispute or any other circumstances beyond our reasonable control.

9.3 We may transfer our rights under this Agreement at any time. You may not transfer your rights under this Agreement.

9.4 There may be other taxes or costs which exist in addition to the sums referred to in this Agreement which are not a condition of the loan or imposed by us.

9.5 The Loan can be paid either by cheque or by CHAPS. If you want payment by CHAPS, an administration fee of £30 will be deducted from the money paid out to cover the processing charge.

9.6 Any delay in enforcing our rights under this Agreement does not affect our rights. We may also accept late payments or partial payments, or cheques and money orders marked payment in full or something similar, without losing any of our rights under this Agreement.

9.7 This Agreement is governed by English law.

PRECEDENT 7
RESPONSE TO A REQUEST UNDER CCA 1974, S.77(1)

ABC Finance Limited
1 Finance Road
Finance Park
Finance Town
FT1 1AB

Mr John Smith
14 The Avenue
Bridford
BD14 3ES

1 November 2011

Response to request under Section 77(1) of the Consumer Credit Act 1974 (the 'CCA 1974')

Dear Mr Smith

Fixed-Sum Loan Agreement dated 8 January 2010 and numbered ABC0000123 between ABC Finance Limited and You (the 'Agreement')

Thank you for your request under Section 77(1) of the CCA 1974 dated 20 October 2011.

1. We enclose with this letter a [reconstituted][**1**] copy of the Agreement including the terms at the date of the Agreement [and your latest terms and conditions][**2**]. [We also enclose a copy of the security document referred to in the terms and conditions.][**3**] This complies with the requirements of the Consumer Credit (Cancellation Notices and Copies of Documents) Regulations 1983 (the **'CC(CNCD)R 1983'**).

2. By Regulation 3(2)(b) of the CC(CNCD)R 1983, the copy can omit any signature box, signature or date of signature. We are not required to produce a copy with your signature on it.

3. [There is no requirement under the CCA 1974 to provide a copy of the original and signed copy of the Agreement. Despite this, we enclose a copy of the pages of the original Agreement which proves a valid signature by you. The prescribed terms of the Agreement would have been validly incorporated into the Agreement on the back of the enclosed sheet or a separate attached sheet.][**4**]

4. We also enclose a signed statement of account separately showing:

    4.1 the total sum paid under the Agreement by you;

    4.2 the total sum which has become payable under the Agreement by you but remains unpaid, and the various amounts comprised in that total sum, with the date when each became due; and

    4.3 the total sum which is to become payable under the Agreement by you, and the various amounts comprised in that total sum, with the date, or mode of determining the date, when each becomes due.

5. By providing the documents enclosed with this letter, we have satisfied our obligations under Section 77(1) of the CCA 1974. The Agreement complies with the requirements of Sections 60 and 61 of the CCA 1974. It is therefore fully enforceable and we will continue to treat it as fully enforceable.

6. We will not be entering into any further correspondence regarding our compliance with Section 77(1) of the CCA 1974.

Yours sincerely

Miss Nicola Pearce
Compliance Manager
For ABC Finance Limited

Notes

[1]   Creditor to delete this word if the original Agreement is provided.
[2]   Creditor to delete these words if the terms and conditions have not changed.
[3]   Creditor to delete this sentence if no other document is referred to in the Agreement.
[4]   Creditor to delete this paragraph if the original and signed Agreement is provided.

PRECEDENT 8
RESPONSE TO A REQUEST UNDER CCA 1974, S.78(1)

ABC Finance Limited
1 Finance Road
Finance Park
Finance Town
FT1 1AB

Mr John Smith
14 The Avenue
Bridford
BD14 3ES

1 November 2011

Response to request under Section 78(1) of the Consumer Credit Act 1974 (the 'CCA 1974')

Dear Mr Smith

Running-Account Credit Agreement dated 5 January 2010 and numbered ABC0000007 between ABC Finance Limited and You (the 'Agreement')

Thank you for your request under Section 78(1) of the CCA 1974 dated 22 October 2011.

1. We enclose with this letter a [reconstituted]**[1]** copy of the Agreement including the terms at the date of the Agreement [and your latest terms and conditions]**[2]**. [We also enclose a copy of the security document referred to in the terms and conditions.]**[3]** This complies with the requirements of the Consumer Credit (Cancellation Notices and Copies of Documents) Regulations 1983 (the **'CC(CNCD)R 1983'**).
2. By Regulation 3(2)(b) of the CC(CNCD)R 1983, the copy can omit any signature box, signature or date of signature. We are not required to produce a copy with your signature on it.
3. [There is no requirement under the CCA 1974 to provide a copy of the original and signed copy of the Agreement. Despite this, we enclose a copy of the pages of the original Agreement which proves a valid signature by you. The prescribed terms of the Agreement would have been validly incorporated into the Agreement on the back of the enclosed sheet or a separate attached sheet.]**[4]**
4. We also enclose a signed statement of account separately showing, from information to which it is practicable for us to refer:

    4.1 the state of the account; and
    4.2 the amount, if any, currently payable by you to us under the Agreement; and
    4.3 the amounts and due dates of any payments which, if you do not draw further on the account, will later become payable by you to us under the Agreement.**[5]**

5. By providing the documents enclosed with this letter, we have satisfied our obligations under Section 78(1) of the CCA 1974. The Agreement complies with the requirements of Sections 60 and 61 of the CCA 1974. It is therefore fully enforceable and we will continue to treat it as fully enforceable.
6. We will not be entering into any further correspondence regarding our compliance with Section 78(1) of the CCA 1974.

Yours sincerely

Miss Nicola Pearce
Compliance Manager
For ABC Finance Limited

Notes

[1]   Creditor to delete this word if the original Agreement is provided.
[2]   Creditor to delete these words if no further terms and conditions have been issued.
[3]   Creditor to delete this sentence if no other document is referred to in the Agreement.
[4]   Creditor to delete this paragraph if the original and signed Agreement is provided.
[5]   If the creditor does not have sufficient information to enable it to calculate the amounts and dates mentioned here, it must explain in the statement of account the basis on which, under the Agreement, they would fall to be calculated.

PRECEDENT 9
RESPONSE TO A REQUEST UNDER CCA 1974, S.79(1)

ABC Finance Limited
1 Finance Road
Finance Park
Finance Town
FT1 1AB

Mr John Smith
14 The Avenue
Bridford
BD14 3ES

4 November 2011

Response to request under Section 79(1) of the Consumer Credit Act 1974 (the 'CCA 1974')

Dear Mr Smith

Consumer Hire Agreement dated 14 November 2010 and numbered ABC0000667 between ABC Finance Limited and You (the 'Agreement')

Thank you for your request under Section 79(1) of the CCA 1974 dated 27 October 2011.

1. We enclose with this letter a [reconstituted]**[1]** copy of the Agreement including the terms at the date of the Agreement [and your latest terms and conditions]**[2]**. [We also enclose a copy of the security document referred to in the terms and conditions.]**[3]** This complies with the requirements of the Consumer Credit (Cancellation Notices and Copies of Documents) Regulations 1983 (the **'CC(CNCD)R 1983'**).

2. By Regulation 3(2)(b) of the CC(CNCD)R 1983, the copy can omit any signature box, signature or date of signature. We are not required to produce a copy with your signature on it.

3. [There is no requirement under the CCA 1974 to provide a copy of the original and signed copy of the Agreement. Despite this, we enclose a copy of the pages of the original Agreement which proves a valid signature by you. The prescribed terms of the Agreement would have been validly incorporated into the Agreement on the back of the enclosed sheet or a separate attached sheet.]**[4]**

4. We also enclose a signed statement of account separately showing, according to the information to which it is practicable for us to refer, the:

   4.1 total sum which has become payable under the Agreement by you but remains unpaid; and

   4.2 various amounts comprised in that total sum, with the date when each became due.

5. By providing the documents enclosed with this letter, we have satisfied our obligations under Section 79(1) of the CCA 1974. The Agreement complies with the requirements of Sections 60 and 61 of the CCA 1974. It is therefore fully enforceable and we will continue to treat it as fully enforceable.

6. We will not be entering into any further correspondence regarding our compliance with Section 79(1) of the CCA 1974.

Yours sincerely

Miss Nicola Pearce
Compliance Manager
For ABC Finance Limited

Notes

[1]   Owner to delete this word if the original Agreement is provided.
[2]   Owner to delete these words if the terms and conditions have not changed.
[3]   Owner to delete this sentence if no other document is referred to in the Agreement.
[4]   Owner to delete this paragraph if the original and signed Agreement is provided.

PRECEDENT 10
REQUEST UNDER CCA 1974, S.80(1)

ABC Finance Limited
1 Finance Road
Finance Park
Finance Town
FT1 1AB

Mr John Smith
14 The Avenue
Bridford
BD14 3ES

1 November 2011

Notice under Section 80(1) of the Consumer Credit Act 1974 (the 'CCA 1974')

Dear Mr Smith

Hire-Purchase Agreement dated 1 January 2010 and numbered ABC0000173 between ABC Finance Limited and You
BMW 318i motor car with registration no. 1 JS (the 'Vehicle')

Please treat this letter as our formal request, under Section 80(1) of the CCA 1974, for you to tell us the Vehicle's location within seven working days after the date that you receive this letter.

If you fail to provide a response to this letter within twenty-one days after the date that you receive it then you will commit a criminal offence under Section 80(2) of the CCA 1974.

Please respond by:

- writing to us at 1 Finance Road, Finance Park, Finance Town, FT1 1AB; or
- emailing us at section80@abcfinance.co.uk; or
- calling us on 01234 567890.

When contacting us, please ensure you quote your agreement.

Yours sincerely

Mr Jack Jones
Collections Manager
For ABC Finance Limited

PRECEDENT 11A
DEFAULT NOTICE UNDER CCA 1974, S.87(1): FIXED-SUM LOAN
AGREEMENT

SSH Finance plc
2 Park Lane
Leeds
LS3 1ES

By First Class Post
Mr John Smith
1 Town Street
Manchester
M60 6HS

5 January 2012

IMPORTANT – YOU SHOULD READ THIS CAREFULLY

Dear Mr Smith

Fixed-Sum Loan Agreement regulated by the Consumer Credit Act 1974 dated 24
December 2008 and numbered ABC12345 between John Smith and SSH Finance plc
(the 'Agreement')

This is a default notice served under Section 87(1) of the Consumer Credit Act 1974.

In breach of clause 4(a) of the Agreement, you have failed to pay the monthly instalments which fell due on 24 October 2011, 24 November 2011 and 24 December 2011 on time and in accordance with the terms of the Agreement. Please remedy your breach of the Agreement by paying those arrears to us, which total £[*amount*], on or before 24 January 2012.

IF THE ACTION REQUIRED BY THIS NOTICE IS TAKEN BEFORE THE DATE
SHOWN NO FURTHER ENFORCEMENT ACTION WILL BE TAKEN IN
RESPECT OF THE BREACH.

IF YOU DO NOT TAKE THE ACTION REQUIRED BY THIS NOTICE BEFORE
THE DATE SHOWN THEN THE FURTHER ACTION SET OUT BELOW MAY BE
TAKEN AGAINST YOU.

If you fail to pay £[*amount*] on or before 24 January 2012, we will enforce our rights and:

- send you a letter terminating the Agreement;
- demand you pay the balance due under the Agreement to us;
- report your default and non-payment to credit reference agencies; and
- issue legal proceedings for judgment for the balance due under the Agreement.

Total Amount Payable under the Agreement:	£[0.00]
Total Amount paid by the date of this notice:	£[0.00]
Total balance outstanding before deducting the rebate (if any):	£[0.00]
Rebate (if any but calculated on the assumption that early settlement takes place on 24 January 2012)	£[0.00]

Balance due under the Agreement on 24 January 2012 (after applying any rebate)	£[0.00]

If the arrears are not discharged and the Agreement is terminated, you must make payment of the balance referred to above as a lump sum. If that lump sum payment is not made on 24 January 2012, the balance will be recalculated as at the date when such payment is actually made or to be made.

In your own interests, you are strongly urged to contact us by telephone on 0113 123 4567 (quoting your reference number shown in this notice) if you cannot pay the total arrears in full.

IF YOU HAVE DIFFICULTY IN PAYING ANY SUM OWING UNDER THE AGREEMENT OR TAKING ANY OTHER ACTION REQUIRED BY THIS NOTICE, YOU CAN APPLY TO THE COURT WHICH MAY MAKE AN ORDER ALLOWING YOU OR ANY SURETY MORE TIME.

You should be aware that if we take you to court and get a judgment against you requiring you to pay us the money you owe us under the agreement, you may have to pay us both the amount of the judgment and interest under the agreement on all the sums owed by you at the date of the judgment until you have paid these in full. This means that even if you pay off the whole amount of the judgment, you may still have a further sum to pay.

IF YOU ARE NOT SURE WHAT TO DO, YOU SHOULD GET HELP AS SOON AS POSSIBLE. FOR EXAMPLE YOU SHOULD CONTACT A SOLICITOR, YOUR LOCAL TRADING STANDARDS DEPARTMENT OR YOUR NEAREST CITIZENS' ADVICE BUREAU.

This notice should include a copy of the current Office of Fair Trading information sheet on default. This contains important information about your rights and where to go for support and advice. If it is not included, you should contact us to get one.

If you would like to speak to us to discuss your arrears or the content of this notice, please contact us on 0113 123 4567.

We look forward to hearing from you.

Yours sincerely

Andrew Collector
Collections & Recoveries
For SSH Finance plc

PRECEDENT 11B
DEFAULT NOTICE UNDER CCA 1974, S.87(1): HIRE-PURCHASE
AGREEMENT

SSH Finance plc
2 Park Lane
Leeds
LS3 1ES

By First Class Post
Mr John Smith
1 Town Street
Manchester
M60 6HS

5 January 2012

IMPORTANT – YOU SHOULD READ THIS CAREFULLY

Dear Mr Smith

Hire-Purchase Agreement regulated by the Consumer Credit Act 1974 dated 24 December 2008 and numbered ABC12345 between John Smith and SSH Finance plc (the 'Agreement')
Volkswagen Golf 1.6 motor car with registration number A1 BCD and VIN/Chassis Number ABCDEFG123456 (the 'Vehicle')

This is a default notice served under Section 87(1) of the Consumer Credit Act 1974.

In breach of clause 4(a) of the Agreement, you have failed to pay the monthly instalments which fell due on 24 October 2011, 24 November 2011 and 24 December 2011 on time and in accordance with the terms of the Agreement. Please remedy your breach of the Agreement by paying those arrears to us, which total £[*amount*], on or before 24 January 2012.

IF THE ACTION REQUIRED BY THIS NOTICE IS TAKEN BEFORE THE DATE SHOWN NO FURTHER ENFORCEMENT ACTION WILL BE TAKEN IN RESPECT OF THE BREACH.

IF YOU DO NOT TAKE THE ACTION REQUIRED BY THIS NOTICE BEFORE THE DATE SHOWN THEN THE FURTHER ACTION SET OUT BELOW MAY BE TAKEN AGAINST YOU.

If you fail to pay £[*amount*] on or before 24 January 2012, we will enforce our rights and:

- send you a letter terminating the Agreement;
- demand you to return the Vehicle and/or pay the balance due under the Agreement to us;
- attempt to recover the Vehicle or, if you have paid more than one-third of the total amount payable under the Agreement, attempt to recover the Vehicle with your informed consent;
- report your default and non-payment to credit reference agencies; and
- issue legal proceedings for the Vehicle's return and/or judgment for the balance due under the Agreement.

BUT IF YOU HAVE PAID AT LEAST ONE-THIRD OF THE TOTAL AMOUNT PAYABLE UNDER THE AGREEMENT SET OUT BELOW (OR ANY INSTALLA-TION CHARGE PLUS ONE-THIRD OF THE REST OF THE AMOUNT PAYABLE), THE CREDITOR MAY NOT TAKE BACK THE GOODS AGAINST YOUR WISHES UNLESS HE GETS A COURT ORDER. (IN SCOTLAND, HE MAY NEED TO GET A COURT ORDER AT ANY TIME.) IF HE DOES TAKE THEM WITHOUT YOUR CONSENT OR A COURT ORDER, YOU HAVE THE RIGHT TO GET BACK ALL THE MONEY YOU HAVE PAID UNDER THE AGREEMENT SET OUT BELOW.

Total Amount Payable under the Agreement:	£[0.00]
Total Amount paid by the date of this notice:	£[0.00]
Total balance outstanding before deducting the rebate (if any):	£[0.00]
Rebate (if any but calculated on the assumption that early settlement takes place on 24 January 2012)	£[0.00]
Balance due under the Agreement on 24 January 2012 (after applying any rebate)	£[0.00]

If the arrears are not discharged and the Agreement is terminated, you must make payment of the balance referred to above as a lump sum. If that lump sum payment is not made on 24 January 2012, the balance will be recalculated as at the date when such payment is actually made or to be made.

In your own interests, you are strongly urged to contact us by telephone on 0113 123 4567 (quoting your reference number shown in this notice) if you cannot pay the total arrears in full.

You have the right to end this agreement at any time before the final payment falls due. Note that this right may be lost if you do not act before the date shown (after which we may take action). If the date for final payment has not passed and you wish to end this agreement, you should write to the person to whom you make your payments. You will need to pay £[*amount to be paid by the debtor calculated in accordance with the provisions of CCA 1974, ss.99(2) and 100 on the assumption that the agreement terminates on 24 January 2012*] if you wish to end this agreement by the date shown and we will be entitled to the return of the goods. You will also be liable for costs if you have not taken reasonable care of the goods. Note that if you end this agreement, this will not necessarily terminate any insurance finance agreements that are linked to this agreement.

IF YOU HAVE DIFFICULTY IN PAYING ANY SUM OWING UNDER THE AGREEMENT OR TAKING ANY OTHER ACTION REQUIRED BY THIS NOTICE, YOU CAN APPLY TO THE COURT WHICH MAY MAKE AN ORDER ALLOWING YOU OR ANY SURETY MORE TIME.

You should be aware that if we take you to court and get a judgment against you requiring you to pay us the money you owe us under the agreement, you may have to pay us both the amount of the judgment and interest under the agreement on all the sums owed by you at the date of the judgment until you have paid these in full. This means that even if you pay off the whole amount of the judgment, you may still have a further sum to pay.

IF YOU ARE NOT SURE WHAT TO DO, YOU SHOULD GET HELP AS SOON AS POSSIBLE. FOR EXAMPLE YOU SHOULD CONTACT A SOLICITOR, YOUR

**LOCAL TRADING STANDARDS DEPARTMENT OR YOUR NEAREST CITI-
ZENS' ADVICE BUREAU.**

**This notice should include a copy of the current Office of Fair Trading information
sheet on default. This contains important information about your rights and where to
go for support and advice. If it is not included, you should contact us to get one.**

If you would like to speak to us to discuss your arrears or the content of this notice, please
contact us on 0113 123 4567.

We look forward to hearing from you.

Yours sincerely

Andrew Collector
Collections & Recoveries
For SSH Finance plc

PRECEDENT 12
PARTICULARS OF CLAIM FOR THE UNPAID BALANCE UNDER A
REGULATED FIXED-SUM CREDIT AGREEMENT FOLLOWING
TERMINATION FOR NON-PAYMENT

IN THE LEEDS COUNTY COURT　　　　　　　CLAIM NO.: _____

BETWEEN

SSH FINANCE PLC

Claimant

and

Mr STEPHEN TAYLOR

Defendant

_____

PARTICULARS OF CLAIM

_____

Parties

1.　The Claimant is a public limited company (company registration number 123456) which is regulated by the Financial Services Authority (financial services authority register number 987654). The Claimant carries on business in (amongst other things) the provision of unsecured personal lending.
2.　The Defendant is an individual and the Claimant's former customer.

Agreement

3.　By a written fixed-sum loan agreement dated 01.04.2007 and numbered ABC1234567890 (the **'Agreement'**), which incorporated the Claimant's standard terms and conditions of business (a copy of the Agreement and standard terms are attached), the Claimant advanced to the Defendant £20,000.00 (the **'Loan'**).
4.　The Claimant will say that:

　　4.1　the Agreement was regulated by the Consumer Credit Act 1974 (the **'CCA 1974'**);
　　4.2　it advanced the Loan to the Defendant;
　　4.3　the total charge for credit for the Loan was £11,094.40 (the **'Charges'**);
　　4.4　the total amount payable by the Defendant to the Claimant for the Loan was £31,094.40 (the **'Total Amount Payable'**); and
　　4.5　the Defendant was required to repay the Total Amount Payable by 120 equal consecutive monthly payments of £259.12 (the **'Monthly Payments'**).

5.　By clause 2.1 of the Agreement, the Defendant was required to promptly pay the Monthly Payments to the Claimant until the whole of the Total Amount Payable and all interest and other monies duly debited to the Agreement are fully paid.
6.　By clause 4.1 of the Agreement, if the Defendant failed to comply with clause 2.1 (time of which was of the essence) then the Claimant could (subject to service of a notice

under the CCA 1974) terminate the Agreement and require the Defendant to immediately pay the balance outstanding of the Total Amount Payable and interest and any other sums due under the Agreement.

7. The Claimant will say that in accordance with the Agreement, the Defendant paid Monthly Payments totalling £11,660.40.

Breach and Termination of the Agreement

8. The Claimant will say that in repudiation of the Agreement, the Defendant cancelled his direct debit and/or stopped paying the Monthly Payments due to the Claimant.
9. The Claimant will say that the Defendant did not pay the Monthly Payments which fell due on or around 01.02.2011 or any later instalment. By 08.05.2011 the Defendant was £1,036.48 in arrears.
10. Because the Defendant failed to pay the Monthly Payments in accordance with clause 2.1, the Claimant served upon him (by first class post) a default notice dated 08.05.2011 in accordance with Section 87(1) of the CCA 1974 (copy attached).
11. Because the Defendant failed to remedy his breach of the Agreement by the time stated in the default notice, the Claimant sent the Defendant a letter (by first class post) dated 29.05.2011 (copy attached) accepting his repudiation, ending the Agreement and demanding payment of the unpaid balance. By 29.05.2011 the Defendant had arrears totalling £1,036.48.

Loss and Damage

12. On termination, the Claimant became entitled to the immediate payment of the unpaid balance of the Total Amount Payable and administration charges (including arrears of £1,036.48 at termination) of £19,434.00.
13. By clause 3.2 of the Agreement, if any sum is not paid on the due date for payment the Defendant must pay interest on that sum from its due date until when it is paid at the APR specified on page 1 of the Agreement both before and after judgment. However, the Claimant is entitled to and claims interest on the total figure shown in paragraph 0 from the date of termination (29.05.2011) until the date of these Particulars of Claim (20.06.2011) at a rate of 8% a year under Section 69 of the County Courts Act 1984. This produces a figure of £97.97.
14. The Claimant is also entitled to further interest from the day immediately after these Particulars of Claim (21.06.2011) until judgment or sooner payment at a daily rate of £4.26.
15. By clause 3.3 of the Agreement, if the Defendant fails to comply with any provision of the Agreement, the Claimant is entitled to recover from the Defendant all expenses, charges and costs (including inquiry costs and legal costs) incurred by the Claimant in the administration of the Agreement, locating the Defendant, communicating with the Defendant and collecting any unpaid sums. By the date of these Particulars of Claim, such expenses are £600.00 including VAT (but excluding the Court issue fee).

AND THE CLAIMANT CLAIMS:

(1) The sum of £20,131.97; and
(2) Further interest and costs as stated in paragraphs 14 and 15 of these Particulars of Claim; or
(3) Damages for breach of the Agreement together with interest under Section 69 of the County Courts Act 1984 on such sums and for such periods and at such rate as the Court thinks fit together with costs; and/or
(4) Further or other relief.

Statement of Truth

The Claimant believes that the facts stated in these Particulars of Claim are true. I am authorised by the Claimant to sign this Statement of Truth on its behalf.

Dated this [   ] day of [*month*] 201[ ]

Signed: Position: [*job title*]

       [*Full name*]

Claimant's Solicitors: Squire Sanders (UK) LLP, 2 Park Lane, Leeds, LS3 1ES; DX: 26441 Leeds; Ref: RJK.

PRECEDENT 13
DEFENCE AND COUNTERCLAIM RESPONDING TO PRECEDENT 12 AND
SEEKING A DECLARATION THAT THE AGREEMENT IS UNENFORCEABLE

IN THE LEEDS COUNTY COURT   CLAIM NO.: _____

BETWEEN

SSH FINANCE PLC

Claimant

and

Mr STEPHEN TAYLOR

Defendant

_____

DEFENCE & COUNTERCLAIM

_____

DEFENCE

1.   In this Defence & Counterclaim:

    1.1   except as expressly admitted, the Defendant requires the Claimant to prove its claims;

    1.2   entirely without prejudice to that requirement and except as expressly admitted, the Defendant denies each and every allegation in the Particulars of Claim; and

    1.3   references to paragraphs in this Defence are to paragraphs in the Particulars of Claim (unless expressly stated otherwise).

2.   Except to the extent that the Defendant denies that the Agreement is enforceable against him under the CCA 1974 and its associated regulations and he is therefore liable to the Claimant as alleged or at all, paragraphs 1 to 7 are admitted.

3.   The Defendant will say that the Agreement was not properly executed within Section 61(1) of the CCA 1974 because it:

    3.1   was not signed by the Defendant in breach of Section 61(1)(a) of the CCA 1974;

    3.2   failed to correctly state the amount of credit in breach of Paragraph 2 of Schedule 6 to the Consumer Credit (Agreements) Regulations 1983 (the **'CC(A)R 1983'**);

    3.3   failed to correctly include the nature of the Agreement in breach of Paragraph 1 of Schedule 1 to the CC(A)R 1983;

    3.4   failed to correctly state the annual percentage rate (the **'APR'**) in breach of Paragraph 15 of Schedule 1 to the CC(A)R 1983; and

    3.5   failed to correctly include a statement of protections and remedies in breach of Form 2 of Part I to Schedule 2 to the CC(A)R 1983.

4.   By virtue of Section 65(1) of the CCA 1974, the Agreement is only enforceable against the Defendant if the Court makes an enforcement order under Section 127(1) of the CCA 1974.

5. By Section 127(3) of the CCA 1974, the Court cannot make an enforcement order under Section 127(1) for the matters alleged in paragraphs 3.1 and 3.2 of this Defence.
6. The Defendant will say that the Court should not make an order under Section 127(1) of the CCA 1974 for the matters alleged in paragraphs 3.3 to 3.5 of this Defence because he has been prejudiced by the Claimant's non-compliance. The Defendant will say that he would not have entered into the Agreement if:

    6.1   the Claimant had correctly recorded that the Agreement was a 'Hire-Purchase Agreement regulated by the Consumer Credit Act 1974' instead of a 'Fixed-Sum Loan Agreement regulated by the Consumer Credit Act 1974';

    6.2   the APR had been correctly recorded on the Agreement; and

    6.3   it had included the correct statement of statement of protections and remedies.

COUNTERCLAIM

7. The Defendant repeats paragraphs 2 to 6 of his Defence.
8. For the reasons set out in the Defence, the Defendant will say that Agreement is:

    8.1   irredeemably unenforceable (for the allegations made in paragraphs 3.1 and 3.2 of this Defence); or

    8.2   unenforceable without the Court's permission (for the allegations made in paragraphs 3.3 to 3.5 of this Defence) and the Court should not make an order under Section 127(1).

9. The Defendant therefore counterclaims for a declaration that the Agreement is unenforceable and/or a declaration that the Claimant is not entitled to enforce the Agreement under Section 142(1) of the CCA 1974 and/or that any further application for an enforcement order under the Agreement will not be entertained.

AND THE DEFENDANT COUNTERCLAIMS:

(1) A declaration under Rule 40.20 of the Civil Procedure Rules 1998 that the Agreement is unenforceable; and/or
(2) A declaration under Section 142(1) of the CCA 1974 that the Claimant is not entitled to enforce the Agreement and/or that any further application for an enforcement order under the Agreement will not be entertained.
(3) Further or other relief.
(4) Costs.

Statement of Truth

The Defendant believes that the facts stated in this Defence & Counterclaim are true.

Dated this [ ] day of [*month*] 201[ ]

Signed: Position: N/A

        Stephen Taylor

Defendant's Solicitors: Taylor & Co LLP, 2 London Road, Leeds, LS25 9EF; Ref: JLG.

PRECEDENT 14
REPLY AND DEFENCE TO COUNTERCLAIM RESPONDING TO
PRECEDENT 13

IN THE LEEDS COUNTY COURT   CLAIM NO.: _____

BETWEEN

SSH FINANCE PLC

Claimant

and

Mr STEPHEN TAYLOR

Defendant

REPLY & DEFENCE TO COUNTERCLAIM

REPLY

1. In this Reply & Defence to Counterclaim·

    1.1 except as expressly admitted, the Claimant requires the Defendant to prove his claims;

    1.2 entirely without prejudice to that requirement and except as expressly admitted, the Claimant denies each and every allegation in the Defence & Counterclaim; and

    1.3 references to paragraphs in this Reply & Defence to Counterclaim are to paragraphs in the Defence & Counterclaim (unless expressly stated otherwise).

2. Paragraph 1 is noted.

3. Paragraphs 2 and 3 are denied. The Claimant will say that the Agreement:

    3.1 was signed by the Defendant (the Claimant attaches a copy of the Agreement, signed by the parties, to this Reply & Defence to Counterclaim);

    3.2 correctly stated the amount of credit in compliance with Paragraph 2 of Schedule 6 to the CC(A)R 1983;

    3.3 correctly stated the nature of the Agreement in compliance with Paragraph 1 of Schedule 1 to the CC(A)R 1983;

    3.4 correctly stated the APR in compliance with Paragraph 15 of Schedule 1 to the CC(A)R 1983; and

    3.5 correctly includes a statement of protections and remedies in compliance with Form 2 of Part I to Schedule 2 to the CC(A)R 1983.

4. Entirely without prejudice to paragraph 3 of this Reply, the Claimant will say that if the APR is incorrectly stated (which is denied) the Claimant relies upon the tolerances set out in Paragraph 1A of Schedule 7 to the CC(A)R 1983.

5. The Claimant admits that paragraphs 4 and 5 correctly state the law but, for the reasons set out in this Reply, will say that the Agreement is properly executed.

6. The Claimant requires the Defendant to prove paragraph 6. Entirely without prejudice

to that requirement, the Claimant denies that the Defendant has been prejudiced either as alleged or at all. If the Court may make an enforcement order under Section 127(1) of the CCA 1974, the Claimant will say it is entitled to such an order:

6.1 the Claimant repeats the matters set out in this Reply;

6.2 the Agreement complies with the CCA 1974 and/or the CC(A)R 1983;

6.3 any breach of the CCA 1974 and/or the CC(A)R 1983 is *de minimus* and/or did not prejudice the Defendant;

6.4 the Claimant advanced the Loan to the Defendant;

6.5 the Defendant has had the use and benefit of the Loan;

6.6 the Claimant has complied with all relevant guidance in the selling and management of consumer credit agreements.

DEFENCE TO COUNTERCLAIM

7. The Claimant repeats paragraphs 2 to 6 of its Reply.

8. The Claimant requires the Defendant to prove paragraphs 7 to 9. Entirely without prejudice to that requirement, and for the reasons set out in the Reply, the Claimant will say that Agreement is wholly enforceable and/or enforceable with the Court's permission (and the Court should give permission under Section 127(1) of the CCA 1974).

Statement of Truth

The Claimant believes that the facts stated in this Reply & Defence to Counterclaim are true. I am authorised by the Claimant to sign this Statement of Truth on its behalf.

Dated this [ ] day of [*month*] 201[ ]

Signed: Position: [*job title*]

     [*Full name*]

Claimant's Solicitors: Squire Sanders (UK) LLP, 2 Park Lane, Leeds, LS3 1ES; DX: 26441 Leeds; Ref: RJK.

PRECEDENT 15
PARTICULARS OF CLAIM FOR RETURN OF GOODS LET UNDER A
REGULATED HIRE-PURCHASE AGREEMENT AND/OR THE BALANCE DUE
UNDER THE AGREEMENT

IN THE LEEDS COUNTY COURT   CLAIM NO.: _____

BETWEEN

SSH FINANCE PLC

Claimant

and

Mr ANTHONY TAYLOR

Defendant

PARTICULARS OF CLAIM

Parties

1. The Claimant is a public limited company (company registration number 123456) which is regulated by the Financial Services Authority (financial services authority register number 987654). The Claimant carries on business in (amongst other things) the provision of credit.
2. The Defendant is an individual and the Claimant's former customer.

Agreement

3. By a written hire-purchase agreement dated 21.11.2007 and numbered 123456789 (the **'Agreement'**) (copy attached together with the Claimant's standard terms and conditions of business) the Claimant let to the Defendant a BMW X5 motor vehicle with registration no. ABC 1 and VIN/Chassis No. ABCDEFG123456 (the **'Vehicle'**) subject to its standard terms and conditions of business.
4. The Agreement was regulated by the Consumer Credit Act 1974 (the **'CCA 1974'**).
5. The following are the particulars required by CPR PD 7B, para.7.2:

    5.1   the date of the agreement: 21.11.2007;
    5.2   the parties to the agreement: the Claimant and the Defendant;
    5.3   the number or other identification of the agreement (with enough information to allow the debtor to identify the agreement): 123456789;
    5.4   where the Claimant was not one of the original parties to the agreement, the means by which the rights and duties of the creditor passed to him: not applicable;
    5.5   the place where the agreement was signed by the Defendant (if known): Good Value Motors Limited, Motor Dealer Row, Leeds, LS1 1ZZ;
    5.6   the goods claimed: the Vehicle;
    5.7   the total price of the goods: £21,975.16;
    5.8   the paid-up sum: £16,549.50;
    5.9   the unpaid balance of the total price: £5,425.66;
    5.10 whether a default notice or a notice under Section 76(1) or Section 98(1) of the

CCA 1974 has been served on the Defendant, and if it has, the date and method of service: default notice dated 20.10.2010, served by first class post;

5.11 the date when the right to demand delivery of the goods accrued: 08.11.2010 or, alternatively, 17.11.2010;

5.12 the amount (if any) claimed as an alternative to the delivery of goods: £5,425.66;

5.13 the amount (if any) claimed in addition to:

5.13.1 the delivery of the goods, or

5.13.2 any claim under sub-paragraph 5.13.1 above,

with the grounds of each claim: see following paragraphs.

6. Under the Agreement, the total price for the Vehicle was:

6.1	cash price (including deposit of £2,430.00)	£19,035.00
6.2	administration fee (payable on date of Agreement)	£208.00
6.3	option fee	£75.00
6.4	interest	£2,657.16
6.5	total amount payable (including deposit)	£21,975.16

7. After paying the deposit of £2,430.00, the balance of the cash price and charges (excluding the administration fee and the option fee) was payable by thirty-six consecutive monthly instalments of £535.06.

8. In accordance with the Agreement, the Defendant paid to the Claimant the deposit of £2,430.00, the administration fee of £208.00, and twenty-five instalments of £535.06 totalling £13,376.50 and an ad hoc payment of £535.00. The total amount paid by the Defendant to the Claimant under the Agreement is therefore £16,549.50.

Default & Termination

9. In breach of clause 3(1) of the Agreement, the Defendant failed to maintain the instalments due under the Agreement and/or within 7 days of them falling due.

10. By a default notice dated 20.10.2010 (copy attached), sent by first class post and in accordance with Section 87(1) of the CCA 1974, the Claimant required payment of the outstanding of arrears of £4,280.54 by 08.11.2010. The Defendant failed to pay that sum, or indeed any sum, by the deadline.

11. Because the Defendant failed to pay the arrears in full by the due date, the provisions of the default notice acted as an automatic acceptance of his repudiation and termination of the Agreement in accordance with clause 7(1) and/or clause 7(2) of the Agreement.

12. Further or alternatively, by a letter dated 17.11.2010 from the Claimant's solicitors to the Defendant (copy attached), the Claimant accepted the Defendant's repudiation and termination of the Agreement in accordance with clause 7(1) and/or clause 7(2) of the Agreement. By the same letter, the Claimant demanded delivery-up of the Vehicle.

13. Despite that letter, the Defendant has failed and/or refused to deliver up the Vehicle to the Claimant.

Loss & Damage

14. By clauses 7(2), 7(3) and 8(1) of the Agreement, the Claimant is entitled to recover from the Defendant:

14.1	unpaid instalments at termination		£4,815.60
14.2	liquidated damages:		
	14.2.1	total amount payable: minus:	£21,975.16	
	14.2.2	payments due at termination	(£21,365.10)	£610.06
14.3	total		£5,425.66

15. Further or alternatively, the Claimant will say that it is entitled to recover from the Defendant, as damages for breach of the Agreement, the sum claimed in paragraph 14.3 of these Particulars of Claim or such other sum as the Court thinks fit.

16. By clause 3(2) of the Agreement, if any repayment is not paid on the due date for payment then the Defendant must pay interest on a day to day basis from the due date for payment until receipt at a rate of 5% above the Finance House Base Rate at that time. However, the Claimant is entitled to and claims interest on the total figure shown in paragraph 14.3 of these Particulars of Claim from the date of termination (08.11.2010) until the date of these Particulars of Claim (01.11.2011) at a rate of 8% a year under Section 69 of the County Courts Act 1984. This produces a figure of £426.92.

17. The Claimant is also entitled to further interest from the date of these Particulars of Claim (01.11.2011) until judgment or sooner payment at a daily rate of £1.19.

18. By clause 3(6) of the Agreement, if the Defendant failed to comply with the terms of the Agreement, the Claimant became entitled to its legal and professional costs of taking any steps to recover the balance due under the Agreement and/or the Vehicle. By the date of these Particulars of Claim, such costs (excluding the Court issue fee but including VAT) are £300.00.

AND THE CLAIMANT CLAIMS:

(1) Delivery-up and/or return of the Vehicle; and/or

(2) The total sum of £6,152.58 due under the Agreement together with further interest as particularised in paragraph 17 of these Particulars of Claim and further costs as particularised in paragraph 18 of these Particulars of Claim; and/or

(3) Damages for breach of the Agreement, interest under Section 69 of the County Courts Act 1984 at such rate and for such period as the Court considers just and costs; and/or

(4) Further or other relief.

Statement of Truth

The Claimant believes that the facts stated in these Particulars of Claim are true. I am authorised by the Claimant to sign this Statement of Truth on its behalf.

Dated this [   ] day of [*month*] 201[ ]

Signed: Position: [*job title*]

     [*Full name*]

Claimant's Solicitors: Squire Sanders (UK) LLP, 2 Park Lane, Leeds, LS3 1ES; DX: 26441 Leeds; Ref: RJK.

PRECEDENT 16
DEFENCE AND COUNTERCLAIM RESPONDING TO PRECEDENT 15 AND
SEEKING A DECLARATION THAT THE VEHICLE WAS REJECTED AS
BEING OF UNSATISFACTORY QUALITY AND/OR DAMAGES FOR BREACH
OF WARRANTY

IN THE LEEDS COUNTY COURT   CLAIM NO.: _____

BETWEEN

SSH FINANCE PLC

Claimant

and

Mr ANTHONY TAYLOR

Defendant

DEFENCE & COUNTERCLAIM

DEFENCE

1. In this Defence & Counterclaim:

    1.1 except as expressly admitted, the Defendant requires the Claimant to prove its claims;

    1.2 entirely without prejudice to that requirement and except as expressly admitted, the Defendant denies each and every allegation in the Particulars of Claim; and

    1.3 references to paragraphs in this Defence are to paragraphs in the Particulars of Claim (unless expressly stated otherwise).

2. Except to the extent that the Defendant denies it is liable to the Claimant either as alleged or at all and/or that the Claimant has terminated the Agreement, the Defendant admits paragraphs 1 to 8.

3. As to paragraph 9, it is admitted that the Defendant failed to maintain the instalments due under the Agreement and/or within 7 days of them falling due but, for the reasons set out below, the Defendant denies that such a failure constituted a breach of the Agreement.

4. The Defendant will say that there were implied conditions in the Agreement that the Vehicle would be of satisfactory quality and/or reasonably fit for purpose by virtue of Section 10 of the Supply of Goods (Implied Terms) Act 1973.

5. The Defendant will say that:

    5.1 on or around 15.01.2010 the Defendant was driving along the M1 motorway between junctions 15 and 16 in the outside lane at between 60 miles an hour and 70 miles an hour;

    5.2 without any prior warning, the Vehicle lost power and immediately decelerated;

    5.3 in an attempt to avoid a collision or accident, the Defendant immediately displayed his hazard warning lights and began to move towards the hard shoulder until the Vehicle was stationary and parked on the hard shoulder;

5.4   shortly after stopping, the Defendant telephoned his breakdown repair company;

5.5   the breakdown repair company attended the scene approximately one hour later and produced an initial diagnostic report (copy attached);

5.6   the breakdown repair company was unable to repair the Vehicle's engine and towed the Vehicle to the Good Value Motors Limited (the **'Dealer'**);

5.7   after inspecting the Vehicle, the Dealer was unable to diagnose and/or repair the problem;

5.8   for the reasons set out in paragraphs 5.1 to 5.7 of this Defence, the Defendant will say that the Vehicle was not of satisfactory quality and/or reasonably fit for purpose at the date of supply. The Defendant was therefore entitled to rescind the Agreement and/or treat it as having been repudiated by the Claimant;

5.9   by a letter dated 17.01.2010 sent to the Dealer and the Claimant (copies attached), the Defendant rescinded the Agreement and/or accepted the Claimant's repudiation of the Agreement.

6.   For the reasons set out in paragraph 5 of this Defence, the Defendant will say that the Claimant was not (and is not) entitled to any further payment under the Agreement either as alleged in paragraphs 10 to 18 or at all. The Defendant therefore denies it is liable to the Claimant either as alleged or at all.

7.   Further or alternatively, if (which is denied) the Defendant is liable to the Claimant under the terms of the Agreement, the Defendant will seek to wipe out or reduce any such liability by such amount as the Defendant is awarded on his counterclaim.

COUNTERCLAIM

8.   The Defendant repeats paragraphs 2 to 7 of his Defence.

9.   The Defendant is entitled to a declaration that the Agreement has been rescinded and repayment of the total sums paid by the Defendant to the Claimant under the Agreement, namely £16,549.50. Further or alternatively, the Defendant is entitled to repayment minus a deduction for his use of the vehicle.

10.   Further or alternatively, for the reasons set out in paragraphs 2 to 7 of his Defence, the Defendant has suffered loss and damage:

10.1   the difference between the Vehicle's value had it been of   £[0.00] satisfactory quality and/or reasonably fit for purpose

10.2   cost of hiring alternative transport   £[0.00]

11.   The Defendant is entitled to (and claims) interest under Section 69 of the County Courts Act 1984 on such sums and for such period and at such a rate as the Court thinks fit.

AND THE DEFENDANT COUNTERCLAIMS:

(1)   A declaration that the Defendant lawfully rescinded the Agreement by his letter dated 17.01.2010 or, alternatively, that the Defendant lawfully accepted the Claimant's repudiation of the Agreement by his letter dated 17.01.2010; or

(2)   Rescission of the Agreement; and/or

(3)   Repayment of £16,549.50 or such other sum as the Court thinks fit plus interest and costs; and/or

(4)   Damages plus interest and costs; and/or
(5)   Further or other relief.

Statement of Truth

The Defendant believes that the facts stated in this Defence & Counterclaim are true.

Dated this [   ] day of [*month*] 201[ ]

Signed: Position: N/A

        Anthony Taylor

Defendant's Solicitors: Taylor & Co LLP, 2 London Road, Leeds, LS25 9EF; Ref: JLG.

PRECEDENT 17
REPLY AND DEFENCE TO COUNTERCLAIM RESPONDING TO
PRECEDENT 16

IN THE LEEDS COUNTY COURT   CLAIM NO.: _____

BETWEEN

SSH FINANCE PLC

Claimant

and

Mr ANTHONY TAYLOR

Defendant

REPLY & DEFENCE TO COUNTERCLAIM

REPLY

1.   In this Reply & Defence to Counterclaim:

   1.1   except as expressly admitted, the Claimant requires the Defendant to prove his claims;

   1.2   entirely without prejudice to that requirement and except as expressly admitted, the Claimant denies each and every allegation in the Defence & Counterclaim; and

   1.3   references to paragraphs in this Reply & Defence to Counterclaim are to paragraphs in the Defence & Counterclaim (unless expressly stated otherwise).

2.   Paragraph 1 is noted.
3.   As to paragraphs 2 and 3, the Claimant repeats the Particulars of Claim and will say that the Defendant's failure to maintain the instalments due under the Agreement and/or within 7 days of them falling due constituted a breach of the Agreement.
4.   Paragraph 4 is admitted.
5.   As to paragraph 5, the Claimant requires the Defendant to prove the matters set out in that paragraph. Entirely without prejudice to that requirement, the Claimant will say that the Vehicle was of satisfactory quality and/or reasonably fit for purpose when supplied. The Defendant will say that:

   5.1   before entering into the Agreement:

      5.1.1   the Defendant inspected the Vehicle for around one hour;

      5.1.2   the Defendant's mechanic inspected the Vehicle;

      5.1.3   any defects that existed at the time of the supply (none being admitted) ought to have been reasonably revealed during those inspections;

   5.2   the Dealer undertook a 140 point check (copy attached) (the **'Check'**) before selling the Vehicle to the Claimant;

   5.3   the Check failed to reveal any issues with the Vehicle;

5.4 the Defendant failed to maintain the Vehicle meaning that any issues that arose with the Vehicle (none being admitted) did not exist on the date of supply.

6. Further or alternatively, if the Vehicle was of unsatisfactory quality and/or not reasonably fit for purpose (which is denied), the Defendant has affirmed the Agreement by keeping and/or using the Vehicle after the Defendant's letter dated 17.01.2010 and/or making an ad hoc payment under the Agreement.

7. In those circumstances, the Claimant denies that the Defendant is entitled to rescind the Agreement and/or purport to accept an alleged repudiation of the Agreement by the Claimant.

DEFENCE TO COUNTERCLAIM

8. The Claimant repeats paragraphs 2 to 7 of its Reply.

9. If, despite the Claimant's contentions to the contrary, the Claimant is liable in damages to the Defendant then the Claimant will seek to set-off any sum against the balance due under the Agreement.

10. For the reasons set out in the Reply, the Claimant denies the Defendant is entitled to the declaratory relief sought either as alleged or at all. Further or alternatively, the Claimant denies it is liable to the Defendant either as alleged or at all. It therefore follows that the Defendant's claim for interest and costs are also denied.

Statement of Truth

The Claimant believes that the facts stated in this Reply & Defence to Counterclaim are true. I am authorised by the Claimant to sign this Statement of Truth on its behalf.

Dated this [   ] day of [*month*] 201[ ]

Signed: Position: [*job title*]

[*Full name*]

Claimant's Solicitors: Squire Sanders (UK) LLP, 2 Park Lane, Leeds, LS3 1ES; DX: 26441 Leeds; Ref: RJK.

PRECEDENT 18
**PARTICULARS OF CLAIM ALLEGING BREACH OF CONTRACT BY THE
SUPPLIER, AND A CLAIM AGAINST THE CREDITOR UNDER CCA 1974,
S.75(1)**

IN THE [*CITY*] COUNTY COURT   CLAIM NO.: [   ]

BETWEEN

[*CLAIMANT'S NAME*]

Claimant

and

(1) [*FIRST DEFENDANT'S NAME*]

(2) [*SECOND DEFENDANT'S NAME*]

Defendants

PARTICULARS OF CLAIM

Parties

1.   The Claimant is a consumer.
2.   The First Defendant is a private company incorporated in England & Wales with
company registration number [   ]. The First Defendant carries on business in the sale of
motor cars.
3.   The Second Defendant is public company incorporated in England & Wales with
company registration number [   ]. The Second Defendant carries on business in
(amongst other things) the provision of credit to consumers.

The Agreement

4.   By a fixed-sum loan agreement dated [*date*] and numbered [   ] (the **'Agreement'**) the
Second Defendant agreed to loan £[*amount*] (the **'Loan'**) to the Claimant subject to its
standard terms and conditions of business (a copy of the Agreement is attached).
5.   The Agreement is regulated by the Consumer Credit Act 1974 (the **'CCA 1974'**).
6.   The Agreement is a debtor-creditor-supplier agreement falling within Section 12(b) of
the CCA 1974.

The Sale Contract

7.   The Agreement financed a contract of sale between the Claimant and the First Defendant dated [*date*] (the **'Sale Contract'**). Under the terms of the Sale Contract (a copy of
which is attached), the First Defendant agreed to sell a [*vehicle make and model*] with
registration no. [   ] (the **'Vehicle'**) to the Claimant for £[*amount*] (the **'Price'**).
8.   The Claimant paid the Price by using the Loan and making a cash payment to the First
Defendant of £[*amount*].

Breach of Sale Contract

9.   By virtue of Section 14(2) of the Sale of Goods Act 1979 (the **'SGA 1979'**), it was implied into the Sale Contract that the Vehicle would be of satisfactory quality. Further or alternatively, and by virtue of Section 14(3) of the SGA 1979, it was implied into the Sale Contract that the Vehicle would be fit for purpose.
10. In breach of the terms implied by Section 14(2) and/or Section 14(3) of the SGA 1979, the Vehicle was neither of satisfactory quality nor fit for purpose:

PARTICULARS

   10.1   [ ]

Claim against First Defendant

11. Because of the First Defendant's breach of the Sale Contract, the Claimant has suffered loss and damage:

PARTICULARS

   11.1   [ ]

12. The Claimant is also entitled to (and claims) interest at such rate and for such period and on such sums as the Court thinks just under Section 69 of the County Courts Act 1984.

Claim against Second Defendant

13. By Section 75(1) of the CCA 1974 the Second Defendant is jointly and severally liable with the First Defendant for the Claimant's losses set out in paragraphs 11 to 12 of these Particulars of Claim.

AND THE CLAIMANT CLAIMS AGAINST BOTH DEFENDANTS:

(1)   Damages;
(2)   Interest;
(3)   Costs;
(4)   Further or other relief.

Statement of Truth

The Claimant believes that the facts stated in these Particulars of Claim are true. I am authorised by the Claimant to sign this Statement of Truth on its behalf.

Dated this [   ] day of [*month*] 201[ ]

Signed: Position: [*job title*]

            [*Full name*]

Claimant's Solicitors: Taylor & Co LLP, 2 London Road, Leeds, LS25 9EF; Ref: JLG.

PRECEDENT 19
DEFENCE AND ADDITIONAL CLAIM RESPONDING TO PRECEDENT 18 BY THE CREDITOR, AND SEEKING AN INDEMNITY FROM THE SUPPLIER

IN THE [*CITY*] COUNTY COURT   CLAIM NO.: [   ]

BETWEEN

[*CLAIMANT'S NAME*]

Claimant

and

(1) [*FIRST DEFENDANT'S NAME*]

(2) [*SECOND DEFENDANT'S NAME*]

Defendants

SECOND DEFENDANT'S DEFENCE &
ADDITIONAL CLAIM AGAINST
FIRST DEFENDANT

DEFENCE

1.   In this Second Defendant's Defence:

1.1   the Second Defendant requires the Claimant to prove his claim;

1.2   entirely without prejudice to that requirement and except as otherwise admitted, the Second Defendant denies the Claimant's claim;

1.3   references to paragraphs in this Second Defendant's Defence are to paragraphs in the Particulars of Claim unless expressly stated otherwise; and

1.4   the Second Defendant adopts the definitions used by the Claimant unless expressly stated otherwise.

2.   Paragraphs 1 to 6 are admitted.

3.   Except to the extent that the Second Defendant admits that the Claimant used the Loan provided under the Agreement to buy the Vehicle, the Second Defendant neither admits nor denies paragraphs 7 to 12 as it has no knowledge of the Claimant's dealings with the First Defendant.

4.   Entirely without prejudice to paragraph 3 of this Second Defendant's Defence, the Second Defendant will say that:

4.1   it is entitled to rely upon any defences to the claim that the First Defendant may have and therefore reserves the right to serve further particulars of its Defence in due course;

4.2   if the Sale Contract was subject to the SGA 1979, it will say that the Claimant has provided no evidence to show that the Vehicle was unsatisfactory contrary to Section 14(2) and/or unfit for purpose contrary to Section 14(3) of the SGA 1979;

4.3 even if the Claimant has such evidence (which is denied), the Vehicle was satisfactory and/or fit for any particular purpose implied into the Sale Contract.

5. In these circumstances, the Second Defendant will say that the Claimant does not have a 'like claim' against the Second Defendant either as alleged or at all.

6. If (contrary to the Second Defendant's position), the Claimant succeeds on liability against the First Defendant, then the Second Defendant requires the Claimant to prove his losses alleged in paragraph 11. If he does so, the Second Defendant also requires him to prove that such losses were caused by the First Defendant and/or the Claimant has mitigated his loss and/or any loss is not too remote.

7. For the reasons set out above, the Second Defendant denies it is liable to the Claimant either as alleged or at all.

SECOND DEFENDANT'S ADDITIONAL CLAIM AGAINST THE FIRST DEFENDANT

8. At all relevant times, the First Defendant was a motor dealer.

9. On or about [date], the First Defendant agreed to sell to the Claimant the Vehicle subject to the terms of the Sale Contract.

10. By Section 14 of the SGA 1979, there were the following implied conditions of the Sale Contract between the Claimant and the First Defendant:

10.1 the Vehicle was of satisfactory quality;
10.2 the Vehicle was reasonably fit for the Claimant's purposes.

11. Under the terms of the Agreement (copy attached), the Second Defendant advanced the Loan to the Claimant to allow him to buy the Vehicle.

12. The Agreement was a debtor-creditor-supplier agreement within the meaning of Section 12(b) of the CCA 1974.

13. By the Particulars of Claim, a copy of which is served with this Defence (together with all other statements of case in the claim to date), the Claimant alleges that the Vehicle was unsatisfactory and/or unfit for purpose and he has suffered loss and/or damage. The Second Defendant will rely upon the particulars stated by the Claimant.

14. The Claimant also alleges that the Second Defendant is jointly and severally liable for such damages to the Claimant by virtue of Section 75(1) of the CCA 1974.

15. By its Defence, the Second Defendant makes no admissions on the Claimant's claim.

16. If, however, by Section 75(1) of the CCA 1974 the Second Defendant is liable to the Claimant, and it is found that the Vehicle was unsatisfactory and/or unfit for purpose, the Second Defendant is entitled to an indemnity and/or a contribution from the First Defendant by Section 75(2) of the CCA 1974.

17. The Second Defendant therefore claims from the First Defendant a contribution and/or an indemnity and/or damages for any loss or damage it suffers for:

PARTICULARS

17.1 the amount of any liability of the Second Defendant to the Claimant;
17.2 any costs ordered to be paid by the Second Defendant to the Claimant;
17.3 the Second Defendant's own costs of the claim between it and the Claimant.

AND THE SECOND DEFENDANT CLAIMS AGAINST THE FIRST DEFENDANT:

(1) An indemnity and/or contribution under Section 75(2) of the CCA 1974 (including but

not limited to the amount it has to pay (if anything) to the Claimant, interest and costs (either the Claimant's costs or its own)) plus its own costs of defending the Claimant's claim; and/or

(2) Damages; and
(3) Interest;
(4) Costs;
(5) Further or other relief.

Statement of Truth

The Second Defendant believes that the facts stated in this Defence & Additional Claim are true. I am authorised by the Second Defendant to sign this Statement of Truth on its behalf.

Dated this [   ] day of [*month*] 201[ ]

Signed: Position: [*job title*]

      [*Full name*]

Claimant's Solicitors: Squire Sanders (UK) LLP, 2 Park Lane, Leeds, LS3 1ES; DX: 26441 Leeds; Ref: RJK/[   ].

PRECEDENT 20
PARTICULARS OF CLAIM INCLUDING A CLAIM FOR AN ENFORCEMENT ORDER UNDER CCA 1974, S.127(1)

IN THE LEEDS COUNTY COURT   CLAIM NO.: _____

BETWEEN

SSH FINANCE PLC

Claimant

and

Mr ANTHONY TAYLOR

Defendant

_____

PARTICULARS OF CLAIM

_____

Parties

1. The Claimant is a public limited company (company registration number 123456) which is regulated by the Financial Services Authority (financial services authority register number 987654). The Claimant carries on business in (amongst other things) the provision of credit.
2. The Defendant is an individual and the Claimant's former customer.

Agreement

3. By a written hire purchase agreement dated 21.11.2007 and numbered 123456789 (the **'Agreement'**) (copy attached together with the Claimant's standard terms and conditions of business) the Claimant let to the Defendant a BMW X5 motor vehicle with registration no. ABC 1 and VIN/Chassis No. ABCDEFG123456 (the **'Vehicle'**) subject to its standard terms and conditions of business.
4. The Agreement was regulated by the Consumer Credit Act 1974 (the **'CCA 1974'**).
5. The following are the particulars required by CPR PD 7B, para.7.2:

   5.1   the date of the agreement: 21.11.2007;
   5.2   the parties to the agreement: the Claimant and the Defendant;
   5.3   the number or other identification of the agreement (with enough information to allow the debtor to identify the agreement): 123456789;
   5.4   where the Claimant was not one of the original parties to the agreement, the means by which the rights and duties of the creditor passed to him: not applicable;
   5.5   the place where the agreement was signed by the Defendant (if known): Good Value Motors Limited, Motor Dealer Row, Leeds, LS1 1ZZ;
   5.6   the goods claimed: the Vehicle;
   5.7   the total price of the goods: £21,975.16;
   5.8   the paid-up sum: £16,549.50;
   5.9   the unpaid balance of the total price: £5,425.66;
   5.10 whether a default notice or a notice under Section 76(1) or Section 98(1) of the

CCA 1974 has been served on the Defendant, and if it has, the date and method of service: default notice dated 20.10.2010, served by first class post;

5.11 the date when the right to demand delivery of the goods accrued: 08.11.2010 or, alternatively, 17.11.2010;

5.12 the amount (if any) claimed as an alternative to the delivery of goods: £5,425.66;

5.13 the amount (if any) claimed in addition to:

5.13.1 the delivery of the goods, or

5.13.2 any claim under sub-paragraph 5.13.1 above,

with the grounds of each claim: see following paragraphs.

6. Under the Agreement, the total price for the Vehicle was:

6.1	cash price (including deposit of £2,430.00)	£19,035.00
6.2	administration fee (payable on date of Agreement)	£208.00
6.3	option fee	£75.00
6.4	interest	£2,657.16
6.5	total amount payable (including deposit)	£21,975.16

7. After paying the deposit of £2,430.00, the balance of the cash price and charges (excluding the administration fee and the option fee) was payable by thirty-six consecutive monthly instalments of £535.06.

8. In accordance with the Agreement, the Defendant paid to the Claimant the deposit of £2,430.00, the administration fee of £208.00, and twenty-five instalments of £535.06 totalling £13,376.50 and an ad hoc payment of £535.00. The total amount paid by the Defendant to the Claimant under the Agreement is therefore £16,549.50.

Default & Termination

9. In breach of clause 3(1) of the Agreement, the Defendant failed to maintain the instalments due under the Agreement and/or within 7 days of them falling due.

10. By a default notice dated 20.10.2010 (copy attached), sent by first class post and in accordance with Section 87(1) of the CCA 1974, the Claimant required payment of the outstanding of arrears of £4,280.54 by 08.11.2010. The Defendant failed to pay that sum, or indeed any sum, by the deadline.

11. Because the Defendant failed to pay the arrears in full by the due date, the provisions of the default notice acted as an automatic acceptance of his repudiation and termination of the Agreement in accordance with clause 7(1) and/or clause 7(2) of the Agreement.

12. Further or alternatively, by a letter dated 17.11.2010 from the Claimant's solicitors to the Defendant (copy attached), the Claimant accepted the Defendant's repudiation and termination of the Agreement in accordance with clause 7(1) and/or clause 7(2) of the Agreement. By the same letter, the Claimant demanded delivery-up of the Vehicle.

13. Despite that letter, the Defendant has failed and/or refused to deliver up the Vehicle to the Claimant.

Loss & Damage

14. By clauses 7(2), 7(3) and 8(1) of the Agreement, the Claimant is entitled to recover from the Defendant:

14.1	unpaid instalments at termination		£4,815.60
14.2	liquidated damages:		
	14.2.1	total amount payable: minus:	£21,975.16
	14.2.2	payments due at termination	(£21,365.10) £610.06
14.3	total		£5,425.66

15. Further or alternatively, the Claimant will say that it is entitled to recover from the Defendant, as damages for breach of the Agreement, the sum claimed in paragraph 14.3 of these Particulars of Claim or such other sum as the Court thinks fit.

16. By clause 3(2) of the Agreement, if any repayment is not paid on the due date for payment then the Defendant must pay interest on a day to day basis from the due date for payment until receipt at a rate of 5% above the Finance House Base Rate at that time. However, the Claimant is entitled to and claims interest on the total figure shown in paragraph 14.3 of these Particulars of Claim from the date of termination (08.11.2010) until the date of these Particulars of Claim (01.11.2011) at a rate of 8% a year under Section 69 of the County Courts Act 1984. This produces a figure of £426.92.

17. The Claimant is also entitled to further interest from the date of these Particulars of Claim (01.11.2011) until judgment or sooner payment at a daily rate of £1.19.

18. By clause 3(6) of the Agreement, if the Defendant failed to comply with the terms of the Agreement, the Claimant became entitled to its legal and professional costs of taking any steps to recover the balance due under the Agreement and/or the Vehicle. By the date of these Particulars of Claim, such costs (excluding the Court issue fee but including VAT) are £300.00.

Enforcement Order

19. For the purposes of these proceedings, the Claimant accepts that the Agreement failed to correctly state the form of statement of protection and remedies required by Regulation 2(3) of the Consumer Credit (Agreement) Regulations 1983 (the **'CC(A)R 1983'**) and Form 7 of Part I to Schedule 2 to the CC(A)R 1983.

20. The Claimant therefore seeks the Court's permission to enforce the Agreement and will say it is entitled to (and therefore seeks) an enforcement order under Section 127 of the CCA 1974. Further, the Claimant will say that it would be just to make an enforcement order in the circumstances.

21. In support of the Claimant's application for an enforcement order, it will rely upon the following facts:

    21.1 the Defendant was in no way prejudiced by the contravention of the CC(A)R 1983 because the Claimant simply failed to properly calculate the amount payable under Section 100 of the CCA 1974 by £0.05;

    21.2 the breach is minor and/or *de minimis*;

    21.3 the Agreement set out the material terms of the agreement;

    21.4 the Claimant has let the Vehicle to the Defendant;

    21.5 the Defendant has had the use and benefit of the Vehicle;

    21.6 letting the Vehicle to the Defendant provided him with a considerable benefit;

    21.7 the Claimant solely bought the Vehicle from the supplying dealer to provide it under the terms of the Agreement to the Defendant;

    21.8 the Claimant could be expected to have generated a return on the Vehicle's price by investing those sums elsewhere had it not paid it to the supplying dealer so it could let the Vehicle to the Defendant;

21.9 it is just and proper for the Defendant to satisfy the balance under the Agreement (either in part or in full).

AND THE CLAIMANT CLAIMS:

(1) An enforcement order under Section 127(1) of the CCA 1974; and
(2) Delivery-up and/or return of the Vehicle; and/or
(3) The total sum of £6,152.58 due under the Agreement together with further interest as particularised in paragraph 17 of these Particulars of Claim and further costs as particularised in paragraph 18 of these Particulars of Claim; and/or
(4) Damages for breach of the Agreement, interest under Section 69 of the County Courts Act 1984 at such rate and for such period as the Court considers just and costs; and/or
(5) Further or other relief.

Statement of Truth

The Claimant believes that the facts stated in these Particulars of Claim are true. I am authorised by the Claimant to sign this Statement of Truth on its behalf.

Dated this [   ] day of [*month*] 201[ ]

Signed: Position: [*job title*]

       [*Full name*]

Claimant's Solicitors: Squire Sanders (UK) LLP, 2 Park Lane, Leeds, LS3 1ES; DX: 26441 Leeds; Ref: RJK.

PRECEDENT 21
FORM N440 – APPLICATION FOR A TIME ORDER

IN THE   COUNTY COURT

Claim no.

IN THE MATTER OF AN APPLICATION FOR A TIME ORDER

Between _____ **Applicant**
(Insert your full name in block capitals)

and _____ **Respondent**
(insert the full name in block capitals of the company to whom you make your payments)

1. I *(Name)* _____

Of *(Address)*

apply to the court for a time order

2. The following are the details of the regulated agreement in respect of which I am asking for a time order.

a. The agreement is dated _____

and the reference number is _____

b. The names and addresses of the other parties to the agreement are:

_____

c. The name and address of the person (if any) who acted as surety

is _____

of _____

_____

d. *(Delete if not applicable)* The rights and duties

of the party named _____

at b. above passed to the respondent

on _____ when *(here give the reasons why you now regard the respondent as your creditor)*

His address is

e. I signed the agreement at *(here give the address of the shop or other place where you signed the agreement)*

_____

f. I agreed to pay instalments

of £ _____ a week ☐   a month ☐

g.   ☐   The unpaid balance due under the
agreement is   £ _____

or   ☐   I do not know the unpaid balance

h.   ☐   I am   £ _____ in arrear
with my payments.

or   ☐   I do not know how much the arrears are.

N440 Notice of application for time order by debtor or hirer (4.99)   *Crown copyright. Reproduced by The Law Society.*

i. On   the Respondent served on me:

☐   a default notice

☐   a notice given under section 76(1)

☐   a notice given under section 98(1)

or I attach a copy of the notice which the Respondent served on me on

j. *You should complete this section if you are applying for time to pay, if not cross it out.*

My proposals for payment are £

to clear the arrears (if any) and then by instalments of £

k. *You should complete this section if you have failed to comply with the agreement in any other respect.*

I am in breach of the following provisions of the agreement:

And my proposals for remedying the breach(es) are as follows:

3. I have answered the questions about my financial circumstances set out in the schedule to this application.

4. The names and addresses of the persons to be served with this application are: *(You must include any sureties)*

5. My address for service is:

6. Signed

(Solicitor for the) Applicant.

Dated

377

Index